Inappropriate Relationships

The Unconventional,
The Disapproved,
&
The Forbidden

LEA's Series on Personal Relationships
Steve Duck, Series Editor

www.erlbaum.com

Inappropriate Relationships

The Unconventional,
The Disapproved,
&
The Forbidden

Edited by

Robin Goodwin
Brunel University
and
Duncan Cramer
Loughborough University

LEA LAWRENCE ERLBAUM ASSOCIATES, PUBLISHERS
2002 Mahwah, New Jersey   London

Lawrence Erlbaum Associates, Inc., Publishers
10 Industrial Avenue
Mahwah, NJ 07430

Cover design by Kathryn Houghtaling Lacey

Library of Congress Cataloging-in-Publication Data

Inappropriate relationships : the unconventional, the disapproved, and
   the forbidden / edited by Robin Goodwin, Duncan Cramer.
          p.   cm.   (LEA's series on personal relationships)
       Includes bibliographical references and index.
ISBN 0-8058-3742-6 (cloth : alk. paper)
ISBN 0-8058-3743-4 (pbk. : alk. paper)
1. Interpersonal relations. 2. Social norms. 3. Sexual ethics. 4. Interpersonal relations and culture. 5. Social change.   I. Goodwin, Robin,
   1964–   . II. Cramer, Duncan, 1948–   .   III. Series.
HM1106 .I54   2002
302—dc21   2001040724
                                                     CIP

Books published by Lawrence Erlbaum Associates are printed on acid-
free paper, and their bindings are chosen for strength and durability.

Printed in the United States of America
10 9 8 7 6 5 4 3 2 1

To our inappropriate relationships ...

Contents

Foreword

The Series on Personal Relationships from Lawrence Erlbaum Associates is intended to review the progress in the academic work on relationships with respect to a broad array of issues and to do so in an accessible manner that also illustrates its practical value. The LEA series includes books intended to pass on the accumulated scholarship to the next generation of students and to those who deal with relationship issues in the broader world beyond the academy. The series thus not only comprises monographs and other academic resources exemplifying the multidisciplinary nature of this area, but also, in the future, will include textbooks suitable for use in the growing numbers of courses on relationships.

The series has the goal of providing a comprehensive and current survey of theory and research in personal relationships through the careful analysis of the problems encountered and solved in research, yet it also considers the systematic application of that work in a practical context. These resources not only are intended to be comprehensive assessments of progress on particular "hot" and relevant topics, but also will be significant influences on the future directions and development of the study of personal relationships. Although each volume is focused and centered, authors all attempt to place the respective topics in the broader context of other research on relationships and within a range of wider disciplinary traditions. The series already offers incisive and forward-looking reviews and also demonstrates the broader theoretical implications of relationships for the range of disciplines from which the research originates. Present and future volumes include original studies, reviews of relevant theory and research, and new theories oriented toward the understanding of personal relationships both in themselves and within the context of broader theories of family process, social psychology, and communication.

Reflecting the diverse composition of personal relationship study, readers in numerous disciplines—social psychology, communication, sociology, family studies, developmental psychology, clinical psychology, personality, counseling, women's studies, gerontology, and others—will find valuable and insightful perspectives in the series.

Apart from the academic scholars who research the dynamics and processes of relationships, there are many other people whose work takes them up against the operation of relationships in the real world. For such people as nurses, police, teachers, therapists, lawyers, drug and alcohol counselors, marital counselors, and those who take care of the elderly, a number of issues routinely arise concerning the ways in which relationships affect the people whom they serve. Examples are the role of loneliness in illness and the ways to circumvent it, the complex impact of family and peer relationships on a drug-dependent's attempts to give up the drug, the role of playground unpopularity on a child's learning, the issues involved in dealing with the relational side of chronic illness, the management of conflict in marriage, the establishment of good rapport between physicians and seriously ill patients, the support of the bereaved, and the correction of violent styles of behavior in dating or marriage. Each of these is a problem that may confront some of the aforementioned professionals as part of their daily concerns and each demonstrates the far-reaching influences of relationship processes on much else in life that is presently theorized independently of relationship considerations.

The present volume is a case in point because it deals with the very definitions of acceptability in relationships. Our assumptions about the viability of relationships are typically grown in the context of the normative and acceptable. When we talk about "friendship" it is usually understood to be a legitimate friendship between people of equal status and roughly equivalent age, for example. For too long the scholarly research has underplayed the kinds of relationships that step over the boundaries into social sanctions of various levels and strengths and yet, as the chapters in this volume confirm, real-life experiences are quite often in disapproved relationships. These can range from the unconventional to the forbidden. As well as illustrating the nature of these suspect relationships, Robin Goodwin and Duncan Cramer present a compelling case for the relevance of understanding "inappropriate" relationships. This book offers an important scholarly counterweight to others that attempt to draw a misleadingly positive picture of everyday relational lives.

This book shines a light into some dark places and in so doing not only increases our practical understanding of those forms of relationship but also enlightens the comprehension of relational life as a whole.

—*Steve Duck*
University of Iowa

Preface

In one of the defining euphemisms of our time, an embattled U.S. President, Bill Clinton, admitted to an "inappropriate relationship" with a White House intern, Monica Lewinsky. At the time, neither of us was particularly convinced by the depth of his sorrow, or his rather euphemistic use of the word *inappropriate*. Reflecting on the word *inappropriate* some months later, we realized that ambiguities over what forms an "inappropriate" relationship were far more than a rather diverting insight into the life of a U.S. president, but actually a fundamental, if rarely discussed, distinction for relationship researchers. It led us to question what constituted an "inappropriate relationship," and to inquire how an understanding of the rules and norms of appropriateness better help us comprehend personal relationships. Continuing our conversation with others in the personal relationships field soon led us to appreciate that what constitutes an "inappropriate" relationship is more than a simple argument about moral behavior—it actually raises a whole series of relational and cultural issues rarely discussed by those working in a field still dominated by the analysis of the (relatively) happy, consensual, undergraduate couple.

This book includes a wide range of contributions that examine the personal and dyadic boundaries of relationships (the negotiated rules that help define acceptable interaction within a romantic dyad of friendship), the norms and taboos demarcated by particular social groups (such as we might find across social class and religious and ethnic groupings), and the wider societal stipulations, whether enshrined in legal frameworks or not, that serve to prohibit particular liaisons. We have attempted to bring together something of the diversity of the concept of "inappropriate relationships" by recruiting authors from a variety of perspectives, including communications, sociology, psychoanalytic studies, and social and clinical psychology. We asked each author, an expert in his or her respective field, to consider a range of questions, including who it is that defines the relationship as inappropriate, why the relationship they describe is considered "inappropriate" and what functions this may serve, for how long (historically) the relationship has been defined as such, and whether or not this is a universal definition across groups and cultures. By doing so, we aimed to examine the power struggles and negotiations that might occur when different individuals or groups fail to see their relationship as "inappropriate," and to explore the manner in which different individuals and groups may buffer themselves against sanctions or even encourage censure as an agent of change.

The book is divided into five sections. The first, entitled "Conceptualizing Inappropriate Relationships," considers theoretical approaches to issues of inappropriateness. In the opening chapter of this volume, Steve Duck and Lise VanderVoort offer a useful conceptual framework for thinking about inappropriate relationships and relational behavior in general, into which the more specific aspects discussed in the sections that follow can be viewed. A particular theoretical perspective for defining inappropriateness, that of evolutionary psychology, is proposed by Pam Regan in the other chapter of this introductory section, which reviews research on the qualities individuals seek in their romantic partner or mate.

Section II contains three chapters, each of which examines a different aspect of what some may consider to be inappropriate in marital relationships. Graham Allan and Kaeran Harrison discuss their thematic analysis of the written comments about "having an affair" made by participants in the British Mass-Observation Archive. Focusing primarily on Black–White romantic relationships in the United States, Stanley Gaines and Jennifer Leaver outline the way in which individuals in such relationships may be stigmatized, and the effects that this stigmatization may have on individuals both within and outside that relationship. Based on their work with committed fans of the music group The Grateful Dead, Rebecca Adams and Jane Rosen-Grandon illustrate the impact of this dedication on marital dynamics, with particular attention to the influence of this commitment on relationships where the other partner does not share this same interest.

In Section III we turn to two examples of counternormative relationships. In his review of the research literature on cross-gender friendships, Roger Baumgarte highlights the difficulties that these relationships pose, particularly in relation to sexual behavior. Andrew Yip examines changing attitudes toward same-sex romantic relationships, and the growing redefinition and acceptance of such relationships as committed partnerships.

Section IV has four chapters dealing with issues of power-discrepant relationships. Tanya Garrett reviews the arguments for and against sexual activity between therapist and patient, both during and after treatment.

Questioning whether necrophilia should be categorized as a psychiatric disorder, Dany Nobus suggests its inappropriateness may reflect taboos concerning death as well as the lack of consensuality. Brian Spitzberg and William Cupach develop an outline for obsessional relational intrusion and stalking, and reflect on shifting attitudes toward intrusive relationship behaviors. Finally, in the last chapter of this section, Dennis Howitt considers why pedophilia should be the focus of growing approbation when attitudes regarding other sexual activities appear to be increasingly tolerant.

In the concluding section and chapter, Robin Goodwin and Duncan Cramer first return to the major dimensions identified by Steve Duck and Lise VanderVoort in the opening chapter to this book, in the light of the various contributions made in this volume. They supplement this analysis with the results of a survey undertaken among their own students into which relationships are considered "inappropriate." They then consider a continuing and vexing question—Why do we find inappropriate relationships so hard to end—before considering some of the wider historical and cultural perspectives on their findings. Finally, they suggest some of the implications this might have for relational counseling, as well as for the development of the field of personal relationships as a discipline overall.

Several people deserve our warm appreciation for the work they did on this book. Linda Bathgate and her colleagues at LEA have been a consistent source of encouragement throughout this enterprise. In addition, we would like to thank the many friends and colleagues who have shared both their academic insights into relational inappropriateness and, just as insightfully, their own experiences of inappropriate relationships, which have greatly contributed to our thinking in this area. Given the nature of these insights we have, however, decided not to list these "silent contributors" here, for fear of legal suits and spousal retributions.

—Robin Goodwin
—Duncan Cramer

Contributors

Rebecca G. Adams, Department of Sociology, University of North Carolina at Greensboro, P.O. Box 26170, Greensboro, NC 27402–6170, USA • Rebecca_Adams@uncg.edu

Graham Allan, School of Social Relations, Keele University, Keele, Staffordshire, ST5 5BG, England • spa27@keele.ac.uk

Roger Baumgarte, Department of Psychology, Winthrop University, Rock Hill, SC 29733, USA • baumrog@charlotte.infi.net

Duncan Cramer, Department of Social Sciences, Loughborough University, Loughborough, LE11 3TU, England • D.Cramer@lboro.ac.uk

William R. Cupach, Department of Communication, Illinois State University, Normal, IL 61790–4480, USA • wrcupac@ilstu.edu

Steve Duck, 151-BCSB, Communication Studies, University of Iowa, Iowa City, IA 52242–1498, USA • steve-duck@uiowa.edu

Stanley O. Gaines, Jr., Department of Human Sciences, Brunel University, Uxbridge, UB8 3PH, England • Stanley.Gaines@brunel.ac.uk

Tanya Garrett, Reaside Clinic, Birmingham Great Park, Bristol Road South, Birmingham, B45 9BE, England • Tanya.G@psycho65.freeserve.co.uk

Robin Goodwin, Department of Human Sciences, Brunel University, Uxbridge, UB8 3PH, England • Robin.Goodwin@brunel.ac.uk

Kaeren Harrison, Department of Social Work Studies, University of Southampton, Southampton, SO17 1BJ, England

Dennis Howitt, Department of Social Sciences, Loughborough University, Loughborough, LE11 3TU, England • D.L.Howitt@lboro.ac.uk

Jennifer Leaver, School of Behavioral and Organizational Sciences, Claremont Graduate University, Claremont, CA 91711–6160, USA

Dany Nobus, Department of Human Sciences, Brunel University, Uxbridge, UB8 3PH, England • Dany.Nobus@brunel.ac.uk

Pamela C. Regan, Department of Psychology, California State University, 5151 State University Drive, Los Angeles, CA 90032–8227, USA • pcregan@beachnet.com

Jane Rosen-Grandon, 3106 Edgewater, Greensboro, NC 27403, USA

Brian H. Spitzberg, School of Communication, San Diego State University, San Diego, CA 92182–4561, USA • spitz@mail.sdsu.edu

Lise VanderVoort, 105-BCSB, Communication Studies, University of Iowa, Iowa City, IA 52242–1498, USA • lise-vandervoort@uiowa.edu

Andrew Yip, Department of Social Sciences, Nottingham Trent University, Burton Street, Nottingham, NG1 4BU, England • a.yip@ntu.ac.uk

I

CONCEPTUALIZING INAPPROPRIATE RELATIONSHIPS

1

Scarlet Letters and Whited Sepulchres: The Social Marking of Relationships as "Inappropriate"

Steve Duck
Lise VanderVoort[1]
University of Iowa

For what reasons and on what grounds is a relationship to be judged "inappropriate"? The term relational "*in*appropriateness" obviously suggests a contrast between appropriateness and inappropriateness of personal relationships, and that relational behavior may be judged accordingly. Why is it customary to judge personal relationships, private behavior, or intimacy as "appropriate" or "inappropriate"? What is "appropriate" behavior, "appropriate" relational behavior, or an "appropriate" relationship? Who decides?

These initial questions suggest further issues that provide some topics for research: Is there a difference between behavior in a relationship and

---

[1]We are grateful to Julia T. Wood, Walter J. Carl, and the editors for their helpful insights and comments on previous drafts of this chapter.

3

the relationship itself? That is, can inappropriate behaviors occur in an appropriate relationship or does the occurrence of those behaviors immediately render the relationship inappropriate? In short, in what ways is a relationship more than the sum of its component behaviors? Other topics include: What is the difference among a relationship, a behavior, and a relational behavior? Does the subjective meaning of the relationship to its partners, or of the relational behavior, make it appropriate or inappropriate in that relationship, or is it the fact of its emergence into the public domain that makes such a judgment suitable? What, if any, is the relationship between public, social codes and the punishment incurred for inappropriateness in what is otherwise a private dyadic arrangement? What marks the seriousness of a relational transgression? What contextual factors affect judgment? What are the social penalties for inappropriateness? What does it mean personally to participants to be in a relationship judged by others to be inappropriate?

We have only a small number of pages within which to consider this large array of questions and their implications, which intersect in complex ways that research will have to unpack for us. Our analysis, drawing heavily on Davis' (1983) interesting volume *SMUT: Erotic reality/obscene ideology*, assumes that any regulation of private behaviors in relationships is central to the maintenance of a broader social order, irrespective of the specific beliefs within any particular social order.[2]

Within a given social order, we must differentiate between inappropriateness judged by the partners and by an observer, considering that partners are unlikely to be in a relationship that they truly consider unjustifiably inappropriate themselves. In this chapter we identify three different levels of inappropriate relationship types, basing this classification on the one hand on a hierarchy of rules that are broken, and on the other hand on a logical ranking by way of levels of disapprobation (counternormative/unconventional relationships, disapproved relationships, and forbidden/inexcusable relationships). Some criteria that outsiders appear to use to make these identifications are judgments of *equity* within a relationship that render, for example, certain sorts of age and resource differentials unacceptable; *duty and obligation* to partners that render certain forms of extra-dyadic relationship inappropriate; and concerns over *instrumentality* that lead to disapproval of some sorts of relationship, especially between people of unequal power, such as boss and employee. Finally, we note that some relationships in Western society are discouraged but not regarded as truly inappropriate, such as enemyship (Wiseman & Duck, 1995), or marriages of convenience

---

[2]For example, although most societies sanction marriage, only one form of system assumes free choice in marriage and relative freedom to leave that marriage under certain conditions. In other societies (as indeed in our own until surprisingly recently), marriages of convenience are much more common than most present Western theories would presume (Goodwin, 1998; Rothman, 1984).

for money or reasons other than "love" (Collins & Coltrane, 1995; Kephart, 1967)—paradoxically, society tolerates these, while disapproving of sexual promiscuity, "swinging," and prostitution.

All these considerations are driven by a discussion of the relevance of the point of view of the observer, especially as this relates to social forces that constrain and enforce norms of appropriateness, such as the practices of gossip and social accounting that promote strong control over the acceptability of relational forms (Bergmann, 1993). We note also the ways in which certain examples of tainted relationships have been differently classified across time, reflecting the social rather than the inherent nature of the relational transgression. Because our analysis taps into some key cultural beliefs/values about equity, power, duty, instrumentality, and the sanctity of written contracts, we also mention some cultural relativities about inappropriateness (although the bulk of our remarks inevitably betray our membership of "Western society" and, specifically, our knowledge of British and American attitudes and social codes in more ways than those so far acknowledged). Our goal is to provide readers with an analysis that may inform and enrich their readings of the specific inappropriate relationships discussed in the subsequent chapters of this book. We also hope that scrutiny of "inappropriateness" may shed light equally on the elements that constitute socially condoned "appropriate" relationships.

FROM SIN TO INAPPROPRIATENESS

"But this is fantastic," he said. "I don't know what I've been thinking about. First to tell you and then to ask you—this. One can't spy on one's wife through a friend—and that friend pretend to be her lover." "Oh, it's not done," I said, "but neither is adultery or theft or running away from the enemy's fire. The not done things are done every day, Henry. It's part of modern life. I've done most of them myself." (Greene, 1951, p. 17)

People have always done bad things to, and with, other people. Likewise, people have always been liable to social criticism for doing so. Moral rules, condemning certain sorts of behavior and approving others, are some of the oldest writings discovered (Ginsburg, 1988), and many of these rules speak of specific relationships (usually between superiors and inferiors, parents and children, or husbands and wives). The criteria for moral judgment of such behaviors have not always been the same, however, and neither have the consequences of transgression, except that the overall effect of the judgments is to reinforce a larger social order through direction and regulation of personal relationships, particularly in respect of sexual behavior (Davis, 1983). For instance, the sexual behaviors that could have rendered a Victorian "ruined" or "disgraced" might today be taken only as a mark of the "freedom" and "progress" of modern sexual identities, thus reflecting and reinforcing a looser and less differentiated social order of sexual hierarchy (Giddens, 1979).

Any exploration of criteria through which relational behavior is commonly designated as wrong encounters two shifts: one from the historical emphasis on the importance of formal (often public) humiliation of the person committing wrong behavior, toward a more recent emphasis on rehabilitation; the second from basically religious grounds for judgment toward secular grounds of "civility" and mutual respect. We also note that the older terms to describe relational transgressions, such as "sinful," once stood where the term "inappropriate" now denotes something deviating from propriety rather than bearing testament to the inherent corruption of the person. We parse the term "inappropriateness" as now connoting not inherent evil so much as misguidance, hence diminishing the impact of the judgment. For example, necrophilia, once regarded as a "Crime against Nature" (Davis, 1983), is now regarded as a psychological disorder, not as evidence of satanic influence (DSM-IV 302.9 classifies necrophilia as a "Paraphilia not otherwise specified").

Although the traditional religious bases still exist for accounts of [un]acceptability, and the current secular labels are often kissing cousins of the older religious ones, the present-day secular basis for judgment is importantly different in two respects. First, it rests not so much on the assumption that the actions of a person disclose the inherent badness of the person (e.g., as a "sinner" whose evil can be remedied through such things as physical pain, symbolizing the excision of the evil; King James, 1612), but instead focuses on the specific behaviors themselves and hence implies a greater extent to which they can be remedied in the future, rather than merely atoned for. Second, the traditional ethic rests on a presumption of the existence of naturally good moral laws whose transgression necessarily implicates the contrarily evil nature of the doer. Recent thought adopts a relativistic position based on the recognition of particular circumstances justifying or not justifying behavior on a particular occasion and taking account of consequences as well as intent. This blend of circumstances and inherent personality traits, rather than the latter alone, has the effect of diminishing the indication of a person's essentially evil nature when considering personal responsibility for inappropriate behavior.

A further central issue in assessments of present-day relationships is disapproval of instrumentality that makes use of relative power of partners. Whereas previously it might have been accepted that the upper and employing classes could [ab]use power over the lower, working classes, today's egalitarianism disapproves of that, just as it disapproves of parents' use of physical punishment of children. It is therefore probably significant that the label "inappropriate" nowadays attaches predominantly, as other chapters in this book indicate, to instances of sexual activity. The focus on matters of sexual resources rather than other relational resources, such as aid and comfort, has a long record in the history of inappropriate relation-ships (at least as far back as Joseph and Potiphar's wife; Genesis 39: 7–20), but is nowadays of particular concern as issues of power and sexual harass-ment gain greater recognition by evoking a spectre of instrumentality ver-sus genuine affection, where sex may be seen as "traded" in nonpeer relationships. Incidentally, it is worth noting that even though treason (see the U.S. Constitutional definition, based on giving aid and comfort to an enemy) is one relationship that is inappropriate and not always based on sex, sexually related metaphors are very often used to describe it (e.g., "sleeping with the enemy"), although we are grateful to Robin Goodwin for noting that sleeping with the enemy often is just that. The metaphor nonetheless implies that the physical is used to corrupt when higher moral goals should take precedence.

Finally, it is important to note that the label "inappropriate" reflects ab-stract and idealized social norms, not actual social practice. In reality, nor-mative behavior is often the exception. For example, although a single marriage lasting until the death of one of the partners may still be pre-scribed as the ideal "appropriate" adult heterosexual relationship in indus-trialized nations, there are relatively few such marriages (Kipnis, 1998). Similarly, although more than 50% of Americans will publicly condemn adultery, more than 50% of Americans (depending on the poll) also pri-vately admit to having committed it more than once (Kipnis, 1998), and we have no reason to believe that Americans are exceptional in this respect. Kipnis, however, noted (p. 293):

> Sexual self-reporting is notoriously unreliable; the statistics on adultery are sim-ply all over the place. Kinsey's reports famously pegged male adultery at 50 per-cent in 1948 and female adultery at 26 percent in 1953. The numbers currently in common usage, based on a 1994 survey by the National Opinion Research Center, are quite low by comparison (21 percent for men, 11 percent for women), but suspicion has been cast on the method for arriving at these figures and the data collection method itself (the interviewers were predominantly white, middle-aged women, for example). One problem is that men seem to over-report and women seem to underreport sexual activity. In the raw numbers gathered for this survey, apparently 64 percent of male sexual contacts can't be accounted for—or, rather, they could if, in a pool of 3,500 responses, 10 different women each had 2,000 partners they didn't record.

INAPPROPRIATE RELATIONSHIPS OR INAPPROPRIATE RELATIONAL BEHAVIOR?

We begin our examination of these issues by exploring the ways in which former President Bill Clinton discussed his relationship with Monica Lewinsky and the terms of the debate that ensued.

Grand Jury Testimony, August 17, 1998

Clinton: When I was alone with Ms. Lewinsky on certain occasions in early 1996, and once in early 1997, I engaged in conduct that was wrong. These encounters did not consist of sexual intercourse. They did not constitute sexual relations, as I understood that term to be defined at my January 17th, 1998 deposition.... But they did involve inappropriate, intimate contact. These inappropriate encounters ended, at my insistence, in early 1997. I also had occasional telephone conversations with Ms. Lewinsky that included inappropriate sexual banter.... I regret that what began as a friendship came to include this contact. (http://www.courttv.com/casefiles/clintoncrisis/clinton_testimony/1.html retrieved on August 5, 2000)

In the impeachment and attempted removal of President Clinton from office, the defense, prosecution, and President himself struggled to define "sexual relations." Yet the other key phrase popularized during the President's troubles—"inappropriate relationship"—met with little definitional debate.

The term "inappropriate relationship" in fact appears not to have been used by President Clinton himself, who referred only to inappropriate conduct, contact, and behaviors. We wonder, therefore, if there is a difference between an inappropriate relationship and inappropriate relational behavior (cf. also Cramer, 2000). The question may seem moot in the case of Clinton and Lewinsky, because the prosecution was most enthusiastic about discovering details of the pair's sexual contact regardless of whether or not their entire relationship was inappropriate. But Clinton himself implied that there is a crucial difference between a relationship and relational behavior when he regretted that "what began as a friendship came to include this conduct." The presumably appropriate relationship of "friendship" was compromised by inappropriate "conduct." (Whether or not a friendship between the President and a young, female White House intern is appropriate was not addressed in the trial.) This attempted distinction suggests at least that it is possible to distinguish between behaviors that are expected in a given type of relationship and those that are proscribed within a given relationship. It also suggests that some types of relationships are mutually incompatible, such as a friendship and a sexual relationship, even though married couples occasionally identify their spouse as their best friend. This paradox might be explained by the hypothesis that there is a social ordering of relationship behaviors and that "lower-order behaviors," such as friendship, are permitted in "higher-order relationships," such as marriage, but that the reverse is not true and renders the relationship de facto an inappropriate instance of its type.

Such common understandings of the boundaries of relationships lie at the root of dilemmas faced by, for example, nonromantic cross-sex friends (Werking, 1997, 2000; Baumgarte, chap. 6, this volume). It is evident that any couple in a nonnormative relationship takes account of (and *needs* to take account of) the beliefs and assumptions of the audience to whom they are communicating the nature of their relationship (e.g., see Masuda, 2000 on the ways in which former romantic partners, now friends, solve the dilemmas of presenting their relationship to different sorts of audiences). The underlying assumption is that the private form of the relationship can remain appropriate even when some of its conduct is not expected within the relational form recognized by the public. That assumption, however, depends on the couple being able to either keep the dynamics of their relationship out of the public domain or else construct a publicly acceptable account of those dynamics.

On the other hand, some inappropriate behaviors are frequently encountered within otherwise appropriate relationships. Spousal abuse and cruelty are examples of inappropriate behavior occurring in an appropriate relationship. Dishonesty, betrayal, public sex acts, and public arguments are other behaviors that are socially condemned yet can occur in socially acceptable relationships. In some cases, single inappropriate behaviors may jeopardize the appropriateness of an entire relationship. A bulletin from the U.S. Federal Bureau of Prisons (1999) identifies such slippery slopes:

> A staff member allegedly used facility weight equipment along with residents. While some staff might see this as innocuous, this establishes an unprofessional relationship with residents and must be avoided.... A staff member allegedly accepted free meals from a resident who worked at a fast food establishment and brought food back to the facility. This establishes an atmosphere in which small favors are exchanged, which easily leads to bribery and/or extortion.... A staff member allegedly purchased an automobile from a resident. This is clearly inappropriate and gives at least the appearance of bribery, even if the staff member paid full value for the automobile. (U.S. Federal Bureau of Prisons, 1999)

These behaviors, although appropriate for friendship, are seen to compromise the staff–resident relationship in a prison.

We appear, then, to be dealing with an implicit taxonomy of relationships and also with a separate implicit hierarchy of relational *behaviors* that are regarded as crossing Rubicons between one form of relationship and a different form. Once the boundary is crossed, the nature of the relationship is changed by these bridging behaviors, and only with great difficulty can the relationship be restored to its previous form. In the earlier example, gift giving is a bridge from properly formal to improperly informal; in the case of nonromantic relationships, sexual conduct is, according to circumstances, a bridge from a "friendship" to either an "inappropriate" sexual relationship or an "appropriate" romantic relationship. Thus, "inappropriate sexual relationship" is implicitly defined in terms of behavior (sex), whereas "appropriate romantic relationship" implies a broader set of legitimate feelings, thoughts, and behaviors.

Interestingly, the converse does not hold. Socially acceptable behavior occurring in a socially inappropriate relationship does not make that relationship appropriate. Examples abound:

- A gay couple seen holding hands does not find that this behavior—appropriate for heterosexual lovers—makes their relationship more acceptable to people who condemn homosexuality (Huston & Schwartz, 1995).
- Deeply committed heterosexual relations between a Catholic priest and a parishioner are condemned however deep, genuine, and long-lasting the love may be.
- Strong, devoted, committed, and exclusive love of a man toward one of his sheep does not make the relationship legally acceptable.

On the contrary, public awareness of such feelings and behaviors brings condemnation, not commendation, and puts people at greater risk for hate crimes and other lesser forms of social disapproval (Mazanec, 2001). Also, whereas "affection" is expected of a man toward his young daughter, "affection" between a pedophile and the same child is interpreted differently and is immediately suspect. The inappropriateness of a relationship is not established by mere absence or breakdown of behaviors paradigmatically expected in that relationship. Loss of respect, waning of love, or decrease in equity of contribution to the relationship do not, in and of themselves, suffice to render inappropriate the relationship that might have been founded on their growth (Duck, 1998). Thus, the behavior itself is not the sole criterion for appropriateness but is interpreted relative to expectations associated with the assumed relational form and other contextual cues provided by the person's role (father, priest, etc.).

Deferring, for the moment, discussion of the importance of these latter contextual cues, the previous discussion challenges us to differentiate between "a relationship" and "relational behavior" and to note that there are types of behavior that society regards as transitional markers between one form of relationship and another (Conville, 1988). This differentiation is no easy task for researchers, because many scholarly attempts at presentation of Paradigmatic Case Formulations and rules of relationships (e.g., Davis & Todd, 1985; Ginsburg, 1988) have focused extensively on *behaviors* as the relevant criteria for differentiating relationship types from each other without positing the notion of *transitional behaviors* (except in terms of quantity—increase of something, such as intimacy, being typically assumed almost exclusively to be the measure of change; Conville, 1988). Yet, in some relationships, an *observer's presumption* of a transition, where there is none according to the relational partners, poses problems for those partners (as shown by Werking, 1997, in her work on nonromantic cross-sex friendships). Werking (2000) noted both the difficulty and the significance of the ways in which partners in cross-sex friendships present their relationship to external audiences such as family and friends. She wrote that "[the] narratives told by research participants about cross-sex friendship are constructed within specific historical cultural and social configurations" (Werking, 2000, p. 130). Werking observed a distinction between public reports of relationships and the private conduct of relationships. This distinction rests partly on the difference between the "outsider view" of a relationship (the way in which it is presented to outsiders) and the "insider view" (the way in which people actually conduct their relationships in private between themselves).

Evidently, one reason for secrecy in a relationship is that insiders recognize the rhetorical problems of reporting about a relationship to certain public audiences (Masuda, 2000). Equally, presentation of a relationship in public can disturb the partners' needs for privacy. For example, there is evidence that, as part of the establishment of very close relationships, partners construct "personal idioms" (e.g., nicknames and pet terms for each other, other people, or behaviors) in order to talk about their experience in a way that is obscure to other people (Hopper, Knapp, & Scott, 1981). Given that the nature of the relationship is already established as close and personal, a main purpose of using such terms is to draw boundaries around the relationship and render it exclusive of other people, thus adding to its sense of private specialty. It is also possible for partners to carry out behaviors that please them personally while recognizing that other people might condemn them—or at the very least there could be problematic rhetorical dilemmas in presenting the relationship to other people without violating its essence as understood by the two partners (e.g., by revelation of partners' private sexual practices).

The acceptability of a relationship's definition to an insider or outsider will depend in part on the purpose for which it is intended to be defined, whether in research or everyday life, and whether by the partners themselves or for the benefit of outsiders (VanderVoort & Duck, 2000). Although there have been many attempts by researchers to define "a relationship" (e.g., Kelley, et al., 1983), all have met with criticism and none is universally accepted. Numerous authors (Acitelli, Duck, & West, 2000; Duck, 1990, 1994; Kelley, 1984; VanderVoort & Duck, 2000) have suggested that the issue of defining the nature of any kind of a close personal relationship is a remaining central problem for the field. Personal codes and private relational behaviors are well-established features of the development and conduct of relationships. Given the central problem of the insider and outsider perspectives on relationships (see Duck, 1990; Surra & Ridley, 1991), the definition of any "relationship" will be problematic, if unobservable private behaviors have a central role in personal relationships yet are never made public for fear of consequences—as in the case of relationships that partners suspect would be seen as inappropriate by others.

A fortiori it is going to be tough to define an "inappropriate relationship," especially because the previous quotations from Bill Clinton and others appear to differentiate behavior from relationship, or else make the assumption that behavior is not itself a relationship but only an indicator or measure of one for specific purposes and at particular times. Yet, as Spitzberg and Cupach (chap. 10, this volume) pointed out, particular behaviors make a relationship only when they are accepted and performed in a mutually acceptable way. If mutuality is the criterion, then Bill Clinton and Monica Lewinsky *did* have a relationship, not just a set of behavioral exchanges. All the same, prostitutes/gigolos and clients carrying out the same sexual behaviors in similar secret and hurried circumstances do not have a relationship in the sense in which "personal relationship" is normally understood in the research literature. Hence, what elements are critical in differentiating relationships from strings of behavior, and how do these help us understand inappropriate relationships?

One element that distinguishes a relationship from a behavior is concatenated extension over time (Hinde, 1981). Relationships are neither zero history nor zero future; instead, they are strings of instances of behaviors. Another element is a mental element: The relevant people both believe that they have a relationship (Duck, 1980). It is not reasonable to suppose that two people have a relationship just because one of them thinks that they do (see Spitzberg & Cupach, chap. 10, this volume) or because other people think they do. A third element of a relationship is that the majority of behaviors carried out within it have similar meaning to both partners and are relational acts. That is, their very performance with the other person under the presumption of shared meaning is the relationship (Duck, 1994). However, these three elements are not transparent to outsiders and may not even be apparent to them. The judgments made by outsiders are thus typically those that take least account of the internal and private dynamics of a relationship, and are also the reference point for the appropriateness of behavior. Thus, as far as judgments of appropriateness are concerned, the relationship is more than the sum of its component behaviors, but, as far as judgments of inappropriateness go, single sorts of behavior (mostly sexual ones) immediately transform a relationship from one sort to another in the minds of the public and partners alike. Such single inappropriate behaviors can apparently render a relationship publicly inappropriate even when they do not do so privately.

In short, the definition of appropriate and inappropriate relationships and behavior is insufficiently established by looking wholly inward to the relational partners (although that in itself is not unhelpful) and at their conjoint actions together. The definition depends on two things: first, the outsiders' views that define what is typically condemned in a given society and rely on the shame caused by public awareness of otherwise private behavior; and second, insiders' internalization of those views by reason of their membership of society. For reasons of such discouragement through public shaming, the police in Manchester, UK, recently began to publish in the newspaper the names and addresses of men caught "kerb-crawling" and soliciting prostitution in an area that the police were attempting to clean up (*The Times*, August, 2000). As Bergmann (1993) argued, gossip (or, much more significantly, the fear of becoming a notorious object of gossip) acts to order any society by laying out and informally enforcing guidelines for propriety. It is through networks and their tools of social communication that individuals and dyads are closely touched by an otherwise abstract "society" (Milardo & Duck, 2000). Such networks act as enforcers of society's norms and preferences, although these are buttressed by the media, pronouncements of religious and moral leaders, and the political and judicial systems.

Given this background, a taxonomy of appropriateness and inappropriateness depends in large part on the degree of stigma attached to the behavior when/if it becomes public, and also on the degrees of formal punishment exacted for such transgression. Public definition of appropriate behavior and inappropriate behavior is ratified by laws, the media, cultural traditions and stories, and an impressive list of "common sense" ideas about relationships (Fitch, 1998). Folk tales, for example, tell of the rewards for loyalty, drudgery, and submission in the Cinderella story, where Cinderella's reward (a handsome prince) follows from her uncomplaining faithfulness to her role as a household servant (not exactly the American dream!). In a search through written literature and folk stories dating back 1,000 years, Contarello and Volpato (1991) identified the same references to defining behaviors of true friendship, such as loyalty, trust, seeking the other's benefit even at the expense of one's own, and so on. Since Cicero's *De Amicitia*, these same consistent themes are clearly ratified as elements of acceptable friendships and are still borne out by scientific studies looking for core, shared, public concepts of friendship in a given society (Davis & Todd, 1985). Also, researchers as far back as Simmel (1950 ed.) have noted that relational partners refer their internal relational dynamics to social norms as well as to their own private evaluations in order to judge relational satisfaction (Duck, 1998). Thus, it would be hardly surprising if these same broad cultural and social norms were not also implicit guides to couples' private expectations about their own relational behavior and form.

For one thing, in sexual and marital relationships there appear to be a number of expectations about appropriateness of partners for one another as judged from public and cultural materials. For example, it is expected that marriage is normative between the ages of about 22 and 28 (Cunningham & Antill, 1995); that partners are both likely to be about the same age (Norton & Moorman, 1987) and very likely from the same social, demographic, religious, and ethnic groups (Kerckhoff, 1974); and that partners are, of course, required to meet social criteria for mental fitness to conduct the enterprise. Reproductive issues frame many social norms concerning sexual relationships. For example, the inappropriateness (as society sees it) of age difference is often articulated as "old enough to be her father" types of statements that invoke the incest taboo. Significant age differences between partners also attract public interest and commentary, especially if the woman in a marriage is markedly older than the man (perhaps because a large age difference is "worse" when the older person is a woman, because she may no longer be able to bear children; Kenrick & Trost, 2000). In much the same way, many ancient concerns over chastity and adultery were tied to the assumed need for certitude of bloodlines.

Equally likely to attract public curiosity and suspicion, if not disapprobation, are weddings after periods of courtship judged excessively long (say, 10 years) or excessively short (say, 3 days). People entering such marriages are held up for display in the newspapers and on TV, a symbolic ratification of the curiosity—if not inappropriateness—of their relationship in the society. Letters about such couplings are written to newspapers, and audience members in popular TV shows featuring unusual relationships scream their disapproval in ways that reinforce the underlying moral beliefs of the culture. Such curiosity does not so often attach to friendships, where large age differences are less marked even though they sometimes arouse suspicion or disapproval. Again, sexual relationships are the kind most likely to attract condemnation (Davis, 1983).

Public disapproval of certain types of sexual relationships clearly changes with the times while retaining some recognizability from age to age. Adultery, for example, has long been disapproved, despite its prevalence. Homosexuality was an acceptable and institutionalized relationship in ancient Greece, but has more often attracted disapproval. Greater and lesser degrees of condemnation attach to mixed marriages (whether mixed across races or religions), depending on cultural, historical, and religious contexts (Gaines & Ickes, 2000; Gaines & Leaver, chap. 4, this volume).

GREEN, YELLOW, AND RED LIGHTS: THE PERMISSIBLE, THE CAUTIONARY, AND THE CONDEMNED

[speaking about a private investigator] It isn't, when you come to think of it, a quite respectable trade, the detection of the innocent, for aren't lovers nearly always innocent? They have committed no crime, they are certain in their own minds that they have done no wrong, "as long as no one but myself is hurt," the old tag is ready on their lips, and love, of course, excuses everything—so they believe, and so I used to believe in the days when I loved. (Greene, 1951, p. 23)

We previously deferred, until this later point, discussion of roles and contexts in the definition and reaction to inappropriate relationships. One oddity we have encountered in our reflections on the notion of inappropriate relationships is that although "relationships" are separated from "behaviors," a given behavior is seldom a neutral element of the equation in deciding relationship appropriateness or inappropriateness. Rather, behavior is given part of its meaning by other contexts available to the judge. For instance, the knowledge that a person is married is sufficient to render sexual behavior appropriate or inappropriate depending on the partner with whom the sex takes place. Likewise, the fact that someone is contextualized by the role of priest renders certain behaviors as inherently debarred (e.g., a passionate kiss) irrespective of the nature of the other factors that would be relevant in judging those same behaviors if one actor were not a priest. The knowledge that people inhabit certain socially defined roles steers the interpretation of their behavior toward particular judgments that either decrease suspicion ("He kissed her because he is her father") or else tend to condemnation ("He is a pedophile and he touched the girl's arm"). Although such role ascriptions are essentially circular ("He did what he did because he is the sort of person he is, namely the sort of person who does what he did"), the ability of an outside observer to pre-ascribe roles to the performers of relational behavior clearly contributes to some of the moral weight attaching to judgments of behaviors and relationships.

In parallel fashion, descriptive terms can be morally loaded and can excuse or accuse the user. As Davis (1983) and Winters and Duck (2001) noted, even the language used to describe sexual acts and bodily parts itself carries such moral weight. The use of Latin names for sexual organs and activity is regarded as acceptable in public discourse or in print, whereas use of Anglo-Saxon terms for the same items is regarded as vulgar, obscene, and common. Davis (1983) noted that no one is barred from using the term *copulate* on TV, but are still discouraged from using "the F-word" (itself a handy euphemism for another term and one that seems to render reference to the activity publicly acceptable). The point is that even the type of language used to describe relational behaviors can be traced to an implicit social order where the learned and professional classes use Latin terms for excretion, copulation, and incest with one's mother, but vulgar common people use other terms. The opprobrium attached to violations of norms and roles is based on the acceptability of high-order codes of speech and the unacceptability of lower-order codes, not the referent per se (see Winters & Duck, 2001 for discussion of the relational implications of swearing).

Given the distinctions that we have already made, there are roles and descriptive terms that contextualize interpretations of behavior; relationships that are a priori inappropriate within the culture; behaviors in a relationship that subsequently render the relationship contaminated; and behaviors that are inappropriate but do not render the relationship an inappropriate one, but instead just render the performer of the behavior morally suspect. Besides these differences, there appears to be a rank ordering of condemnation from the merely curious to the utterly irredeemable. This rank ordering interacts with the roles of the participants and judgment of their acts (consensual seduction of a patient by a doctor is judged more seriously than is consensual seduction of an unmarried schoolteacher by an unmarried neighbor). Cramer (2000) made a similar observation.

The ranking of relational inappropriateness reflects social attitudes toward the circumscriptions of certain roles, but it is also reflected in social codes broken and punishments incurred. Punishments can be social, religious, or legal, and can include anything from gossip to excommunication to lynching or the death penalty. With the exceptions of stalking and physical abuse, which are now unacceptable in any kind of relationship, a large number of these condemnations attach specifically to sexual relationships rather than to friendship or other forms of more general intimacy. However, as we have already observed, the distinction among roles, behaviors, and relationships is critical.

At the very edge of moral reproof are behaviors that are regarded as relational nuisances but hardly sufficient grounds for condemning the relationship itself unless compounded with other nefarious behaviors. Privacy and secrecy about self, for example, are not much praised as relational behaviors in an age where self-disclosure and emotional expressiveness are offered as the foundations of emblematically successful relationships (Duck, 1998). All the same, a tendency to such closedness would be unlikely in itself to render a relational partner "inappropriate," although it could lead to judgments of lack of skill. (A relationship where one partner is so unskilled as to create difficulty for the other person in all private settings is a class of inappropriate relationship, but not one that we deal with here.)

On the other hand, because it is clearly important that people engaging in private behaviors that (they fear/know) would attract public stigma keep their relational activities private, secrecy about the relationship is likely to be a major management issue for people who recognize that outsiders might view them as acting inappropriately together. For example, in Nathaniel Hawthorne's (1850) *The Scarlet Letter,* the 17th-century priest Dimmesdale does not wish to hide his adulterous relationship with Hester Prynne and wants to wear the scarlet letter A (for adulterer) as she is forced to do, but Hester dissuades him, saying his congregation would be devastated: "to destroy their faith would be a greater sin." Hester's secret is revealed but she is bound to keep two other men's secrets (Dimmesdale's and her returned husband-blackmailer's), leaving her alone with her shame. A question raised by this dilemma is whether Hester is more or less miserable than the two men because she bears her shame publicly. In related fashion, the matter of gays and lesbians "coming out" is a major life issue: whether to learn to live a double life and lie constantly, or to be open and risk being targeted in hate crimes (Huston & Schwartz, 1995). In such cases the pressures of a relationship's nature create identity stresses for the partners, based on the tension between private behavior and public expectations. Partners in inappropriate relationships have to establish their own rules and boundaries, leading perhaps a more examined life than do others. It takes work and commitment to stay in an inappropriate relationship, because the stakes are so high. The conduct of inappropriate relationships therefore depends very largely on each person's degree of trust in the other as a keeper of the secret.

A relationship is not inappropriate merely because it includes unskilled people or bad behaviors, but also because the behaviors are inconsistent with social expectations for that relationship type. Therefore, exposure of the behaviors would jeopardize the social integrity of the performers. One subtle reason for condemning relationships as inappropriate appears to be based on the extent to which this inconsistency threatens other public modes of acting at a deeper level than the dyad and hence threatens social order. Those acts that imply more general profaning of relationships and of the society's structures are most censoriously regarded, whereas those with more localized effects—dismissible as particular to the persons involved or due to some mismatch of criteria for good relationships—are less reprovable.

Given our tripartite distinction among relationships and behaviors, insider–outsider perspectives, and the prescriptive nature of role expectations of certain kinds, we now offer the following categorization of relationships and relational behavior on a continuum guided by degree of social disapproval as expressed in legal, religious, social, and informal punishments. We believe that this ordering reflects a deeper structure of social values and the intent to sustain them (cf. Davis, 1983). Table 1.1 summarizes these categories.

The least opprobrious of tainted relationships and behaviors are merely *Unconventional (noteworthy, suspicious)*. Such relationships and behaviors stretch the norms in some way and may inspire unpleasant gossip, but do not break any codified (written-down) rules. Some standard examples are cross-sex friendships (see Baumgarte, chap. 6, this volume); large age difference, overshort or overlong courtship, class mismatch, culture mismatch (see Adams & Rosen-Grandon, chap. 5, this volume), Internet-initiated relationships (Parks & Roberts, 1998), relationships based on personal advertisements (Goodwin, 1990), those Western marriages arranged between people who have never met the partner before or clearly do it for the money offered by TV shows, enemyship (Wiseman & Duck, 1995), hatred, rivalry (Zorn, 1995), and too great a frequency of legal marriages and divorces (e.g., Liz Taylor or Larry King). Likewise, marrying "not for love" is, within Western society, an unconventional form even though Kephart (1967) showed that over half of American women would consider it (a

TABLE 1.1

A Taxonomy of Inappropriate Relationships and Behaviors

Unconventional *[noteworthy, suspicious]*	These stretch the norms in some way and inspire unpleasant gossip, but do not break any codified rules (e.g., cross-sex friendships, large age difference, overshort or overlong courtship, class mismatch, culture mismatch, Internet initiated, personal ad initiated, hatred, rivalry, numerous marriages and divorces, marriage of "convenience")
Disapproved	
notable but not necessarily deleterious to social reputation	No formal role ascriptions are violated, but dispreferred or instrumental behaviors are performed (e.g., serial casual seduction, green card marriage, consensual sadomasochism, prostitution)
scandalous and damaging to social reputation because of violation of prescribed roles	Formal role ascriptions are violated, codified rules or practices are broken; punishment may include social ostracism, and legal or institutional reprimand (e.g., doctor–patient sexual relationships, teacher–student sexual relationships, extra-marital affairs)
Forbidden *(totally intolerable or inexcusable)*	Reprehensible, taboo, illegal, and usually leading to significant formal punishment (e.g., incest, pedophilia, stalking, abuse, rape)

Note: Relationships that vary significantly in their position in this taxonomy (or may not even appear in it), depending on the observer, are homosexual relationships, interracial relationships, and polygamy. For some observers, these relationships are reprehensible and yet for others they are entirely acceptable.

finding partially disputed by Simpson, Campbell, & Berscheid, 1986). It is important to note that there is a difference between marrying "not for love" (but out of loneliness, say) and marrying "for the money" or for some other instrumental motive, which is more firmly censured because it is seen as debasing both the partner and the institution rather than merely employing it unconventionally.

The next rank of tainted relationships is *disapproved*, and takes two subforms. The first is *notable but not necessarily deleterious to social reputation*, because no formal role ascriptions are violated but rather dispreferred or instrumental behaviors are carried out. Some examples are serial casual seduction, green-card marriage, consensual sadomasochism, and prostitution. The more serious subform is *scandalous and damaging to*

social reputation because of violation of prescribed roles. These relationships and behaviors break some codified rules or practices and are seen as
deviating from the prescriptions of one or the other partner's role obligations. The perpetrators may be punished by ostracism and severe damage
to a reputation (e.g., eloping with a friend's fiancé/e). The most serious
cases can lead to legal and institutional reprimand (e.g., loss of a job,
grounds for divorce). Some standard examples are doctor–patient sexual
relationships (see Garrett, chap. 8, this volume), teacher–student sexual
relationships, and extra-marital affairs (see Allan & Harrison, chap. 3, this
volume).

The most serious category of inappropriate relationships is *forbidden
(totally intolerable or inexcusable).* These are reprehensible, taboo, illegal,
and usually lead to significant formal punishment, irrespective of the roles
of the persons concerned, with the single exception that establishment of
mental incompetence might mitigate the consequences of having perpetrated the behavior. Some standard examples are incest, pedophilia (see
Howitt, chap. 11, this volume), stalking (see Spitzberg & Cupach, chap.
10, this volume), abuse, and rape.

Relationships that vary in their position on the continuum (or may not
ever appear on it) depending on the observer are homosexual relationships
(see Yip, chap. 7, this volume), interracial relationships (see Gaines &
Leaver, chap. 4, this volume), and polygamy. For some observers, these relationships are entirely acceptable and yet for others they are entirely reprehensible.

BOONS, BANES, BONDS, AND BINDS OF APPROPRIATE AND INAPPROPRIATE RELATIONSHIPS

> Woe to you, scribes and Pharisees, hypocrites! For you are like whited
> sepulchres, which on the outside appear beautiful, but within they are full of the
> bones of the dead and of all kinds of filth. So you also on the outside appear righ-
> teous to others, but within you are full of hypocrisy and iniquity. (Matthew
> 23:27–28)

We hesitate to suggest that society is now, or has ever been, guilty of over-
much consistency in attitudes toward the inappropriateness and appropriateness of other people's relationships. Absence of love is not always
accepted as a reason for declaring a marital relationship inappropriate.
Presence of deep love is not yet universally accepted as a measure of appropriateness of relationships—homosexual, or adulterous relationships, or
marriages themselves, in several cultures, are not always rendered acceptable no matter how deep the love. We note that the 1994 U.S. Defense of
Marriage Act denied marriage to gays on the grounds that it would "morally

degrade the institution" (although widespread adultery apparently does not). It is also a paradox that whereas marriage is terrifically popular, it is not particularly successful as judged from the increasing rate of divorce (Fine & Demo, 2000). Indeed, it has reached the point where previously normative relationships become exceptions—we applaud marriages that last and are awed by them (Pearson, 1996). An inappropriate relationship usually does not enjoy a large social network and therefore depends to a much greater extent on the strength of the particular bond between the two partners (Milardo & Allan, 2000; see also Allan & Harrison, chap. 3, this volume). The absence of such a network is both a boon and a bane: Decreased needs to play secret games to larger numbers of people are balanced against the lack of support for the relationship by other people. Thus, some inappropriate relationships may in part be bound together by the "us versus them" feeling, and by the paradox that expected public reproof of the relationship is both a bind and a bond.

Given these disparities, we might hope that judgment of appropriateness based on the notions of civility and instrumentality might act as a useful—if variable—criterion. However, norms for clarifying issues of instrumentality are set by the powerful, not by the powerless. Those laws and codes that are instituted to protect the powerless (e.g., sexual harassment laws) also have the side effect of silencing them by discounting their consent and by implicit ascription of the people to other roles that have less power. For example, in a famous recent case, a Seattle high school teacher was found to have been having a consensual sexual relationship with one of her pupils. The boy was excused for being "a minor," and the teacher was excused for being "a woman"—both parties being excused on the basis of their powerlessness! However, when the teacher later broke the terms of her probation and became pregnant by the boy, the punishment was heavy on her, despite acknowledged mutual consent.

This case ends our analysis by returning us to one of our initial questions: Why is it customary to judge personal relationships, private behavior, or intimacy as "appropriate" or "inappropriate"? What is the social function of policing private relationships? Why is it so compelling to label relationships as "inappropriate"? Moralists, cynics, and feminists say that the issue is power (e.g., Kipnis, 1998), whereas others offer the variant that unrestrained sex is seen as threatening social structure (e.g., Davis, 1983). It is not a matter of whether a particular marriage is safe, but instead whether the institution itself is viable, possible, and reasonable. Does it fit other current social values such as independence, self-actualization, women's rights, and so on, or is it effectively outmoded in Western society now that birth control is so reliable, whether inside or outside of marriage? Perhaps it is that society senses that inappropriate relationships point to the very unsustainability of appropriate relationships, or to the contradictions in norms of love and marriage. The label "inappropriate" perhaps points to the impossibility of universal adherence to idealized norms and at the same time to the dire consequences for breaking them (Kipnis, 1998). Our point, paralleling Davis (1983) and Kipnis (1998, 2000), is that the question "Was he faithful to his wife?" masks, and is substituted for, the question "Is marriage a viable social institution?" Society prefers condemnation of specific adultery—in the face of its widespread occurrence—as a way to avoid evaluating the premise that the relationship of marriage is equivalent to or sustained by the specific behaviors of fidelity or the particular role requirements of "husband" and "wife." Thus, as Milardo and Wellman (1992) argued, the personal *is* the social, or rather scarlet letters are painted on the whited sepulchres as a warning to everyone.

SUMMARY

This chapter has attempted to define some criteria for regarding relationships—particularly sexual relationships—as "inappropriate." We differentiated between behaviors and relationships, noting that no behavior by itself renders a relationship inappropriate, but instead various contextual factors add to its import in a given set of circumstances. We suggested that the judgment of relationship behaviors is moving from the view that behavior is inherently bad toward the adjustment of moral comment on circumstances and contexts. Roles, social expectations, and the implicit threat of the behavior to social institutions are all relevant to the adjudication of relationship behavior, but the underlying nervousness about "inappropriate" behaviors or relationships comes from the threat of such activity to underlying social orders.

REFERENCES

Acitelli, L. K., Duck, S. W., & West, L. (2000). Embracing the social in personal relationships and research. In W. Ickes & S. W. Duck (Eds.), *Social psychology and personal relationships* (pp. 215–227). Chichester, UK: Wiley.

Bergmann, J. R. (1993). *Discreet indiscretions: The social organization of gossip.* New York: Aldine de Gruyter.

Collins, R., & Coltrane, S. (1995). *Sociology of marriage and family: Gender, love and property.* Chicago: Nelson Hall.

Contarello, A., & Volpato, C. (1991). Images of friendship: Literary depictions through the ages. *Journal of Social and Personal Relationships, 8,* 49–75.

Conville, R. (1988). Relational transitions: An inquiry into their structure and functions. *Journal of Social and Personal Relationships, 5,* 423–437.

Cramer, D. (2000, July). *Towards a conceptual framework for studying 'inappropriate' relationships and relationship behaviors?* Paper presented in the Symposium on Inappropriate Relationships at the Second Joint Conference of the International Society for the Study of Personal Relationships and the International Network on Personal Relationships, Brisbane, Australia.

Cunningham, J. D., & Antill, J. K. (1995). Current trends in non-marital cohabitation: In search of the POSSLQ. In J. T. Wood & S. W. Duck (Eds.), *Under-studied relationships: Off the beaten track [Understanding relationship processes 6]* (pp. 148–172). Thousand Oaks, CA: Sage.

Davis, K. E., & Todd, M. J. (1985). Assessing friendship: Prototypes, paradigm cases and relationship description. In S. W. Duck & D. Perlman (Eds.), *Understanding personal relationships* (pp. 17–38). London: Sage.

Davis, M. S. (1983). *SMUT: Erotic reality/obscene ideology*. Chicago: University of Chicago Press.

Duck, S. W. (1980). Personal relationships research in the 1980s: Towards an understanding of complex human sociality. *Western Journal of Speech Communication, 44*, 114–119.

Duck, S. W. (1990). Relationships as unfinished business: Out of the frying pan and into the 1990s. *Journal of Social and Personal Relationships, 7*, 5–29.

Duck, S. W. (1994). *Meaningful relationships: Talking, sense, and relating*. Thousand Oaks: Sage.

Duck, S. W. (1998). *Human relationships* (3rd ed.). London: Sage.

Fine, M. A., & Demo, D. (2000). Divorce: Societal ill or normative transition? In R. Milardo & S. W. Duck (Eds.), *Families as relationships* (pp. 135–156). Chichester, UK: Wiley.

Fitch, K. L. (1998). *Speaking relationally: Culture, communication, and interpersonal connection*. New York: Guilford.

Gaines, S., & Ickes, W. (2000). Perspectives on interracial relationships. In W. Ickes & S. W. Duck (Eds.), *The social psychology of personal relationships* (pp. 55–79). Chichester, UK: Wiley.

Giddens, A. (1979). *Central problems in social theory: Action, structure and contradiction in social analysis*. Berkeley: University of California Press.

Ginsburg, G. P. (1988). Rules, scripts and prototypes in personal relationships. In S. W. Duck (Ed.), *Handbook of personal relationships* (pp. 23–39). Chichester, UK: Wiley.

Goodwin, R. (1990). Dating agency members: Are they "different"? *Journal of Social and Personal Relationships, 7*, 423–430.

Goodwin, R. (1998). Personal relationships and social change: The "realpolitik" of cross-cultural research in transient cultures. *Journal of Social and Personal Relationships, 15*, 227–247.

Greene, G. (1951). *The end of the affair*. Harmonsworth, UK: Penguin.

Hawthorne, N. (1850). *The scarlet letter*. Boston: Houghton Mifflin.

Hinde, R. A. (1981). The bases of a science of interpersonal relationships. In S. W. Duck & R. Gilmour (Eds.), *Personal relationships 1: Studying personal relationships* (pp. 1–22). London: Academic Press.

Hopper, R., Knapp, M. L., & Scott, L. (1981). Couples' personal idioms: Exploring intimate talk. *Journal of Communication, 31*, 23–33.

Huston, M., & Schwartz, P. (1995). Lesbian and gay male relationships. In J. T. Wood & S. W. Duck (Eds.), *Under-studied relationships: Off the beaten track [Understanding relationship processes 6]* (pp. 89–121). Thousand Oaks, CA: Sage.

Kelley, H. H. (1984). Affect in personal relations. In P. Shaver (Ed.), *Review of personality and social psychology* (Vol. 5, pp. 89–115). Newbury Park, CA: Sage.

Kelley, H. H., Berscheid, E., Christensen, A., Harvey, J., Huston, T. L., Levinger, G., McClintock, D., Peplau, L. A., & Peterson, D. (1983). *Close relationships*. San Francisco: Freeman.

Kenrick, D. T., & Trost, M. R. (2000). Evolutionary approaches to relationships. In W. Ickes & S. W. Duck (Eds.), *The social psychology of personal relationships* (pp. 156–178). Chichester, UK: Wiley.

Kephart, W. M. (1967). Some correlates of romantic love. *Journal of Marriage and the Family, 29,* 470–474.

Kerckhoff, A. C. (1974). The social context of interpersonal attraction. In T. L. Huston (Ed.), *Foundations of interpersonal attraction* (pp. 61–77). New York: Academic Press.

King James, I & VI. (1612). *Malleus maleficarum* [The hammer of witches]. London: Regis Books.

Kipnis, L. (1998). Adultery. *Critical Inquiry, 24,* 289–327.

Kipnis, L. (2000, May). *Kissing and telling.* Paper presented at the Civility Symposium, Iowa City, Iowa.

Masuda, M. (2000). *Post-dissolution relationships.* Doctoral thesis, University of Iowa, Iowa City.

Mazanec, M. (2001). *Hysteria and attraction.* Doctoral prospectus, University of Iowa, Iowa City.

Milardo, R. M., & Allan, G. (2000). Social networks and marital relationships. In R. M. Milardo & S. W. Duck (Eds.), *Families as relationships* (pp. 117–134). Chichester, UK: Wiley.

Milardo, R. M., & Duck, S. W. (2000). Families as relationships In R. Milardo & S. W. Duck *Families as relationships* (pp. 1–7) Chichester, UK: Wiley.

Milardo, R. M., & Wellman, B. (1992). The personal is social. *Journal of Social and Personal Relationships, 9,* 339–342.

Norton, A. J., & Moorman, J. E. (1987). Current trends in marriage and divorce among American women. *Journal of Marriage and the Family, 49,* 3–14.

Parks, M. R., & Roberts, L. D. (1998). "Making MOOsic": The development of personal relationships on-line and a comparison of their off-line counterparts. *Journal of Social and Personal Relationships, 15,* 517–537.

Pearson, J. C. (1996). Forty-forever years? In N. Vanzetti & S. W. Duck (Eds.), *A lifetime of relationships* (pp. 383–405). Pacific Grove, CA: Brooks/Cole.

Rothman, E. (1984). *Hands and hearts: A history of courtship in America.* New York: Basic Books.

Simmel, G. (1950). *The sociology of Georg Simmel.* New York: Free Press.

Simpson, J. A., Campbell, B., & Berscheid, E. (1986). The association between romantic love and marriage: Kephart (1967) twice revisited. *Personality and Social Psychology Bulletin , 12,* 363–372.

Surra, C. A., & Ridley, C. (1991). Multiple perspectives on interaction: Participants, peers and observers. In B. M. Montgomery & S. W. Duck (Eds.), *Studying interpersonal interaction* (pp. 35–55). New York: Guilford.

U.S. Federal Bureau of Prisons. (1999, September 27). *Community update: Notes to BOP's local partners.* Retrieved May 8, 2000 from the World Wide Web: http://www.bop.gov/ccdpg/ccdcu23/html

VanderVoort, L. A., & Duck, S. W. (2000). Talking about relationships: Variations on a theme. In K. Dindia & S. W. Duck (Eds.), *Communication and personal relationships.* (pp. 1–12) Chichester, UK: Wiley.

Werking, K. (1997). *Just good friends: Cross-sex friendships.* New York: Guilford.

Werking, K. (2000). Cross-sex friendship research as ideological practice. In K. Dindia & S. W. Duck (Eds.), *Communication and personal relationships* (pp. 113–130) Chichester, UK: Wiley.

Winters, A. M., & Duck, S. W. (2001). You ****!!! Swearing as an aversive and a relational activity. In R. Kowalski (Ed.), *Behaving badly: Aversive behaviors in interpersonal realtionships* (pp. 59–77). Washington, DC: APA Books.

Wiseman, J. P., & Duck, S. W. (1995). Having and managing enemies: A very challenging relationship. In S. W. Duck & J. T. Wood (Eds.), *Confronting relationship challenges [understanding relationship processes 5]* (pp. 43–72). Thousand Oaks, CA: Sage.

Zorn, T. (1995). Bosses and buddies: Constructing and performing simultaneously hierarchical and close friendship relationships. In J. T. Wood & S. W. Duck (Eds.), *Under-studied relationships: Off the beaten track [understanding relationship processes 6]* (pp. 122–147). Thousand Oaks, CA: Sage.

2

Functional Features: An Evolutionary Perspective on Inappropriate Relationships

Pamela C. Regan
California State University

All relationships, whether short term or long term, carry the potential to benefit or harm us—as individuals, as a society, and as a species. This chapter explores the factors (or functional features) that render long-term, romantic relationships "appropriate" from an evolutionary (i.e., adaptive) perspective. Research conducted within and across a variety of cultures and historical times reveals extensive similarities in the preferences and choices that men and women make as they seek to attract and retain a long-term mate. In particular, individuals who possess various dispositional (e.g., intelligence, openness, emotional stability), physical (e.g., fertility, health), interpersonal (e.g., mutual attraction, similarity, fidelity), and social (e.g., status) characteristics are overwhelmingly preferred, sought after, and chosen as mates. These attributes may, in the ancestral past, have conferred certain survival or reproductive benefits.

That is, it is likely that people in our ancestral environment who possessed these functional features, and/or who selected their partners on the basis of these features, were more likely to survive and reproduce than were those who selected partners on the basis of other characteristics. The former's offspring, in turn, would tend to demonstrate these preferences and characteristics. Thus, an examination of contemporary mating themes provides a window into the evolutionary heritage of our species.

EVOLUTIONARY MODELS OF HUMAN MATING

> The mind is a set of information-processing machines that were designed by natural selection to solve adaptive problems faced by our hunter-gatherer ancestors. (Cosmides & Tooby, 1997, p. 1)

All of the contemporary theories of human mating considered in this chapter are predicated on the theoretical principles of evolutionary psychology, encapsulated in the previous quotation. Specifically, according to noted evolutionary theorists Cosmides and Tooby (1997; also see Tooby & Cosmides, 1992), evolutionary psychology focuses on the design of the human mind (the neural circuits we have that process information). In addition, evolutionary psychologists conceptualize the human mind as composed of many, specialized processing systems. For example, we possess neural circuitry specialized for mate selection, which is different from the circuitry we possess for food selection or language acquisition. Evolutionary psychology also acknowledges that the human mind—our specialized neural circuitry—was designed by the processes of natural and sexual selection originally articulated by Darwin (1859, 1871). Relatedly, evolutionary psychologists believe that the human mind was designed to solve adaptive problems (i.e., recurrent problems in our evolutionary history that had implications for reproduction and survival, including how to select, attract, and retain an "appropriate" mate). And finally, evolutionary psychology—and, therefore, all models of human mating based on evolutionary principles—is oriented toward our species' very distant past. Insofar as natural selection takes time, the human mind was designed to solve problems that existed thousands of years ago, and that affected the daily existence of our hunter-gatherer forbears.

With these principles in mind, evolutionary models of human mating consider the ways in which mating behavior is influenced by psychological heuristics or mechanisms that were selected because they overcame obstacles to reproduction located in the human ancestral past, and enabled our ancestors to make "appropriate" relational decisions. From an evolutionary perspective, an "appropriate" relational decision is one that results in a high(er) probability of gene replication and the production of viable offspring (i.e., offspring who survive to reach reproductive maturity). By the same token, an "inappropriate" relational decision is one that produces a low(er) chance of reproductive success for the individual. Thus, an appropriate decision is simply an adaptive one, or one that enhances reproductive success, and an appropriate partner is one who possesses attributes that enhance, and/or who lacks attributes that hinder, reproductive success.

It is important to recognize that the evolutionary judgment of what constitutes "appropriate" and "inappropriate" is based solely on the concepts of adaptation and reproductive success, and makes no claims of moral correctness. In addition, simply because one type of relational decision may be "inappropriate" from an evolutionary standpoint does not preclude the possibility that individuals living in present-day societies will make just such decisions, or the possibility that those "inappropriate" decisions may produce positive consequences for the individual (and, conversely, that seemingly "appropriate" decisions may produce negative consequences). For example, as discussed in the chapters on same-sex relationships and pedophilia included in this volume, some men and women prefer and select as mates individuals with whom they cannot reproduce (e.g., children who have not yet reached reproductive maturity, or same-sex partners); these relationships would be considered "inappropriate" by evolutionary, but not necessarily by moral or societal, standards.

WHO IS AN "APPROPRIATE" MATE?

Relational decisions must be made on a number of levels, including whom to select as a potential mate; how to attract or communicate one's interest to that particular individual; how to retain the partner, once chosen; and how to fend off potential competitors for his or her affections. At any given step, an "inappropriate" decision can be made. The rest of this chapter focuses on the first major reproductive decision that an individual faces—whom to select as a long-term partner. Evolutionary principles and contemporary models of mate selection suggest four major types of functional feature that have implications for reproductive success, outlined next.

Emotional Fitness Features

When considering a potential long-term mate, emotional fitness is of paramount importance. Grounded in the principles of attachment originally proposed by Bowlby (1973), evolutionary models recognize that the human biological design favors the formation of enduring relationships and few sex differences in long-term mating behavior (e.g., Cunningham, Druen, & Barbee, 1997; Miller & Fishkin, 1997; Zeifman & Hazan, 1997). Specifically, because human offspring are characterized by a period of dependency that extends well beyond infancy, successful pairbonding and childrearing depend for both sexes on the ability to select a mate who can and will provide sustained social and emotional support. Consequently, both men and women are presumed to be particularly desirous of long-term partners who possess prosocial personality characteristics that indicate an ability and willingness to emotionally commit to the reproductive partner, the reproductive relationship, and the resulting offspring.

Empirical evidence strongly supports these theoretical suppositions. Numerous studies reveal a robust preference pattern such that men and women—irrespective of their sexual orientation—overwhelmingly prefer intelligent, honest, dependable long-term partners who are emotionally stable and possess a "good" personality (e.g., Howard, Blumstein, & Schwartz, 1987; Regan & Berscheid, 1997; Regan, Levin, Sprecher, Christopher, & Cate, 2000). For example, in one of the earliest documented examinations of mate preference, Hill (1945) asked a sample of college students to rank order a list of 18 characteristics in terms of their importance in a dating partner. The most important attributes, according to his participants, were "dependable character," "emotional stability," and "pleasing disposition." As illustrated in Table 2.1, other researchers have since replicated these results using the same list of features (e.g., Hudson & Henze, 1969; McGinnis, 1958). More recently, Regan (1998b) asked men and women to indicate their ideal mate preferences for a larger variety of characteristics. For both sexes, the "perfect" long-term romantic partner possessed high amounts of humor, friendliness, and sociability.

In addition, these same preferences are seen in men and women from a variety of cultures (e.g., Hatfield & Sprecher, 1995). For example, Buss et al. (1990) conducted a large-scale survey involving over 10,000 men and women from a wide variety of countries and cultures (e.g., Africa, Asia, Eastern Europe, North America, Western Europe, and South America). Each participant in the study received a list of traits similar to the ones in Table 2.1, which they rated in terms of importance. There were some fairly strong cultural differences. Attributes related to domestic skills and domesticity (e.g., "good housekeeper" and "desire for home and children") were most highly desired by people in African countries (including Zambia and Nigeria) and in South America (Brazil, Colombia, and Venezuela). Men and women from North American cultures (i.e., the United States and Canada), as well as those living in most Western European countries (e.g., England, Ireland, France, Italy, Belgium, and Norway) placed low value on these characteristics. Despite these differences, however, men and women from *all* cultures emphasized a dependable character and emotional stability when evaluating a potential marriage partner.

Not only do men and women from around the world desire similar intra-individual features when considering a potential long-term mate, but they are equally discriminating. Regan (1998a) asked a sample of young adults to indicate their minimum mate selection standards, or the lowest amount of various

TABLE 2.1

The Stability of Long-Term Mate Preferences Over Time

	Rank Order					
	Men			Women		
Characteristic	1945	1958	1969	1945	1958	1969
Dependable character	1	1	1	2	1	2
Emotional stability	2	2	3	1	2	1
Pleasing disposition	3	4	4	4	5	4
Mutual attraction	4	3	2	5	6	3
Good health	5	6	9	6	9	10
Desire for home/children	6	5	5	7	3	5
Refinement/neatness	7	8	7	8	7	8
Good cook/housekeeper	8	7	6	16	16	16
Ambition/industriousness	9	9	8	3	4	6
Chastity	10	13	15	10	15	15
Education/intelligence	11	11	10	9	14	7
Sociability	12	12	12	11	11	13
Similar religious background	13	10	14	14	10	11
Good looks	14	15	11	17	18	17
Similar educational background	15	14	13	12	8	9
Favorable social status	16	16	16	15	13	14
Good financial prospect	17	17	18	13	12	12
Similar political background	18	18	17	18	17	18

Note: Participants rank ordered these characteristics from most preferred (1) to least preferred (18). Numbers indicate the mean ranking given to each characteristic.
Adapted from Hill (1945); Hudson and Henze (1969); McGinnis (1958).

characteristics that they would consider acceptable when selecting a long-term romantic (e.g., marriage) partner. The results revealed that neither men nor women would consider marrying someone unless he or she was well above average (the 50th percentile) on such dispositional features as agreeableness (67th percentile for men, 70th percentile for women), emotional stability (64th percentile for men, 67th percentile for women), and sociability (57th percentile for men, 58th percentile for women). Similar results were reported by Kenrick, Groth, Trost, and Sadalla (1993). When it comes to selecting a long-term mate, both sexes appear to be highly selective with respect to that person's dispositional qualities.

The universal preference for a mate who possesses prosocial dispositional attributes seems eminently "appropriate" from an evolutionary standpoint. Although we cannot travel back in time to examine whether those early humans who selected agreeable, intelligent, emotionally stable mates actually achieved higher rates of reproductive success than did those who selected disagreeable, unintelligent, unstable partners, we *can* examine the interpersonal correlates of various personality attributes in modern societies. Research indicates, for example, that emotional instability (also called *neuroticism*; McCrae & Costa, 1997) is implicated strongly in several long-term relational outcomes, including dissolution (e.g., Cramer, 1993; Eysenck, 1980; Jockin, McGue, & Lykken, 1996; Kurdek, 1993; Tucker, Kressin, Spiro, & Ruscio, 1998) and satisfaction or adjustment (e.g., Bouchard, Lussier, & Sabourin, 1999; Karney & Bradbury, 1997; Newton & Kiecolt-Glaser, 1995).

In one classic longitudinal investigation, Kelly and Conley (1987) followed a sample of 249 married couples from the time of their engagement in the late 1930s to 1980. Prior to marriage, the members of each couple were rated by acquaintances on various personality traits, including neuroticism. Over the next 45 years, the researchers collected information on marital stability (i.e., divorce) and at various times also asked the couples to assess their marital satisfaction (e.g., participants indicated their overall satisfaction with the relationship, whether they had ever regretted the marriage, and whether they had considered divorce or separation from the partner). Both marital outcomes were predicted by premarriage levels of emotional instability. Not only did the men and women who divorced have higher premarriage levels of neuroticism did than those who remained married, but their neuroticism seemed to play a causal role in the dissolution of their marriages. Specifically, when asked by the researchers why they decided to divorce, over one third (37%) cited their own or their partner's emotional instability, irritability, emotional overreactions, or some other manifestation of neuroticism. Marital satisfaction also was related to neuroticism. Men and women high in neuroticism at the beginning of the study were unhappier and less satisfied with their marriages than were those characterized by lower levels of the trait.

This personality trait, with its associated negativity and "moodiness," also contributes to dysfunctional exchanges between relational partners. Pasch, Bradbury, and Davila (1997) explored the relationship between neuroticism and supportive behavior in newlywed couples. In this study, couples were audiotaped during an interaction in which one spouse discussed something he or she wished to change about him or herself and the other provided feedback. These verbal exchanges were then examined for various positive and negative elements. The researchers found that husbands and wives with higher levels of neuroticism gave their spouses less reassurance and encouragement—and conveyed less concern, love, and esteem—than did those with lower neuroticism levels. Emotional instability thus appears to manifest itself in maladaptive behaviors that hinder long-term pairbonds.

Although research with contemporary humans cannot directly speak to the question of whether or not any given preference has evolved, it certainly supports the evolutionary hypothesis that preferences for partners who demonstrate emotional stability and other prosocial personality characteristics confer certain reproductively relevant benefits to the individual.

Physical Fitness Features

In addition to dispositional attributes or emotional fitness, a potential partner also must be evaluated in terms of his or her physical fitness. A consideration of evolutionary principles suggests that reproductive success is dependent, for both sexes, on selecting a sexually mature, healthy individual who is capable of reproduction, will pass on "good" genetic material to any resulting offspring, and is physically able to contribute to the reproductive relationship, the partner, and the offspring. Insofar as physical appearance may function as an external indicant of underlying genetic fitness, reproductive status, and health (e.g., Fisher, 1958; Gangestad, 1993), appearance attributes may play an important role in the mating decisions of both sexes.

Empirical investigations of partner preferences do, in fact, suggest that physical attractiveness and appearance variables are considered relatively important by men and women when considering a potential long-term mate. For example, both sexes indicate preferring a spouse or dating partner who is physically appealing (e.g., Hatfield & Sprecher, 1995; Regan, 1998a). Although researchers who utilize self-report paradigms generally find that men emphasize external appearance more than do women (e.g., Goodwin, 1990; Regan & Berscheid, 1997; Sprecher, Sullivan, & Hatfield, 1994; for a meta-analytic review of this finding, see Feingold, 1990), experimental evidence suggests that both sexes are strongly (and equally) influenced by this partner attribute (e.g., Sprecher, 1989). Indeed, when asked to reveal what they seek in a "perfect" long-term mate, men and women demonstrate the same preference pattern—both desire a partner who is well above average (i.e., ranking in the 84th percentile) in terms of physical attractiveness (Regan, 1998b). Interestingly, Darwin himself predicted this pattern, suggesting that when existing environmental conditions create the opportunity to choose from among an array of potential mates, *both* sexes will select partners "not for mental charms, or property, or social position, but almost solely from external appearance" (1871, p. 368).

Although Darwin did not speculate as to the adaptive significance of this emphasis on appearance, a growing body of research indicates that there are some physical attributes that may serve a utilitarian function. One of these morphological features is body fat distribution, which reliably can be assessed by computing a waist-to-hip ratio (WHR). Before puberty, both sexes exhibit a similar WHR; however, after puberty, women deposit more fat in the gluteofemoral region (buttocks and thighs) whereas men deposit more fat in the central and upper body regions (shoulders, abdomen, and nape of the neck). Typically, the WHR ranges from .67 to .80 in healthy, premenopausal women (an hourglass shape), and from .80 to .90 in healthy men (a straighter, more tubular shape). Research on preferences for targets with varying WHRs reveals that men and women from different ages, races, and cultural backgrounds prefer as romantic partners (and find most attractive) individuals who possess a typical or normal WHR (e.g., Furnham, Tan, & McManus, 1997; Henss, 1995; Singh, 1993, 1994, 1995; Singh & Luis, 1995).

In addition, WHR appears to be an accurate physical indicant of both health and reproductive status (for a review of this literature, see Singh, 1993, 1995). For example, men and women who possess an atypical WHR are at greater risk for a variety of diseases, including ulcers, gallbladder and liver disease, stroke, hypertension, diabetes, and cancer. WHR also is correlated with reproductive status and fertility. In women, a higher WHR is associated with greater difficulty in becoming pregnant, ovarian cysts, and the cessation of reproductive capability (i.e, menopause). In men, a lower WHR is correlated with prostate cancer, hypogonadism, and increased age (and, by inference, decreased fertility). Thus, attractive mates (i.e., those with WHRs in the normal range) are healthier mates, and a preference for these individuals is eminently "appropriate" from an evolutionary perspective.

However, other aspects of appearance—most notably facial characteristics—are not linked as clearly as is WHR to physical fitness. Certainly there are particular facial features that seem to be universally preferred. For example, men and women throughout the world find "average" faces with symmetrical features to be particularly desirable (e.g., Grammar & Thornhill, 1994; Jones & Hill, 1993; Langlois & Roggman, 1990). In addition, although the superficial facial features (e.g., skin tone and pigment, eye color, lip size) that are considered attractive vary widely, there are specific *configurations* of features that most adults find appealing. Cunningham and his colleagues (e.g., Cunningham, 1986; Cunningham, Barbee, & Pike, 1990) provided compelling evidence that the most attractive male and female faces possess a combination of three types of attribute: neonate or babyish features (e.g., relatively large, wide-set eyes, a smallish nose), sexually mature features (prominent cheekbones and thinner cheeks, and, in men, a strong chin), and expressive features (including a wide smile and high eyebrows). But do these attractive facial features actually signal health or reproductive status?

Some theorists have proposed that appealing facial features might signal the possession of parasite-resistant, "good" genes that can be passed along to offspring. For example, Thornhill and Gangestad (1993) noted that prominent cheekbones depend on high levels of sex hormones, which actually inhibit immune functioning; thus, they argue that only extremely fit individuals can afford to develop these costly features, and their possession serves as an "honest badge" of fitness. Other theorists suggest that facial features reveal important information about a person's health status (e.g., Symons, 1979). Unlike the data for WHR, however, the evidence in support of these theoretical suppositions is less clear. For example, Kalick, Zebrowitz, Langlois, and Johnson (1998) collected facial photographs taken in late adolescence of a group of men and women who were part of a longitudinal study on health and aging. The photographs were converted to slides and evaluated by raters in terms of their overall level of attractiveness. Then, the attractiveness ratings were correlated with participants' health status at three points in time: adolescence (age 11 to 18), middle adulthood (age 30 to 36), and later adulthood (age 58 to 66). The researchers found no significant association between facial attractiveness in adolescence and health at any of the three time periods in question. However, attractiveness was related to *perceived* health status; in other words, attractive faces were believed to be healthier faces, although in reality they were not.

So, is an attractive partner an "appropriate" one, from an evolutionary perspective? On the one hand, there certainly seem to be functional elements involved in selecting a mate based on physical appearance as indexed by such morphological features as WHR. On the other hand, attractive facial features do not seem to indicate health or genetic fitness. However, as Kalick et al. (1998) noted, "the strong correlations we observed between facial attractiveness and perceived health suggest a possible earlier epoch when attractive features did signify actual health" (p. 12). In the ancestral environment where disease and ill health were not quite so easily managed (or disguised) as they are today, those who paid attention to a potential mate's physical appearance (and, consequently, to his or her health and vitality) may have increased their chances of reproductive success. Of course, this point remains speculative.

Relational Fitness Features

A third class of adaptively significant or functional features includes those interpersonal attributes that promote the successful formation and maintenance of a committed pairbond. An "appropriate" partner is one who not only possesses emotional and physical fitness, but who additionally demonstrates relational fitness—the ability and motivation to become exclusively attached to one particular individual, ignore the temptations posed by other individuals, and confine his or her reproductively relevant behaviors to the primary relationship. A number of characteristics are indicative of relational fitness, including mutual attraction or love, exclusivity, and similarity between partners.

The emotional experience of *passionate or romantic love* for another appears to be implicated strongly in the establishment and maintenance of long-term, exclusive pairbonds. Cross-cultural evidence points to the universality of the experience of passionate love (Jankowiak & Fischer, 1992; Sprecher, Aron, et al., 1994) and to the importance of mutual attraction or requited love in partner choice (Buss et al., 1990). Survey data from contemporary Western societies reveal that the majority of young men and women refuse to even consider marrying unless they are in love with their partner, and view loss of love as an adequate reason for terminating a marriage (Simpson, Campbell, & Berscheid, 1986). A similar trend is occurring around the world. Cultures with a strong tradition of arranged marriage—including China, Africa, Russia, and the Middle East—increasingly are adopting a matrimonial system based on love and individual choice (e.g., Xu & Whyte, 1990; for reviews, see Goodwin, 1999; Hatfield & Rapson, 1996). In addition, longitudinal studies conducted with Western samples indicate that the amount of love the members of a couple actually feel for each other predicts such important future relational events as marriage and relationship endurance. Hill and Peplau (1998) followed a sample of couples over a 15-year period and reported that those who experienced greater love at the beginning of their study were more likely to actually get married and to stay married than were those who were less in love.

Exclusivity, or the expectation that one will confine various reproductively relevant activities (e.g., economic, social, emotional, and sexual) to the primary long-term relationship, is another important component of relational fitness. Evidence for the importance (and possible adaptive significance) of exclusivity comes from research that focuses on identifying and comparing the mating systems (i.e., the norms that govern partner selection) that exist across cultures. A number of mating systems have been identified, including endogamy (i.e., inbreeding or the pairing of genetically related individuals), exogamy (i.e., outbreeding or the pairing of genetically unrelated relatives), polygyny (i.e., a mating system in which men pair with multiple women), polyandry (i.e., a system in which women pair with multiple men), and monogamy (i.e., a system in which two individuals pairbond).

Despite the panoply of systems that may govern individuals' partner choices, some universals in human pairbonding exist. For example, monogamy is one of the most common mating arrangements throughout the world (Betzig, 1992). In fact, even societies that practice polygyny, which far outnumber those that are exclusively monogamous (Daly & Wilson, 1983), are more appropriately characterized as primarily monogamous—the majority of men pairbond with one woman, whereas a very few men pairbond with multiple women (Betzig, 1992). In addition, all known human societies practice marriage or some other form of socially sanctioned, long-term pairing between men and women (Daly & Wilson, 1983; Goodwin, 1999). Similarly, extramarital relationships (sexual relationships that occur outside of, and in addition to, the primary reproductive pairbond) are forbidden in most societies; are subject to numerous limiting proscriptions in the few societies that openly permit them; and generally result in moderate to severe punishment for both sexes (Frayser, 1989). Indeed, across cultures, infidelity is cited as one of the leading causes of marital dissolution (e.g., Amato & Rogers, 1997; Betzig, 1989; Charny & Parnass, 1995; Davis & Aron, 1988; Kelly & Conley, 1987).

Certainly mating arrangements that emphasize mutual attraction and partner exclusivity are more likely to enhance individuals' reproductive success than are those that lack those characteristics. *Similarity* is a third attribute that has implications for relational fitness. Many courtship theorists propose that similarity plays a key role in the process of mate selection and the establishment of an enduring pairbond. Kerckhoff and Davis (1962), for instance, suggest that potential partners initially are evaluated (or "filtered") in terms of similarity on various social and demographic attributes. Once a potential mate has been screened on the basis of these attributes, he or she then is then assessed for value consensus, or similarity in terms of attitudes and values. Only individuals who possess the requisite degree of social and attitudinal similarity are chosen as mates.

Reiss's Wheel Theory of Love (e.g., 1960, 1980) makes a similar supposition. According to this theory, the initial stage of mate selection involves the establishment of feelings of rapport between potential partners. This process is assumed to be facilitated by similarity. Reiss suggested that we are most able to feel rapport for those who resemble us on key social and cultural variables. In much the same way, Lewis' (1972, 1973) model of dyadic formation proposes that the initial phase of romantic relationship development involves the perception of similarities. During this stage, individuals assess the extent to which they resemble one another in demographic background, values and interests, and personality. The perception of similarity, in turn, induces other positive emotional and behavioral responses that further propel a couple along the courtship trajectory. Theoretically, then, similarity is assumed to provide the fuel that drives the mate selection and pairbond process.

Although empirical investigations of individuals' actual preferences for similarity in potential mates are rare, Regan (1998b) found that heterosexual women prefer as romantic partners men who resemble them on attributes related to family orientation, social status, intellect, and interpersonal skill (in other words, men who possess attribute levels similar to the women's own). More recently, Regan et al. (2000) reported that when making mating decisions both men and women appear to consider the likelihood that they are compatible with a potential partner along various dimensions. Similarity, although not rated as highly as many other attributes, nonetheless was considered quite desirable by their participants, who viewed similarity in personal values and attitudes as most important, followed by similarity in interests and activities, social skills, and background (e.g., demographic) characteristics.

Indeed, regardless of our preferences, we ultimately do seem to pair with similar others. As noted earlier, the majority of cultures practice monogamy, or the bonding of two individuals in a committed relationship. The most typical form of monogamous pairing that occurs is *homogamy*. Also called *assortative mating* or *assortment*, homogamy is defined as the pairing of similar individuals; that is, persons who resemble one another on one or more characteristics. With the exception of biological sex, such that men tend to prefer to mate with women and vice versa, individuals assort along a large variety of dimensions. For example, reviews of the literature on assortment generally reveal positive correlations between marital partners on such characteristics as age, race, ethnicity, education level, socioeconomic status, religion, and physical attractiveness, as well as on a host of personality traits and cognitive abilities (e.g., Berscheid & Reis, 1998; Murstein, 1980; Vandenberg, 1972).

In sum, it would have behooved our ancestors to pay close attention not only to emotional and physical fitness when considering a potential mate, but also to relational fitness. Those early humans who chose to pursue and establish a relationship with an individual who did not reciprocate their feelings of attraction, who did not confine his or her sexual and emotional activities to the primary relationship, and/or whose characteristics were not compatible with their own would have experienced lower levels of reproductive success than would have those men and women who selected a more "appropriate" partner.

Social Fitness Features

The final category of functional feature that may have served to promote reproductive success in the ancestral environment concerns social fitness. Men and women who selected mates on the basis of their ability to successfully negotiate the social hierarchy and to provide tangible resources in the form of food, shelter, and physical protection would have increased their chances of reproductive success.

Interestingly, research on preferences suggests that men and women living in contemporary societies do not consider social fitness to be as important as emotional, physical, and relational fitness. For example, both sexes hold lower minimum standards, and express greater willingness to compromise their ideal standards, for social fitness attributes (e.g., popularity, high social status, material possessions, wealth, good earning capacity) than for characteristics related to the other three fitness dimensions (Regan, 1998a, 1998b). Both sexes also seem quite willing to exchange a potential partner's social fitness for other functionally significant features. Cunningham and colleagues (e.g., 1997) conducted several studies exploring the trade-offs that men and women make when faced with a choice between partners who possess different constellations of positive characteristics. Cunningham et al.'s results revealed that both men and women selected individuals who combined physical attractiveness with a pleasing personality over those who possessed the mix of physical attractiveness and wealth or the combination of a pleasing personality and wealth. Similarly, a series of studies by Jensen-Campbell, Graziano, and West (1995) revealed that the impact of dominant behavior on a man's perceived dating desirability was moderated by his level of agreeableness. Specifically, women participants preferred dominant men, but only if they also demonstrated high levels of prosocial behavior.

Although research on preferences suggests that social fitness is not of primary importance in the mating decisions of contemporary men and women (who no longer face many of the physical challenges that existed in the ancestral environment), most individuals do, in fact, pairbond with others of similar social status (see the earlier discussion on homogamy). In addition, those ancestral humans who based their reproductive decisions at least partly on social fitness considerations—who selected as mates individuals with strong ties to the existing community, some degree of status or position within that community, and the ability to procure tangible resources—would have enjoyed a higher degree of reproductive success than would have those ancestral humans who chose to ignore or to undervalue social fitness.

CONCLUSIONS

The purpose of this chapter was to explore functional features, defined as those attributes or characteristics that might have provided reproductive benefits to our human forebears. A consideration of evolutionary principles, as well as of the preferences and mating decisions of men and women living in contemporary societies, suggests at least four classes of functional feature that are implicated in reproductive success and render a relationship "appropriate" from an adaptive perspective. In particular, features related to *emotional fitness* (e.g., emotional stability, agreeableness, and dependable character) indicate that an individual can and will provide the sustained emotional and social support necessary for long-term pairbonding and childrearing. Attributes related to *physical fitness*, including health and appearance, serve to signal that a potential mate is capable of reproduction and is physically able to contribute to the reproductive relationship, the partner, and the resulting offspring. *Relational fitness* features (e.g., mutual attraction, fidelity, and similarity) suggest that an individual possesses the ability and motivation to become exclusively attached to the primary long-term partner, confine his or her reproductively relevant behaviors to the primary relationship, and avoid the temptations posed by other potential partners. And finally, characteristics related to *social fitness* (e.g., ambition, social status, and material possessions) signify the capacity to successfully negotiate the social hierarchy and provide tangible resources to the reproductive partner and offspring.

Although other attributes undoubtedly were important in the mating decisions of early men and women, it is likely that ancestral humans who possessed these functional features, and who selected their partners on the basis of these features, were more likely to survive and reproduce than were those who did not. We will, of course, never know for certain. Nonetheless, an examination of contemporary mating themes allows us a glimpse, however fleeting, into the evolutionary heritage of our species.

REFERENCES

Amato, P. R., & Rogers, S. J. (1997). A longitudinal study of marital problems and subsequent divorce. *Journal of Marriage and the Family, 59*, 612–624.

Berscheid, E., & Reis, H. T. (1998). Attraction and close relationships. In D. T. Gilbert, S. T. Fiske, & G. Lindzey (Eds.), *The handbook of social psychology* (4th ed., pp. 193–281). Boston: McGraw-Hill.

Betzig, L. (1989). Causes of conjugal dissolution: A cross-cultural study. *Current Anthropology, 30*, 654–676.

Betzig, L. (1992). Roman polygyny. *Ethology and Sociobiology, 13*, 309–349.

Bouchard, G., Lussier, Y., & Sabourin, S. (1999). Personality and marital adjustment: Utility of the five-factor model of personality. *Journal of Marriage and the Family, 61*, 651–660.

Bowlby, J. C. (1973). *Attachment and loss. Vol. 2: Separation: Anxiety and anger.* London: Hogarth Press.

Buss, D. M., et al. (1990). International preferences in selecting mates: A study of 37 cultures. *Journal of Cross-Cultural Psychology, 21*, 5–47.

Charny, I. W., & Parnass, S. (1995). The impact of extramarital relationships on the continuation of marriages. *Journal of Sex and Marital Therapy, 21*, 100–115.

Cosmides, L., & Tooby, J. (1997). *Evolutionary psychology: A primer.* On the Internet at: http://www.psych.ucsb.edu/research/cep/primer.html.

Cramer, D. (1993). Personality and marital dissolution. *Personality and Individual Differences, 14*, 605–607.

Cunningham, M. R. (1986). Measuring the physical in physical attractiveness: Quasi-experiments on the sociobiology of female facial beauty. *Journal of Personality and Social Psychology, 50*, 925–935.

Cunningham, M. R., Barbee, A. P., & Pike, C. L. (1990). What do women want? Facialmetric assessment of multiple motives in the perception of male facial physical attractiveness. *Journal of Personality and Social Psychology, 59*, 61–72.

Cunningham, M. R., Druen, P. B., & Barbee, A. P. (1997). Angels, mentors, and friends: Trade-offs among evolutionary, social, and individual variables in physical appearance. In J. A. Simpson & D. T. Kenrick (Eds.), *Evolutionary social psychology* (pp. 109–140). Mahwah, NJ: Lawrence Erlbaum Associates.

Daly, M., & Wilson, M. (1983). *Sex, evolution, and behavior* (2nd ed.). Belmont, CA: Wadsworth.

Darwin, C. (1859). *On the origin of the species by means of natural selection, or, preservation of favoured races in the struggle for life.* London: J. Murray.

Darwin, C. (1871). *The descent of man, and selection in relation to sex.* London: J. Murray.

Davis, B., & Aron, A. (1988). Perceived causes of divorce and postdivorce adjustment among recently divorced midlife women. *Journal of Divorce, 12*, 41–55.

Eysenck, H. J. (1980). Personality, marital satisfaction, and divorce. *Psychological Reports, 47*, 1235–1238.

Feingold, A. (1990). Gender differences in effects of physical attractiveness on romantic attraction: A comparison across five research paradigms. *Journal of Personality and Social Psychology, 59*, 981–993.

Fisher, R. A. (1958). *The genetical theory of natural selection* (2nd ed.). Oxford, UK: Clarendon.

Frayser, S. G. (1989). Sexual and reproductive relationships: Cross-cultural evidence and biosocial implications. *Medical Anthropology, 11*, 385–407.

Furnham, A., Tan, T., & McManus, C. (1997). Waist-to-hip ratio and preferences for body shape: A replication and extension. *Personality and Individual Differences, 22*, 539–549.

Gangestad, S. W. (1993). Sexual selection and physical attractiveness: Implications for mating dynamics. *Human Nature, 4*, 205–235.

Goodwin, R. (1990). Sex differences among partner preferences: Are the sexes really very similar? *Sex Roles, 23*, 501–513.

Goodwin, R. (1999). *Personal relationships across cultures.* London: Routledge.

Grammar, K., & Thornhill, R. (1994). Human (*homosapiens*) facial attractiveness and sexual selection: The role of symmetry and averageness. *Journal of Comparative Psychology, 108*, 233–242.

Hatfield, E., & Rapson, R. L. (1996). *Love and sex: Cross-cultural perspectives.* Needham Heights, MA: Allyn & Bacon.

Hatfield, E., & Sprecher, S. (1995). Men's and women's preferences in marital partners in the United States, Russia, and Japan. *Journal of Cross-Cultural Psychology, 26*, 728–750.

Henss, R. (1995). Waist-to-hip ratio and attractiveness: Replication and extension. *Personality and Individual Differences, 19*, 479–488.

Hill, C. T., & Peplau, L. A. (1998). Premarital predictors of relationship outcomes: A 15-year follow-up of the Boston Couples Study. In T. N. Bradbury (Ed.), *The developmental course of marital dysfunction* (pp. 237–278). New York: Cambridge University Press.

Hill, R. (1945). Campus values in mate-selection. *Journal of Home Economics, 37*, 554–558.

Howard, J. A., Blumstein, P., & Schwartz, P. (1987). Social or evolutionary theories? Some observations on preferences in human mate selection. *Journal of Personality and Social Psychology, 53*, 194–200.

Hudson, J. W., & Henze, L. F. (1969). Campus values in mate selection: A replication. *Journal of Marriage and the Family, 31*, 772–775.

Jankowiak, W. R., & Fischer, E. F. (1992). A cross-cultural perspective on romantic love. *Ethnology, 31*, 149–155.

Jensen-Campbell, L. A., Graziano, W. G., & West, S. (1995). Dominance, prosocial orientation, and female preferences: Do nice guys really finish last? *Journal of Personality and Social Psychology, 68*, 427–440.

Jockin, V., McGue, M., & Lykken, D. T. (1996). Personality and divorce: A genetic analysis. *Journal of Personality and Social Psychology, 71*, 288–299.

Jones, D., & Hill, K. (1993). Criteria of facial attractiveness in five populations. *Human Nature, 4*, 271–296.

Kalick, S. M., Zebrowitz, L. A., Langlois, J. H., & Johnson, R. M. (1998). Does human facial attractiveness honestly advertise health? Longitudinal data on an evolutionary question. *Psychological Science, 9*, 8–13.

Karney, B. R., & Bradbury, T. N. (1997). Neuroticism, marital interaction, and the trajectory of marital satisfaction. *Journal of Personality and Social Psychology, 72*, 1075–1092.

Kelly, E. L., & Conley, J. J. (1987). Personality and compatibility: A prospective analysis of marital stability and marital satisfaction. *Journal of Personality and Social Psychology, 52*, 27–40.

Kenrick, D. T., Groth, G. E., Trost, M. R., & Sadalla, E. K. (1993). Integrating evolutionary and social exchange perspectives on relationships: Effects of gender, self-appraisal, and involvement level on mate selection criteria. *Journal of Personality and Social Psychology, 64*, 951–969.

Kerckhoff, A. C., & Davis, K. E. (1962). Value consensus and need complementarity in mate selection. *American Sociological Review, 27*, 295–303.

Kurdek, L. A. (1993). Predicting marital dissolution: A 5-year prospective longitudinal study of newlywed couples. *Journal of Personality and Social Psychology, 64*, 221–242.

Langlois, J. H., & Roggman, L. A. (1990). Attractive faces are only average. *Psychological Science, 1*, 115–121.

Lewis, R. A. (1972). A developmental framework for the analysis of premarital dyadic formation. *Family Process, 11*, 17–48.

Lewis, R. A. (1973). A longitudinal test of a developmental framework for premarital dyadic formation. *Journal of Marriage and the Family, 35*, 16–25.

McCrae, R. R., & Costa, P. T., Jr. (1997). Personality trait structure as a human universal. *American Psychologist, 52*, 509–516.

McGinnis, R. (1958). Campus values in mate selection: A repeat study. *Social Forces, 35*, 368–373.

Miller, L. C., & Fishkin, S. A. (1997). On the dynamics of human bonding and reproductive success: Seeking windows on the adapted-for-human-environmental interface. In J. A. Simpson & D. T. Kenrick (Eds.), *Evolutionary social psychology* (pp. 197–235). Mahwah, NJ: Lawrence Erlbaum Associates.

Murstein, B. I. (1980). Mate selection in the 1970s. *Journal of Marriage and the Family, 42*, 777–792.

Newton, T. L., & Kiecolt-Glaser, J. K. (1995). Hostility and erosion of marital quality during early marriage. *Journal of Behavioral Medicine, 18*, 601–619.

Pasch, L. A., Bradbury, T. N., & Davila, J. (1997). Gender, negative affectivity, and observed social support behavior in marital interaction. *Personal Relationships, 4*, 361–378.

Regan, P. C. (1998a). Minimum mate selection standards as a function of perceived mate value, relationship context, and gender. *Journal of Psychology and Human Sexuality, 10*, 53–73.

Regan, P. C. (1998b). What if you can't get what you want? Willingness to compromise ideal mate selection standards as a function of sex, mate value, and relationship context. *Personality and Social Psychology Bulletin, 24*, 1288–1297.

Regan, P. C., & Berscheid, E. (1997). Gender differences in characteristics desired in a potential sexual and marriage partner. *Journal of Psychology and Human Sexuality, 9*, 25–37.

Regan, P. C., Levin, L., Sprecher, S., Cate, R., & Christopher, S. (2000). Partner preferences: What characteristics do men and women desire in their short-term sexual and long-term romantic partners? *Journal of Psychology and Human Sexuality, 12*, 1–21.

Reiss, I. L. (1960). Toward a sociology of the heterosexual love relationship. *Marriage and Family Living, 22*, 139–145.

Reiss, I. L. (1980). *Family systems in America* (3rd ed.). New York: Holt, Rinehart & Winston.

Simpson, J. A., Campbell, B., & Berscheid, E. (1986). The association between romantic love and marriage: Kephart (1967) twice revisited. *Personality and Social Psychology Bulletin, 12*, 363–372.

Singh, D. (1993). Adaptive significance of female physical attractiveness: Role of waist-to-hip ratio. *Journal of Personality and Social Psychology, 65*, 293–307.

Singh, D. (1994). Body fat distribution and perception of desirable female body shape by young Black men and women. *International Journal of Eating Disorders, 16*, 289–294.

Singh, D. (1995). Female judgment of male attractiveness and desirability for relationships: Role of waist-to-hip ratio and financial status. *Journal of Personality and Social Psychology, 69*, 1089–1101.

Singh, D., & Luis, S. (1995). Ethnic and gender consensus for the effect of waist-to-hip ratio on judgment of women's attractiveness. *Human Nature, 6*, 51–65.

Sprecher, S. (1989). Importance to males and females of physical attractiveness, earning potential, and expressiveness in initial attraction. *Sex Roles, 21*, 591–607.

Sprecher, S., Aron, A., Hatfield, E., Cortese, A., Potapova, E., & Levitskaya, A. (1994). Love: American style, Russian style, and Japanese style. *Personal Relationships, 1*, 349–369.

Sprecher, S., Sullivan, Q., & Hatfield, E. (1994). Mate selection preferences: Gender differences examined in a national sample. *Journal of Personality and Social Psychology, 66*, 1074–1080.

Symons, D. (1979). *The evolution of human sexuality.* New York: Oxford University Press.

Thornhill, R., & Gangestad, S. W. (1993). Human facial beauty: Averageness, symmetry, and parasite resistance. *Human Nature, 4*, 237–269.

Tooby, J., & Cosmides, L. (1992). The psychological foundations of culture. In J. H. Barkow, L. Cosmides, & J. Tooby (Eds.), *The adapted mind: Evolutionary psychology and the generation of culture* (pp. 19–136). Oxford, UK: Oxford University Press.

Tucker, J. S., Kressin, N. R., Spiro, A., III, & Ruscio, J. (1998). Intrapersonal characteristics and the timing of divorce: A prospective investigation. *Journal of Social and Personal Relationships, 15*, 211–225.

Vandenberg, S. G. (1972). Assortative mating, or who marries whom? *Behavior Genetics, 2*, 127–157.

Xu, X., & Whyte, M. K. (1990). Love matches and arranged marriages: A Chinese replication. *Journal of Marriage and the Family, 52*, 709–722.

Zeifman, D., & Hazan, C. (1997). A process model of adult attachment formation. In S. Duck & W. Ickes (Eds.), *Handbook of personal relationships* (2nd ed., pp. 179–195). Chichester, UK: Wiley.

II

INAPPROPRIATE MARRIAGES

Marital Affairs[1]

Graham Allan
Keele University

Kaeren Harrison
University of Southampton

As other chapters in this book demonstrate, there are many forms of inappropriate relationships. However, aside from incest, few can have received the uniformity of moral censure that adultery has attracted across different cultures and different time periods. In numerous societies, any form of nonmarital sexual relationship is seen as morally inappropriate, but adultery often carries a particularly high degree of stigma and opprobrium. There are many accounts from different places and times of those who are known (or believed) to have committed adultery being penalized, often through forms of social and/or economic ostracism, but at times in more extreme fashion (Betzig, 1989; Goodwin, 1999; Hatfield & Rapson, 1996). In this regard, it would seem that adulterous relationships represent an undermining of social cohesion and a threat to moral order, with those involved often portrayed as weak, selfish, and unprincipled, if not actually evil.

[1]We gratefully acknowledge the support of the Economic and Social Research Council (Grant number: R000222722) and of the Trustees of the Mass-Observation Archive at the University of Sussex.

Yet such a perspective is far too simple, for whereas adultery is frequently represented as immoral and undermining social order, there are also times when it is tolerated and seen as a matter of personal rather than public concern. In the preface to this book, Robin Goodwin and Duncan Cramer referred to former President Bill Clinton's "inappropriate relationship" with Monica Lewinsky. Around that time, the British Foreign Secretary, Robin Cook, was also receiving a good deal of critical media scrutiny for an extramarital relationship he had been conducting that led to his marriage ending amid much public acrimony, fueled by his wife's revelations about his previous behavior. In contrast, in France shortly after President Françios Mitterand's death it was revealed that he had fathered a child within an adulterous relationship, yet in France this was not seen as a matter worthy of much publicity or warranting critical comment.

Although it would be foolhardy to jump too readily to conclusions on the basis of marital indiscretions committed by well-known politicians, these examples do indicate the degree of variation there is in responses to adultery. Put slightly differently, religious and moral "rules" against adultery are applied more readily to some people, and to some groups, than others. An obvious example of this is the degree to which husbands' and wives' extramarital liaisons are traditionally understood differently, with any marital "misbehavior" by husbands often being condoned more than that of their wives (Frayser, 1985; Goodwin, 1999). Interestingly, for example, in Britain a husband's adultery was only recognized as sufficient grounds for divorce in 1923, in marked contrast to the legal consequences of a wife's adultery (Gibson, 1994).

Equally, responses to adultery are shaped by the current understandings of marriage in the society and the social circle in question. Thus, in agricultural societies, marriage and kinship—with their associated land rights—often represent the key structures around which social and economic organization is built. In this context, adultery is a threat to social order as well as to marital relationships, and so is often condemned through the range of religious, moral, and social sanctions available. In other circumstances, marriage is not necessarily defined as monogamous in practice, even if it is in principle. Thus, it is arguable that historically within English (and other) upper-class marriages there has been a greater acceptance of adulterous relationships than in more "respectable" middle- or working-class marriages. Within the former, husbands and wives tended to construct lives in which more time was spent apart, for example in their different town or country houses. Furthermore, marriage was not always defined as a relationship in which personal commitment and fidelity played a large part (MacFarlane, 1986; Stone, 1979).

However, the changes that were occurring in the construction of marriage in industrialized societies like Britain and America in the middle of the 20th century resulted in marital fidelity being assigned a heightened significance. With the rise in ideologies of companionate marriage in the period before and after World War II, more emphasis than previously was placed on the emotional satisfactions and rewards of a more genuine partnership (Finch & Summerfield, 1991). Although this ideology did not represent any radical transformation in the gendered character of marital tasks and responsibilities, it did signify a greater level of personal compatibility, commitment, and trust. Within this, adultery came to represent a betrayal not simply of the marriage contract with its vows of exclusivity, but more specifically of the personal ties through which the couple were united. To put this differently, just as it can be argued that the rise in companionate marriage represented the beginning of a shift away from marriage as a social institution to marriage as a personal construction, so too as a consequence there was a comparable shift in the ways in which adultery came to be portrayed and understood.

And, of course, changes continue in the ways marriage is constructed beyond the development of companionate ideologies. Indeed, within Britain and other similar societies, the shifts occurring in marriage in the late 20th and early 21st centuries have been significantly more radical than those that developed in the mid-20th-century period. This can be recognized most readily at a demographic level. Not only have divorce rates been rising substantially since 1970, but at the same time the age at which people first marry has increased. (This is in direct contrast to the falling age-of-marriage characteristic of the growth of the companionate marriage model throughout the rest of the century.) Equally, the numbers of people choosing to get married has been falling quite markedly over the last 30 years. Most importantly, there has been a very rapid and significant growth in rates of cohabitation. Not only do the majority of couples now cohabit as a prelude to marriage, but an increasing number are choosing cohabitation rather than marriage in the long term (Allan & Crow, 2001; McRae, 1999). As part of this demographic change—which itself can be interpreted as a reordering of sex, marriage, and childbirth (Kiernan, Land, & Lewis, 1998)—the very language used has altered. In many contexts, it is often no longer sensible to discuss marriage as such; instead, the emphasis needs to be on "partnerships" or on marriage and "marriagelike relationships."

Within sociology, these changes in the demography of partnership formation and dissolution more widely have led to reappraisals of the nature of contemporary marital and partner commitment. In particular, theorists concerned with understanding the impact that the structural transformations of late modernity are having on personal life have focused on the character of those solidarities that contemporary sexual/domestic partnerships embody. In the context of examining adultery as an "inappropriate" relationship, the framework Anthony Giddens provided in his discussion of *The Transformation of Intimacy* (1992) is particularly interesting, even if in many regards the arguments he forwarded are contentious (Duncombe &

Marsden, 1993; Jackson, 1995; Jamieson, 1998, 1999; Smart & Neale, 1999). Like others such as Beck (Beck, 1992; Beck & Beck-Gernsheim, 1995), Giddens argued that the social and economic developments of late modernity have fostered a more individualistic orientation that influences the ways in which different partnership relationships are framed and, importantly, results in a reevaluation of the appropriateness of more traditional moral standards governing relational commitment.

In developing this, Giddens focused on the ways in which sexual partnership and marital commitment are currently being remodeled, pointing to the transformations he saw occurring in the character of sexual love. Building on ideas about companionate marriage, Giddens maintained that, until recently, "romantic love" was the main form of partnership commitment. Deeply rooted in notions of lifelong compatibility and marital stability, it was this form of love that dominated couple formation throughout the mainstream period of industrial capitalism. However, Giddens suggested that this mode of love is no longer so congruent within contemporary society, as gender inequalities are becoming less marked due to labor market changes as well as increased contraceptive efficiency. Instead, we are seeing the development of "confluent love" which embodies an ethic and morality quite distinct to "romantic love."

The essence of confluent love, as Giddens defined it, lies in its contingency. Whereas romantic love incorporates a "once-and-for-always" commitment, with confluent love it is the continuing quality of the relationship and each individual's desire to remain involved with the other that matter. The relationship's legitimation, in other words, lies in its meeting the varied and changing needs of the individuals involved; sustained dissatisfaction with the tie is of itself sufficient reason for ending it. It is in this sense that commitment is contingent. The moral high ground no longer attaches to those who stay in a moribund or conflictual tie; rather, the new, emergent morality of confluent love recognizes the rights of the individual to happiness and the appropriateness of ending relationships that are no longer experienced as fulfilling. Moreover, within confluent love, sexual exclusivity may or may not be significant, depending on the understandings negotiated by those involved.

It is not at all difficult to criticize Giddens' ideas about the growth of confluent love. Individuals are rarely as free of constraint as his model suggests. Ending relationships and moving on nearly always carry emotional and practical costs, which can be quite heavy once children, housing, and the other paraphernalia of longer-term domestic involvement are considered (see Jamieson, 1998; 1999; Smart & Neale, 1999). Importantly too, whereas women's dependence on men has been altering, the changes in social and economic life have, at best, ameliorated rather than eradicated the structural advantages accruing to men. Nonetheless, there have evidently been changes in patterns of partnership commitment. The shifts in marriage and divorce rates, cohabitation, and lone parenthood are all indicative of the emergence of different understandings of partnership matters. Whether or not Giddens was correct in the detail of his argument, he was surely right to highlight the development of ideologies of individualism in which the morality of partnership commitment is understood differently from the past (Beck & Beck-Gernsheim, 1995; Jackson, 1993, 1995; Jamieson, 1989, 1999). As mentioned earlier, the once-strong relationships between sex, marriage, and childbearing no longer hold as they did, a transformation that signifies shifting cultural conceptions of marital commitment.

Such views about transformations in the character of commitment in marital and other broadly equivalent partnerships clearly carry implications for contemporary understandings of adultery, although these are not as straightforward as they might initially seem. Of itself, a movement toward confluent love as the underpinning of longer-term relationships does not indicate that infidelity within partnerships is more acceptable than it was. It can be argued, indeed, that monogamy—albeit serial rather than lifelong monogamy—remains highly salient within the construction of partnerships because of the additional emphasis now placed on continued personal compatibility and satisfaction as their rationale. At the same time, however, the recognition that marriage and other such partnerships are not necessarily lifelong and that individuals have a right, and perhaps a responsibility, to seek fulfilment within their personal relationships creates a cultural climate in which the exploration and development of new relationships is socially more acceptable than it once was.

Popular discourses around adultery reflect these complexities. Most noticeably, as with *marriage* and *partnership*, the language employed is itself altering. So far in this chapter we have deliberately used the term *adultery*. However, like *living in sin*, this is a term that now seems far less appropriate than it once did. Many people find its connotations too moralistic and judgmental to reflect their own understandings of these situations. So, too, the term *infidelity* is used far less than it was, because it seems too old-fashioned and rigid a characterization for contemporary times. Instead, language has been modified so that people now refer more commonly to *affairs*, a term that carries far fewer moral connotations. Whereas *committing adultery* clearly expresses wrongdoing, *having an affair* carries a more ambiguous and muted moral message. So, too, phrases such as *having a relationship* or *being involved with someone else* have come into greater prominence, serving less as clear-cut euphemisms for *adultery* than as expressions conveying a greater tolerance and moral relativity. Even *being unfaithful*, although clearly retaining a strong sense of disapproval, lacks the rigidity of a term like *infidelity*.

In the rest of this chapter we concern ourselves with these issues, and in particular with how contemporary understandings of marital affairs/adultery are patterned. To date, there have been relatively few studies of marital affairs in Britain (Lawson, 1987; Lawson & Samson, 1988; Reibstein & Richards, 1992). We seek to add to this research by exploring the different interpretations and responses there are to affairs, and by assessing the ways in which extramarital sexual relationships are constructed as "inappropriate." Clearly, obtaining data on marital affairs raises significant methodological problems, in particular around issues of access and sampling. Previous studies have sought to overcome these difficulties in different ways. For example, some—like Shackelford and Buss (1997)—have relied on people's responses to hypothetical scenarios. Others—like Lawson (1987) and Prins, Buunk, and VanYperen (1993)—used advertisements and media publicity to attract a sample. Reibstein and Richards (1992) obtained a sample through personal contacts. The data on which we are basing this analysis consists of written accounts of people's experiences of affairs generated from the panel of correspondents maintained by the Mass-Observation Archive at the University of Sussex, UK.

MASS-OBSERVATION ARCHIVE

The Mass-Observation Archive has a long history and tradition within British social science research. It was established initially in 1937 as an archive for recording aspects of people's everyday lives, and has always emphasized the importance of understanding the constructed *meanings* individuals attach to activities and behavior, as well as the changing nature of people's beliefs and attitudes over time. From its inception, correspondents have been invited to record their experiences, feelings, and views about a whole range of contemporary issues, with the principal aim of making these available to future researchers as a way of reconstructing "ordinary life." After a period of inactivity, the Archive began operating again in 1981. Since then, by sending out three "Directives" a year to their national panel of voluntary writers, the Archive has built up an enormous bank of written material (over 640,000 pages of typed or handwritten pages) representing the contributions of over 2,800 men and women who have contributed to the Archive for periods of various lengths (Sheridan, 1993).

The Archive's Directives are not questionnaires, but instead a series of open-ended questions or prompts designed to encourage correspondents to express themselves freely and with as much candor as possible. This approach, combined with the Archive's commitment to running the project with a high degree of anonymity and confidentiality, has consistently generated response rates in the region of 70% and more. The method also produces material that is highly reflexive, detailed, and intimate; correspondents frequently reveal a great deal about their private and personal lives, providing data of a scope and depth that would be difficult to achieve through other survey methodologies. The three key features of the Mass-Observation Archive of reflexivity, anonymity, and autonomy were major advantages for investigating extra-marital affairs and their meaning within marriage. We required information about people's understandings of affairs within marriage at a detailed and intimate level that, due to both its sensitivity and its peculiarity, would have been hard to obtain using a more structured approach.

Consequently, in collaboration with the Archive's staff, in the spring of 1998 a Directive focusing specifically on "having an affair" was constructed and mailed out to the Archive's correspondents. The resultant data set contained a wide range of candid material reflecting the correspondents' beliefs and values, as well as their direct and indirect experiences of affairs. Some of the correspondents drew heavily on personal experience, and discussed in detail the various love triangles in which they, or those they know, have been involved. A large number claimed not to have had an affair, although others (see Table 3.1) did not disclose either way, preferring instead to frame their replies in more general terms. Two hundred and forty-six responses were received from the 354 Directives sent; 185 from women and 61 from men. The respondents ranged in age from 19 to 87. Importantly, the Archive's correspondents are not a cross-section of the British population. By the nature of the Archive, they are a relatively well-educated, articulate, and middle-class grouping. Moreover, because of their different methodologies, it is difficult to make any comparison with data from larger-scale studies of sexual attitudes and activities, such as Wellings, Fields, Johnson, and Wadsworth (1994). Nonetheless, through their commitment to the Archive's mission, the Archive's correspondents collectively offer a valuable resource for generating personal and reflexive data (see Shaw, 1996; Sheridan, 1993; Stanley, 1995).

What Counts as an Affair?

There was some degree of variation in people's definitions of what counted as an affair. One correspondent completed a major section of her letter under the heading "Our Affair," but revealed that they had never

TABLE 3.1

Correspondents Reporting Affairs

	Women	Men
Have had an affair	28	8
Spouse/partner has had affair	17	2
Both self and spouse/partner have had an affair	14	1
No affair specified	126	50

actually made love (S1399, female, 48).[2] Another correspondent wrote about her father-in-law's affair, explaining that 'It was not an affair in the real sense of the word. I think he was more sort of hedging his bets—in case the marriage broke down, he wanted a spare woman in reserve' (A2212, female, 41). Clearly, the definition of an affair is not clear-cut in the minds of these correspondents. (See Wellings et al., 1994, for a discussion of definitional ambiguities around sexual activities generally.) Similarly, whether an affair is regarded as taking place depends in part on whether one of those involved is also involved in a committed or marriagelike relationship. Some respondents, for example, reported having "affairs" when they were separated from their spouses but did not know whether these really counted as "affairs."

Along with problems of definition came the related problem of interpretation. A large group of correspondents—approximately one third of the total panel—neither admitted nor denied personal involvement in an affair (Table 3.1). Although some letters began (and ended) with an abrupt statement like "Sorry. Can't manage this one" (L2881, female, 66), other writers pointed out that despite the anonymity and confidentiality of the Archive, "Some things should be kept secret—and treasured as a secret" (R2144, female, 62). Another respondent wrote: "Even after several decades, some things are still too sensitive to write about" (P2546, female, 72). As in all autobiographical expression, responses are interesting for what they reveal, but are equally fascinating for what they do not (Heilbrun, 1989). It is difficult to tell what has been omitted from a letter and, even where it is suspected that something has, to judge just how significant it was for the correspondent. By their very nature, affairs are conducted secretly. "Successful" affairs might arguably be those that have been managed without discovery. For example, explaining her nonparticipation in the Directive, one female correspondent wrote: "Not that I have had any relevant personal experience in the last 22 years, but I have been married for 39 years and intend to stay that way!" (P1326, female, 61).

An Inappropriate Relationship?

The great majority of correspondents replying to the Directive on marital affairs saw them as inappropriate. Very few conveyed an overall sense that affairs were a positive element within the construction of long-term partnerships, although, as we shall discuss later, some expressed more sympathy for their occurrence than did others. Yet how their inappropriateness was expressed varied a good deal, reflecting different beliefs about the na-

---

[2]The alphanumeric numbers used to identify correspondents are those used by the Mass-Observation Archive. The identities of correspondents are only known to staff at the Archive.

ture and character of long-term relationships within contemporary life-styles. Some correspondents held relatively firm religious beliefs in which marriage was viewed as a sacrament based on principles from which there could never be justification for deviating. The most extreme example of this was provided by a 53-year-old female correspondent whose reply to the Directive consisted solely of four quotations from the Christian gospels expressing the sinfulness of adultery, followed by the remark: "*My views, opinions and personal experience on this subject are irrelevant.*" (S1983). A further set of correspondents paid less heed to the role of religion but emphasized the inappropriateness of infidelity within marriage by appeal to "traditional" moral codes or principles that they saw as the bedrock of stable and ordered family life. They perceived the increase in marital breakdown, with all its harmful consequences, as a result of people failing to take their avowed commitments sufficiently seriously:

> I think affairs are hurtful, secretive and sordid, although I have personally never had one—thank goodness (W729, female, 40)

> I think any affair is wrong, there cannot be shades of wrongness and no affair can be positive or enriching. An affair is basically dishonesty and can only bring pain, suffering, especially when there are children involved. (B1426, male, 62)

> I have never had the time or the inclination for sex outside marriage, believing that when one contracts to remain faithful to a partner one has an obligation to do so, unless things become so unbearable that divorce is the only option (R1760, female, 67)

In contrast, there were a small number of correspondents who took a more "open" and liberal view of partnership infidelity. For them, affairs were not necessarily inappropriate, and not always damaging, although often their accounts contained riders that specified particular "rules" governing how such infidelities should be managed. A few correspondents described being in "open relationships" in which affairs with others were acceptable, especially if the involvement was defined as essentially sexual rather than emotional. Other correspondents—and proportionately more men than women—reported viewing involvement in affairs as acceptable provided that the affairs remained hidden from their spouses. Some portrayed a traditional perspective of marital commitment; others argued that a single relationship cannot meet all the needs and desires an individual has, particularly over an extended period.

As would be expected, most of those responding to the Directive took a less "permissive" view than this, generally emphasizing the damage that affairs can do, without adopting the moralistic perspective of those cited earlier. For many correspondents, there was a recognition that the complexities of contemporary "coupledom" meant that judgments about third-party relationships should not be made too readily. In particular, correspondents reflected on the ease with which marriages can become stale and the extent to which individuals' needs and personalities change over time. Interestingly, too, a number of correspondents reported how their perceptions on affairs had altered, often as a result of particular experiences, some becoming more "liberal" and others more "traditional" in their outlooks.

It is difficult to succinctly summarize the diversity of the views expressed by correspondents. Nonetheless, a number of themes consistently emerged from the accounts that shed light on people's interpretation and construction of affairs as inappropriate relationships. These include issues concerning trust, betrayal, and guilt; change; and ambiguity. We discuss each of these in turn. In doing this we have not separated male and female correspondents. There were significant gender differences in the responses received, although these were more to do with the conduct of affairs than with their inappropriateness, the focus of this chapter. Gender issues in people's experiences of affairs are analyzed fully in a separate paper.

Trust, Betrayal, and Guilt

A strong theme presented in the correspondents' accounts of marital affairs concerned issues of trust, betrayal, and guilt (Lawson, 1987; Morgan, 2000). There was a powerful view that any adulterous act represented a form of betrayal of both the partner and the partnership:

> What is immoral about affairs is not the sex, but the deception, lies, emotional manipulation and the raising of false hopes. (A2212, female, 41)

> Few marriages can continue unscathed the discovery of unfaithfulness, because it means that trust is almost impossible for the future. (B2710, male, 68)

> I believe it is absolutely vital to remain sexually faithful in a long-term relationship as once that is lost then so is every other ingredient lost—truthfulness and trust cannot ever be regained once thrown out of a marriage. (L1290, female, 55)

As these quotes indicate, sexual fidelity continues to be seen by many as the cornerstone of marriage. Sexual relations with another person undermines the trust on which marriage—and, in particular, a successful and rewarding marriage—is normatively based (Holmes & Rempel, 1989). Within this viewpoint, however, different elements were expressed by different correspondents, depending in part on their own experiences.

To begin with, many of the correspondents who wrote that neither they nor, as far as they knew, their spouses had had affairs echoed the comments just quoted. They indicated that even if they were tempted, the maintenance of trust was too important a feature of their relationship to put at risk. Sometimes this was presented as primarily a matter of *duty* and *responsibility*. The promise of sexual fidelity had been made; to disregard this would be dishonorable. For others, however, fidelity was expressed less as a contractual issue and more as a betrayal of the partner and his or her continuing commitment. The other did not deserve to be treated in such a fashion, and to do so would irreparably harm an otherwise secure and satisfying relationship. For these respondents, the immediate satisfactions of fresh sexual experiences could not compensate for the damage that would be caused to their existing relationships.

Not surprisingly, many correspondents also referred to feelings of guilt. In particular, those who held the view that sexual infidelity was antithetical to marital trust frequently indicated that a prime reason they would not contemplate being unfaithful was that they would be unable to cope with the consequent guilt such actions would generate. In addition to guilt associated with betrayal, correspondents also reflected on the broader damage that affairs can have on family life. More specifically, the harm potentially caused to children within the family by the threat that an affair presented to a marriage was frequently mentioned, especially by those who had never been unfaithful to their spouses. Often assuming that marital infidelity once known about would inevitably lead to separation, these correspondents argued that they would be unable to manage the guilt that would ensue from causing their children so much emotional disruption and unhappiness. In their view, no affair could be worth the risk of damaging their children to this degree.

Correspondents whose marriages had been affected by affairs also frequently wrote about their feelings of betrayal and guilt, often at some length. A large proportion of those whose spouses or partners had become involved in another relationship expressed poignantly the sense of betrayal and rejection they experienced. For them, the trust on which their relationship was premised had been polluted, sometimes to the point of destruction, by their partners' actions. As the quotes that follow indicate, these respondents felt demeaned and belittled by what had happened. With knowledge of the affair, a significant element of their self-esteem and self-security had been undermined in ways that could not easily be rectified:

The pain of knowing my husband had an affair was indescribable. I couldn't say anything, I just froze. In fact, it's very difficult to talk about it. (B1424, female, 73)

When I learned, age 30, that my husband had been unfaithful a number of times, I found his mendacity and betrayal impossible to forgive. I do not know how I would have reacted to a single infidelity. (R2247, female, 49)

Oddly enough, the affair itself was immaterial to me … it was the loss of trust that was the over-riding concern. (M1593, male, 51)

Sadly, even after all this time [two and a half years], I no longer feel the same way about him as he totally abused my trust…. It isn't the only reason I no longer want to be with him but it is a large part of it. (M2811 female, 30)

Equally, many, although not all, of those who reported having had affairs recognized with regret that they had betrayed their partners' trust in ways that were difficult to justify. For these people, the affair itself might have been highly significant, but they nonetheless recognized that because of it they had abused the trust on which their marriages were based. As a result, many were left with strong feelings of guilt, which sometimes remained potent long after the affair was over:

… but I don't think he ever really forgave me and it caused him a lot of pain. I don't believe that affairs are immoral, but hurting other people is. This makes having affairs very risky for people in permanent relationships. (M2164, female, 70)

I've had 14 affairs, some brief.… As I move into my late sixties, with a partner I love, who is in his own way vulnerable, I am certain there will be no more affairs. I could not deceive or hurt him. I dislike the lying and deceit that accompany these tangles. (N1592, female, 66)

I find this Directive hard to write about. To admit to. Even though it was in the 60's. I still feel so ashamed. Ashamed of the way I hurt my husband, a kind and trusting young man who didn't deserve all the shock, pain, humiliation I introduced him to. (W853, female, 62)

A quite different perspective on trust was taken by a small minority of correspondents who argued that sexual fidelity was only one element, and not necessarily a particularly important one, within the trust on which contemporary marriages needed to be built. Whereas for them marital commitment certainly embodied trust, it was a trust that ran much deeper than sexual exclusivity. Indeed, for these correspondents, rather than lifelong fidelity being the symbol *par excellence* of commitment, an affair represented more a hurdle or "blip" that, given a sufficient degree of trust, couples should be able to overcome. This was captured most graphically by a 38-year-old female correspondent who wrote: "People also confuse trust with fidelity—when the spouse or partner is unfaithful the first thing said is that they've abused their trust—what world are these people living in! Trusting them never to be unfaithful is unrealistic" (P2819, female, 38).

Change and Loss

A further powerful theme present in the correspondents' accounts was that an affair would so alter the basis of marriage that it could never again be the same. Clearly this sense of irrevocable change is tied in with the correspondents' feelings about betrayal and trust discussed in the previous section. Many of those who stated that they had no experience of an affair highlighted their belief that their marriage would not survive an affair intact. Some thought any affair would automatically result in separation.

Others were less certain on this, but nonetheless recognized that they would see their partners in a quite different light if they ever were unfaithful. In particular, they felt that even if they tried to sustain the marriage, it would have a distinctly different dynamic. They would no longer be able to give their spouses the unreflexive trust they now did, nor overcome the harm done to their sense of security and self-esteem. The following quotes, taken from correspondents making no claim of involvement in affairs, illustrate these themes:

> I cannot imagine being able to cope if my husband were to have an affair. It would be so out of character, so degrading and hurtful. I would feel disgusted, cheapened, humiliated. I would possibly be able to forgive it eventually but I would never have the same feelings for him again and I don't think our marriage would survive. (S2207, female, 46)

> I think if my husband had a public affair I would leave him. I couldn't stand to be humiliated in front of friends and family. (B2066, female, 57)

> I've never had an affair, or wanted one. If I discovered my husband had been disloyal, it would be a divorce. There is no excuse for disloyalty in any form of partnership. (C2653, female, 34)

This sense of irredeemable change to the marital relationship following an affair was expressed most vividly by many of those who had direct experience of these matters. This applied most obviously to those marriages in which the affairs eventually led to separation and divorce. Although with hindsight an affair was not always seen as the sole reason for the marriage ending—sometimes it was viewed as a symptom of marital disharmony as much as a cause especially by those who had had the affair—the affair almost invariably played a significant role in the accounts these correspondents gave of their separations. The marriage might have ended anyway, but knowledge of the affair(s) became the catalyst for, and symbol of, the disunity that prevailed within the marriage.

Correspondents who knew of their spouses' affairs often described how their sense of commitment had changed as a result. As the following quotes indicate, these correspondents experienced this in a variety of ways. Some people quickly recognized that they had no desire to carry on with the marriage, a position that was particularly marked if the affair continued in any way. Others were more prepared to try to save the relationship but found this extremely difficult, even when their spouses also appeared committed to this. They had problems putting the image of the other person aside, or found that suspicions reemerged whenever their spouses were late coming home or away for any period. A number wrote that they could not forgive their spouses for what had happened, however hard they tried. Other correspondents reported being able to understand and forgive but not able to forget. Some emphasized an abiding sense of injustice; others focused more on the damage the affair had done to their self-esteem or the humiliation they had experienced as knowledge of the affair became public. However expressed, the reality for this group of correspondents was that their marriages were unlikely to be the same again. To use a biblical metaphor, the apple had been bitten and innocence lost. For these respondents, the *status quo ante* was extremely difficult to reestablish.

Nonetheless, some of these correspondents attempted to rebuild their marriages, although a number were successful in this for only a short period. The structural cracks the affair had revealed or generated in their relationships ran too deep to be plastered over. Others reported being more successful. Although the period after the affair had been an extremely difficult one with much argument and emotional trauma involved in renegotiating their relationships, the marriages had nonetheless withstood these pressures. Eventually, new concordances came to be established. Although this often involved lowered senses of intimacy, expectation, and commitment, it nonetheless rendered the marriages tolerable and (at the least) provided sufficient satisfaction for their continuation. In addition, there were very occasional examples of marriages becoming stronger as a result of an affair. As with the final quote in the list that follows, the affair resulted in the relationship being refashioned in a manner that led to increased satisfaction and renewed commitment:

> My first husband had many affairs and I hated it, but was unable to stop loving him, and I think he took advantage of that. I never really felt the same about him though, as I felt there was nothing left about him that wasn't known by loads of others as well as me. (B2760, female, 63)

> My husband had an affair with his secretary, when he was in his forties. It was a terrible shock when he told me and although I don't think about it much now (fourteen years later) you can never forget completely.... I got depression and had to take anti-depressants, even feeling suicidal for a short time. (C2078, female, 53)

> I never ever thought that I'd ever have an affair, but I did. It lasted 3 years. My husband and I had not got on well for years, he insulted me, refused to take me out anywhere and drank to excess.... I told my husband about the affair.... From that day he has been caring and considerate and tells me that he loves me every single day. Our relationship now is much stronger than it has ever been. He has stopped drinking, and we go out together often. Indirectly the affair saved our marriage. (S2442, female, 60)

Ambiguity

As we have seen, some correspondents took a "traditional" view of marital infidelity. Whether validated in terms of vows or personal commitment, for them, the "rules" of marriage were clear: Any act of adultery was morally wrong. Other correspondents, however, took a less judgmental and dogmatic approach than this. Although they also saw infidelity as damaging to marriage, they nonetheless conveyed a greater willingness to understand affairs contextually rather than see them simply in terms of rule breaking and wrongdoing. At the heart of this lies different understandings of the nature of marriage. From the traditional perspective, marriage is a contract in which binding agreements are made that govern the conduct of the relationship. Those correspondents adopting a more interpretive or contextual stance also accepted the significance of normative convention but equally viewed marriage as a dynamic relationship in which the feelings the spouses have for one another are liable to change, as are their needs and the extent to which these can be met by the spouse.

In line with this, many correspondents recognized that marriages can easily become taken for granted, with the routine demands of everyday domestic life coming to dominate to the extent that the relationship no longer offers sufficient emotional, sexual, or other fulfilment. As would be expected, some argued that at such times what was required was greater vigilance: Marriages needed to be "worked at" if they were to be successful, although few went on to discuss explicitly the degree to which such "emotion work" or "relationship vigilance" was bound up with gender (Duncombe & Marsden, 1993, 1995; Hochschild, 1990). Rather more interestingly, other respondents reported a growing sense that, no matter what effort was put into a particular relationship or however committed a spouse was, it was unlikely one relationship could ever fully meet an individual's needs over the life course. In this context, affairs became understandable—unfortunate but understandable. The following quotes capture this view:

> No man can be all things to any woman, nor can any woman be all things to any man. Once this fact can be realised and accepted one has to make up one's mind to accept the discrepancies in one's life—or not. (H2506, male, 78)

> I have been changing my mind about these issues for some time now. It might be very idealistic to think so, but I believe if you're married to the right person, you won't want to have an affair.... I'm feeling at the moment, after observing myself and my friends, that one special partner is probably not a possibility for a lot of people, and for the best motives. In my own case, I feel I have become a completely different person to who I was 10, 20, 30 years ago, and I want different things from different people.... Although I couldn't say I'm actually looking for an affair, I am in that state of dissatisfaction with my marriage that makes me feel it would be a possibility. (A1706, female, 52)

> The sad thing is that we all have such complicated needs, many of which we may not realize until well on in life; and if one does then find a man or woman who meets these needs the temptation to reach out to them can be irresistible. (D996, female, 71)

> I have been married 41 years and my views have naturally changed during this long relationship.... At certain ages/times and for certain people affairs may be a necessity.... (L1884, female, 66)

The majority of those correspondents who reflected a more interpretive perspective on affairs were certainly not condoning them. For most, there was little suggestion that affairs were beneficial or positive. However, unlike many of those who took a more judgmental stance, their accounts were often characterized by ambiguity and moral dilemmas. In particular, many of their responses reflected a tension between marriage as a long-term commitment and an individual's need for self-actualization and fulfilment. People had some right to seek happiness in their personal, domestic, and sexual lives, but at the same time, marital commitment should not be treated lightly. Correspondents recognized that all marriages experience "rocky patches" in which one or both partners became dissatisfied, but during such periods the spouses needed to "work at" their marriage rather than seeking what was generally perceived as likely to be short-term solace with someone else, however attractive such new relationships might seem (Dindia & Canary, 1993; Duck & Wood, 1995). Others argued that although affairs were understandable, it was important that they remained secret. Most of these correspondents thought it better not to have an affair but, if one developed, those in it had a responsibility to keep it clandestine so as not to hurt their spouses or children. Thus, in these accounts, the tension between marital commitment and self-realization was "resolved" by trying to ensure that the affair did the least possible damage:

> Sometimes affairs can be enriching if the long-term partner does not find out. If it's short or [a] one-off fling it can be flattering to know someone else fancies you. It can make you look at yourself in a different way. (H2816, female, 39)

> Quite often, one partner may have a "dalliance" elsewhere but I think the secret is in fact secrecy. Why tell your partner if you've had an encounter with someone else? What would it achieve? It might clear your conscience but surely, nine times out of ten it can only damage what might otherwise be a very sound relationship. Jealousy, suspicion and even mere doubt can be killers, so you must do nothing to put them into the other person's mind. (D1602, male, 55)

> Ideally people should be committed to a long-term marriage.... A very private affair is only acceptable if *no* one gets hurt ... but this is, I think, rarely possible and would involve the holding of secret knowledge for ever.... Some things should be kept secret—and treasured as a secret. (R2144, female, 62)

CONCLUSION: ALWAYS INAPPROPRIATE?

At the beginning of this chapter, we pointed out that marital affairs are nearly always seen as inappropriate, although tolerance of them varies significantly across cultures and contexts (Goodwin, 1999). In this study, the dominant view of the Mass-Observation Archive's correspondents was that affairs were wrong, damaging, and best avoided. Yet, the accounts they provided of both their own affairs and those of others they knew also contained other judgments, opening up the issue of whether all aspects of affairs, and all types of affairs, are seen as similarly inappropriate. It was clear that when affairs became known, they were nearly always harmful for marriages, and usually resulted in a good deal of anguish and pain. At the same time, affairs could be experienced as important and highly rewarding for those directly involved. The affair(s) had added elements to respondents' lives that they perceived to be otherwise missing, be this excitement, sexual satisfaction, validation of the self, or emotional fulfilment. They may not perceive what they did as right or moral, but it was frequently understood as experientially important within the context of their lives. Thus, even when correspondents clearly regretted the harm an affair had caused, their accounts often still conveyed a strong sense of the affair being enriching for them personally.

Correspondents recognized that there are different types of affairs, some producing quite complex categorizations. However, as well as differences between short flings and more long-lasting affairs, the main distinction made was between love and lust—affairs of the heart and affairs of the loin. There were clearly differences in the ways these were viewed. Affairs that were defined predominantly in terms of sexual gratification were seen as inappropriate and damaging, but often not to the same degree as affairs that were emotionally charged. Yet, although these latter types were understood to be "inappropriate" within the dominant construction of contemporary marriage, from other perspectives they were not always seen as wholly so. As noted earlier, some correspondents felt that affairs had enriched their lives, adding dimensions that would otherwise be missing. They had found pleasure in them, pleasure that—from their perspective—outweighed any damage done. However, this was generally only so because their spouses and children had been protected from knowledge of the affairs. Equally, some correspondents recognized that for people in the wrong marriage, an affair could be a route to change that was ultimately judged as beneficial, although most felt it better for the marriage to end before a new relationship was started.

Finally, even though most correspondents highlighted the damage that affairs wrought, many also emphasized the complexity of human relationships and the dangers of passing judgments too readily. In part, this may be a characteristic of the Mass-Observation panel, as continued participation fosters reflexivity above any simple dogmatism. Nonetheless, this perspective on affairs can be read as signifying a movement toward Giddens' model of confluent love, plastic sexuality, and pure relationships. Certainly, there was an emphasis within many of the more detailed Mass-Observation Archive responses that individuals should not be locked into unsatisfactory marriages. Most appeared to believe that people had a right to personal happiness; yet, they also believed that marital commitments needed to be taken seriously, especially during periods of disharmony. If the couple really were unsuited, then separation and a fresh start with someone new was an acceptable solution. To this degree, these correspondents did reflect the new moralities of love and commitment portrayed by Giddens and others, which is, perhaps, not really surprising given the socioeconomic makeup of the Archive's volunteer writers. Nevertheless, we also found a strong emphasis in the responses on the importance of marital commitment. As their comments on betrayal and trust indicate, correspondents of all ages emphasized that marriage should not be taken lightly. Perhaps, most significantly, the majority of those whose marriages had ended because of affairs recounted the pain and hurt that this had generated. Although there was acknowledgment that young people were less sexually constrained now than in the past, there was little evidence to suggest that people now treated the ties of marriage and partnership as only loose bindings.

REFERENCES

Allan, G., & Crow, G. (2001). *Families, households and society.* London: Macmillan.

Beck, U. (1992). *Risk society.* London: Sage.

Beck, U., & Beck-Gernsheim, E. (1995). *The normal chaos of love.* Cambridge, UK: Polity.

Betzig, L. (1989). Causes of conjugal dissolution: A cross-cultural study. *Current Anthropology, 30,* 654–676.

Dindia, K., & Canary, D. (1993). Definitions and theoretical perspectives on maintaining relationships. *Journal of Social and Personal Relationships, 10,* 163–174.

Duck, S., & Wood, J. (1995). For better, for worse, for richer for poorer. In S. Duck & J. Wood (Eds.), *Confronting relationship challenges* (pp. 1–21). London: Sage.

Duncombe, J., & Marsden, D. (1993). Love and intimacy. *Sociology, 27,* 221–241.

Duncombe, J., & Marsden, D. (1995). Workaholics and whingeing women: Theorising intimacy. *Sociological Review, 43,* 150–169.

Finch, J., & Summerfield, P. (1991). Social reconstruction and the emergence of companionate marriage, 1945–59. In D. Clark (Ed.), *Marriage, domestic life and social change* (pp. 7–32). London: Routledge.

Frayser, S. (1985). *Varieties of sexual experience: An anthropological perspective on human sexuality.* New Haven, CT: HRAF Press.

Gibson, C. (1994). *Dissolving Wedlock.* London: Routledge.

Giddens, A. (1992). *The transformation of intimacy.* Cambridge, UK: Polity.

Goodwin, R. (1999). *Personal relationships across cultures.* London: Routledge.

Hatfield, E., & Rapson, R. (1996). *Love and sex: Cross-cultural perspectives.* Boston: Allyn & Bacon.

Heilbrun, C. (1989). *Writing a woman's life.* London: Woman's Press.

Hochschild, A. (1990). *The second shift.* London: Piatkus.

Holmes, J., & Rempel, J. (1989). Trust in close relationships. In C. Hendrick (Ed.), *Review of personality and social psychology* (vol. 10, pp. 187–220). London: Sage.

Jackson, S. (1993). Even sociologists fall in love: an exploration in the sociology of emotions. *Sociology, 27,* 201–220.

Jackson, S. (1995). Women and heterosexual love. In L. Pearce & J. Stacey (Eds.), *Romance revisited* (pp. 49–62). London: Lawrence and Wishart.

Jamieson, L. (1998). *Intimacy*. Cambridge, UK: Polity.

Jamieson, L. (1999). Intimacy transformed? *Sociology, 33*, 477–494.

Kiernan, K., Land, H., & Lewis, J. (1998). *Lone motherhood in twentieth century Britain*. Oxford, UK: Oxford University Press.

Lawson, A. (1987). *Adultery*. Oxford, UK: Blackwell.

Lawson, A., & Samson, C. (1988). Age, gender and adultery. *British Journal of Sociology, 39*, 409–440.

MacFarlane, A. (1986). *Marriage and love in England 1300–1840*. Oxford, UK: Blackwell.

McRae, S. (Ed.). (1999). *Changing Britain: Families and households in the 1990s*. Oxford, UK: Oxford University Press.

Morgan, D. (2000, April). *How brief an encounter? Time and relationships, pure or otherwise*. Paper presented to the BSA Conference, Making Time/Marking Time, University of York, York, UK.

Prins, K., Buunk, B., & VanYperen, N. (1993). Equity, normative disapproval and extramarital relationships. *Journal of Social and Personal Relationships, 10*, 39–53.

Reibstein, J., & Richards, M. (1992). *Sexual arrangements: Marriage and affairs*. London: Heinemann.

Shackelford, T., & Buss, D. (1997). Anticipation of marital dissolution as a consequence of spousal infidelity. *Journal of Social and Personal Relationships, 14*, 793–808.

Shaw, J. (1996). Surrealism, mass-observation and researching imagination. In E. S. Lyon & J. Busfield (Eds.), *Methodological imaginations* (pp. 1–16). London: Macmillan.

Sheridan, D. (1993). Writing to the archive: Mass-observation as autobiography. *Sociology, 27*, 27–40.

Smart, C., & Neale, B. (1999). *Family fragments?* Cambridge, UK: Polity.

Stanley, L. (1995). *Sex surveyed 1949–1994*. London: Taylor & Francis.

Stone, L. (1979). The family, sex, and marriage in England 1500–1800. Harmondsworth: Penguin.

Wellings, K., Fields, J., Johnson, A., & Wadsworth, J. (1994). *Sexual behaviour in Britain*. London: Penguin.

Interracial Relationships[1]

Stanley O. Gaines, Jr.
Brunel University

Jennifer Leaver
Claremont Graduate University

Among interethnic relationships (i.e., relationships involving partners who differ in their racial, cultural, and/or religious group memberships; Baptiste, 1984), interracial relationships are especially likely to engender ambivalence, if not outright hostility, from relationship outsiders in the United States (Perlman, 1997). For example, unlike same-race couples among whom partners do not share a common cultural or religious background, mixed-race couples (who may or may not share cultural and religious backgrounds) frequently are targeted for abuse by strangers in public (Gaines & Ickes, 1997). Obviously, within many segments of American society, interracial relationships (approximately 5% of all marriages; Suro, 1999) are regarded as "inappropriate."

[1]An earlier version of this chapter was presented at the 2000 joint conference of the International Society for the Study of Personal Relationships and the International Network on Personal Relationships, University of Queensland, Brisbane, Australia, June 27–July 2, 2000. Preparation of this chapter was facilitated by a Fulbright Scholars Grant to the first author. The authors are indebted to Robin Goodwin and Duncan Cramer for their insightful comments regarding earlier versions of this chapter. Please address all correspondence to: Stanley O. Gaines, Jr., who currently is at the Department of Human Sciences, Brunel University, Uxbridge, Middlesex UB8 3PH, United Kingdom.

Interracial relationships are not the only interethnic relationships that are deemed "inappropriate" in America; partners in interreligious relationships also face strong opposition within some communities and families (Heaton & Pratt, 1990; Sussman & Alexander, 1999; see also Whyte, 1990). Nevertheless, the negative impact of societal disapproval on intermarriage seems to be magnified within interracial relationships. For example, consistent with Allport's (1954/1979) observation that religious differences were decreasing in salience relative to racial differences, Levinger and Rands (1985) reported that the interreligious marriage rate had risen relative to the interracial marriage rate. In addition, by the late 1990s, the divorce rate for Jewish–Gentile marriages (i.e., approximately one third) was double the divorce rate for Jewish–Jewish marriages (Sussman & Alexander, 1999), but only *half* the divorce rate for interracial marriages (see Gaines & Ickes, 1997). The rate of intermarriage for Jewish persons in the United States (most estimates exceed 50%; e.g., see Heaton & Pratt, 1990; Sussman & Alexander, 1999; but see also Soskis, 2000) is particularly instructive. With the exception of Native Americans (50% of whom marry outside their racial group; Alba, 1995), no racial minority group approaches such a high intermarriage rate (although, among Asian Americans, the Japanese American intermarriage rate is 50%; Lee & Fernandez, 1998; see also Sung, 1990). Moreover, although more than 50% of European Americans are in "interethnic" marriages (if one includes marriages that cross the lines of religious denomination and nation of origin), only 2% of European Americans are in "interracial" marriages (Alba, 1995).

In the present chapter, we consider the historical and contemporary circumstances that have allowed "old-fashioned" and "modern" racists alike (see Dovidio & Gaertner, 1991) to deem interracial dating and marital relationships—especially Black–White dating and marital relationships—as "inappropriate." Specifically, we examine the processes by which stigmatization (i.e., the marking of individuals as inferior by virtue of their membership in socially devalued groups; Goffman, 1963) simultaneously affect nonstigmatized and stigmatized individuals alike. We focus primarily on the United States, partly because virtually all of the published research on interethnic marriage is based on U.S. samples (especially U.S. census sample data; e.g., Blackwell & Lichter, 2000; Crowder & Tolnay, 2000; Hwang, Saenz, & Aguirre, 1997; Lee & Fernandez, 1998), and partly because Black–White intermarriage rates in the United States are among the lowest for all Western nations (Pettigrew, 1988). Furthermore, we focus primarily on Black–White romantic relationships, partly because the Black–White dichotomy underlies most of the race-based empirical studies on stigmatization (see Jones et al., 1984), and partly because most of the published research on interethnic marriages has dealt specifically with Black–White marriages (Blackwell & Lichter, 2000; for a cautionary note regarding generalizations from Black–White marriages to other interracial marriages, see Lee & Fernandez, 1998).

WHO SAYS THAT INTERRACIAL RELATIONSHIPS ARE "INAPPROPRIATE"?

The United States Congress never explicitly outlawed miscegenation (i.e., sex and marriage between persons designated by society as belonging to different racial groups). Nevertheless, 37 of the 50 states had antimiscegenation laws at some time, 22 of the 37 states with antimiscegenation laws focused solely on Black–White marriage, and 29 of the states had antimiscegenation laws throughout most of their history (i.e., from the time that they were admitted as states; Spickard, 1989). At the time that the United States Supreme Court ruled in *Loving v. Virginia* (1967) that all existing antimiscegenation laws were null and void, every former Confederate state still had such laws. Thus, most state legislatures in the United States have said at one time that interracial marriage was "inappropriate."

Prior to the 1960s, one of the most common arguments against federal civil rights legislation in the United States was that "stateways cannot change folkways"—a saying attributed to sociologist William Graham Sumner (Allport, 1954/1979, p. 469). Despite Sumner's proclamation to the contrary, the legacy of antimiscegenation laws helped solidify antimiscegenation attitudes among White Americans. It was only after state antimiscegenation laws were abolished within a larger environment that fostered tremendous social change, such as the Civil Rights Movement and the liberalization of immigration laws, that antimiscegenation attitudes began to change (Lee & Fernandez, 2000). For example, in 1970 (a few years after the aforementioned *Loving v. Virginia* decision), 52% of White Americans supported antimiscegenation laws; by 1990 (a generation after *Loving v. Virginia*), only 23% of White Americans supported antimiscegenation laws (Tucker & Mitchell-Kernan, 1995). We hasten to add that the lack of support for antimiscegenation laws does not necessarily reflect tolerance for interracial marriage; in 1991, 66% of White Americans said that they would oppose marriage between their close relatives and Black Americans (Pinkney, 1993).

American society is patriarchal, and "father figures" disproportionately are personified by White males. By and large, White males in the United States have shaped the prism through which interracial romance is viewed. For instance, White male–Black female romantic relationships generally have been deemed as less "inappropriate" than have Black male–White female relationships (Gaines & Ickes, 1997). When a White male dates or marries a Black female, no fundamental change in power within the American social structure is perceived as taking place. In contrast, when a White female dates or marries a Black male, the Black male often is perceived as attaining higher social status (i.e., the White woman is viewed as the Black man's "prize," stolen from the more deserving White man). One result of White male paranoia concerning such supposed trophy-stealing behavior by Black males is the creation and transmission of ugly racial stereotypes depicting Black men as savage animals who want nothing more than to bed (if not wed) White women (Gaines & Ickes, 1997). According to Foeman and Nance (1999), such stereotypes were embedded within much of the social-scientific theorizing on interracial relationships prior to the 1980s, without any efforts at hypothesis testing or empirical disconfirmation (see also Tucker & Mitchell-Kernan, 1990).

In contrast, most persons of color do *not* say that interracial marriage is inappropriate. Even among Black Americans, who are less likely to marry across racial boundaries (approximately 5%) than are other persons of color (as many as 30% of Latinas/os and 33% of Asian Americans; Alba, 1995), approximately two thirds indicated in 1991 that they would neither oppose nor support marriage between their close relatives and White Americans (Pinkney, 1993). Furthermore, at no time in the history of the United States has a majority of Black Americans supported state antimiscegenation laws (National Research Council, 1989).

Black Americans' attitudes toward interracial marriage involving family members may have been shaped in part by the fact that Whiteness (unlike Blackness) never has been stigmatized in American society. However, even if we take stigmatization into account, Black Americans historically have not displayed ethnocentrism to the same degree as have White Americans (Gaines & Reed, 1994, 1995; Reed & Gaines, 1997). Those Blacks who do harbor negative attitudes toward "race mixing" involving family members appear to differ from the majority of Black Americans by virtue of nationalistic political views, rather than by socioeconomic status (Porterfield, 1978). Overall, Blacks and other persons of color tend not to say that interracial marriage is "inappropriate," even if such marriage potentially involves their own relatives.

In their review of the literature on social stigma, Crocker, Major, and Steele (1998) discussed various predicaments of stigmatized individuals, with each predicament ultimately involving potential threats to stigmatized persons' self-esteem. In general, persons of color have been aware throughout their lives that at any time when they are in public view, they are potential targets of racial stereotyping, prejudice, and discrimination (see also Fiske, 1998). Most White Americans, in contrast, have no direct experience as victims of racial stereotyping, prejudice, or discrimination— that is, unless they have dated or married across racial lines (Rosenblatt, Karis, & Powell, 1995).

If individuals who date and marry interracially tend to internalize negative stereotypes about themselves, then one might expect those individuals to suffer from low self-esteem, relative to individuals who date within their race. However, empirical studies of persons in interracial versus intraracial relationships have yielded inconclusive results. Shibazaki and Brennan (1998) found that persons in mixed-race relationships tended to score significantly lower in self-esteem than did persons in same-race relationships; whereas Gurung and Duong (1999) failed to replicate this significant interracial–intraracial difference in self-esteem. The lack of clear evidence concerning self-esteem differences raises doubts as to whether persons who date and marry interracially have internalized the "tribal stigma" that, according to Goffman (1963), Western societies impose upon interracial couples.

WHAT MAKES INTERRACIAL RELATIONSHIPS "INAPPROPRIATE"?

More than any other type of social contact that crosses the "color line," interracial marriage symbolizes social equality among the races (Fang, Sidanius, & Pratto, 1998; Hwang et al., 1997). In the United States, a common conversation-stopping response to advocates for civil rights legislation prior to the 1960s was the question, "Would you want your daughter to marry one?" (Allport, 1954/1979). The symbolic importance of interracial marriage was not lost on White Americans during the pre-Civil Rights Era. For example, during the World War II years, many Southern White men held the erroneous belief that Southern Black men were more concerned with obtaining sex and marriage with White women than with obtaining equal employment opportunity (Myrdal, 1944; see also Zebroski, 1999).

Due largely to the "peculiar institution" of slavery, Blacks historically have been treated as members of an inferior caste in the ostensibly classless United States. To this day, Blacks in American society are stigmatized as the descendants of slaves (Jones, 1997); and those Whites who marry Blacks are stigmatized literally through guilt by association (Gaines & Ickes, 1997; Goffman, 1963). In a vivid illustration of White Americans' negative attitudes toward interracial marriage involving kin, many Whites—especially White women—in Black–White marriages report that their families of origin have disowned them (Porterfield, 1978; Rosenblatt et al., 1995). However, the exact percentage of White women and men who have experienced such ostracism is not clear.

Without a doubt, American society maintains a taboo against interracial marriage. This taboo is evident in popular culture. Just as antimiscegenation laws guided most of the United States at one point, so too did the Hays Office Code, which prohibited implicit or explicit depictions of miscegenation in motion pictures, guide Hollywood prior to World War II (Guerrero, 1993). Even in the years during and after the Civil Rights Era, the American motion picture industry rarely has dealt with Black–White romance—and in those few exceptions, Black–White romance has been depicted either as marriage without sex (e.g., *Guess Who's Coming To Dinner?* in 1967) or as sex without marriage (e.g., *Jungle Fever* in 1991; see Gates, 1991).

On commercial network television, a major milestone regarding interracial romance include the first interracial kiss depicted on the science fiction series *Star Trek* (whose protagonist, Captain James T. Kirk, proclaimed that he and his crew would "boldly go where no man has gone before" regarding intergalactic relations!) in the 1960s. Another important milestone was the first interracial married couple depicted on the situation comedy *The Jeffersons* in the 1970s and 1980s. More recent examples of interracial romance include storylines on the medical drama *ER*, and on the comedy-drama *Ally McBeal*, in the 1990s. Like the "big screen" of cinema, the "small screen" of television still tends to dichotomize Black–White romance as sex without marriage (e.g., *ER*, *Ally McBeal*) or as marriage without sex (e.g., *The Jeffersons*).[2] All in all, interracial relationships violate a long-standing taboo in American society that, in turn, reflects past stateways and present folkways concerning miscegenation (Gaines & Liu, 2000).

According to Crocker et al. (1998), stigmatized individuals implement an array of strategies for coping with the predicaments of stigmatization. These coping strategies are similar to the strategies that nonstigmatized individuals implement in response to threats to self-esteem. Although Crocker et al. (1998) did not use the term specifically, the concept of *self-serving bias* (i.e., the tendency for individuals to attribute personal successes to factors within themselves, yet attribute personal failures to factors outside themselves; Baumeister, 1998) neatly captures the essence of the relevant coping strategies. An individual person of color might respond to a failure of impression management (e.g., presenting oneself as a likable person, only to find that a White stranger yells racial epithets at him or her without provocation) by concluding, "I'm not the one with low self-esteem; that racist is the insecure one." Similarly, two interracial spouses might respond to a failure of impression management (e.g., presenting themselves as a happy couple, only to have a White stranger declare that they do not "belong" together) by concluding, "We aren't the ones with low self-esteem; that racist is the insecure one" (for a detailed discussion of impression management, see Goffman, 1959). To our knowledge, attributional processes such as self-serving bias have not been examined systematically among interracial couples.

---

[2]The interracial taboo seems to be enforced more rigidly on commercial network television than in syndicated programs or on public television in the United States. Outside of commercial network television, the syndicated action-adventure series, *Xena*, depicted a Black male–White female romance over the short term; whereas the public television documentary, *An American Love Story*, dealt candidly with the private as well as public lives of a Black male–White female married couple (Gaines & Brennan, 2001).

WHOM DOES IT SERVE TO DEFINE INTERRACIAL RELATIONSHIPS AS "INAPPROPRIATE"?

According to Gaines, Chalfin, Kim, and Taing (1998), the middle-age, middle-class, heterosexual, Protestant, White male stands at the point of intersection among the "spheres of prejudice" that include ageism, classism, heterosexism, religious dogmatism, racism, and sexism in American society. In fact, it is difficult for such an individual to avoid communicating prejudice, even in personal or close relationships. Historically, White men have been the primary beneficiaries of the American racial spoils system. For example, (a) White men who are convicted of killing Blacks are far less likely to receive the death penalty than are Black men who kill Whites; (b) every federal employee who has been elected within the executive branch of government has been a White male, and the vast majority of federal employees who have been elected within the legislative branch or appointed within the judicial branch have been White males; and (c) White males dominate the big screen and small screen. This is not to say that a majority of White males in the United States are racists, or that members of other socially defined groups (e.g., White women, Black men, Black women) are immune from harboring racist attitudes. Nevertheless, those American White males who *are* racists have been in a unique position to manifest their racism individually, institutionally, and culturally.

Conversely, "antiracists" are *not* well-served by defining interracial relationships as "inappropriate." According to J. M. Jones (1997), the concept of antiracism is not synonymous with "reverse racism," the latter of which implies that one simply can replace White privilege with, say, Black privilege. Rather, *antiracism* refers to the active rejection of racism. With regard to interracial marriage, an antiracist essentially would take a pro-choice position—that is, the decision to marry interracially should be made by the romantic partners themselves, rather than by relationship outsiders (Penn, Gaines, & Phillips, 1993; Phillips, Penn, & Gaines, 1993).

Throughout most of this chapter, we have discussed stigmatization processes primarily from the standpoint of stigmatized persons. However, in order to understand the ways that individual, institutional, and cultural racists benefit psychologically from defining interracial relationships as "inappropriate," we must consider stigmatization processes from the standpoint of the nonstigmatized person as well. Crocker et al. (1998) not only identified several functions of stigma for the nonstigmatized individual but also invoked the concept of *ingroup-outgroup bias* (i.e., the tendency for individuals to view members of their ingroup as having more desirable personal characteristics and greater heterogeneity than do members of outgroups; see also Brewer & Brown, 1998) to explain the psychological origins of those functions. For example, a would-be Klansman might bolster his own shaky self-esteem by yelling the epithet "Nigger!" (thus affirming the racist's "White pride") at a Black man on the opposite side of the street. Similarly, the would-be Klansman might inflate his ego temporarily by yelling the epithet "Nigger-lover!" at a White woman who meets and kisses the Black man—her husband—on the opposite side of the street. Despite the conceptual appeal of ingroup-outgroup bias as an explanation for the behavior of virulently racist outsiders toward interracial couples, we do not know of any research that has addressed attributional biases of outsiders vis-à-vis interracial relationships.

HAVE INTERRACIAL RELATIONSHIPS ALWAYS BEEN "INAPPROPRIATE"?

At first glance, the long history of state antimiscegenation laws in the United States might lead one to conclude that interracial relationships always have been deemed "inappropriate" in American society. However, Staples and Boulin Johnson (1993) identified three periods in American history during which antimiscegenation laws generally "were ignored or did not exist" (p. 147). First, early in the Colonial Era, antimiscegenation laws did not exist; with Black women in short supply, many Black male indentured servants and, later, slaves married White female indentured servants. Second, during the Civil War, the large numbers of White men who went off to wage battle prompted many White women and Black men to ignore those antimiscegenation laws that were in effect at the time (largely in the North). Third, early in the modern-day Civil Rights Era (i.e., before the aforementioned *Loving v. Virginia* decision in 1967), the changing political climate led many individuals—especially White women and Black men—to defy those antimiscegenation laws that still were in effect at the time (almost exclusively in the South).

All of the seemingly anomalous periods in American history identified by Stapes and Boulin Johnson (1993) are distinct because they involved relatively large numbers of Black male–White female sexual and marital pairings. In fact, one enduring legacy of the tumultuous 1960s has been a dramatic increase in the number of Black male–White female marriages, relative to the number of White male–Black female marriages (Tucker & Mitchell-Kernan, 1990). The reasons for such a shift among Black–White marriages appear to be twofold. First, in the aftermath of reformed immigration laws in the United States in 1965, Asian American women have become the interracial marriage partners of choice for European American men (Blackwell & Lichter, 2000). Second, in the aftermath of the 1967 *Loving v. Virginia* decision by the United States Supreme Court, many of the sociolegal constraints that had targeted Black male–White female marriages began to lose their potency (Gaines & Ickes, 1997).

In the pre-Civil War South, White male masters routinely took Black female slaves—who increasingly were viewed as prized "commodities" as the slave trade escalated—as concubines, either through mutual consent or (more commonly) by force (Spickard, 1989). Moreover, prior to the modern-day Civil Rights Era, White male–Black female married couples in the North as well as the South typically were not punished as harshly for violating state antimiscegenation laws as were Black male–White female married couples. As a result, until the 1960s, White male–Black female marriages outnumbered Black male–White female marriages in the United States (Tucker & Mitchell-Kernan, 1995).

UNRESOLVED ISSUES CONCERNING RELATIONSHIP SATISFACTION AND STABILITY AMONG INTERRACIAL COUPLES

Crocker et al. (1998) discussed the consequences of stigma for the social and psychological well-being of stigmatized individuals. For example, one effect of the accumulation of encounters with racial stereotyping, prejudice, and discrimination over the years may be lowered overall satisfaction among Black Americans than among White Americans. Similarly, multiple encounters with racial stereotyping, prejudice, and discrimination across time may result in lowered marital satisfaction and, subsequently, lowered marital stability among interracial couples than among intraracial couples. However, evidence for the negative consequences of stigma for the social-psychological well-being of stigmatized couples is indirect at best. On the one hand, approximately two thirds of interracial married couples eventually divorce, compared to approximately one half of American married couples overall (Gaines & Ickes, 1997). On the other hand, we do not know of any evidence that persons in mixed-race marriages are less satisfied with their marriages than are persons in same-race marriages.

According to Rusbult and her colleagues (e.g., Rusbult & Arriaga, 1997; Rusbult, Drigotas, & Verette, 1994), any impact of marital satisfaction on marital stability is mediated by spouses' *commitment*, or psychological attachment, to each other. Thus, even in the absence of direct evidence that the high divorce rate among interracial couples is due to high marital dissatisfaction, it is conceivable that spouses in interracial marriages are less committed than are spouses in intraracial marriages. Despite the intuitive appeal of such a hypothesis, to our knowledge evidence that interracial marriage partners are less committed than are intraracial marriage partners is nonexistent. Unfortunately, much of the literature on interracial relationships is long on anecdotes and speculation, and short on quantitative data and samples large enough to permit rejections of the null hypothesis (for exceptions, see Gurung & Duong, 1999; Shibazaki & Brennan, 1998).

If the *consequences* of interracial partners' marital satisfaction are unclear, then the *antecedents* of interracial partners' marital satisfaction are
equally unclear. For example, according to *mate selection theory*
(Kerckhoff & Davis, 1962), individuals "screen" potential marriage partners initially on the basis of similarity concerning demographic characteristics, and subsequently on the basis of similarity concerning psychological
characteristics. After couples progress from dating to matrimony, spouses'
demographic and psychological similarity—that is, broadly speaking,
spouses' similarity in personality (see Wiggins, 1979)—ostensibly influences spouses' marital satisfaction (Levinger & Rands, 1985). Indeed, results of a study by Heaton and Pratt (1990) indicated that among
interdenominational Christian marriages, religious homogamy is associated positively with marital satisfaction. Unfortunately, the study by
Heaton and Pratt (1990) did not include a sufficient number of Jewish
spouses to permit examination of Jewish–Christian marriages.[3]

Based on mate selection theory, one might predict that a lack of personality similarity and a lack of satisfaction will plague interracial relationships. However, such a prediction does not take into account the facts that
(a) interracial partners tend to be similar in socioeconomic status (a demographic characteristic; Gaines & Ickes, 1997), and (b) interracial partners
tend to be similar in the cluster of attitudes known as romanticism (a psychological characteristic; Gaines et al., 1999). Levinger and Rands (1985)
summarized the issue of interracial (and interreligious) marital compatibility succinctly: "Racial and religious similarity are merely two instances of
macrolevel factors that affect the building of a permanent relationship.
They affect initial perceptions of another's availability, eligibility, and desirability, but they do not inevitably have a huge impact on later interaction" (p. 316).

DIRECTIONS FOR FUTURE RESEARCH

Our review of the literature on the "inappropriateness" of interracial relationships in American society leads us to suggest potentially fruitful directions for future research. First, research on the self-esteem of individuals
who are dating interracially versus intraracially (Gurung & Duong, 1999;
Shibazaki & Brennan, 1998) has produced inconclusive results. Future researchers might find it useful to extend self-esteem research to individuals
who are married interracially. Indirect evidence against the notion of interracial partners' self-esteem as threatened by relationship outsiders can be
found in a study by Gaines, Granrose et al. (1999) concerning attachment
style. In a sample in which 75% of the interracial couples were married, a

---

[3]Among Jewish–Christian marriages, religiosity, ethnic identity, and other-group orientation
all were unrelated to spouses' satisfaction (Sussman & Alexander, 1999).

majority of men and women in all major racial/ethnic groups were classified as securely attached and, presumably, high in self-esteem. Nevertheless, direct research on interracial married partners' self-esteem is in order,
especially with couples other than Black–White pairs. After all, more than
75% of all interracial couples in the United States involve either Whites
paired with persons of color other than Blacks, or persons of color paired
with other persons of color (Gaines & Ickes, 1997).

Second, research on interracial couples' strategies for coping with predicaments of stigmatization and on outsiders' cognitive responses to interracial couples seems to be nonexistent. Virtually all of the relevant
research on attributional biases has been based on targets and perceivers *as
individuals*, rather than targets or perceivers as members of romantic couples (see Crocker et al., 1998), although strictly individual-level
attributional biases certainly are informative in their own right. Earlier in
this chapter, we described certain attributional biases (e.g., self-serving
bias among relationship insiders, ingroup-outgroup bias among relationship outsiders) that might be especially relevant to the study of interracial
relationships. Such attributional processes are termed *biases*, because they
represent departures from normative information processing and are distinguished by the systematic overuse or underuse of information about self
and environment (Fiske & Taylor, 1991). All in all, we believe that attributional biases should receive increased attention within the literature on interracial relationships.

CONCLUSION

At the outset of this chapter, we noted the strong tendency for relationship outsiders in the United States to define interracial sex and marriage
as "inappropriate." Such a tendency begs the question of how (or if) relationship outsiders can be persuaded to redefine interracial sex and marriage as "appropriate." One approach might be to appeal to the cultural
values of *individualism* (i.e., an orientation toward the welfare of oneself) and *romanticism* (i.e., an orientation toward the welfare of one's romantic relationship pair or dyad) that Whites and persons of color tend to
hold with equal fervor (Gaines, Gilstrap, et al., 1999). That is, if individuals truly are free to "do their own thing," and if couples really are free to
prove that "love can conquer all," then relationship outsiders have no
business interfering with the private lives of interracial couples. However, it is likely that *socioeconomic* parity among the races will be necessary, albeit not necessarily sufficient, for persons of African descent to
achieve *socioemotional* parity with persons of European descent in American society. In the meantime, mass media potentially can play a con-
structive role in reshaping relationship outsiders' thoughts and feelings
toward interracial couples.

REFERENCES

Alba, R. D. (1995). America's quite tide. *Public Interest, 119*, 3–18.

Allport, G. W. (1954/1979). *The nature of prejudice*. Reading, MA: Addison-Wesley.

Baptiste, D. A., Jr. (1984). Marital and family therapy with racially/culturally inter-married stepfamilies: Issues and guidelines. *Family Relations, 33*, 373–380.

Baumeister, R. F. (1998). The self. In D. T. Gilbert, S. T. Fiske, & G. Lindzey (Eds.), *The handbook of social psychology* (4th ed., vol. 1, pp. 680–740). Boston: McGraw-Hill.

Blackwell, D. L., & Lichter, D. T. (2000). Mate selection among married and cohabiting couples. *Journal of Family Studies, 21*, 275–302.

Brewer, M. B., & Brown, R. J. (1998). Intergroup relations. In D. T. Gilbert, S. T. Fiske, & G. Lindzey (Eds.), *The handbook of social psychology* (4th ed., vol. 2, pp. 554–594). Boston: McGraw-Hill.

Crocker, J., Major, B., & Steele, C. (1998). Social stigma. In D. T. Gilbert, S. T. Fiske, & G. Lindzey (Eds.), *The handbook of social psychology* (4th ed., vol. 2, pp. 504–553). Boston: McGraw-Hill.

Crowder, K. D., & Tolnay, S. E. (2000). A new marriage squeeze for Black women: The role of racial intermarriage. *Journal of Marriage and the Family, 62*, 792–817.

Dovidio, J. F., & Gaertner, S. L. (1991). Changes in the expression and assessment of racial prejudice. In H. J. Knopke, R. J. Norrell, & R. W. Rogers (Eds.), *Opening doors: Perspectives on race relations in contemporary America* (pp. 119–148). Tuscaloosa: University of Alabama Press.

Fang, C. Y., Sidanius, J., & Pratto, F. (1998). Romance across the social status contin-uum. *Journal of Cross-Cultural Psychology, 29*, 290–305.

Fiske, S. T. (1998). Stereotyping, prejudice, and discrimination. In D. T. Gilbert, S. T. Fiske, & G. Lindzey (Eds.), *The handbook of social psychology* (4th ed., Vol. 2, pp. 357–411). Boston: McGraw-Hill.

Fiske, S. T., & Taylor, S. E. (1991). *Social cognition* (2nd ed.). New York: McGraw-Hill.

Foeman, A. K., & Nance, T. (1999). From miscegenation to multiculturalism: Percep-tions and stages of interracial relationship development. *Journal of Black Studies, 29*, 540–557.

Gaines, S. O., Jr., & Brennan, K. A. (2001). Interracial couples. In J. H. Harvey, R. A. E. Wentzel (Eds.), *Close romantic relationships: Maintenance and enhancement* (pp. 237–253). Mahwah, NJ: Lawrence Erlbaum Associates.Gaines, S. O., Jr., with Buriel, R., Liu, J. H., & Rios, D. I. (1997). *Culture, ethnicity, and personal relation-ship processes*. New York: Routledge.

Gaines, S. O., Jr., Chalfin, J., Kim, M., & Taing, P. (1998). Communicating prejudice in personal relationships. In M. L. Hecht (Ed.), *Communicating prejudice* (pp. 163–186). Thousand Oaks, CA: Sage.

Gaines, S. O., Jr., Gilstrap, S., Kim, M., Yi, J., Rusbult, C. E., Holcomb, D., Gaertner, L., & Lee, J. (1999, June). *Cultural value orientations: Measurement and manifestation in responses to accommodative dilemmas*. Paper presented at the 1999 joint confer-ence of the International Network on Personal Relationships and the International So-ciety for the Study of Personal Relationships, University of Louisville, KY.

Gaines, S. O., Jr., Granrose, C. S., Rios, D. I., Garcia, B. F., Page Youn, M. S., Farris, K. R., & Bledsoe, K. L. (1999). Patterns of attachment and responses to accommoda-tive dilemmas among interethnic/interracial couples. *Journal of Social and Personal Relationships, 16*, 277–287.

Gaines, S. O., Jr., & Ickes, W. (1997). Perspectives on interracial relationships. In S. Duck (Ed.), *Handbook of personal relationships: Theory, research, and interventions* (2nd ed., pp. 197–220). Chichester, UK: Wiley.

Gaines, S. O., Jr., & Liu, J. H. (2000). Multicultural/multiracial relationships. In C. Hendrick & S. S. Hendrick (Eds.), *Close relationships: A sourcebook* (pp. 97–108). Thousand Oaks, CA: Sage.

Gaines, S. O., Jr., & Reed, E. S. (1994). Two social psychologies of prejudice: Gordon W. Allport, W. E. B. Du Bois, and the legacy of Booker T. Washington. *Journal of Black Psychology, 20*, 8–28.

Gaines, S. O., Jr., & Reed, E. S. (1995). Prejudice: From Allport to Du Bois. *American Psychologist, 50*, 96–103.

Gaines, S. O., Jr., Rios, D. I., Granrose, C. S., Bledsoe, K. L., Farris, K. R., Page Youn, M. S., & Garcia, B. F. (1999). Romanticism and interpersonal resource exchange among African American/Anglo and other interracial couples. *Journal of Social and Personal Relationships, 16*, 277–287.

Gates, H. L., Jr. (1991). Jungle fever; or guess who's not coming to dinner? In S. Lee & D. Lee (Eds.), *Five for five: The films of Spike Lee* (pp. 163–169). New York: Stewart, Tabori & Chang.

Goffman, E. (1959). *The presentation of self in everyday life*. Garden City, NY: Doubleday Anchor.

Goffman, E. (1963). *Stigma: Notes on the management of spoiled identity*. Englewood Cliffs, NJ: Prentice-Hall.

Guerrero, E. (1993). *Framing Blackness: The African American image in film*. Philadelphia: Temple University Press.

Gurung, R. A. R., & Duong, T. (1999). Mixing and matching: Assessing the concomitants of mixed-ethnic relationships. *Journal of Social and Personal Relationships, 16*, 639–657.

Heaton, T. B., & Pratt, E. L. (1990). The effects of religious homogamy on marital satisfaction and stability. *Journal of Family Issues, 11*, 191–207.

Hwang, S.-S., Saenz, R., & Aguirre, B. E. (1997). Structural and assimilationist explanations of Asian American intermarriage. *Journal of Marriage and the Family, 59*, 758–772.

Jones, E. E., Farina, A., Hastorf, A. H., Markus, H., Miller, D. T., & Scott, R. A. (1984). *Social stigma: The psychology of marked relationships*. New York: Freeman.

Jones, J. M. (1997). *Prejudice and racism* (2nd ed.). New York: McGraw-Hill.

Kerckhoff, A. C., & Davis, K. E. (1962). Value consensus and need complementarity in mate selection. *American Sociological Review, 27*, 295–303.

Lee, S. M., & Fernandez, M. (1998). Trends in Asian American racial/ethnic intermarriage: A comparison of 1980 and 1990 census data. *Sociological Perspectives, 41*, 323–342.

Levinger, G., & Rands, M. (1985). Compatibility in marriage and other close relationships. In W. Ickes (Ed.), *Compatible and incompatible relationships* (pp. 309–331). New York: Springer-Verlag.

Myrdal, G. (1944). *An American dilemma: The Negro problem and modern democracy*. New York: Harper Brothers.

National Research Council (1989). *A common destiny: Blacks and American society*. Washington, DC: National Academy Press.

Penn, M. L., Gaines, S. O., Jr., & Phillips, L. (1993). On the desirability of own group preference. *Journal of Black Psychology, 19*, 303–321.

Perlman, J. (1997). Multiracials, intermarriage, ethnicity. *Society, 34*, 21–24.

Pettigrew, T. F. (1988). Integration and pluralism. In P. A. Katz & D. A. Taylor (Eds.), *Eliminating racism: Profiles in controversy* (pp. 19–30). New York: Plenum.

Phillips, L., Penn, M. L., & Gaines, S. O., Jr. (1993). A hermeneutic rejoinder to ourselves and our critics. *Journal of Black Psychology, 19*, 350–357.

Pinkney, A. (1993). *Black Americans* (4th ed.). Englewood Cliffs, NJ: Prentice-Hall.

Porterfield, E. (1978). Black and White mixed marriages. Chicago: Nelson-Hall.

Reed, E. S., & Gaines, S. O., Jr. (1997). Not everyone is "different-from-me": Toward an historico-cultural account of prejudice. *Journal of Black Psychology, 23*, 245–274.

Rosenblatt, P. C., Karis, T. A., & Powell, R. D. (1995). *Multiracial couples: Black and White voices*. Thousand Oaks, CA: Sage.

Rusbult, C. E., & Arriaga, X. B. (1997). Interdependence theory. In S. Duck (Ed.), *Handbook of personal relationships: Theory, research, and interventions* (2nd ed., pp. 221–250). Chichester, UK: Wiley.

Rusbult, C. E., Drigotas, S. M., & Verette, J. (1994). The investment model: An interdependence analysis of commitment processes and relationship maintenance phenomena. In D. J. Canary & L. Stafford (Eds.), *Communication and relational maintenance* (pp. 115–139). San Diego: Academic Press.

Shibazaki, K., & Brennan, K. A. (1998). When birds of different feathers flock together: A preliminary comparison of intra-ethnic and inter-ethnic dating relationships. *Journal of Social and Personal Relationships, 15*, 248–256.

Soskis, B. (2000). Faith-based. *New Republic, 222*, 42.

Spickard, P. R. (1989). *Mixed blood: Intermarriage and ethnic identity in twentieth-century America*. Madison: University of Wisconsin Press.

Staples, R., & Boulin Johnson, L. (1993). *Black families at the crossroads: Challenges and prospects*. San Francisco: Jossey-Bass.

Sung, B. L. (1990). Chinese American intermarriage. *Journal of Comparative Family Studies, 21*, 337–352.

Suro, R. (1999). Mixed doubles. *American Demographics, 21*, 56–62.

Sussman, L. M., & Alexander, C. M. (1999). How religiosity and ethnicity affect marital satisfaction for Jewish–Christian couples. *Journal of Mental Health Counseling, 21*, 173–185.

Tucker, M. B., & Mitchell-Kernan, C. (1990). New trends in Black American interracial marriage: The social structural context. *Journal of Marriage and the Family, 52*, 209–218.

Tucker, M. B., & Mitchell-Kernan, C. (1995). Social structural and psychological correlates of interethnic dating. *Journal of Social and Personal Relationships, 12*, 341–361.

Whyte, M. K. (1990). *Dating, mating, and marriage*. New York: Aldine de Gruyter.

Wiggins, J. S. (1979). A psychological taxonomy of trait-descriptive terms: The interpersonal domain. *Journal of Personality and Social Psychology, 37*, 395–412.

Zebroski, S. A. (1999). Black–White intermarriages. *Journal of Black Studies, 30*, 123–132.

5
Mixed Marriages: Music Community Membership as a Source of Marital Strain[1]

Rebecca G. Adams
University of North Carolina

Jane Rosen-Grandon
Rosen Grandon Associates, Inc.

The Grateful Dead, a North American rock band that stopped performing in 1995 after 30 years together, was as well known for its fans as it
was for its music. Deadheads, as these fans are called, traveled from venue
to venue to hear the band play, sometimes staying "on tour" with them for
extended periods of time. For a variety of reasons, on which we elaborate
later, members of the cultural mainstream viewed the relationship that
Deadheads had with the band and the community surrounding it as inappropriate. Many Deadheads spent a great deal of time and money following the band, appeared to value collective experiences more than
individual material success, dressed in "hippie" clothing, and either used or
approved of the use of psychedelic drugs. These values and behaviors,

[1]The authors would like to thank Samantha Ammons and Jeffrey Meyers for their assistance
with the bibliographic research.

along with Deadheads' "questionable" musical taste, led the cultural main-stream to stigmatize these fans.

Although Deadheads generally prefer endogamous unions, some of them enter "mixed" or "cross-community" marriages (Stringer, 1994). Some of these mixed marriages have been quite successful. Non-Dead-heads serve as confidantes and allies to their Deadhead spouses, filling the role that Goffman (1963) called "the wise." Sometimes, however, these relationships are problematic, both because of the stigma associated with membership in the Deadhead community and because of marital conflict over lifestyle issues. In this chapter, after describing the data on which our analysis is based, we discuss the Dead and their fans, elaborate on our observations about the basis of the stigma assigned to Deadheads, and outline the ways in which these mixed marriages are sometimes problematic for the participants. Then we discuss the importance of considering the problems of mixed marriages from a life-course perspective. Subsequently, we present a series of descriptions of mixed marriages to illustrate the problems caused by stigma, lifestyle issues, and changes in life-course stage. We end the chapter with a discussion of the theoretical and clinical implications of this case study of a deviant community in which some members enter exogamous marriages.

THE DATA

We did not intentionally collect data to examine the topic of mixed marriages. Rather, the topic emerged as one of importance from data collected as part of Adams' multimethod Deadhead Community Project (see Adams, 1998a, for a discussion of the theoretical and pedagogical goals of this project). Background data derived from this study are supplemented here by Rosen-Grandon's clinical records. Rosen-Grandon is a therapist in private practice who has treated clients who were Deadheads involved in problematic mixed marriages. In this report, we present seven examples of problematic mixed marriages, most of which were derived from Rosen-Grandon's records. The data on which this chapter is based are therefore anecdotal and suggestive rather than systematic and conclusive. Although we present the problems facing each couple fully and accurately, we changed their names and some of the details about their backgrounds and lives to protect their anonymity.

The data collected as part of the Deadhead Community Project include Adams' observational notes from 91 Grateful Dead shows and nine Jerry Garcia Band concerts (Jerry Garcia was the Dead's lead guitarist who also had his own band) between 1989 and 1995; her notes from Deadhead social gatherings and concerts at which survivors of the Grateful Dead, jam bands, and Dead cover bands performed between 1995 and 2000; and reports of 21 of her students on each of four Dead shows during the summer of 1989. She also interviewed key members of the Deadhead community and of the Grateful Dead organization, received responses to three mail questionnaires with open-ended questions (total $N = 177$) between 1990 and 1996, and has access to 77 open-ended interviews conducted by her students during the summer of 1989. When Jerry Garcia died, approximately 150 Deadheads wrote letters and e-mail messages to Adams about their experience mourning for him. In addition, Adams received a file drawer of letters and more than 21 megabytes of electronic correspondence from Deadheads; downloaded online conversations among Deadheads from rec.music.gdead (an electronic discussion list) for 11 years beginning with the summer of 1989; and has access to artifacts, photos, videotapes, audiotapes, Deadhead media, and mainstream media about Deadheads. These qualitative data are supplemented by quantitative analysis of responses to a questionnaire with closed-ended questions her students distributed in the parking lots of Dead shows during the summer of 1987 ($N = 286$) and one distributed by Grateful Dead Productions in 22 cities during Furthur Festival, a series of concerts at which surviving members of the band performed as the Other Ones during the summer of 1998 ($N = 6,020$).

THE DEAD AND THEIR FANS

The roots of this migrating subculture are in the hippie culture that grew up in the Western United States during the 1960s. Known as the Warlocks for a spring, summer, and autumn, the band became the Grateful Dead in December of 1965. They were the "house band" for the Acid Tests, public psychedelic celebrations held in 1965 and 1966 before LSD (lyserg saure diethylamid) was illegal. By late 1966, the Dead were headquartered in San Francisco, California, at 710 Ashbury, near its intersection with the Haight, the symbolic heart of the hippie community. From this address, it was a short walk to Golden Gate Park where the Dead often gave free concerts for their increasing crowd of fans (Adams, 1991; for more detailed histories of the Grateful Dead, see Gans, 1991; Gans & Simon, 1985; Jackson, 1983; Perry, 1984; Troy, 1991).

Although there is still a large concentration of Deadheads in the San Francisco Bay Area, there are now Deadheads everywhere in the United States and in many foreign countries as well. This is not surprising, because during their career the band played at least once in 45 states and 13 foreign countries (Adams, 1998b; Scott, Dolgushkin, & Nixon, 1997).

The subculture continued to grow in size after its inception in the 1960s, but the band did not become a commercial success until their 1987 album, *In the Dark*, hit the charts. By the 1990s, the Dead was considered the most successful touring band in concert history. It was the top-grossing touring act in 1991 and 1993 and finished in third place in 1995, despite having completed only two of their typical three tours (Adams, 1991). They played 2,314 shows during their career, often to sellout crowds of more than 50,000 people (Scott et al., 1997; Simon, 1999).

The Grateful Dead organization now distributes information to approximately 290,000 Deadheads (C. Sears, President, Grateful Dead Productions, personal correspondence, fall 1998). Their mailing list is far from complete. In the summer of 1998, half of the Deadheads who attended performances of the Other Ones, a band consisting of most of the surviving members of the Dead and three new players, indicated that they did not receive *The Grateful Dead Almanac*, which the Dead organization mails at no cost to their fans (Adams, 1998b). It is less likely that Deadheads who did not attend one of the performances of the Other Ones are on the mailing list than those who did, suggesting that there are considerably more than a half-million Deadheads. Even this is probably a very conservative estimate.

The Deadhead community is not only remarkable among music communities because of the length of time it has survived, how geographically dispersed it is, and how large it is; it is also noteworthy because of the length and intensity of involvement of individual fans. On the average, the fans who the Dead surveyed in 1998 saw their first show in 1984 or 1985, 13 or 14 years before they were surveyed (or 10 or 11 years before the Dead stopped playing together). Fifty percent of them had seen their first show at least 11 years previously, 8 or 9 years before the Dead stopped playing together (Adams, 1998b).

Not only had these fans been involved in the community over a long period of time, they were intensely involved. The respondents who indicated the furthest they had ever traveled to hear a member of the Dead ranged from those who had not traveled at all to those who had traveled 20,000 miles. The average Deadhead had traveled 1,223 miles to attend a show, and half of them had traveled 800 miles. More than 10% of the respondents had traveled more than 2,750 miles, which is approximately the furthest anyone in the United States has to travel to get to San Francisco. The average respondent had attended 61 shows, and exactly half of the respondents had attended 25. One percent had attended 400 or more. One "deadicated" respondent had attended 1,350 (Adams, 1998b).

Lest the reader be misled to think that Deadheads have an extreme tolerance for repetition, it is important to mention that unlike most rock bands who play the same show repeatedly during a given tour, the Dead never played the same show twice (Shank & Simon, 2000). The Dead rarely rehearsed, were almost always on tour, and played different songs, in a different order, in different ways, each night (Adams, 1991). Even Deadheads who were constantly on tour thus did not perceive themselves as repeatedly having the same experience (Freeman, 2000). As one Deadhead said: "Every show is the first one. After you get into it, you see what's different about each show. It seems to be better and better." The uncertainty about when particular songs or combinations of songs would be played and about when the band would play particularly well provided Deadheads with incentive to go to as many shows as possible (Adams, 1991).

Deadheads did not attend shows merely for entertainment or to socialize with like-minded people. Many of them reported having spiritual experiences at shows, which provided them with an additional motivation to attend (Sutton, 2000). Although the spiritual experiences of Deadheads varied widely and included feelings of déjà vu, out-of-body experiences, connecting with a higher power, and living through the cycle of death and rebirth, the most commonly mentioned experiences were inner and outer connectedness—self-revelation and unity with others (Adams, 1991). Although dancing and drugs surely contributed to these experiences for some Deadheads, others attributed their occurrence, at least in part, to the power and trajectory of the music (Goodenough, 1999; Hartley, 2000). "Getting it" is an expression Deadheads use to describe the process of learning to perceive shows as spiritual experiences and to understand "these spiritual experiences as inseparable from the music, the scene, and a cooperative mode of everyday existence" (Adams, as quoted in Shenk & Silberman, 1994, p. 106).

The feelings of unity and empathy that Deadheads experienced at shows often were extended to the band. Some Deadheads claim that the band was psychically "connected" to the audience. Not only did the band influence the experiences Deadheads had through the music that they played, some Deadheads said that the audience "controlled" the band (Carr, 1999). These Deadheads believe that they influenced the selection of songs, the way they were played, and thus the trajectory of the music. John Barlow, one of the Dead's lyricists, confirmed Deadhead beliefs that band members did not know what they were going to play before a performance but were rather guided by "the groupmind" in selecting songs while they were on stage (Shenk & Silberman, 1994, p. 56).

Thus, by having spiritual experiences at many shows over a long period of time, Deadheads developed feelings of closeness and a high level of commitment to the band and other members of the community. The intensity of this relationship was most obvious after Jerry Garcia died in 1995 (Adams, 1999; Wilgoren, 1999). Immediately after his death, fans held vigils all over the country. Many flocked to Golden Gate Park to celebrate Garcia's life with those who worked and lived with him. Deadheads developed tribute web sites (Gans, 1995) and contributed to memorial issues of magazines (e.g., *Dupree's Diamond News*, 1995).

THE BASIS OF STIGMA

As Goffman (1963) observed, a stigma has its origins in a discrepancy between opinions about the way people should live their lives and perceptions of the way they do. Some people are stigmatized because of physical deformities or character flaws (Goffman, 1963). Regardless of their own individual characteristics, others are assigned what Goffman called a "tribal stigma." In other words, expectations regarding individual behavior and evaluations of a person's moral worth are extrapolated from impressions of the larger group to which the individual belongs.

The cultural mainstream applies a tribal stigma to Deadheads because they do not appear to be what they should be. Although the diversity of the Deadhead population is great, the majority of Deadheads occupy or have opportunities to occupy privileged positions in our society. They tend to be Caucasian men from middle- and upper-middle class backgrounds. Given these demographic characteristics, Deadheads should be successful, hard-working, well-groomed, law-abiding citizens (Adams, 1991)

The global impressions held by members of the cultural mainstream about Deadheads come mainly from the media. Deadheads were typically depicted as lazy, unwashed throwbacks to the 1960s who used illegal drugs, dressed unconventionally, and valued collective experiences more than individual material success. Paterline (2000) found that there were variations in how the media depicted Deadheads in the 40 American cities where the Dead played in 1989 and 1990. Newspapers in less populated communities, Southern communities, and higher-status communities had a more negative reaction to the Deadhead subculture. Nonetheless, the coverage almost everywhere was more negative than positive. Given the opportunity most Deadheads had for success, outsiders could not understand how they could "throw it all away" to follow a band from venue to venue.

The stigma was particularly salient for older Deadheads who "should have grown up" and "gotten lives." The stereotypical rock music fan is college aged, but this is not so with Deadheads. According to the Terrapin Station survey, which was conducted in 1998 (2½ years after the Dead stopped playing together), Deadheads' average age was about 32 years and most of them were in mid-life. Only a small percentage of Deadheads were younger than 22 years old (15.7%). Almost a quarter of them were more than 40 years of age (24.4%). Outsiders did not understand why anyone would want to be a groupie during mid-life (Adams, 1998b).

There is some truth to the stereotype of Deadheads portrayed in the media. Deadheads sometimes wear subcultural dress such as tie-dyed shirts, Guatemalan pants, home-sewn calico jumpers and halters, and Indian gauze skirts. Sometimes, especially when they are "on tour," they do not bathe. Many Deadheads use marijuana and other psychedelic drugs or accept their use by others. The cultural mainstream interprets these behaviors of some Deadheads as signs that they reject the Protestant work ethic, a major North American value (Williams, 1951).

The irony is, however, that most Deadheads are successful and hard-working by mainstream standards. Rather than reject the mainstream value of individual material success, they supplement it with an appreciation of collective experientialism. Although their hippie forebears are of-ten described as members of a "counterculture," Deadheads comprise a "subculture" (Hall, Clarke, Jefferson, & Roberts, 1976). The vast majority of Deadheads eventually obtain college degrees, and many of them finish graduate school. Although some employed Deadheads are pink- or blue-collar workers, most of them are professionals or fill white-collar po-sitions (Adams, 1991). Even the young "tourheads" who made their living selling food and hand-crafted items in the parking lot worked hard to sup-port themselves and their "show families" (Sheptoski, 2000). Despite these facts, the negative stereotype of Deadheads prevails.

Tribal stigmata generally apply to people who share ethnic origin (Goffman, 1963). Race and nationality, which could each form the basis for a tribal stigma, are generally ascribed characteristics. In contrast, member-ship in the Deadhead community is "achieved" or voluntary. Research shows that voluntary membership in a stigmatized group is likely to evoke a more negative reaction from outsiders than is membership in a group in which membership is not voluntary (Rush, 1998; Weiner, Perry, & Magnusson, 1988). When participation and identity are voluntary, as with religious groups in contemporary Western society or as with the Deadhead commu-nity, the idea is that people who do not want to experience stigma can simply end their affiliation or hide their beliefs. Although outsiders might consider religion a serious enough affiliation that members could not be expected to deny their involvement to avoid stigma, most members of the mainstream do not know how important the spiritual rewards of community member-ship are to many Deadheads, and would probably not regard this as an im-portant consideration even if they did. It is thus fair to expect that the stigma assigned to Deadheads is relatively potent.

PROBLEMATIC MARRIAGES

Mixed marriages between Deadheads and non-Deadheads are sometimes problematic. The problems specific to this type of relationship are some-times related to the effects of the global tribal stigma and sometimes result from marital conflict over lifestyle issues. The effects of global tribal stigma can result from discrimination due to community membership, the fear of such discrimination, or efforts to conceal Deadhead identity. Life-style issues can provoke a negative response from both the non-Deadhead and Deadhead spouses. The non-Deadhead spouse is sometimes irritated by the expenditure of family resources for subcultural activities and illegal behavior. The Deadhead spouse is sometimes upset by the non-Deadhead partner's inability to understand why subcultural membership is impor-tant and meaningful. If their values and interests diverge significantly, noncouple socializing can also be problematic. These issues become more salient when the members of the couple become older, more established, concerned about career issues, and parents.

Tribal Stigma

Some tribal stigmata are inherited and thus "equally contaminate all members of a family" (Goffman, 1963, p. 4). The children and spouses of Deadheads are not, however, necessarily members of the community. Nonetheless, as Goffman (1963) observed, "the wise" often receive a "courtesy stigma" by virtue of their affiliation with a community member. Thus, the Deadhead tribal stigma becomes a source of stress not only for the Deadhead, but for his or her family members as well.

The way in which tribal stigma affects families depends on whether people in their social circle know that a member of the couple is a Deadhead. Goffman distinguished between the "discredited" (those whose community membership is known) and the "discreditable" (those for whom exposure is a possibility). For the "out" Deadhead, tribal stigma can result in actual discrimination. For example, police profiles for cars to stop without reason include those with Dead stickers on them (Eagan, 1990). When wearing subcultural dress and behaving as she generally does in professional circumstances, Adams has been refused a seat in a restaurant, had a gun trained on her while purchasing a soda in a convenience store, and been told that she and her husband could not take a guest to visit briefly with them in their room in an expensive hotel. For the "closeted" Deadhead the issue is concealment and "passing." Of course, Deadheads might be "out" in one context and "closeted" in another. The issue is whether "to display or not to display; to tell or not to tell; to let on or not to let on; to lie or not to lie; and in each case, to whom, how, when, and where" (Goffman, 1963, p. 42). Another approach could be to "cover" how intensely involved the Deadhead is in the community.

Lifestyle Issues

Not all of the problems Deadheads in mixed marriages face are related to the global tribal stigma assigned to members of the subculture. Some of these problems result directly from disagreement between the Deadhead and non-Deadhead spouses over lifestyle issues (see Leichter, 1997, for a discussion of lifestyle correctness). Unlike tribal stigma, which is only relevant in marriages in which one partner belongs to a deviant or undesirable community, the lifestyle issues that create tensions between Deadheads and their non-Deadhead spouses are similar to problems other couples also face, especially when the partners do not share interests in the same leisure activities. The main sources of potential strain in Deadhead mixed marriages are the costs of participation in the community, both in terms of time and money, participation in illegal activities (i.e., drug use), and noncouple socializing.

Maintaining active involvement in the Deadhead community was costly, both in terms of time and money. When the Dead were touring, the largest Deadhead expenses were tickets and travel to shows. Surveys conducted in years during which the Dead played all three tours consistently report that an average Deadhead saw about nine shows a year. Given that Deadheads sometimes traveled great distances to these shows, attending this many per year took a great deal of time. Although it is impossible to calculate the annual expenses of a typical Deadhead accurately, it is estimated that the average Deadhead spent between $720 and $1,170 per year on tickets, subsistence, and transportation for attending shows (Adams, 1991). The respondents to *Deadbase Feedback '94* (Scott, Dolgushkin, & Nixon, 1995) provided a higher estimate. For travel, tickets, lodgings, and food in 1994, they reported spending on average approximately $1,300.00 per year. Of course, expenses varied widely depending on tour habits.

The costs of tickets and travel to shows were not the only ones Deadheads incurred. In addition to these expenses, Deadheads often spent money on music recordings, stereo equipment, subcultural clothing and accessories, magazines, books, and drugs. Although data estimating the average cost of these additional expenses per year are not available, some suggestive information is. For example, in *Deadbase X* (Scott et al., 1997), a book that reports on the setlists of Grateful Dead shows, their readers reported having an average of 774 hours of Grateful Dead audiotapes and owning a stereo costing an average of $2,000 on which to play them.

The cost of illegal drugs was an issue in some mixed marriages, and so was the use of them. Although many Deadheads have never taken drugs or have ceased using them, many others do. According to Adams' students' 1987 survey, the following percentages of Deadhead respondents had taken each of the following drugs at a Grateful Dead concert at least once in their lives: marijuana ("pot"; 93.8%); LSD ("acid"; 78.9%), psilocybin mushrooms ("shrooms"; 77.5%), nitrous oxide ("laughing gas" or "hippie crack"; 37.1%), and MDMA ("ecstasy"; 34.4%). All five of these drugs were available for purchase in the parking lot of Dead shows from wandering vendors who announced the name of the drug they had for sale or, in the case of nitrous oxide, from vendors with tanks in their vans or automobile trunks. The use of the first three drugs—marijuana, LSD, and mushrooms—is generally condoned by a large proportion of the members of the subculture, whether they personally use them or not. There is less normative consensus on the advisability of inhaling nitrous oxide and taking ecstasy, because it is the belief within the subculture that both involve more substantial physical risk.

In general, Deadheads do not condone the use of physically addicting drugs such as cocaine or heroin, which they call "white powder" drugs, although some members of the subculture have used such drugs at some point in their lives. These drugs are disliked not only because they are physically addictive, but also because they are escapist. As Goode (1984) pointed out, proponents of psychedelic drugs argue that they offer a direct confrontation with reality rather than an escape from it.

Although some non-Deadhead spouses traveled to shows and other subcultural events with their Deadhead husbands or wives, sometimes the Deadhead spouses traveled alone or with other friends, including members of the opposite sex. Deadheads referred to their regular traveling companions as "show buddies" or "show families," and sometimes to show buddies of the opposite sex as "show wives" or "show husbands." Some non-Deadhead spouses accepted these arrangements, pleased that their husband or wife had a trustworthy companion with whom to travel to shows. Other times, these tour relationships caused marital conflict, raising issues of fidelity, loyalty, or at least the relative importance of family and Deadhead community membership.

LIFE-COURSE ISSUES

Tribal stigma and life-course issues sometimes do not become problematic for spouses in mixed marriages until they are older, become more serious about their careers, and have children. As discussed earlier, many Deadheads are middle-aged professionals. Even when Adams' students surveyed a relatively young sample of Deadheads in 1987, 8% of them had children. The percentage of all Deadheads who had children then was probably higher and the percentage of those who have children has inevitably increased since this survey was conducted. In other words, a substantial number of Deadheads remain loyal fans throughout their adulthood and have to decide how to present themselves to others and how extensively to participate in the community once they have "something to lose."

Although David (2000) reported that the adult development of Deadheads is not significantly different from the development of non-Deadheads, Deadheads in mixed marriages face issues that others do not. In some cases, even when the partners originally met in the context of the Grateful Dead community, one spouse ceases to identify with the subculture while community membership remains central to the other's self-concept. For some fans, attending Grateful Dead concerts might fall into the category of "youthful experimentation." In contrast, those who are genuine fans of the Grateful Dead seem to have an unqualified love of the music, the concert atmosphere, and the Grateful Dead themselves. "Deadicated" fans are sometimes reluctant to conceal their Deadhead identities or to limit their involvement in the subculture in order to further their careers, protect their children from the effects of stigma, or to please their non-Deadhead spouses who might prefer a lifestyle more acceptable to the mainstream. This refusal to cooperate often irritates their non-Deadhead spouses and causes marital strife. Conversely, Deadheads who do remain closeted, limit their involvement, or admit their identity only to some people or to some extent often feel that their identity is diminished and correspondingly become depressed or disengaged.

ILLUSTRATIVE MIXED MARRIAGES

The following descriptions of mixed marriages illustrate the effects of tribal stigma, the disagreements over lifestyle issues that can occur between Deadhead and non-Deadhead spouses, and the importance of viewing mixed marriages from a life-course perspective. Some of these descriptions are more detailed than others, but each provides insight into the challenges facing couples in which one member belongs to a deviant community and the other does not. It is important to remember that many marriages between non-Deadheads and Deadheads are not problematic. We chose these cases to illustrate the range of problems that can occur, not as representative examples of typical mixed marriages.

Couple #1: "Just Don't Tell Anyone You're a Deadhead."

When Carol and David started dating, David knew that Carol considered herself a Deadhead, but he underestimated the importance of the Grateful Dead to her. When they decided to get married, David was a young man with high aspirations who carefully made all of his decisions based on their potential impact on his career growth. In the effort to adapt to being married, Carol became accustomed to David's social instructions. He was concerned with all aspects of propriety and was especially concerned with making a good impression on his bosses, co-workers, relatives, and even their friends. In no time, Carol found herself dressing according to David's high-fashioned tastes. Although it was a pleasure to be pampered with new clothes, Carol soon grew tired of the constant pressure to dress for success. She was beginning to long to resume her previously casual and fun life, which often included attending Grateful Dead concerts.

Carol described the first time she broached the topic of attending a concert in a nearby town. In her words, David reacted as though Carol had suddenly become disloyal to him. In his mind, Carol was being trained to be the wife of a successful businessman. There was no way that he could condone having a wife who considered herself to be a Deadhead. Carol described this as the moment she came face to face with David's unconscious marital contract. Little by little, he was limiting and controlling her outside interests and behaviors.

In an act of desperation, Carol turned to her parents for support, boldly sharing her thoughts about the possibility of divorce because she knew she would need their support to leave the marriage. But when she approached them with her explanation of David's overbearing and judgmental requirements, they surprisingly took her husband's side, reminding her of his financial future and admonishing her not to create any kind of a scandal. Carol was horrified to think that her parents had bought into David's materialistic, wealth-conscious image. In a last-ditch effort, Carol demanded that her husband join her in marital therapy, where the two engaged in rigorous counseling in order to reconcile their differences enough to achieve a working compromise. As part of the solution to the problem, this couple made a list of those individuals who could know and those who should never know of Carol's fondness for the Grateful Dead.

Couple #2: The Problem of Making Friends

Relocation is sometimes problematic for the closeted Deadhead, who must face the task of making new friends. This was the case of Eric and Joan, who were informed by the company that employed them both that they would be relocated across the country to start a new division. According to their boss, they were the perfect employees to do the job, and besides, because they were married, it would save the company money in moving expenses. Whereas Joan was pleased to be making the move, Eric was concerned about his ability to make new friends. As a closeted Deadhead, it had taken him literally years to find other closeted Deadheads to whom he could relate.

Anticipating the move, he could not help but recall his discomfort in socializing with new people. He was uncomfortable talking with people who either had no interest in music or expressed a dislike for the music of the Grateful Dead (although none had actually attended a live concert). For Eric, true friendships required a shared musical interest. Although Joan did not consider herself a Deadhead, she was at least willing to accompany Eric to concerts and did not criticize their music.

Couple #3: "Drugs Are the Issue."

Sarah and Jim had also met at a Grateful Dead concert. During the early years of their courtship, they both occasionally experimented with LSD and smoked marijuana on a fairly regular basis. Over time, they got married and had two children, who at the time of this case were 2 and 4 years of age. These days, Sarah no longer smoked marijuana, but allowed Jim to imbibe in this habit on the back porch when the children were not around. As far as Sarah knew, hard-core drugs, such as cocaine, were no longer an enticement for Jim. From his perspective, many years had passed since he experimented with cocaine. Besides, cocaine was not the "drug of choice" for most Deadheads.

When Sarah agreed to allow Jim to go on tour with some of his male friends, neither of them knew that these particular male friends had recently taken a liking to cocaine. At first, Jim was offered free snorts of cocaine. But in very little time, Jim became more interested in scoring cocaine from these so-called friends and less interested in the concerts. Several thousands of dollars later, Jim awoke in a hospital looking up at Sarah. It was obvious that she had been crying for days. He had been comatose due to a drug overdose and had almost died.

Ramifications of this relapse extended throughout their life. He was court-ordered to enter a treatment program for substance abuse, lost time at work, lost a certain amount of status in the community, lost opportunities for career advancement, and lost the trust of many of his friends and family members. Fortunately, this couple was able to draw on their resilience as a team. Determined to earn back his sense of credibility with Sarah, Jim offered to never again attend a concert. To her credit, Sarah countersuggested that instead of avoiding concerts, the two of them could attend concerts together and learn to enjoy the music drug-free.

Couple #4: "You Need to Get Things Done at Home."

Pete and Wendy met while he was playing guitar for a heavy metal band. Pete had been a Deadhead since earlier in his youth, but was not at the time actively participating in the community. After they were married, he joined a jam band that had a Deadhead audience. Soon the band was touring during most of the year and Pete was rarely at home. Wendy had never understood the spiritual importance the show experience had for Pete. On one occasion, Wendy asked him not to attend a celebration at which his band was playing, because she wanted him to work on their home remodeling project. The issue was particularly salient, because the band was playing free of charge for the event. The issue was temporarily resolved when Pete's Deadhead friends came to help him remodel the day before he left for the event. During the event, he was obviously worried about whether Wendy was really satisfied with the compromise. This was a theme that came up repeatedly in their marriage.

Couple #5: "It's a Matter of Money."

In the case of Elliot and Roxanne, both had been Deadheads for many years. Both Elliot and Roxanne adored the Grateful Dead's music, the concert atmosphere, and decorated their home with many festive symbols and souvenirs from concerts. They named their dogs after song lyrics, named their newborn son for a member of the band, and proudly decorated their newborn's nursery in tie-dyed everything. These doting parents were proud of their "little Deadhead," and frequently played the music of the Grateful Dead for his (and their) entertainment at home and in the car.

Problems arose for this couple when they fell on hard times financially. Just as they were investing in baby furniture and diapers, Elliot lost his job. As a result, Roxanne was forced to cut her maternity leave short and work longer hours to support the family. Initially, both Elliot and Roxanne were pleased with their nontraditional gender roles in which Elliot was the stay-at-home parent, but soon Roxanne's resentment began to grow. It seemed that as long as both spouses were focused on the needs of their child, things between them were fine. It was not until Elliot suggested they get a babysitter and attend a few concerts together that mayhem broke out between them.

When describing the situation, the partners emphasized different aspects of the situation. Roxanne was upset, feeling that Elliot was obviously not aware of the financial strain she was experiencing. As a Mom who was hoping to stay home and take care of her infant for a little while longer, Roxanne found herself in a constant state of conflict between her desire to be at home with her baby, and the very real need for her to support the family until Elliot was employed. As a result, she felt completely offended by both Elliot's suggestion that they hire a babysitter for a night and the idea of spending money on attending a concert. At the root of their problems, Roxanne no longer liked the role division in the family and was distancing herself from both Elliot and their common interests.

From Elliot's perspective, he felt the increasing emotional distance between himself and Roxanne and wanted to spend more time alone with her, as they had in the past. Grateful Dead concerts had always been a bonding experience for them as a couple, and he longed to renew their intimacy in that way. Like so many couples who are under stress due of time and money, they were in great in danger of growing apart.

Couple #6: "You Cheated on Me."

Sheila and Kirk had been involved since high school. Although they had never married, they had been together for so long that they would have qualified as common-law partners in many states. They both attended Grateful Dead concerts and had many friends who did also, but Kirk was more committed to the lifestyle and music than Sheila was. Kirk attended college for awhile, but dropped out due to a drug problem that was soon thereafter resolved. He eventually reenrolled in college, made new friends, and began touring with them frequently while Sheila stayed at home and held down a regular nine-to-five job. This issue did not appear to create problems for the couple until he developed a close relationship with a woman who regularly toured with him. When Sheila realized how deep this other relationship was, she expressed a willingness to continue their partnership but demanded that he cease seeing the other woman. Many of Kirk's new friends knew the other woman better than they knew Sheila, so it was difficult for him to break off the relationship. Jerry Garcia died at about this time, which made it possible for Kirk to sever his ties with his touring friends. He remained in touch with his "tour wife" by e-mail, but they ceased traveling together. Sheila and Kirk are still together.

Couple #7: "Will It Hurt the Kids?"

Marvin had been a hard-core Deadhead in his youth, intensely involved in the Haight-Ashbury experience in the 1960s. He left the scene to become an accomplished artist, returning to shows years later as a self-described "born-again Deadhead." When Adams called his home to invite him to participate in a creative project she was undertaking, his wife answered the telephone. His wife asked questions to ascertain whether she was a legitimate researcher, and said Marvin could participate as long as it would not hurt their children. She went on to say that she did not want them to suffer from the discrimination experienced by Deadheads. (Note that this project never materialized, so "Marvin's" real name does not appear on Adams' curriculum vitae.)

DISCUSSION

Mainstream society considers the all-consuming relationship that Deadheads had with the Grateful Dead and their involvement in the community surrounding the band as inappropriate. Marriages in which one spouse is a Deadhead and one is a non-Deadhead are problematic for two interrelated reasons. First, the tribal stigma associated with membership in the Deadhead community creates issues for both those who belong and their spouses and families as well. The stigma is particularly potent because "Deadhead" is a voluntary identity rather than an inherited disability or ascribed social characteristic. This tribal stigma sometimes leads to discrimination against Deadheads and their families, causes some of these families to fear discrimination, and sometimes forces Deadheads to conceal their community identity to protect their families. Second, the ways in which Deadheads lead their lives can also create tension within their marriages to non-Deadheads. The investment of time and money required for full involvement in the community, participation in illegal activities, noncouple socializing, and the lack of understanding some non-Deadhead spouses demonstrate regarding the spiritual importance of show experiences also can cause marital strife. Both types of issues—those arising from the general effects of tribal stigma and those related to behaviors and attitudes of both spouses—become more salient as Deadheads age, establish themselves professionally, and have children.

In these conclusions, we discuss the theoretical and clinical implications of this case study of a music community in which some members enter exogamous marriages. Although some of the problems discussed in this chapter are probably specific to mixed marriages involving a Deadhead, the general point is that music subculture identity is a powerful influence on people's lives and on their relationships as well. A more general point is that when only one partner in a relationship is intensely involved in a community—whether it is based on music, another leisure activity, religion, politics, or whatever—marital strain is a possible result. Especially for Caucasians from middle- or upper-class backgrounds without any strong ethnic identity, voluntary membership in a community in which people share their interests and beliefs can be particularly appealing. Although Deadheads are freer to deny their identity than are members of ascribed groups, many of the problems Deadheads reported are similar to problems reported by members of different racial and ethnic groups who marry each other (e.g., Johnson & Warren, 1994; Khatib-Chahidi, Hill, & Paton, 1998; Lee, 1994; Luke, 1994). Now that modern communications technology has made it possible for people who share the same tastes in music or other activities to communicate with each other frequently and regularly, music and other leisure communities are larger and less likely to be local. As illustrated here, participants in these communities sometimes share values and beliefs in addition to taste in leisure activities. For this reason, when partners do not affiliate with the same voluntary communities, marital strain can result. The literatures on stigma, marital satisfaction, and counseling have largely ignored this increasingly important dimension of identity and its potential effects on relationships.

Theoretical Issues

This research highlights several areas of the theoretical literatures on stigma and relationships that need elaboration. First, although some research has been conducted on the difference in societal reaction to involuntary and voluntary membership in a stigmatized group (Rush, 1998; Weiner et al., 1988), we still know very little about this topic. As this case study suggests, stigma may operate differently when the stigmatized have the option of abandoning membership in a community either temporarily or permanently when the need arises.

Second, most of the research on the effects of stigma focuses on the person who is stigmatized rather than on others who are implicated. Although Goffman (1963) recognized that people affiliated with a stigmatized individual often receive a "courtesy stigma," very little research has been conducted on this topic (Birenbaum, 1992; Lewis, 1998) or on the pressure those with courtesy stigmata place on the stigmatized to manage their identities in ways that decrease these negative effects (Weinberg & Vogler, 1990).

Third, these findings suggest the importance of studying stigma and the marital problems associated with it in the context of the life course. Just as the stigma associated with Deadhead community membership becomes more salient as couples age, the power of other stigmata may change over the life course as well. For example, physical stigmata may become less salient as the stigmatized age and begin to associate with more mature people.

Fourth, stigma may be context dependent rather than an enduring trait (Brown, 1998; Donnan, 1990; Waldren, 1998). This observation is supported by the tendency of Deadheads to reveal their identity in some contexts and not in others, and for their spouses to support this compromise.

Finally, most of the literature on deviant spouses focuses on the problems the deviant spouse creates in a marriage. This research suggests that the nondeviant member of a couple sometimes creates marital tension by failing to accept the deviant spouse's worldview or beliefs as legitimate or at least as important. Researchers are able to view relationships from the perspectives of both spouses and should take advantage of this theoretical opportunity to consider deviance systemically.

Clinical Issues

In this chapter, we have stated the case for considering marriages between Deadheads and non-Deadheads as mixed or cross-community marriages. In doing so, we have proposed that one partner's participation in a music subculture or another type of deviant or leisure activity can become a source of conflict between spouses, similar to the more widely studied sources of marital stress stemming from racial, ethnic, and religious affiliation. Although the consequences of voluntary membership in a community (i.e., being a Deadhead) are distinctly different from those of membership in an ascribed community, psychotherapists are encouraged to consider the interpersonal differences just as seriously.

In the following section, consideration is given to therapists, both those who are and those who are not familiar with the Deadhead community. Although the process illustrated here describes how therapists might best work with couples in mixed marriages where one spouse is a Deadhead, these concepts are applicable to working with couples in other types of mixed marriages as well. For our purposes, discussion is limited to the following three elements of therapeutic relationships with couples: trust, identification of the major issue, and language.

Trust. When working with any couple, marriage counselors are challenged to establish trust and rapport with both members of a couple, regardless of their issues. In Rosen-Grandon's practice, couples are seen conjointly for their initial consultation so that both spouses will make the decision whether they can work together with this particular therapist. The value of this practice is that it forces the couple to reach a consensus and take equal responsibility for selecting a therapist with whom they are willing to discuss their marital conflicts.

When working with couples, therapists are challenged to both validate the clients' problem as a legitimate source of conflict and demonstrate a lack of bias toward one spouse over the other. When therapists themselves are Deadheads, awareness of the Deadhead subculture provides a rich source of information, but it can also be perceived as bias against the non-Deadhead client and lead to premature termination of therapy. Similarly, therapists who are not Deadheads must be cautious not to communicate either disapproval or minimization of the presented problem. In general, therapists are wise to remain impartial, process-oriented, and neutral, at least until the couple has become fully engaged in the therapeutic process.

Identification of the Major Issue.   As with other cultural differences, therapists are wise to note the nature of interpersonal differences as early as possible in the therapeutic process. Milton Erickson (Erickson & Rossi, 1979) was often asked about the collection of different artifacts in his office. He claimed that these various toys and artistic objects were useful as both diagnostic tools and sources of metaphors. Concurring with this view, Rosen-Grandon's clinical office is also decorated with a variety of souvenirs and symbols that attract the interest of her clients, including a variety of photos, paintings, diplomas, rocks, and art objects. Pertinent to the present discussion, the walls of Rosen-Grandon's office host two subtle mementos of the Grateful Dead: A picture-postcard of band members during their younger years, and a flyer that advertises the art of Jerry Garcia. Deadheads are usually quick to notice these artifacts. Once recognized, they serve as a catalyst for discussion and assessment of whether this is a mixed marriage or one in which spouses share a common interest in the Grateful Dead.

In contrast, therapists who are not familiar with the Grateful Dead may have a more difficult time identifying the source of conflicts in Deadhead mixed marriages. Closeted members of the Deadhead community tend to exercise a great deal of discretion. If therapists fail to ask the right questions, they may also fail to discover the deeper underlying sources if conflicts in these marriages. All therapists, however, can learn to recognize the subtle but observable symbols of the Deadhead subculture, such as modes of dress, concert T-shirts, hairstyles, bumper stickers, symbols, or the use of language that suggests an interest in the Grateful Dead. By acquainting oneself with symbols of this and other subcultures, therapists are then in a position to inquire about their meaning.

Using Humphrey's (1983) model of marital therapy, Rosen-Grandon employs an approach that is designed to help her learn about clients as both individuals and members of a couple. Once couples are seen conjointly during the initial session, individual appointments are scheduled for second sessions, in order to permit individual assessments. It is during these individual sessions that the therapist gets to know the clients as individuals; it is also a time when spouses feel most free to self-disclose. In her practice, Rosen-Grandon has frequently been forewarned about certain "sensitive" marital subjects during these individual sessions. As a rule of thumb, whenever the mention of the Grateful Dead or any other topic evokes a negative emotional reaction in one spouse, the topic becomes fertile ground for exploring deeper issues related to the identity conflicts of the individuals who comprise the marriage.

Language.   As members of a subculture that grew out of music appreciation, many Deadheads incorporate lyrics from Grateful Dead songs into their everyday vocabulary. In the effort to establish rapport with clients, therapists who are familiar with the lyrics of Grateful Dead songs may find themselves with a unique but dangerous advantage. Deadhead therapists may skillfully be able to employ the use of Deadhead lyrics and metaphors when communicating with these couples, but, if overused, the employment of dialect may arouse concerns in the non-Deadhead spouse that the therapist is forming an alliance or coalition with the Deadhead spouse that excludes him or her.

On the other hand, non-Deadhead therapists can miss important messages if they fail to inquire about the special meaning associated with various phrases. If the therapist chooses to ignore these phrases, a great opportunity may be lost to establish trust and rapport with the Deadhead client.

Judiciously used, Grateful Dead lyrics may be an excellent way to communicate with Deadhead clients. For example, one couple was convinced that their relationship was hopeless. After an extensive evaluation, the couple asked the therapist how she viewed the possibility of their marital survival. Spontaneously, the words of the Grateful Dead song "China Doll" offered what seemed like the best response. The words "pick up your china doll … it's only fractured … just a little nervous from the fall" (Hunter, 1990) afforded the couple a renewed sense of hope and a stronger sense of commitment to repairing their marriage. By learning about and using the in-group language associated with various subcultures, therapists can achieve similar rapport with partners involved in other volunteer communities.

Closing Comments

It is important to remember that the examples of marriages described in this chapter were chosen because they were problematic. We did not attempt to determine how common these problems were or what proportion of all marriages between a Deadhead and non-Deadhead are problematic. Our goal was to illustrate the range of potential problems and to discuss their implications for the theoretical literature and for clinical practice. Deadheads comprise only one example of a music community whose members enter exogamous unions despite their strong subcultural identities. More systematic research on marriages between people who do not both belong to the same music subculture might address their prevalence, how frequently they are problematic, and how sources of problems vary across music subcultures. Eventually it would be useful if this research were considered in the context of the broader issue of how voluntary identities in general affect relationships.

In this chapter, we have attempted to raise the awareness of therapists to recognize and understand one type of mixed marriage. Marriage counselors face the daily challenge of establishing a therapeutic relationship with both spouses, while remembering that their actual patient is the marital relationship. As we have illustrated, this requires sensitivity to the subcultural group memberships of each spouse, validation of the couple's difficulties, and an appreciation of the perspective of each partner. Needless to say, the issues of cultural differences in these mixed marriages usually extend far beyond differences in musical tastes.

Here we have illustrated the types of theoretical insights regarding stigma and relationships that can be derived from studies of mixed marriages. We have also suggested some counseling strategies for dealing with Deadheads whose spouses are not members of their community. It is our hope that researchers and therapists with knowledge of other music subcultures will contribute to the literature by describing the additional issues that affect such marriages. A comparison of these case studies should lead to a greater understanding of the core theoretical and clinical implications of identification with music subcultures.

Of course, music subcultures are only one of many types of voluntary affiliations that can contribute to marital problems. In this chapter, we have presented case studies of marriages that are mixed by virtue of differences in musical affiliations in order to consider their implications for marriage and highlight the enduring effects of Deadhead affiliation on one's personal identity and lifestyle. In this postmodern age, which offers such diverse opportunities for group affiliation, we must develop a greater understanding of these voluntary identities and their implications for our relationships and participation in a variety of overlapping social circles. Although it is challenging and complicated to examine interpersonal relationships in context, it is critical to understanding our society.

REFERENCES

Adams, R. G. (1991). *Deadheads: Community, spirituality, and friendship.* Unpublished manuscript.

Adams, R. G. (1998a). Inciting sociological thought by studying the Deadhead community: Engaging publics in dialogue. *Social Forces, 77*(1), 1–25.

Adams, R. G. (1998b). *Terrapin station.* Final report for an audience development study sponsored by Grateful Dead Productions.

Adams, R. G. (1999). We haven't left the planet yet. In J. Rocco (Ed.), *Dead reckonings: The life and times of the Grateful Dead* (pp. 141–146). New York: Schirmer.

Birenbaum, A. (1992). Courtesy stigma revisited. *Mental Retardation, 30*(5), 265–268.

Brown, L. (1998). Ethnic stigma as a contextual experience: A possible selves perspective. *Personality and Social Psychology Bulletin, 24*(2), 163–172.

Carr, R. (1999). Deadhead tales of the supernatural: A folklorist analysis. In R. Weiner (Ed.), *Perspectives on the Grateful Dead: Critical writings* (pp. 203–212). Westport, CT: Greenwood.

David, M. (2000). An Ericksonian perspective on the journey into adulthood. In R. G. Adams & R. Sardiello (Eds.), *Deadhead social science: You ain't gonna learn what you don't want to know* (pp. 215–225). Lanham, MD: AltaMira.

Donnan, H. (1990). Mixed marriages in contemporary perspective: Gender and power in Northern Ireland and Pakistan. *Journal of Comparative Family Studies, 21*(2), 207–225.

Dupree's Diamond News. (1995). *Garcia: A Grateful Celebration* [special issue].

Eagan, J. M. (1990). *A speeder's guide to avoiding tickets.* New York: Avon.

Erickson, M. H., & Rossi, E. L. (1979). Hypnotherapy: An exploratory casebook. New York: Irvington.

Freeman, R. (2000). Other people play the music: Improvisation as social interaction. In R. G. Adams & R. Sardiello (Eds.), *Deadhead social science: You ain't gonna learn what you don't want to know* (pp. 75–107). Lanham, MD: AltaMira.

Gans, D. (1991). *Conversations with the Dead: The Grateful Dead interview book.* New York: Citadel.

Gans, D. (Ed.). (1995). *Not fade away: The on-line world remembers Jerry Garcia.* Berkeley, CA: Thunder's Mouth.

Gans, D., & Simon, P. (1985). *Playing in the band: An oral and visual portrait of the Grateful Dead.* New York: St. Martin's Press.

Goffman, E. (1963). *Stigma: Notes on the management of spoiled identity.* Englewood Cliffs, NJ: Prentice-Hall.

Goode, E. (1984). *Drugs in American society* (2nd ed.). New York: Knopf.

Goodenough, M. (1999). Grateful Dead: Manifestations from the collective unconscious. In R. Weiner (Ed.), *Perspectives on the Grateful Dead: Critical writings* (pp. 175–182). Westport, CT: Greenwood.

Hall, S., Clarke, J., Jefferson, T., & Roberts, B. (Eds.). (1976). *Resistence through rituals.* London: Hutchinson.

Hartley, J. (2000). "We were given this dance": Music and meaning in the early unlimited devotion family. In R. G. Adams & R. Sardiello (Eds.), *Deadhead social science: You ain't gonna learn what you don't want to know* (pp. 129–155). Lanham, MD: AltaMira.

Humphrey, F. G. (1983). *Marital therapy: A clinician's manual for treating couples in conflict.* Englewood Cliffs, NJ: Prentice-Hall.

Hunter, R. (1990). China doll. In *A Box of Rain: Collected Lyrics of Robert Hunter* (p. 36). New York: Penguin.

Jackson, B. (1983). *Grateful Dead: The music never stopped.* New York: Delilah Books.

Johnson, W. R., & Warren, D. M. (1994). *Inside mixed marriage: Accounts of changing attitudes, patterns, and perceptions of cross-cultural and interracial marriages.* Lanham, MD: University Press of America.

Khatib-Chahidi, J., Hill, R., & Paton, R. (1998). Chance, choice, and circumstance: A study of women in cross-cultural marriages. In R. Breger & R. Hill, (Eds.). *Cross-cultural marriage: Identity and choice* (pp. 49–66). New York: Oxford University Press.

Lee, R. M. (1994). *Mixed and matched: Interreligious courtship and marriage in Northern Ireland.* Lanham, MD: University Press of America.

Leichter, H. M. (1997). Lifestyle correctness and the new secular morality. In A. M. Brandt & P. Rozin, *Morality and health* (pp. 359–378). London: Routledge.

Lewis, M. (1998). Shame and stigma. In P. Gilbert & B. Andrews, (Eds.). *Shame: Interpersonal behavior, psychopathology, and culture* (pp. 126–140). New York: Oxford University Press.

Luke, C. (1994). White women in interracial families: Reflections on hybridization, feminine identities, and racialized othering. *Feminist Issues, 14*(2), 49–72.

Paterline, B. (2000). Community reaction to Deadhead subculture. In R. G. Adams, & R. Sardiello (Eds.), *Deadhead social science: You ain't gonna learn what you don't want to know* (pp. 183–201). Lanham, MD: AltaMira.

Perry, C. (1984). *The Haight Ashbury: A history.* New York: Random House.

Rush, L. L. (1998). Affective reactions to multiple social stigmas. *Journal of Social Psychology, 138*(4), 421–430.

Scott, J., Dolgushkin, M., & Nixon, S. (1995). *Deadbase '94.* Hanover, NH: Authors.

Scott, J., Dolgushkin, M., & Nixon, S. (1997). *Deadbase X: The complete guide to Grateful Dead song lists.* Hanover, NH: Authors.

Shank, G., & Simon, E. (2000). The grammar of the Grateful Dead. In R. G. Adams & R. Sardiello (Eds.), *Deadhead social science: You ain't gonna learn what you don't want to know* (pp. 51–73). Lanham, MD: AltaMira.

Shenk, D., & Silberman, S. (1994). *Skeleton key: A dictionary for Deadheads.* New York: Doubleday.

Sheptoski, M. (2000). Vending at Dead shows: The bizarre bazaar. In R. G. Adams & R. Sardiello (Eds.), *Deadhead social science: You ain't gonna learn what you don't want to know* (pp. 157–181). Lanham, MD: AltaMira.

Simon, E. (1999). *Useless deadstats.* Available from stats@Gdead.berkeley.edu.

Stringer, P. (1994). Cross-community marriage in Northern Ireland: Social support and social constraints. *Sexual and Marital Therapy, 9*(1), 71–86.

Sutton, S. (2000). The Deadhead community: Popular religion in contemporary American culture. In R. G. Adams & R. Sardiello (Eds.), *Deadhead social science: You ain't gonna learn what you don't want to know* (pp. 109–127). Lanham, MD: AltaMira.

Troy, S. (1991). *One more Saturday night: Reflections with the Grateful Dead, dead family, and dead heads.* New York: St. Martin's Press.

Waldren, J. (1998). Crossing over: Mixing, matching and marriage in Mallorca. In R. Breger & R. Hill (Eds.), *Cross-cultural marriage: Identity and choice.* (pp. 33–48). Oxford University Press.

Weinberg, T. S., & Vogler, C. C. (1990). Wives of alcoholics: Stigma management and adjustments to husband–wife interaction. *Deviant Behavior, 11,* 331–343.

Weiner, B., Perry, R. P., & Magnusson, J. (1988). An attributional analysis of reactions to stigma. *Journal of Personality and Social Psychology, 55*(5), 738–748.

Wilgoren, R. (1999). The Grateful Dead as a community. In R. Weiner (Ed.), *Perspectives on the Grateful Dead: Critical writings* (pp. 191–202). Westport, CT: Greenwood.

Williams, R. (1951). *American society: A sociological interpretation.* New York: Knopf.

III

COUNTERNORMATIVE
RELATIONSHIPS

6
Cross-Gender Friendship: The Troublesome Relationship

Roger Baumgarte
Winthrop University

There is something inappropriate about cross-gender friendships. They can incite jealousies in a romance or a marriage, confuse friends and family members, and be emotionally perplexing to the partners themselves (O'Meara, 1989; Rawlins, 1982). Relationship researchers disagree on whether men and women can truly be "just friends" (Werking, 1997a). Most societies find such friendships "inappropriate," discouraging them in anyone past the age of puberty. This discouragement often takes the form of gossip, direct expressions of disapproval (Allan, 1989), or clearly understood cultural norms, as in societies with high levels of gender segregation. Even in societies with fluid boundaries regarding gender and relationships, there is often the suspicion that at least one of the partners in a cross-gender friendship is harboring, consciously or unconsciously, romantic or sexual aspirations for the other, rendering the relationship something other than simply friendship.

This chapter reviews the recent literature on cross-gender friendships and, consistent with the theme of this text, highlights the difficulties posed by this form of relationship. Rawlins (1982) and O'Meara (1989) wrote convincingly about the challenges presented by cross-gender friendships, but direct tests of these challenges have led at least one group of researchers to question whether they are "much ado about nothing" (Monsour, 1992; Monsour, Harris, Kurzweil, & Beard, 1994). Other researchers of close relationships have, until very recently, simply avoided the study of cross-gender friendship (Werking, 1997b). Those who have focused their professional energies on these relationships have tended to cast them in a rather positive light. In fact, recent reviews of the literature on this topic have emphasized the advantages of cross-gender friendships, citing such benefits as doubling one's potential number of friends, gaining insider information about the opposite gender, improving understanding and acceptance across the genders and thereby reducing sexism and sexual harassment, validating oneself as attractive to someone of the opposite gender, breaking down the old boys' network in the workplace, and gaining the enrichment that stems from having a friend who is different than oneself (Kaplan & Keys, 1997; Monsour, 1997; Werking, 1997a). Although it is true that the difficulties and risks of these relationships have been addressed, they are typically viewed as "challenges" (O'Meara, 1989; Rawlins, 1982) or "impediments" (Werking, 1997a), which can and must be "managed." The use of such terms, and the general tenor of the writing in this field, have tended to understate the potential problems that can occur when a man and a woman try to develop a friendship.

This chapter takes the position that the difficulties of cross-gender friendships are significant enough to deserve a closer look. Sufficient data exist to suggest that cross-gender friendships have a dark side that needs to be understood and appreciated more fully. The focus of this review is on the initiation and maintenance of the relationship itself, rather than on the public scrutiny that cross-gender friends face from romantic partners, family, work colleagues, and other friends. Because of pervasive prior cultural conditioning about gender and romance, a man and a woman trying to develop a friendship must negotiate a minefield of potential hazards even beyond society's tendency to disapprove. A number of recent studies shed new light on these risks.

The definition of friendship employed here reflects the thinking of Fehr (1996), Rawlins (1992), and Wright (1982), who saw it as a close personal relationship between equals characterized by reciprocal caring, openness, and a desire to enjoy each other's company. Two individuals engaged in a friendship have agreed on the nature of their relationship and what this commitment implies. The key elements of this definition of equality, reciprocity, openness, and mutual agreement about the nature of the relationship serve to focus our discussion about the nature of cross-gender friendships. Following the lead of O'Meara (1989), cross-gender friendships can be defined as a "non-romantic, non-familial, personal relationship between a man and a woman." To distinguish them from romantic relationships, the latter are characterized by exclusivity and fascination. As shown later, in addition to these distinguishing characteristics, these three forms of relationships (friendships, cross-gender friendships, and romantic relationships) have much in common.

Although some of the studies include adults of varying ages, this review focuses primarily on young adults, because it is during this time period when such friendships are most frequent, and the data are the most available and insightful. Cross-gender friendships hardly exist, at least overtly, during the grade-school years, and tend to taper off in importance in middle and later adulthood (see Monsour, 1997). During young adulthood, especially for those who attend college, cross-gender friendships are more common, and social sanctions against such relationships are weaker. As one commits to marriage, children, and career, one has less time for friends in general, and the social pressures of spouse and family make the cultivation of cross-gender friendships even more difficult. Yet despite their relative acceptability during young adulthood, social pressures create tensions and problems between cross-gender friends, rendering these relationships as something other than friendship (as the term has been defined earlier). Stated briefly, this chapter concludes that cross-gender friendships often lack key characteristics of a genuine friendship. Each of these missing elements are examined in turn.

LACK OF A CULTURAL SCRIPT FOR CROSS-GENDER FRIENDSHIPS

Rawlins (1982) was the first to outline the challenges one encounters in a cross-gender friendship. Much of the difficulty, he pointed out, stems from the close similarity between romantic relationships and cross-gender friendships. In both cases, key aspects of the relationship are negotiated in private, both are pursued to meet social and intimacy needs, and both require an emotional investment and a high degree of loyalty. In addition, both are characterized by caring, trust, enjoyment, mutual respect, enhanced self-esteem, and companionship (Bleske & Buss, 2000; Helgeson, Shaver, & Dyer, 1987). Furthermore, the norm for many, especially those of middle-class socioeconomic status, is to think of one's romantic partner as one's best friend (Allan, 1989). All of these similarities blur the distinctions between friendship and romance.

However, society holds a rather clear definition for romantic relationships. Well-defined cultural scripts serve to guide the behaviors and destinies of those who fall in love (Rose & Frieze, 1993): A heterosexual man and woman who find themselves attracted to each other begin by dating and then fall in love. The dating becomes more exclusive as they present themselves as a "couple" to friends and family, they become engaged, and eventually they marry in a ceremony full of ritual and symbolism recognizing their love and commitment, and the culturally defined position they will take in society.

By comparison, friendships of any sort represent a very weak set of cultural norms. Only very ill-defined scripts exist for this type of relationship. Especially in U.S. culture, for example, the term *friend* itself can be used in a variety of contexts and can mean almost anything, from a new acquaintance one met at a convention last week to a person one has held dear since early childhood (Stewart & Bennett, 1991). As for cross-gender friendships specifically, literally no such cultural script exists (O'Meara, 1989; Rawlins, 1982). There are no cultural icons, no cinematic or literary models of cross-gender friendship that don't evolve into romance or failed attempts at romance. The idea of a man and a woman being close friends without a romance looming over the horizon has not been conditioned into our cultural consciousness (Booth & Hess, 1974; Rawlins, 1983). The dominance of romantic notions of these relationships can even be detected in the descriptors used by relationship researchers for friendship. Reeder (2000) cleverly pointed out that common definitions of friendship tend to stress notions of equality, mutuality, and positive affect, whereas definitions of cross-gender friendships attempt to differentiate them from romance by referring to them as nonromantic, nonsexual, or nonpassionate. (The definitions offered earlier reflect this common practice.)

Blurred distinctions between romance and heterosexual friendship—and the lack of a cultural script—result in an uncharted path for partners pursing this sort of friendship. From society's perspective, the way is clearer for those who confine their friendships to the work context (Lobel, Quinn, Clair, & Warfield, 1994); for those who are single, because their friendships can be conceived as precursors to the romantic script (Booth & Hess, 1974; Rawlins, 1993); or for friendships between married or committed couples (Allan, 1989). Others are left on their own to define the nature and boundaries of their relationships (Rawlins, 1982; O'Meara, 1989): Is this love? Is this friendship? Is this sex? Given that these three concepts are anything but mutually exclusive (Cupach & Metts, 1991), people engaged in a cross-gender friendship are faced with a very difficult task. This task is more difficult in cultures that have traditionally espoused separation of the sexes in public institutions. In a cross-cultural study involving university students from five countries, Baumgarte, Lee, and Kulich (2001) found that cross-gender friendships were most common in the European countries of Romania and France and least common in South Korea. Respondents from all five cultures reported being less acquainted with the family members of their cross-gender friends compared to their same-gender friends, a pattern of results undoubtedly reflecting societal pressures to keep cross-gender friendships out of public scrutiny (Baumgarte, Lee, & Kulich, 1999).

The salience and dominance of romantic conceptions of cross-gender relationships suggest that there will be a natural tendency for the friendship to take on features of romantic relationships. These may consist of superficial gestures reflecting societal customs about gender roles, such as who opens the door or who pays for the dinner. But each partner's perceptions of the relationship could be influenced by romantic norms in more subtle and profound ways. The partners could come to see each other in ways that resemble the "couple identity" of romantic relationships more than friendships. Resisting the romantic script for partners in a cross-gender friendship would require a clear understanding of each other's intentions and a strong commitment to friendship.

LACK OF META-RELATIONAL TALK IN CROSS-GENDER FRIENDSHIPS

Complicating this task is the fact that, for most couples, broaching these topics in casual conversation is not easy. Afifi and Burgoon (1998), Baxter and Wilmot (1985), and Swain (1992) have found that meta-relational discussions—or discussions that attempt to clarify the nature of their relationships—represent the most taboo and avoided topics between cross-gender friends. An established principle in social psychology is that people seek to reduce uncertainty in their lives. This principle applies, in most cases, to reducing uncertainty between partners in close relationships (Berger & Calabrese, 1975). People in romantic relationships, for example, want to feel that they know their partners well, that their behaviors are predictable, and that they feel some certainty about the state of their relationship. Relationship maintenance consists primarily of reciprocal expressions of love that serve to reassure each other regarding the state and the future of their relationship.

This desire to reduce uncertainty does not seem to apply to cross-gender friendships (Afifi & Burgoon, 1998; Swain, 1992). Perhaps it is better not to know than to have one's perceptions and expectations violated. Partners tend not to engage in meta-relational talk or directly seek information to clarify the state of their relationship. Despite the common stereotype about women's expertise in the maintenance of relationships, women—even more than men—find direct talk about these issues difficult in their cross-gender developing relationships (Baxter & Wilmot, 1985). Instead of directly addressing these critical issues, Baxter and Wilmot (1984) found that partners in uncertain cross-gender friendships—which most are—often resort to "secret tests" to determine the nature of their relationships. These researchers have identified several of these tests, such as the "endurance test" (acting in an obnoxious fashion to see if the friendship survives), or the "triangle test" (arranging for the friend to be in the company of someone with romantic intentions to see how they react). Far from clarifying the state of their relationship, such tests seem counterproductive and antithetical to notions of openness, trust, and caring, which are thought to characterize the nature of true friendship.

To summarize the arguments thus far, a man and a woman attempting to pursue a friendship are venturing into uncharted territory, without cultural norms or models to guide them about what could be considered normal or appropriate for this type of friendship. The close similarity between cross-gender friendship and romance leaves plenty of opportunity for the friendship to take on romantic characteristics, because cultural norms for that style of relationship are quite well conditioned into everyone's expectations about cross-gender relationships. The tension produced by trying to forge a friendship from the materials typically used to construct a romantic relationship leave the partners with a great deal of uncertainty about the nature of their relationship. This uncertainty could be relieved by candid, self-disclosing conversation that attempts to clarify the feelings of each partner and the state of their relationship. Yet, research suggests that partners in these uncertain relationships typically avoid such clarifying meta-relational talk. In general, they lack both openness and a mutual understanding about the nature of their relationship—key characteristics in defining a friendship.

LACK OF AGREEMENT ABOUT THE NATURE OF FRIENDSHIP

People pursuing a cross-gender friendship often discover that men and women have differing expectations about the nature of friendship itself. In describing these gender differences, researchers have referred to men's tendency toward agentic or instrumental friendship and women's preference for intimacy and emotional exchange (e.g., Canary, Emmers-Sommer, & Faulkner, 1997; Fehr, 1996). Expressed more graphically, Wright (1982) suggested that men cultivate side-by-side friendships, whereas women cultivate face-to-face friendships. Some researchers, noting the persistent findings of lower levels of satisfaction attributed to male friendships compared to female friendships, have referred to men as "deficient" (Huyck, 1982, p. 480) or "impoverished" (Tognoli, 1980, p. 273) in their friendship skills. Others have warned against overstating these differences, arguing instead that intragender differences are sufficiently great to render cross-gender differences as relatively insignificant (e.g., Burleson, 1997; Canary et al., 1997). Recent studies, however, suggest that these gender differences are rather large and pervasive, especially in the realm of established friendships (Bank & Hansford, 2000; Dindia & Allen, 1992; Schneider & Kenny, 2000). Regardless, all theorists working in this field acknowledge that gender differences in close relationships are far more complex than what appears on the surface.

To clarify these gender differences, it is important to acknowledge first that men and women hold very similar ideas about what it means to be close to someone, to have someone as a close friend (Helgeson, Shaver, & Dyer, 1987; Monsour, 1992). Both men and women prefer friendships that are characterized by emotional expressiveness, unconditional support, trust, shared activities, and so on. Research suggests, for example, that both men and women find their friendships more satisfying when they are characterized by greater self-disclosure and emotional expressiveness (Fehr, 1996; Reisman, 1990). However, although men prefer these elements in their close friendships, they typically don't report experiencing them in their friendships with other men (Bank & Hansford, 2000). Communication among male friends tends to be more group oriented and to revolve around matters external to the relationship: sports, cars, and activities. Men are comfortable talking about themselves, but only as these self-references pertain to things such as achievements (Hacker, 1981). The competitive world of male society prevents them from speaking about vulnerabilities or failures (Hess, 1979). By contrast, communication among women friends tends to be more dyadic in structure, and more intimate, expressive, and supportive in content.

Interestingly, existing data suggest that men are capable of being emotionally expressive if the situation calls for it (Leaper, Carson, Baker, Holliday, & Myers, 1995; Reis, 1988). Leaper et al., for example, found that when close friends were asked to discuss how their relationships with their families had changed since coming to college, the men in this study actually self-disclosed more than did the women. Thus, it is clear that men are capable of intimacy, but simply do not always exhibit it. One reason for this reticence is that they typically don't talk about issues that lend themselves to self-disclosure (Martin, 1997). Another reason could be that, respecting the masculine stereotype, listeners do not reinforce men when they do self-disclose (Leaper et al., 1995). Other reasons have been delineated in a recent study by Bank and Hansford (2000) that focused on male friends. Bank and Hansford found that men inhibited expressions of intimacy and support because of homophobia and personality factors related to parental modeling. That is, men with emotionally expressive personalities and less masculine self-identities, who were not afraid of appearing homosexual and who had fathers with close friendships, were more likely to be intimate and supportive with their male friends. These same factors are likely to determine their tendencies toward intimacy and support in cross-gender friendships as well. In fact, a rather extensive literature suggests that androgynous men tend to have more intimate and satisfying interpersonal relationships than do typically masculine men (see Fehr, 1996, for a review).

So what happens when these two styles of friendship meet in a cross-gender friendship? How does the agentic, side-by-side male style of friendship mesh with the more emotionally expressive, self-disclosing, supportive female style of friendship? Most of the literature suggests that men find friendships with women more satisfying than their friendships with other men, especially when these studies focus on the dimensions of intimacy and emotional support (e.g., Canary et al., 1997; Fehr, 1996; Rawlins, 1992; Werking, 1997a). By contrast, women in these relationships often end up disappointed. For example, Buhrke and Fuqua (1987) found that women do not feel that the men in their close relationships understand them as well as do the women with whom they are close. When under stress, men will often seek out the company of their cross-gender friends and receive emotional support. Women in the same situation typically find that men often do not reciprocate this support. It is worth noting that there are women who prefer the activity-oriented friendship style stereotypically attributed to men, and there are men who prefer the intimacy and supportive exchange that tend to characterize the friendships of women. Although men's appreciation of their friendships with women has been rather thoroughly explored, no one has yet examined why some women prefer the male style of friendship.

In summary, men and women typically carry very different expectations and predispositions into their cross-gender relationships. Although both genders agree on what defines a close relationship and rate a relationship as more satisfying when these elements are present, women are more likely to bring these characteristics to their friendships than are men. One of the defining characteristics of friendship proposed earlier was that both partners have agreed on the nature of their relationship and what this commitment implies. The data reviewed in this section indicate that cross-gender friendships often do not meet this criterion.

LACK OF CLEAR MOTIVES ABOUT FRIENDSHIP VERSUS ROMANCE

As heterosexual friends attempt to sort out the nature of their relationship, one area that often presents the greatest difficulty is determining whether or not they will eventually become romantically involved. Afifi and Burgoon (1998) concluded that most cross-gender friends think of their relationship as having little romantic potential. In this same study, however, only 18% indicated "no" romantic interest. On the other end of the continuum, 28% indicated more than just a mild romantic interest in their friends. Reeder (2000) found that the desire to be friends with someone of the opposite gender was correlated with romantic and sexual interest in that person. Thus, there is sufficient data to suggest that romantic interests play at least some role in most of these friendships.

There are a number of findings that make this fact troublesome. For one thing, Afifi and Burgoon (1998) found that the level of romantic interest of one partner in a cross-gender friendship is uncorrelated with the interest of the other. This finding suggests that cross-gender friendships can be one-sided affairs with respect to romance. For many cross-gender friends, the reason they are labeling it a friendship instead of a romance is probably because their romantic overtures have not been reciprocated. What makes this arrangement more problematic is that these same researchers have found that romantic interest is correlated with relational state certainty. That is, the more one is romantically interested in a cross-gender friend, the more certain one is about the definition of the relationship. Given the tendency of people to idealize romantic relationships (Martz et al., 1998; Murray, Holmes, & Griffin, 1996), it is likely that the partner with romantic interests feels relatively certain that the relationship is moving in a romantic direction, regardless of the reality of the situation. The flip side of this correlation is also relevant to this discussion: Those who are not romantically interested are more uncertain about the definition of their relationship. The romantically uninterested party is receiving a variety of verbal and nonverbal signals from the romantically interested party, leaving the former confused and the latter frustrated.

Recent studies reporting both interview and survey data reinforce this assertion. Reeder (2000) found that one-sided romantic feelings were far more detrimental to a cross-gender friendship than unreciprocated feelings of physical or sexual attraction. Schneider and Kenny (2000) found that friendships between men and women who were formerly lovers tend to involve lingering romantic interests on the part of at least one partner. The greater the romantic interest, the more likely they were to report jealousy, criticism and nagging. Friends who were formerly lovers also reported greater costs and fewer benefits in their friendships compared to those who had purely platonic relationships.

Harboring romantic interests in one's cross-gender friend seems to characterize men more than women (Afifi & Burgoon, 1998; Bleske & Buss, 2000; Schneider & Kenny, 2000). In fact, men in general hold stronger ideological beliefs about romance. On measures of romanticism, men are more likely to agree with such ideas as "love overcomes all" (Sprecher & Metts, 1989). Furthermore, Rawlins (1982) showed that although men make clear distinctions between their male friends and their female friends, they tend to make only very weak distinctions between their female friends and their romantic partners. For women, this pattern is reversed. In other words, for a man, the woman he is in love with has much in common with the woman he sees as a friend. For a woman, these are very distinct relationships with much less in common. More recent research has reinforced these findings (Rawlins, 1993; Werking, 1997a). Men's tendency to romanticize relationships with women and their inability to distinguish between friendship and love suggest that they bring a great deal of motivational and romantic confusion to their cross-gender friendships.

To render this scenario in the form of a typical example, the man's romantic interests and overtures to a female acquaintance are not reciprocated. Attempting to find a compromise, they agree on a "friendship" instead, although he is certain all along that this is merely a step on the path to genuine romance. Accustomed to greater intimacy in her close relationships, the woman offers him a version of friendship that feels much warmer and supportive than what he is accustomed to associating with friendship. This warmth and acceptance further increases his romantic desire, and he begins to feel more certain about the eventual outcome of his efforts. She, meanwhile, finds his mixed signals perplexing. He speaks of friendship, but acts too possessive and romantic.

Given the lack of meta-relational talk (as reviewed earlier), and the mixed messages that are being expressed, more attention is drawn to interpreting each other's nonverbal cues. Guerrero (1997) found that partners in cross-gender friendships attempt to monitor the nonverbal cues they are projecting to each other more than do same-gender friends or romantic partners. When the respondents were interacting with their cross-gender friends, they were more anxious and concerned about making a good impression. Although there were some differences in the types of cues participants projected to their romantic partners (e.g., more touching, longer silences) compared to their cross-gender friends, the results were dominated by similarities of the nonverbal behaviors displayed in these two contexts. Hence, rather than clarify the romantic intentions of the cross-gender friends, these nonverbal cues are likely to be a source of confusion and misinterpretation. This tendency for miscommunication is likely to be greatest for each other's gestures of affection (Maltz & Borker, 1982), the aspect of nonverbal communication of greatest importance for partners trying to sort out each other's romantic intentions. The context in which the cross-gender friends typically spend their time may also contribute to the confusion. Rather than cultivating their friendships as part of larger groups, Werking (1997a) found that most of her respondents reported meeting face to face, often eating meals together, a context that is typically associated with romantic dating.

The example given earlier describes a man pursuing his romantic interests and a woman wanting platonic friendship, because that is the pattern found to be more common. Yet the roles can be reversed. Regardless, most cross-gender friends report at least a minimal degree of romantic interest in each other. Disparate motives regarding romance are not uncommon in cross-gender friendships. The more a friend experiences romantic feelings, the more that person feels certain about the romantic potential of the relationship, whether justified or not. These one-sided romances are also associated with more conflict and greater costs, leading both partners to find the relationship frustrating and unsatisfying. Their inability to discuss these issues openly, and the potential for confusion in the realm of nonverbal gestures, simply amplify the inclination for miscommunications. Hence, there are a variety of factors that coalesce to produce a relationship that is ripe for difficulty. It should not be surprising that, across cultures, cross-gender friendships tend to be of shorter duration and reflect a higher degree of conflict than do same-gender friendships (Baumgarte et al., 1999).

LACK OF CLEAR MOTIVES ABOUT SEXUALITY

These difficulties in communication are revealed in a more concrete fashion in the realm of sexuality. A number of studies have attempted to investigate how sexual interests and behaviors evolve in cross-gender relationships, including friendships. First of all, it would be unrealistic to think that sexual issues and tensions do not play a role in cross-gender friendships. Kaplan and Keys (1997), for example, found that 58% of their sample of college students had at least some sexual interest in their cross-gender friend. Roughly two thirds of Sapadin's (1988) sample of professional adults reported sexual tensions and feelings in their relationships, with over three fourths saying that sexual feelings complicated their friendships in a negative fashion. For 23% of their respondents, it was what they disliked most about their cross-gender friendships. In another study of adults in the workplace, half admitted some level of sexual attraction to their friends (Lobel et al., 1994).

Studies have also looked at the frequency with which cross-gender friends, in otherwise platonic relationships, actually engage in sex. Specific estimates have been made for college populations in the United States and they vary widely depending how the questions are posed. In studies where respondents were asked about a variety of issues in addition to sexual activity within a specific nonromantic friendship, Bleske and Buss (2000) found that roughly 15% of their respondents had had sex. In a study aimed explicitly at the impact of sexual activity in cross-gender friendships, where respondents were asked whether they had ever had sex with someone they had no intentions of dating at the time, Afifi and Faulkner (2000) found that 51% of their sample had done so. Of these, less than half reported that the sexual experience was a prelude to the subsequent development of a romantic relationship. Two thirds who had sex saw it as beneficial to the relationship, regardless of its romantic outcome. Afifi and Faulkner did not expand on the remaining one third of their respondents, who evidently did not find these sexual experiences beneficial.

Some theorists have considered the possible benefits of sex in cross-gender friendships. Afifi and Faulkner (2000), for example, claimed that engaging in sex could be seen as helping relational members overcome "the sexuality boundary that often stunts friendship development" (p.

208). Rubin (1985) suggested that, for a few cross-gender friends, having sex would reduce the tension and liberate their relationship, with the idea of "getting it over with" and helping them to move beyond this "distraction" (p. 150). However, most theorists, including Rubin, generally see it as detrimental, at least as far as the friendship is concerned (Allan, 1989; Cupach & Metts, 1991; Egland, Spitzberg, & Zormeier, 1996; Lampe, 1985; O'Meara, 1989; Rawlins, 1982; Werking, 1997a). Messman, Canary, and Hause (2000) found that most cross-gender friends avoid sex as a way of maintaining their relationship.

To highlight the potential damage that can result from sexual engagement in a cross-gender friendship, it is important to note that the act of having sex by itself is probably not as critical as the meaning that each partner assigns to the act (Duck, 1994). Here, again, gender is often cited as an issue, because men and women tend to assign very different meanings to sexual encounters. To begin with, men tend to have a higher degree of sexual interest in their cross-gender friends, and see having sex with them as more beneficial to themselves, than do women (Bleske & Buss, 2000; Rose, 1985). Kaplan and Keys (1997) found that not only do men report greater current and past sexual interest in their supposedly platonic cross-gender friends, this interest is greater in men who are already in committed romantic relationships. That is, sexual interest in his cross-gender friend is not just the province of the single, romantically "available" male.

Monsour (1992) found that men were more likely than women to see sexuality as a way of expressing intimacy to their otherwise platonic, cross-gender friend. Although other factors in this study were rated as more important than sex for expressing intimacy, this gender difference suggests that men, more than women, find sexuality as more acceptable outside the context of an exclusively romantic relationship. Thus, for the man, feelings of sex tend to be intertwined with feelings of intimacy, which can provide a rationale for or perhaps some confusion about becoming sexually involved with one's cross-gender friend. Men are more likely to initiate sex in a cross-gender relationship (McCormick & Jesser, 1982), and are more likely to start a friendship out of sexual motivation (Kaplan & Keys, 1997; Rose, 1985). However, men's tendency to harbor sexual feelings for their cross-gender friend appears to be more relevant at the beginning of their relationship compared to later on. For the woman, similar feelings, when they occur, seem to be unrelated to the length of their relationship (Kaplan & Keys, 1997). A woman's interest in having sex with her cross-gender friend may continue for years.

So how do these sexual interests get expressed and negotiated in the context of a cross-gender friendship? The explanations offered earlier in the context of sorting out romantic feelings apply to the realm of sexuality as well. Cross-gender friends are reticent to discuss relationship issues directly, and thus resort to a variety of "secret tests," flirtations, innuendo, and jokes to communicate their intentions. These forms of communication are intrinsically ambiguous, and rendered even more so by the fact that research in naturalistic settings suggest that they do not distinguish between romantic relationships and friendships (Afifi & Johnson, 1999; Egland et al., 1996). Further complicating this issue, evidence also suggests that men tend to interpret the friendly behaviors of women in a sexual fashion, often seeing seduction where none is intended (Shotland & Craig, 1988).

Although both men and women report enjoying flirting and teasing in their cross-gender friendships, men report enjoying this game more than do women (Sapadin, 1988; Swain, 1992). More often than not, women are in the position of interpreting these intrinsically vague cues. They must decide whether to play along and reciprocate, or reject the supposed advances and risk inappropriately dampening the ongoing ambiance of the friendship. The enigmatic nature of flirtation allows the flirter to claim that he was only joking and to accuse his friend of being too defensive or prudish. In addition, despite their fear of embarrassment and losing face, men do not find sexual rejection in the context of a cross-gender friendship to be terribly discouraging (Bleske & Buss, 2000; Metts, Cupach, & Imahori, 1992). Women in these contexts tend to prefer only moderately direct forms of rejection, such as "I don't think I am ready for this right now" (Metts et al., 1992, p. 8). But because men are less upset and deterred by this form of rejection compared to more direct forms, their sexual ambitions may not be sufficiently constrained.

Metts et al. (1992) suggested that one disturbing implication of this pattern of findings is that some men may perceive women's initial resistance as "token" and feel less inhibited to continue their advances because ultimately they expect to succeed. Although accurate statistics on the frequency of unwanted sex or sexual assault in the context of "friendship" are difficult to determine, such outcomes represent a real risk that should be acknowledged (Murnen, Perot, & Byrne, 1989; Sorenson, Stein, Siegel, Golding, & Burnam, 1987). It is worth noting that in Afifi and Faulkner's (2000) study, 55% of those who had sex with their otherwise platonic cross-gender friend did so while under the influence of alcohol.

But, one could argue, can't sex between two friends simply remain as "friendly sex?" Does it have to be dichotomized between romantic sex and unwanted sex? In his typography of cross-gender relationships, Rawlins (1982) considered this possibility and labeled it "friendship love." Bradae (1983) created the term "flovers" to refer to friends who occasionally or frequently have sex but prefer to think of their relationship more in terms of friendship than romance. Empirical support for the existence of flovers can be seen in the work of Afifi and Faulkner (2000), who found that of the 51% of their respondents who had sex with their otherwise platonic friends, 34% did so on multiple occasions either in the same friendship or in a number of friendships. The authors noted that this phenomenon might be a direct result of the lack of a cultural script or a set of societal mores concerning what is appropriate and normal in a cross-gender friendship. Given the lack of "rules," these friends construct their own "knowledge structure" (Afifi & Faulkner, 2000, p. 218), which reflects how each person conceptualizes the nature of his or her cross-gender friendship. For some, this conceptualization included an open attitude about sex.

However, it is important to note that most theorists and researchers have argued that a flover-type relationship is easier to effect for men compared to women (Bleske & Buss, 2000; Helgeson et al., 1987; Rawlins, 1982; Sapadin, 1988). Rawlins (1982) argued that this form of relationship is inherently unstable and not likely to survive for long. Rubin (1985) concluded that it produces possessiveness that is antithetical to friendship. Bleske and Buss (2000) found a high correlation between the situation in which a female friend was interested in moving toward a romantic relationship but the man wasn't, and the man having sex with that woman. Stated more directly, this finding implies that men will take sexual advantage of women who are romantically interested although the men have no romantic interest themselves. This correlation did not exist for women in the study, suggesting that women are less likely to engage in sex with a man who is romantically interested when she isn't. Taken together, these findings suggest that men are more likely than women to exploit a flover-type relationship for their own sexual benefit (Lampe, 1985).

To summarize, sexual tensions tend to complicate most cross-gender friendships. For those who do engage in sex and the relationship does not develop into a romance, most theorists predict a negative outcome for the friendship. Men tend to sexualize their relationships with women, a tendency that may apply especially to their cross-gender friendships. Findings suggest men are more likely to initiate a cross-gender friendship out of sexual interest, more motivated to have sex with their friends, and more likely to initiate sex, yet are less clear about their motives and feelings about the relationship. The role of sexuality in their relationship is often not discussed. Rather, it often takes place in an atmosphere of unclear motives, confusing nonverbal cues, and alcohol, resulting in an experience that could be considerably less than consensual. Even sex that is kept at an entirely friendly level has the strong potential of being exploitive.

THE LACK OF EQUALITY

Most relationships are inherently hierarchical, and this principle applies to cross-gender relationships as well. Various analyses of romantic relationships, for example, have concluded that they tend to reflect a differential of power and control (Argyle & Furnham, 1983; Cates & Lloyd, 1992). By contrast, friendship, as defined earlier here and by most theorists, is a relationship between equals (Allan, 1989; Rawlins, 1992; Werking 1997a).

Even when friendship occurs between people of widely different ages or statuses, some elements in the relationship serve as levelers to compensate for these inequalities (Rawlins, 1992). The issue for this section is whether cross-gender friendships reflect the equality assumed to define friendship, or whether they experience the inequality typical of cross-gender relationships. Monsour et al. (1994) found that most cross-gender friends do not see themselves as unequal. However, power differentials are complex and subtle forces in close relationships and are not always evident to the partners themselves (Winter, 1973).

McWilliams and Howard (1993) provided an analysis of how masculine and feminine stereotypes might influence the perception of power in cross-gender friendships. They argued that status differences arise from the differing stereotypes society holds for men and women. For example, when a man gives advice, it is assumed to stem from his stereotype as agentic and instrumental. This tendency toward activity is perceived as expertise and authority, which in turn promotes a sense of hierarchy in the relationship between the giver and the receiver of the advice. By contrast, a woman's advice giving, based again on commonly held stereotypes, is seen as stemming from her nurturant and communal orientation, which in turn promotes a sense of solidarity between advice giver and advice receiver. McWilliams and Howard asserted that hierarchy (inequality, authority) and solidarity (feelings of closeness) are inversely correlated, working as opposing forces. When a man and a woman are in a close relationship, her solidarity style (reflecting closeness and nurturance) and his hierarchical orientation (reflecting inequality and authority) will typically result in an unequal relationship. Although intriguing, this is an idea that needs to be tested empirically.

Along a similar vein, Maccoby (1990) maintained that girls are socialized to be enabling—agreeing, taking turns, acknowledging, and so on—a strategy appropriate for communal, dyadic relationships. Boys, by comparison, are socialized to be restrictive—derailing interactions by boasting, contradicting, shortening, and so on—a strategy suitable for large, hierarchically organized group activities, like sports. Helgeson et al., (1987) found that when a distancing experience such as conflict occurs in cross-gender relationships, men tend to pursue arguments that end in victory, self-justification, or dominance, compared to women who think more often in terms of restoring closeness. Both of these findings—being socialized in hierarchical activities such as sports and employing conflict strategies aimed at winning—suggest that the relationship styles of men and women tend to reinforce a higher status for men in cross-gender relationships.

Others have looked more specifically at cross-gender friendships. In Sapadin's (1988) study, the patronizing attitude of their friend was a complaint received only from women in the context of a cross-gender friendship. This response was never given by men or by women in same-gender friendships. Most of the friendships studied by Booth and Hess (1974) reflected a high degree of equality in terms of age, education, status, and so on. But when cross-gender dyads were not equal, they tended to follow the same pattern as romantic relationships, with men being older and of higher status than their cross-gender friends. Men who had higher educational status than their cross-gender friends were more willing to confide in these friends than when the friends were of similar or higher educational status. This implies that the cross-gender friendships are seen as most comfortable, for men at least, when they reflect the same status hierarchy typically found in romantic relationships. The pattern of an older male and a younger female in cross-gender friendships also seems to cut across cultures. In a study involving university students in five cultures, only 18% of cross-gender friendships involved an older woman with a younger man (Baumgarte et al., 1999). Taken together, these theoretical arguments and empirical data suggest that there tend to be status differences in cross-gender relationships in general, and cross-gender friendships in particular.

Other studies have focused more specifically on the inequality of the exchange processes in cross-gender friendships. Hacker (1981) and Swain (1992) noted that men will self-disclose and seek consultation more from female friends than women will from male friends. They also found that, relative to each other, men will hide their weaknesses and women their strengths in cross-gender friendships. These patterns of exchange suggest that men expect and receive more social support from women than women obtain from men. Rose (1985) asserted that men can gain intimacy and acceptance from their female friends, but that women do not typically receive these benefits from their male friends. In fact, the only benefit in which women in this study reported gaining more than men in cross-gender friendships was companionship, which Rose interpreted as women's desire for increased status. Reviewing somewhat different literatures led Rawlins (1982), Schneider and Kenny (2000), and Winstead, Derlega, and Rose (1997) to conclude that equitable cross-gender friendships are impossible or quite difficult to negotiate.

Given the clear advantages and benefits that these relationships provide for men, it should not be surprising that every study investigating this topic has found that men consistently report larger numbers of cross-gender friends than do women. This difference appears to be consistent across cultures (Baumgarte et al., 2001). Given that these studies are always comprised of men and women drawn from the same populations, this difference in the reported number of cross-gender friends must represent inconsistent perceptions about who is friends with whom. In fact, Rubin (1985) found that two thirds of the women who were identified as close friends of the men she interviewed did not consider that characterization of their relationship as appropriate. That is, they did not see themselves as close friends with the men who claimed them as such. In fact, some women felt they hardly knew them. Hence, the question emerges of whether it is appropriate to call it a friendship if both partners don't agree they have one.

CONCLUSIONS

The lack of a cultural script about friendship in general and cross-gender friendships specifically leaves individuals without a sense of what it means to be friends with someone of the opposite gender. Furthermore, the existence of very powerful societal norms for romance and the resemblance of these two types of relationships cause the friendship to take on romantic characteristics. Evidence suggests that cross-gender friends typically harbor at least some degree of romantic interest, and these interests often go unreciprocated. A tendency to avoid discussion of these issues and a heightened focus on ambiguous nonverbal cues result in a relationship that is characterized by misunderstandings or at least a lack of agreement about the nature of the relationship. This lack of agreement is likely to be frustrating and unsatisfying for both partners.

For most cross-gender friends, sexual tensions and particularly men's tendency to sexualize these relationships impact the friendship in a detrimental fashion. Although some friends engage in sex, and some of these find it beneficial to their relationship, the risk of exploitation is clearly in evidence. With respect to emotional support, men and women want and seek similar affective benefits. However, men's reticence to demonstrate equivalent emotional support and intimacy implies that these relationships often become unequal. In fact, with respect to both status differentials and the nature of the exchange, cross-gender friendships are characterized by inequality. On nearly all dimensions that have been studied, men benefit from these relationships more than women do. The definition of friendship offered at the beginning of this chapter stressed the requirements of equality, reciprocity, and mutual agreement about the nature of the relationship. Cross-gender friendships, according to the literature reviewed here, often seem to lack all three of these requirements.

RECOMMENDATIONS

Taken together, the evidence suggests ample reason to be cautious about pursuing a friendship with someone of the opposite gender. This warning applies especially to women, for whom these relationships are at risk of becoming emotionally or sexually exploitive. Although the benefits and adaptive aspects of cultivating a cross-gender friendship have been thoroughly explored in other reviews of this literature, this chapter has focused exclusively on the problems associated with these relationships, arguing that it may be inappropriate to think of them as genuine friendships. Although pessimistic in tenor, this analysis does imply some adaptive recommendations.

The factors that cause cross-gender friendships to be something less than friendship are evident. Stated in the briefest form, cross-gender friendships tend to be unequal relationships lacking in the openness of communication needed to sort out exactly what it means to be a friend, and how romantic feelings and sexual interests are to be negotiated within the relationship. The pervasiveness of the evidence for these difficulties suggests that many people may not be capable of a genuine cross-gender friendship. Yet, by exploring all of the avenues by which a cross-gender friendship can go awry, one can gain insight about what would be required to make them more functional, satisfying, and enjoyable relationships for both partners. Many people, especially young adults, are pursuing this type of relationship, and it is important to determine what can be done to improve their chances of success.

This review implies some rather clear recommendations concerning cross-gender friendships. These recommendations are given from the perspective of what could be considered the ideal, realizing of course that relationships in the real world often fall short of such fantasies. First, our society needs more television programs, Hollywood movies, or best-selling novels in which the main characters are involved in a cross-gender friendship that has no hint of a past or future romance. The characters might well be involved in committed, romantic relationships, but the friendship itself should be a dominant feature of the plot. These could be dramas, comedies, war stories, science fiction stories, or whatever. In fact, the more varied the genre, the wider the potential appeal. But the main characters should be attractive, popular individuals who cultivate a close, communicative, enjoyable relationship with someone of the opposite gender. Sexuality could be depicted with delight and humor, but also with clarity and sensitivity about each other's intentions. Above all, the friendship should be portrayed as a relationship between equals in which the costs and benefits are shared equally. A very wide range of media images exists for romantic relationships. Why have friendships been so persistently stereotyped as same-gender buddy stories? It is time that modern societies consider widening their relationship horizons.

For those engaged in a cross-gender friendship, the clear and pervasive implication from this review is the importance of open and honest talk, especially talk aimed at understanding and clarifying the nature and state of the relationship. This principle would apply especially to those experiencing discomfort with the mixed signals they are receiving from their partners. The strong inhibition against talking about these issues could, itself, be discussed. Of course, this type of talk is much easier for the partner who is clear about his or her own goals and intentions for the relationship. Achieving such clarity of self may be more difficult for the young adult, whose identity isn't fully established, and also for the person who has lingering romantic interests that are at risk of being rebuffed. Yet mutual self-disclosures in the context of a committed friendship should allow the partners to weather such uncertainties. It is important to realize that such clarity in cross-gender friendships does increase over time (Monsour et al., 1994; Reeder, 2000; Werking, 1997a). The longer the friendship endures, the lower the inhibition partners experience in discussing the state of their relationship and the easier it is to talk about romantic and sexual issues. Of course, relationships are dynamic, organic phenomena that progress, evolve, regress, fluctuate, digress, and may decline over time. Given the lack of cultural models for cross-gender friendships, the importance of monitoring these changes and each other's conceptions and aspirations for the relationship are more important than what they would be for a same-gender friendship.

Men will have to make a special effort to clarify their own motives and to approach the relationship with care and candor. They must be honest and forthright about their romantic interests or lack thereof. With respect to sexuality, it is important that men understand and appreciate their own tendency to sexualize the friendly behaviors of their female friends. Men must be sensitive to their friends' reactions to their sexual overtures, no matter how oblique or charming they perceive their gestures to be. Sexuality can add humor and spice to the relationship, or it can be annoying (Cupach & Metts, 1991). It is important to distinguish the difference. Simply asking from time to time how one's sexually oriented gestures are being perceived would go a long way to clear the air and solidify the basis for a satisfying friendship. It is important for women to realize that, as Leaper et al. (1995) showed, men's attempts at self-disclosure and intimate talk are often insufficiently encouraged. For both, committing to the relationship as a friendship and agreeing on the implications of this commitment would be essential. Most important, perhaps, men must give to these friendships in proportion to what they take from them, especially in the realm of emotional support and intimacy. After any significant interaction with a female friend, men should ask themselves: Who was supported more in this interaction? Who was more nurturing, caring, and encouraging? Who honestly knows the other better? Having an egalitarian relationship, which friendships are supposed to be, will only occur when men are as emotionally expressive, receptive, and supportive as their female friends are.

REFERENCES

Afifi, W. A., & Burgoon, J. K. (1998). "We never talk about that": A comparison of cross-sex friendships and dating relationships on uncertainty and topic avoidance. *Personal Relationships, 5,* 255–272.

Afifi, W. A., & Faulkner, S. L. (2000). On being 'just friends': The frequency and impact of sexual activity in cross-sex friendships. *Journal of Social and Personal Relationships, 17*(2), 205–222

Afifi, W. A., & Johnson, M. L. (1999). The use and interpretation of tie signs in a public setting: Relationship and sex differences. *Journal of Social and Personal Relationships, 16*(1), 9–38.

Allan, G. (1989). *Friendship: Developing a sociological perspective.* Boulder, CO: Westview.

Argyle, M., & Furnham, A. (1983). Sources of satisfaction and conflict in long-term relationships. *Journal of Marriage and the Family, 34,* 481–493.

Bank, B. J., & Hansford, S. L. (2000). Gender and friendship: Why are men's best same-sex friendships less intimate and supportive? *Personal Relationships, 7,* 63–78.

Baumgarte, R., Lee, N.-M., & Kulich, S. (1999). *Cross-gender friendships in five cultures.* Unpublished manuscript.

Baumgarte, R., Lee, N.-M., & Kulich, S. (2001). Friendship patterns among university students in five cultures. *The International Scope Review, 3,* [Online serial]. Available at www.internationalscope.com.

Baxter, L. A., & Wilmot, W. W. (1984). "Secret tests": Social strategies for acquiring information about the state of the relationship. *Human Communication Research, 11*(2), 171–201.

Baxter, L. A., & Wilmot, W. W. (1985). Taboo topics in close relationships. *Journal of Social and Personal Relationships, 2,* 253–269.

Berger, C. R., & Calabrese, R. J. (1975). Some explorations in initial interaction and beyond: Toward a developmental theory of interpersonal communication. *Human Communication Research, 1,* 99–112.

Bleske, A. L., & Buss, D. M. (2000). Can men and women be just friends? *Personal Relationships, 7,* 131–151.

Booth, A., & Hess, E. (1974). Cross-sex friendship. *Journal of Marriage and the Family, 36,* 38–47.

Bradae, J. J. (1983). The language of lovers, flovers, and friends: Communicating in social and personal relationships. *Journal of Language and Social Psychology, 2,* 141–162.

Buhrke, R. A., & Fuqua, D. R. (1987). Sex differences in same- and cross-sex supportive relationships. *Sex Roles, 17*(5/6), 339–352.

Burleson, B. R. (1997). A different voice on different cultures: Illusion and reality in the study of sex differences in personal relationships. *Personal Relationships, 4,* 229–241.

Canary, D. J., Emmers-Sommer, T. M., & Faulkner, S. (1997). *Sex and gender differences in personal relationships.* New York: Guilford.

Cates, R. M., & Lloyd, S. A. (1992). *Courtship.* Newbury Park, CA: Sage.

Cupach, W. R., & Metts, S. (1991). Sexuality and communication in close relationships. In K. McKinney & S. Sprecher (Eds.), *Sexuality in close relationships* (pp. 93–110). Hillsdale, NJ: Lawrence Erlbaum Associates.

Dindia, K., & Allen, M. (1992). Sex differences in self-disclosure: A meta-analysis. *Psychological Bulletin, 112,* 106–124.

Duck, S. (1994). *Meaningful relationships: Talking, sense, and relating.* Thousand Oaks, CA: Sage.

Egland, K. L., Spitzberg, B. H., & Zormeier, M. M. (1996). Flirtation and conversational competence in cross-sex platonic and romantic relationships. *Communication Reports, 9*(2), 105–117.

Fehr, B. (1996). *Friendship processes.* Thousand Oaks, CA: Sage.

Guerrero, L. K. (1997). Nonverbal involvement across interactions with same-sex friends, opposite-sex friends and romantic partners: Consistency or change? *Journal of Social and Personal Relationships, 14*(1), 31–58.

Hacker, H. M. (1981). Blabbermouths and clams: Sex differences in self disclosure. *Psychology of Women Quarterly, 5,* 385–401.

Helgeson, V. S., Shaver, P., & Dyer, M. (1987). Prototypes of intimacy and distance in same-sex and opposite-sex relationships. *Journal of Social and Personal Relationships, 4*, 195–233.

Hess, B. (1979). Sex roles, friendship, and the life course. *Research on Aging, 1*, 494–515.

Huyck, M. H. (1982). From gregariousness to intimacy: Marriage and friendship over the adult years. In T. M. Field, A. Huston, H. C. Quay, L. Troll, & G. E. Finley (Eds.), *Review of human development* (pp. 471–484). New York: Wiley.

Kaplan, D. L., & Keys, C. B. (1997). Sex and relationship variables as predictors of sexual attraction in cross-sex platonic friendships between young heterosexual adults. *Journal of Social and Personal Relationships, 14*(2), 191–206.

Lampe, P. E. (1985). Friendship and adultery. *Sociological Inquiry, 55*(3), 310–324.

Leaper, C., Carson, M., Baker, C., Holliday, H., & Myers, S. (1995). Self-disclosure and listener verbal support in same-gender and cross-gender friends' conversations. *Sex Roles, 33*(5/6), 387–404.

Lobel, S. A., Quinn, R. E., St. Clair, L., & Warfield, A. (1994). Love without sex: The impact of psychological intimacy between men and women at work. *Organizational Dynamics, 23*, 5–16.

Maccoby, E. (1990). Gender and relationships: A developmental account. *American Psychologist, 45*, 513–520.

Maltz, D. N., & Borker, R. A. (1982). A cultural approach to male–female miscommunication. In J. J. Gumperz (Ed.), *Language and social identity* (pp. 196–216) Cambridge, UK: Cambridge University Press.

Martin, R. (1997). "Girls don't talk about garages!": Perceptions of conversation in same- and cross-sex friendships. *Personal Relationships, 4*, 115–130.

Martz, J. M., Verette, J., Arriaga, X. B., Slovik, L., Cox, C. L., & Rusbult, C. E. (1998). Positive illusion in close relationships. *Personal Relationships, 5*, 159–181.

McCormick, N. B., & Jesser, J. C. (1982). The courtship game: Power in the sexual encounter. In E. R. Allgeier & N. B. McCormick (Eds.), *Changing boundaries: Gender roles and sexual behavior* (pp. 64–86). Palo Alto, CA: Mayfield.

McWilliams, S., & Howard, J. (1993). Solidarity and hierarchy in cross-sex friendships. *Journal of Social Issues, 49*(3), 191–202.

Messman, S. J., Canary, D. J., & Hause, K. S. (2000). Motives to remain platonic, equity, and the use of maintenance strategies in opposite-sex friendships. *Journal of Social and Personal Relationships, 17*(1), 67–94.

Metts, S., Cupach, W. R., & Imahori, T. T. (1992). Perceptions of sexual compliance-resisting messages in three types of cross-sex relationships. *Western Journal of Communication, 56*(Winter), 1–17.

Monsour, M. (1992). Meanings of intimacy in cross- and same-sex friendships. *Journal of Social and Personal Relationships, 9*, 277–295.

Monsour, M. (1997). Communication and cross-sex friendships across the life cycle: A review of the literature. In B. R. Burleson & A. W. Kunkel (Eds.), *Communication Yearbook, 20* (pp. 375–414). Thousand Oaks, CA: Sage.

Monsour, M., Harris, B., Kurzweil, N., & Beard, C. (1994). Much ado about nothing: Challenges confronting cross-sex friendships. *Sex Roles, 31*, 55–77.

Murnen, S. K., Perot, A., & Byrne, D. (1989). Coping with unwanted sexual activity: Normative responses, situational determinants, and individual differences. *Journal of Sex Research, 26*, 85–106.

Murray, S. L., Holmes, J. G., & Griffin, D. W. (1996). The benefits of positive illusions: Idealization and the construction of satisfaction in close relationships. *Journal of Personality and Social Psychology, 70*, 79–98.

O'Meara, J. D. (1989). Cross-sex friendships: Four basic challenges of an ignored relationship. *Sex Roles, 21*, 525–543.

Rawlins, W. K. (1982). Cross-sex friendship and the communicative management of sex-role expectations. *Communication Quarterly, 30*(4), 243–352.

Rawlins, W. K. (1983). Negotiating close friendships: The dialectic of conjunctive freedoms. *Human Communication Research, 9*, 255–266.

Rawlins, W. K. (1992). *Friendship matters*. New York: Aldine de Gruyter.

Rawlins, W. K. (1993). Communication in cross-sex friendships. In L. P. Arlis & D. J. Borisoff (Eds.), *Women and men communicating* (pp. 51–70). Orlando: Harcourt Brace.

Reeder, H. M. (2000). 'I like you … as a friend': The role of attraction in cross-sex friendship. *Journal of Social and Personal Relationships, 17*(3), 329–348.

Reis, H. T. (1988). Gender effects in social participation: Intimacy, loneliness, and the conduct of social interaction. In R. Gilmour & S. Duck (Eds.), *The emerging field of personal relationships* (pp. 91–105). Hillsdale, NJ: Lawrence Erlbaum Associates.

Reisman, J. M. (1990). Intimacy in same-sex friendships. *Sex Roles, 23*, 65–82.

Rose, S. M. (1985). Same- and cross-sex friendships and the psychology of homosociality. *Sex Roles, 12*, 63–74.

Rose, S., & Frieze, I. H. (1993). Young singles' contemporary dating scripts. *Sex Roles, 28*, 499–509.

Rubin, L. B. (1985). *Just friends*. New York: Harper & Row.

Sapadin, L. A. (1988). Friendship and gender: Perspectives of professional men and women. *Journal of Social and Personal Relationships, 5*, 387–403.

Schneider, C. S., & Kenny, D. A. (2000). Cross-sex friends who were once romantic partners: Are they platonic friends now? *Journal of Social and Personal Relationships, 17*(3), 451–466.

Shotland, R. L., & Craig, J. M. (1988). Can men and women differentiate between friendly and sexually interested behavior? *Social Psychology Quarterly, 51*, 66–73.

Sorenson, S. B., Stein, J. A., Siegel, J. M., Golding, J. M., & Burnam, M. A. (1987). The prevalence of adult sexual assault: The Los Angeles epidemiologic catchment area project. *American Journal of Epidemiology, 126*, 1154–1164.

Sprecher, S., & Metts, S. (1989). Development of the "Romantic Beliefs Scale" and examination of the effects of gender and gender-role orientation. *Journal of Social and Personal Relationships, 6*, 387–411.

Stewart, E. C., & Bennett, M. J. (1991). *American cultural patterns: A cross-cultural perspective*. Yarmouth, ME: Intercultural Press.

Swain, S. O. (1992). Men's friendships with women: Intimacy, sexual boundaries, and the informant role. In P. M. Nardi (Ed.), *Men's friendships* (pp. 153–172). Newbury Park, CA: Sage.

Tognoli, J. (1980). Male friendship and intimacy across the life span. *Family Relations, 29*, 273–279.

Werking, K. (1997a). *We're just good friends*. New York: Guilford.

Werking, K. (1997b). Cross-sex friendship research as ideological practice. In S. Duck (Ed.), *Handbook of personal relationships (2nd ed.)*. New York: Wiley.

Winstead, B. A., Derlega, V. J., & Rose, S. (1997). *Gender and close relationships*. Thousand Oaks, CA: Sage.

Winter, D. G. (1973). *The power motive*. New York: Free Press.

Wright, P. (1982). Men's friendship, women's friendships and the alleged inferiority of the latter. *Sex Roles, 8*, 1–20.

7
Same-Sex Relationships

Andrew K. T. Yip
Nottingham Trent University

A person engaging in homosexual behavior therefore acts immorally. To choose someone of the same sex for one's sexual activity is to annul the rich symbolism and meaning, not to mention the goals, of the Creator's sexual design. Homosexual activity is not a complementary union, able to transmit life.... When they engage in homosexual activity they confirm within themselves a disordered sexual inclination which is essentially self-indulgent. As in any moral disorder, homosexual activity prevents one's own fulfilment and happiness by acting contrary to the creative wisdom of God.

There is morality between all sexual activity within a faithful, committed, and monogamous relationship between two people of any gender, regardless of whether or not it has received the stamp of approval from the Church or the State.

The above quotes represent two starkly contrasting views on homosexuality and same-sex relationships.[1] The former is taken from an official

---

[1]In this chapter, *homosexuality* is defined as erotic, emotional, and sexual attraction to, or preference for, same-sex members. Unless specified, it is used generally to refer to both male and female homosexuality. *Same-sex relationship*, on the other hand, refers to a close relationship involving two (although not necessarily so) same-sex members, over an extended period of time, with shared meaning between the partners regarding such a relational status. This distinction is important. Theoretically, it is probable for someone, throughout his or her life, to engage in fleeting and episodic homosexual relational behaviors (e.g., "cottaging" for (continued on next page)

statement of the Roman Catholic Church that labels the homosexual orientation or inclination as an "objective disorder," and genital acts between members of the same sex as "intrinsically disordered" (Congregation for the Doctrine of the Faith, 1986). The latter, on the other hand, was expressed by a respondent in a postal survey of Roman Catholics I conducted in the United Kingdom (Yip, 1997a). These two views, although framed exclusively by a Christian religious vocabulary, are nevertheless instrumental as I proceed to explore in general various aspects of the "inappropriateness" of same-sex relationships. I incorporate into the discussion some data drawn from my various research projects on non-heterosexual Christians in the United Kingdom.[2]

It is undeniable that same-sex relationships are in general faced with moral opprobrium and social disapproval. However, the level of disapprobation is contingent on the geographical, historical, and sociocultural contexts, as well as how different social audiences perceive these relationships. For instance, research evidence suggests that in Western societies the older generation is more intolerant of this issue than is the younger generation. In general, women are more tolerant of homosexuality compared to men; and lesbianism is more tolerated than male homosexuality. Religiously conservative people, on the other hand, are more disapproving compared to their religious liberal or nonreligious counterparts. People in cities are also found to be more tolerant of sexual diversity compared to their counterparts in the countryside (Baker, 1997; Johnson, Wadsworth, Wellings, Field, & Bradshaw, 1994). In addition, many would not mind tolerating same-sex relationships in the name of human rights, as long as they are conducted within the context of private life, but not in the public sphere. Neighbors of a same-sex couple might be polite enough to keep a respectable distance, but they might express disapproval if the same-sex partners start to display affection physically (e.g., hugging, kissing) on the front lawn! For homosexuals, therefore, the private represents the boundary of social tolerance (Richardson, 1996, 1998, 2000).

On the whole, I think it is accurate to argue that despite the increasing visibility and "normalization" of homosexuality through mass media and

---

[1](continued)   homosexual men) without establishing a "close or personal relationship" (as understood in the literature in this area). Unless absolutely necessary, I avoid using terms like *gay* and *lesbian*, which increasingly are subject to cross-cultural critique as being Western construction of *homosexual* (that they hold a distinct sexual identity, and invariably express this identity through their involvement in the same-sex community and political activism). This point is elaborated in the section on cultural and historical angles.

[2]The first project, using quantitative and qualitative methods, examines the dynamics of 68 gay male Christian partnerships in the United Kingdom. The second project involves a postal membership survey of Quest, the UK organization for gay and lesbian Roman Catholics. Most of the findings of these two projects have been published, and are referred to in this chapter. The third project involves 565 gay, lesbian, and bisexual Christians in the United Kingdom. All respondents completed postal questionnaires, and a subsample of 61 respondents was interviewed. The findings of this project are currently being published.

socio-political reform, same-sex relationships are still faced with distant and uninterested tolerance at best, and discrimination and even violence at worst. Underlying this is an entrenched perception that same-sex relationships are "inappropriate," both morally and biologically.

LEVELS AND BASES OF DISAPPROBATION

In Western societies, factors that accord same-sex relationship an "inappropriate" status can be examined on two levels. On the level of popular and religious discourses, the "inappropriateness" of same-sex relationships is predicated on an ideology of sexuality that defines heterosexuality as the sole morally and biologically acceptable form of human sexuality. This accords it a hegemonic position, thus authenticating it as *the* referential framework for the discourses of sexuality, intimacy, and erotic relating. This ideology problematizes other forms of human sexuality, because they depart from the "heterosexual norm." On this level, the disapprobation of same-sex relationships has little to do with the dynamics or nature of the *relationship* itself. What renders it problematic is the partners' *sexuality*, which is perceived as psychopathological and "deviant," whether it is practiced within a relationship context or not. Therefore, I would argue that, in order to understand the basis for the "inappropriateness" of same-sex relationships, we must first of all unpack the ideology of sexuality that defines homosexuality itself (as sexual orientation and behavior) as "inappropriate."

On the legislative level, however, the discourse seems to have moved forward to addressing same-sex relationships specifically, having accepted that homosexuals are entitled to the basic human right of forming relationships. Even then, a same-sex relationship is still not on equal footing with a heterosexual one. There remain elements that render it not as "appropriate" as a heterosexual one, for instance, in the area of childrearing. Thus, although certain governments (e.g., Iceland, Denmark, Norway, and Vermont in the United States) legally recognize same-sex relationships as "registered partnerships" or even accord them a "marriage" status, there are limits to such a concession. On this level, a same-sex relationship is not labeled as "inappropriate" because of the sexuality of the partners, but instead because it is an "inappropriate" context for certain aspects of "healthy" family life. Childrearing is an example *par excellence*.

It's Not Natural!

In Western societies, one of the most vehement arguments put forward for the disapproval of same-sex relationships is that homosexuality itself is against the God-ordained law of nature. A same-sex relationship therefore becomes the context that concretizes and affirms the partners' pathological or morally depraved sexuality. This is explicitly expressed by Christian religious authority structures, whose voice is the loudest among those who stigmatize homosexuality and same-sex relationships. This is clearly shown in the first quote that opens this chapter. (For a more detailed review of the Roman Catholic official documents regarding this issue, see Jordan, 2000. For a good discussion of official statements of other Christian denominations, see Brash, 1995; Hartman, 1996.) Of course, this ideology is also implicitly assumed by people in the street, who might not be entirely aware and questioning of the impact of the Judeo-Christian tradition on their values and beliefs about sex, sexuality, and relationships.

In the history of Western societies, Christianity was once a powerful force, both on the macro level of politics and government as well as on the micro level, in shaping individuals' moral conscience (Harrocks, 1997). Much of the normalized and naturalized notions and understanding of human sexuality that we take for granted are informed by this religious tradition. Viewed from this established ideological standpoint, homosexuality is unnatural because it falls outside the framework of normality that recognizes heterosexuality as the only natural human sexuality. Homosexuality (more specifically homosexual genital *acts*, on which the discourse seems to focus) involves partners of the same sex, and does not have the potential for procreation. Homosexuals themselves are perceived to be psychopathological, incapable of human intimacy and the formation of long-standing relationships. One of the most distorted stereotypes of gay men is that they live a life of casual and unfulfilling sexual promiscuity, unable to construct nurturing and committed relationships, which is reflexive of their own pathological sexuality.

We must not forget that it was as recent as 1973 when the American Psychiatric Association removed homosexuality from its official *Diagnostic and Statistic Manual of Mental Disorder.* Similarly, only in 1975 did the American Psychological Association declare that homosexuality does not imply impairment of judgment, stability, reliability, or general social or vocational capabilities (Isay, 1989). In spite of this, even a cursory examination of the ideological underpinnings of the Christianity-inspired "ex-gay movement" will show that such perception of homosexuals as psychologically maladjusted individuals continues to persist. This underlies the movement's attempt to "reform" homosexuals to leave "the homosexual lifestyle," with spiritual intervention.[3] Underpinning such an ideology is the conception of homosexuality as isolated sexual acts. It is a reductionist

---

[3]The broadly termed "ex-gay movement" embraces groups with various degrees of fundamentalism. Some groups insist that homosexuals should be "cured" and bisexuals should confine to heterosexual "practice." Other less fundamentalist groups assert that "curing" need not be a definite outcome. Thus, abstinence, with spiritual discipline, is a more realistic objective. In the United States, Exodus International and New Hope Ministry are prime examples. Within the United Kingdom, the Courage Trust and the Trust Freedom Trust are most well known. For a good evaluation of the ex-gay ministry, see Green, Harrison, and Innes (1996) and Ponticelli (1996).

view of homosexuality as mere nonprocreative genitalization, against the perceived norm of heterosexual marital intercourse. Such a view is incapable of conceiving same-sex relationship dynamics, beyond the sexual behavior of the individual partners.

Such a perception of homosexuality does not promote accurate understanding of same-sex relationships. It also contradicts what research evidence has consistently shown, that same-sex relationships can be a healthy and rewarding relationship alternative. In my survey of 565 nonheterosexual Christians in the United Kingdom, I found that 51.9% of the sample are in long-standing relationships ranging from one to 45 years, with a mean of 7 years and 5 months. Further, 86.9% consider a long-term committed relationship the most desired relationship arrangement, and only 1.9% considers casual and short-term relationship as such.

Nevertheless, I would like to turn now to the social construction of heterosexuality itself, for it is by examining what constitutes "normality" that we enhance our understanding of "abnormality." The binary or dualistic conception of human sexuality means that heterosexuality presupposes the complimentarity of a femininity and a masculinity. Human erotic desires are therefore defined as only desires of difference (thus heterosexual). Homosexual desires, on the other hand, are desires of sameness. This disrupts and transgresses the normative way of erotic relating. Homosexual relating therefore assumes an "Otherness" that is both disturbing and corrupting,[4] disrupting heterosexuality as the referential framework for human sexuality. In other words, homosexuality disrupts the normative understanding of sex, sexuality, intimacy, and erotic relating. In England, for instance, "buggery," legally defined as only possible between men, used to be a hanging offense because it signified an unnatural sexuality. This punishment, however, did not apply to sex between men and women (as natural and normal sexuality), no matter how abusive or violent the context within which that sex took place (Smart, 1996).

To some, the thought of two partners of the same sex in a relationship is simply off-putting. This is due to the normative understanding that such a relationship should involve partners of different sex, complementing each other to form a "union." Much of this is based on the traditional and implicit assumption of the "active-passive" or "dominant-submissive" model that could be traced back to Christianity, which constitutes the cultural heritage of Western societies. This assumption generates the misunderstanding that one of the partners in a same-sex relationship adopts the "feminine" role, whereas the other takes the "masculine" role. Many find it

---

[4]This is clearly demonstrated in the arguments put forward in the English Parliamentary debates by those opposing lowering of the age of consent for gay sex to 16. It was argued that lowering of the age of consent would be capitalized by older men to corrupt gullible young men. Interestingly, the same argument was not applied to the case of women.

off-putting to envisage such "gender inversion" within a gay male relationship, because one of the men behaves like a "woman." Ironically, a lesser
degree of "inappropriateness" is attached to a lesbian relationship, in
which, according to this model, one of the partners assumes a "man's" role.
Cross-gender behavior on the part of a woman has always been less censured compared to that of a man. This further illustrates the discrepancy in
social understanding of gender roles, and the ideological underpinnings of
the gender order and erotic relating.

In what is widely regarded as the first study of female homosexuality,
the following claim was made:

> Many lesbian relationships between two women become the equivalent of a hus-
> band–wife relationship. The mannish or overt lesbian likes to take on the role of
> the "husband" and generally attaches herself to a female partner who is feminine
> in physique and personality. She regards her mate as her "wife." (Caprio, 1954,
> p. 18; cited in Richardson, 1996, p. 3)

This description is, of course, based on an outdated assumption that is
not consistent with many cross-sex relationships in late modern society
(e.g., Beck & Beck-Gernsheim, 1995; Giddens, 1992), let alone same-sex
relationships. In the last two decades, there has been a growing corpus of
research evidence from both sides of the Atlantic showing that although
there are same-sex couples who choose to conform to this traditional
model, most aspire to an "ethic of equality." Many same-sex couples consider "best friendship," characterized by role reciprocity rather than role
complimentarity, as the most accurate description of the dynamics of their
relationships (e.g., Dunne, 1997, 1999; Huston & Schwartz, 1995;
Mackey, O'Brien, & Mackey, 1997; Weeks, Donovan, & Heaphy, 1999;
Weeks, Heaphy, & Donovan, 2001; Yip 1997b).

Another implicit assumption underlying the disapproval of same-sex relationships pertains to the mechanics of sex itself. Traditionally, sex acts are
unquestioningly defined as a heterosexual act, culminating in vaginal penetration. Thus, a normative sexual intercourse is understood as one that involves a man and a woman, culminating in his penis penetrating her vagina.
When this is used as the referential framework to perceive same-sex couples, particularly gay male couples, many automatically assume that it involves penetration of the anus, which they find repulsive to say the least.
Derogatory stereotypes and names about gay men illustrate this narrow
understanding of sexual activity. Research evidence shows that not all gay
male couples practice penetrative anal sex, or consider that indispensable
in a sexual intercourse (e.g. Johnson et al., 1994; Yip, 1997b).[5] Way back in

---

[5]In my own research on 68 gay male Christian couples (see Yip 1997b), "insertive anal sex" is
ranked fifth and "receptive anal sex" seventh on a list of 10 most frequently employed sexual techniques. At the top of the list is "receptive oral sex."

1976, Harry argued that "participation in gay sexual activities encourages sexual flexibility rather than the sexual role specialization that psychoanalytic or popular conceptions would have us believe" (1976, p. 151).

In recent years, heterosexuality has been subjected to rigorous critique and theorizing, demonstrating that heterosexuality is far from a "natural" sexuality, and that heterosexual relationships are the only form of "appropriate" relationships for humankind. Both the theoretical and empirical literature shows that heterosexuality "is institutionalized as a particular form of practice, and relationships, of family structure and identity" (Richardson, 1996, p. 2). This process itself is fraught with religious and political ideologies (for good critiques of heterosexuality from the feminist perspective, see Hawkes, 1996; Jeffreys, 1990; Richardson, 1996; and from a gay and lesbian perspective, see Katz, 1995; Kitzinger & Wilkinson, 1994; Segal, 1997). The following quotes encapsulate this body of critique that problematizes cultural assumptions of sex and sexuality:

> At the core of heterosexuality is the gendering of desire—the idea that we should be attracted to "the opposite sex." Because homosexuality involves the "wrong" choice of sexual partner, it has often been seen as a "gender disorder." (Jackson, 1999, p. 154)

> Heterocentrism lies at the heart of this system of prejudice [against homosexuals]. Heterocentrism leads to the conviction that heterosexuality is *the* normative form of human sexuality. It is the measure by which all other sexual orientations are judged. All sexual authority, value and power are centred in heterosexuality. (Jung & Smith, 1993, p. 14)

Recognized but not Equal

I have argued here that, on religious and popular levels, the "inappropriateness" of same-sex relationships rests primarily on the sexuality of the partners, rather than the nature of the relationship itself. Much of the discourse on this level remains within the "right and wrong" framework of homosexuality as sexual acts. It has not proceeded to addressing the "inappropriateness" of same-sex relationships. Nevertheless, recent legal and political discourses, located primarily within a "human rights" framework, show that on this level at least, some governments are extending some of the rights and benefits of heterosexual married couples to same-sex couples. What is conspicuously missing in this package of affirmation is the right to child adoption and parenting. This highlights the limit of legislative tolerance, that homosexuals have the rights to construct relationships and be accorded some rights and benefits. Seemingly vulnerable and gullible children, however, should be left out of the picture. Segments of society that support this express concern that children growing up in same-sex families would be confused about the parental roles, as a result of having two "mommies" or "daddies." In the worst scenario, children of same-sex families might be subjected to ridicule and ostracism in various social contexts such as school.

Underpinning this is the well-established view that the family structure most "appropriate" and healthiest for the nurturing of children is the traditional nuclear family. Parenting should involve a man and a woman. This, alas, marginalizes not only same-sex families, but also the burgeoning sector of single-parent families. It also diverts attention from the fact that a traditional nuclear family need not be a safe haven for children, given the high degree of reported child abuse in such a setting.

FUNCTIONS OF DISAPPROBATION

For those who disapprove of same-sex relationships, or homosexuality implicitly, social censure serves as a means to safeguard "family values" from the "moral decline" of an increasingly permissive and ambivalent society. This is clearly illustrated in public and political debates on the validity and the level of legal recognition that should be accorded to same-sex relationships. In the United Kingdom, this is clearly demonstrated in the debates on the age of consent and Section 28 of the Local Government Act in both the House of Commons and the House of Lords. Opponents to the repeal of Section 28, for example, label same-sex relationships as "pretended families," aspiring to be the "normal" (heterosexual) family, but nevertheless falling short of the ideal. Thus, the main function of the disapprobation of same-sex relationships is to prevent the perceived corrosive forces of homosexuality on the moral health of society.

From another standpoint, however, the disapprobation of same-sex relationships is a blatant sociopolitical attempt to silence sexual minorities and to deny them human rights, with the intention to maintain the hegemony of what Rich (1980) called "compulsory heterosexuality." In the same vein, Jeffreys (1990) argued that such an attempt aims to uphold "heteropatriarchy," a social order that privileges heterosexual men. Social policies, therefore, become instruments of disciplinary power used by the state to promote the normality of heterosexuality, and prevent the normalization of homosexuality by denying same-sex couples of social and economic resources taken for granted by heterosexual couples. From a Foucauldian perspective, such an ideology of sexuality normalizes and naturalizes cross-sex relationships, and in turn disciplines and punishes variant forms of close relationship and controlling their access to social and economic resources. (For a good application of this perspective, see Carabine, 1996. See also Foucault, 1979, 1990, from which Carabine drew heavily.) The institution of heterosexuality and cross-sex relationships—buttressed by the legal, religious, and political systems as "authorities of delimitation"—label same-sex relationships as "inappropriate" and therefore less (or not) deserving of legal and social support.

CULTURAL AND HISTORICAL ANGLES

Anthropologists and ethnographers have shown convincingly that social perception of, and therefore responses to, homosexuality and same-sex relationships vary cross-culturally (e.g., Blackwood, 1986; Blackwood & Wieringa, 1999; Hekma, 2000; Herdt, 1981, 1984; Murray, 1995; Murray & Roscoe, 1997; Schmitt & Sofer, 1992; Seabrook, 1999; Williams, 1992). The dominant contemporary understanding of homosexuality is predicated on Western understanding of sexuality, that an individual has a distinct sexual identity, primarily consistent with his or her sexual behavior. Thus, a person engaging in homosexual activity is assumed to possess a lesbian or gay identity, and the organization of his or her life is at least partially informed by this aspect of his or her identity. Yet, anthropological research demonstrates that, in certain cultures, homosexual activity takes place within a framework that is very different from that of the Western framework, and so are the social responses to it.

Homosexuality takes different forms of expression. Some result in a significant and permanent relationship, and some are of a more transient nature. The opportunity to establish a relationship is much contingent on the social climate. In some sociocultural contexts, there are no safe meeting places for homosexuals, let alone legal and social resources for the establishment of a sustained relationship. In general, homosexuals in non-Western societies do not have such resources that their Western counterparts increasingly possess (I elaborate on this later). Thus, they encounter more difficulty in realizing their probable intention to establish open and long-standing relationships.

Greenberg (1988) stated that there are primarily three expressions of homosexual activity and relationships in various cultures and historical periods. The first is "transgenerational" (or what some call "age structured"), where one of the partners is significantly older than the other, and the former predominantly leads and shapes the nature of the relationship. This is prevalent in ancient Greek culture, sub-Sahara Africa, and some Melanesian cultures (e.g. Halperin, 1990; Murray, 1995).

The second is "transgenderal" (some prefer the term "gender-defined"), where one partner assumes an "active/dominant/masculine" role, and the other the "passive/submissive/feminine" role. The *berdache* in American Indian culture and the *hijra* in the Indian culture are good examples of partners playing the "feminine role," often donning woman's clothing. Another good example is men who play the *pasivo* role in some Mediterranean and Latin American cultures. In this case, the partner who is "active," unlike his "passive" counterpart, is not socially labeled as "homosexual" because he is playing an active role like a heterosexual man (see, e.g., Murray, 1995; Whitehead, 1993).

The last expression is most common in Anglo-European and American societies, where both partners are in general committed to the ethic of equality, with a high degree of role reciprocity, rather than role complimentarity that is characteristic of the first two. Murray (1995) also argued for a fourth expression, which is profession defined. A good example of this is a spirit healer who engages in homosexual activity with young dancing boys or actors.

As Herdt (1981, 1984) and many other anthropologists have shown, the social status of homosexuality and same-sex relationship on the morality spectrum is much contingent on social perception. In the Sambia tribe in New Guinea, for instance, homosexual activity between older men and young boys is part of the initiation process into manhood, without carrying any stigma. In that culture, younger boys perform oral sex on older men and swallow their semen as a symbol of buttressing their emerging masculinity, in preparation for the adult male role. When they are grown men, they form heterosexual relationships but initiate the next generation of boys through the same ritual. Such a cultural activity would be unthinkable in Western societies.

As we have seen in the case of Christianity, religion is a prominent cultural force that shapes the perception of homosexuality and same-sex relationship. It is therefore interesting to note that in some religious cultures, like that of Buddhism, another perception is evident. Cabezón (1993) and Runzo and Martin (2000) argued that Buddhism on the whole is neutral on the issue of homosexuality, thus more tolerant than, say, Christianity, of a variety of human sexual expression. Thailand is a very good example of such sexual tolerance.

Social historians have also made their contribution to demonstrate that the "inappropriate" status of homosexuality and same-sex relationships is not consistent across time and space. Boswell (1980)—who analyzed legal, literary, theological, and artistic sources in 12 languages—reported that in Roman society in the beginning of the Christian era, homosexuals did not constitute a distinguished group as we understand now, and homosexual practices were considered an ordinary part of human eroticism. Hostility to homosexuals in Western Europe only became noticeable between the 3rd and 6th centuries, with increased governmental regulation of private morality. It was not until the 12th century that explicit hostility to homosexuals was expressed in popular, theological, and legal literature. In another historical analysis, Boswell (1994) also noted the existence of Catholic and Orthodox liturgies for same-sex unions from Platonic Greece to Rome and Christianized Europe. These ceremonies, reminiscent of heterosexual nuptial services, seem to suggest that same-sex relationships were sanctioned religiously in Western Europe for a substantial period of time.

Using the same historicosociological approach, Leupp (1995) discovered that male–male sexuality was a highly institutionalized social phenomenon in Japanese society during the preindustrial Tokugawa period (1603–1868). Such sexuality was celebrated and practiced in formally organized institutions such as samurai mansions, *kabuki* theatres, and Buddhist monasteries. The male–male sexuality during this period seems to have taken the "gender-defined" and "age-structured" models, reflective of power hierarchy in the society. Leupp lamented that the disapproval of homosexuality and same-sex intimacy in modern Japanese society is primarily due to the import of Western homophobia. On the other hand, Thadani's (1999) analysis of ancient texts (e.g., the Rig Veda) also confirms that lesbian relating was accepted and more visible in the prepatriarchal Indian society prior to 1500 B.C. However, since the Islamic invasion of India between 500 B.C. and 1200 A.D., followed by British rule, female sexualities became more rigidly controlled. In modern India, there is no living language that describes woman-to-woman sexual and kinship relationships. Words that previously denoted female erotic bonding also lost their sexual meanings (see also Vanita & Kidwai, 2000).

In sum, anthropological and historical literature appears to show that there are variations in the forms and expressions of homosexuality across time and culture. Therefore, there are different "social scripts" for the expression of sexuality and sexual relationships. Similarly, what constitutes a same-sex relationship also varies, and the social response to it is therefore dependent on social perception. It is undeniable that homosexual relating is not "normative" (as a practice for the majority) in the known societies studied. However, evidence also suggests that the perception and responses to homosexuality and same-sex relationships within a society are socially constructed, subject to cultural and historical forces. The meaning of "appropriate" sexuality and relationship form is not constant. It shifts in response to social change. Even Western societies, whose Judeo-Christian tradition underlies their disapproval of this contentious issue, have to face up to the far-reaching and profound sociocultural changes in the sexual and moral landscape. To this theme we now turn.

TURNING THE TABLES

It is undeniable that the social perception of homosexuality and same-sex relationships is still beset with much prejudice and misunderstanding. Nevertheless, in certain parts of the late modern Western world at least, the situation is gradually improving. This is due to the burgeoning social confidence and visibility of homosexuals, as individuals and a community, coupled with the "normalization" of homosexuality in mass media and legislation (Neumaier, 2000). This takes place against a shifting moral and sexual landscape that recognizes the reality of increasing pluralism and diversity (Weeks, 1995). The meta-narrative that underpins the "inappropriateness" of homosexuality and same-sex relationship is therefore increasingly subjected to questioning and critique. In this last section, I present evidence to support my optimism that the level of disapprobation for same-sex relationships is decreasing, as the basis of its "inappropriateness" is gradually being weakened.

On a religious (specifically Christian) level, the traditional stance of Church authorities has been subjected to vigorous theological scrutiny. The last two decades have witnessed the growth of gay- and lesbian-affirming literature that constitutes a credible reverse discourse, challenging and weakening the moral authority and intellectual rigor of the Churches' dominant discourse on homosexuality and same-sex relationships (e.g., Sample & DeLong, 2000; Seow, 1995; Stuart, 1995). This corpus of literature affirms the compatibility of homosexuality and Christianity, and that same-sex relationships, like heterosexual relationships, have the potential for spiritual nurturing and growth. Theologians argue that Churches' "theology of sexual acts" must give way to a more wholesome "theology of relationships." The latter emphasizes interpartner mutuality, relationality, and emotional commitment, and not what people do in bed. It further argues that it is the quality, rather than the sexual form, of a relationship, that should be the criterion for the evaluation of acceptability (John, 1993; Nelson, 1992; Shallenberger, 1998; Stuart, 1996; Waun, 1999). The Churches increasingly find such reverse discourse unavoidable in the assessment of their own official stances.

Among lay believers, there are also signs that individuals are increasingly inclined to reevaluate the traditional Christian stance on this issue. Homosexual Christian groups and organizations report an increase in the number of heterosexuals expressing support for homosexuals in monogamous, faithful, and stable same-sex relationships, because, in their view, these are the important Christian values worth affirming.

I believe that in years to come, the Churches will draw up official lines that are less vocal about the "inappropriateness" of same-sex relationship, although, unlike other "secular" institutions, the religious authority structures will be slow in affirming such a relationship. This sense of confidence is demonstrated on an individual level, illustrated by the following quotes, taken from my own research (Yip, 2000):

> I endeavour to be Christian and I try to incorporate Christian principles into my life. It has got to influence the way I live with [his partner], the way I treat [his partner]. When we had problems in the relationship, I prayed for the relationship, and eventually things had been improved. And that's what made me convinced in myself. I have received help in this relationship when we needed it. If what we are doing is totally against God, he wouldn't have answered my prayers.

God created us in his own image, homosexual. He doesn't make mistakes. Our essential Christian vocation is the same as everyone else's, to receive love and to give love. Most human beings are clearly called to a loving sexual, one-to-one relationship with another. We are, too. It is our duty to fulfil our vocation to give love and to receive love in stable relationships. The church is quite wrong in what it says about this.

These narratives typify those of the vast majority of respondents in my various research projects, illustrating the confidence and maturity that they have developed in rattling the cage of religious orthodoxy. Monolithic religious dogma and moral absolutes that affirm "heteronormativity" and impose "compulsory heterosexuality" are subjected to sophisticated reverse discourse. Religious authority structures are increasingly pressured to respond in a more positive way, not just in the area of homosexuality, but also other moral and sexual matters. The important point is, if religious nonheterosexuals, who operate within arguably the most stigmatizing of environments (i.e., the Christian community), could arrive at this positive stage, their nonreligious counterparts would probably arrive at this stage even earlier and more confidently.

This is demonstrated in the rapid growth of safe geographical space for the homosexual community. Organizations such as Stonewall in the United Kingdom (more so in the case of North America) have developed sophisticated strategies to effect positive legal and political changes. Businesses, on the other hand, are increasingly aware of the power of the "pink pound." As the economic and political power of this community continues to grow, so do their visibility and the process of "normalization" (Adam, Duyvendak, & Krouwel, 1999; Blasius & Phelan, 1997; Mabry & Theil, 1996).

Weeks (1993) argued that homosexuality is increasingly tolerated in late modern society because of three main factors. The first factor pertains to the secularization of sex. There has been a constant shift of authority from religious structures to "secular" structures (e.g., the medical and psychiatric professions) in defining the normality of sexuality. Many would consider the Churches' discourse outdated, predicated on the interpretation of ancient texts. It lacks the scientific credibility of discourses within the medical and psychological fields, predicated on the lived experiences of homosexuals themselves.

I personally believe that religious authorities will encounter greater challenge as sociological research continues to produce evidence to support the workability and strength of same-sex relationships, which is capable of informing social policy. On the other hand, psychological research continues to demonstrate that being homosexual does not damage one's ability to function as a healthy and fulfilled human being. This kind of development will change the course of debate, and increases the level of social acceptance for same-sex relationships.

The second factor is the liberation of attitudes toward sexual and moral matters. Although the conservative segment of the society might label such development as moral decline, most people are increasingly aware that the well-established understanding of sexuality is somewhat limited, and that a greater degree of tolerance for difference is called for. Such liberal attitudes are often wrapped within a vocabulary of political correctness and social inclusion (Power, 1998).

Finally, the late modern society in which we live poses to us a challenge of diversity. People are becoming increasingly informed about the existence of diverse lifestyles, and the importance of respecting one another's privacy. People are inclined to see same-sex relationships as "alternative families" or "families of choice," capable of love, stability, and growth, just as with heterosexual relationships. This challenge of diversity is much helped by the increased and more positive representation of homosexuals in the mass media, particularly television and films. All this contributes to the reduction of prejudice (Ellis & Vasseur, 1993).

I do share Weeks' optimism. These developments are enveloped within a late modern society with significant characteristics. One of these is the shift of authority from without (e.g., religious authority structures) to within, namely, the self (Heelas, 1996). In an increasingly detraditionalized, diverse, and risk-laden society, life decisions and choices are made increasingly on the basis of self-reflexivity, rather than traditions and structures. What authenticates one's existence and being is primarily personal experience, and not external structures (Bauman, 1999; Giddens, 1991; Giddens & Pierson, 1998).

In a postal survey I conducted, involving 565 nonheterosexual Christians in the United Kingdom (see footnote 2), almost 81.9% of the respondents consider "personal experience" the most important element of their religious identity, against 16.8% who consider "church authority" to be primary. Similarly, 78.2% consider "personal experience" the most important basis of their sexual ethics, against 9.7% who rate "church authority" as the most important. What this kind of research evidence shows is that the individual's reliance on the self rather than authority structures reduces the moral authority and credibility of the Churches' grand narrative. The following narratives, drawn from various research projects (e.g., Yip, 1997c, 1999), consistently illustrate this point:

I think basically on sexuality as a whole they [the Church] are screwed up and they have got it wrong. The spirit is somehow for some reasons not revealed through the Church as a whole. They have got the issue wrong.

One has to go by one's own conscience. I don't pay much attention to what church leaders say because they can be wrong. They have been wrong in the past about other things. It's rather like contraception. A lot of good Christian people practice birth control. They just think the Vatican is wrong on that particular thing. I think that is the case with being gay. I think they have no experience with gay people. I think any institution that is run by professional bachelors is a bit odd. They have just this thing about sex. I think things have got to change there.

You have to use your reason to think and evaluate the situation. You read the bible, and you ought to ask yourself, "Why was it written, and in what context was it written?" … You then tie this to your personal experience, which itself needs to be governed by objectivity. As for church authority, well, take it with a bucket of salt. You are an autonomous human being. You are real and your freedom is valuable. You don't jump just because the church authority tells you to. God gives you these gifts. Use them and not be submissive to any church authority. Exercise responsibility, and take into account the fact that you are a person in your own right, who is loved by god and who is responsible to god.

There are also positive developments in the wider "secular" society. Already we witness that the commercial sector is becoming more open in recognizing employees in same-sex relationships. For instance, Sainsbury's, one of the larger supermarket chains in the United Kingdom, announced in September 2000 that it would extend pension rights and employment benefits to their employees in same-sex relationships. British Airways is another big corporation that demonstrates such a commitment. Businesses targeting specifically at homosexuals, including those in same-sex relationships, are growing. This is very much a response to the economic reality that gay male couples, who are primarily without children, have the highest disposable income and spend a larger proportion of income on leisure compared to other types of couples. These changes contribute toward the "normalization" of homosexuality and same-sex relationships.

The birth of the Human Rights Act in the United Kingdom on October 2, 2000, incorporating the European Convention on Human Rights, also signposts a positive development in this process of "normalization." This has been hailed as the biggest change to UK law since the 1688 Bill of Rights. This act, which upholds 16 articles on basic human rights, provides same-sex couples increasing recourse to seek legal protection under Article 8: "the right to respect for a private and family life." Legal observers are optimistic that this act will in many ways contribute to the increasing recognition and acceptance of same-sex relationships (e.g., Campbell, 2000a, 2000b; Hamilton, 1998). On September 4, 2001, the mayor of London launched the Partnerships Register for both cross-sex and same-sex couples. One lesbian couple and one gay male couple participated in this historic event, to wide media coverage. Although this Register does not confer any legal rights, it is a symbolically significant step that will pave the way for important legal reform.

Other European countries and the state of Vermont in the United States have gone even further in legalizing same-sex relationships. In 1989, Denmark became the first country in the world to legalize "registered partnerships" for same-sex couples. This guarantees same-sex couples all the rights accorded to heterosexual married couples, except in the area of child adoption. Other European countries (i.e., Iceland, Norway, Finland, the Netherlands, Germany, France, and Sweden) have since followed suit. On the other hand, in March 1999, the state of Vermont in the United States began to issue marriage licences to same-sex couples to form "civil unions" that entitle them to 300 state benefits or privileges available to married people. Going one step further, on April 1, 2001, the Netherlands, fundamentally reformed their civil marriage laws. The phrase *husband and wife* in the laws was replaced with the word *partners*, thus effectively making marriage legal and equal for both heterosexuals and homosexuals (including the right to adopt children). This is a first in the world, and a significant step forward compared to the "registered partnerships" currently on offer in other countries.

It must be mentioned that we should not assume that all homosexuals are in favor of same-sex marriage. Although the extension of legal protection and rights to same-sex couples is enthusiastically welcomed, many object to the notion of marriage as a "heterosexual model" for relationship. Space does not permit a detailed discussion on this. Suffice it to say that such a reality needs to be recognized in order to understand the diversity within the homosexual community (for good discussions on this, see Oliver, 1996; Sullivan, 1997). The significant point is that, as the debate of homosexuality and same-sex relationship moves from a predominantly religious framework to a medical/psychiatric framework and then to one of human rights, same-sex relationships will lose much of their stigma.

As homosexuality and same-sex relationship are normalized and incorporated into mainstream society and social policy, the level of social disapprobation will decrease. Of course, there will always be segments of the society, subjecting themselves to the forces of conservatism, that attempt to swim against these social currents. However, evidence from different fields, and most of all the late modern society that cherishes diversity and difference, will slowly but surely embrace same-sex relationships as just a variant relationship form, chosen by individuals whose rights need to be protected.

SUMMARY

Notwithstanding the increasing social visibility of homosexuality in Western societies, same-sex relationships are still generally labeled as "inappropriate," or even sinful and pathological. This "inappropriate" status is primarily predicated on the predominant ideology that naturalizes and normalizes heterosexuality as the only morally and biologically acceptable sexuality. Heterosexuality has long been supported religiously, particularly by Christianity, as *the* sexuality for humankind. Thus, same-sex relationships are perceived, particularly by the religiously and politically conservative quarters, as the expression of a psychopathological and "deviant" sexuality that does not have the potential for procreation, and against the law of nature. Such ideology serves to silence diversity in erotic relating and relationship forms. Nevertheless, in recent years, such social perceptions have been subjected to increasing academic and popular critiques. Anthropologists and historians confirm that the perception and treatment of same-sex sexuality and relationships vary cross-culturally. Theologians also expose the misunderstanding and homophobia embedded in the moral meta-narratives of the Churches about the "inappropriateness" of same-sex relationships. Psychologists and sociologists, on the other hand, show that same-sex relationships can be as fulfilling and positive as are cross-sex relationships. These positive changes, alongside the increased economic and political power of the homosexual community and the legal reform initiated by some governments, "normalize" homosexuality and same-sex relationships. This process of "normalization" is also aided by the increasing awareness and acceptance of sexual diversity and moral pluralism in late modern society.

REFERENCES

Adam, B. D., Duyvendak, J. W., & Krouwel, A. (1999). *The global emergence of gay and lesbian politics: National imprints of worldwide movement*. Philadelphia: Temple University Press.

Baker, M. (1997). *Sex lives: A sexual self-portrait of America*. New York: Pocket Books.

Bauman, Z. (1999). *In search of politics*. Cambridge, UK: Polity.

Beck, U. , & Beck-Gernsheim, E. (1995). *The normal chaos of love*. Cambridge, UK: Polity.

Blackwood, E. (1986). *The many faces of homosexuality: Anthropological approaches to homosexual behavior*. New York: Haworth.

Blackwood, E., & Wieringa, S. E. (1999). *Female desires: Same-sex relations and transgender practices across cultures*. New York: Columbia University Press.

Blasius, M., & Phelan, S. (1997). *We are everywhere: A historical sourcebook of gay and lesbian politics*. London: Sage.

Boswell, J. (1980). *Christianity, social tolerance and homosexuality*. Chicago: University of Chicago Press.

Boswell, J. (1994). *Same-sex unions in premodern Europe*. New York: Villard.

Brash, A. (1995). *Facing our differences: The churches and their gay and lesbian members*. Geneva: World Council of Churches.

Cabezón, J. I. (1993). Homosexuality and Buddhism. In A. Swidler (Ed.), *Homosexuality and world religions* (pp. 81–101). Valley Forge, PA: Trinity.

Campbell, R. (2000a, July). Family matters. *Gay Times*, pp. 72–73.

Campbell, R. (2000b, August). No Kidding. *Gay Times*, pp. 54–55.

Caprio, F. (1954). *Female homosexuality: A psychodynamic study of lesbianism*. New York: Citadel.

Carabine, J. (1996). Heterosexuality and social policy. In D. Richardson (Ed.), *Theorising heterosexuality* (pp. 55–74). Buckingham, UK: Open University Press.

Congregation for the Doctrine of the Faith. (1986). *Letter to the bishops of the Catholic Church on the pastoral care of homosexual persons*. London: Catholic Truth Society.

Dunne, G. A. (1997). *Lesbian lifestyles: Women's work and the politics of sexuality*. London: Macmillan.

Dunne, G. A. (1999). A passion for "sameness"?: Sexuality and gender accountability. In E. B. Silva & C. Smart (Eds.), *The new family?* (pp. 66–82). London: Sage.

Ellis, A. L., & Vasseur, R. B. (1993). Prior interpersonal contact with and attitudes towards gays and lesbians in an interviewing context. *Journal of Homosexuality, 25*, 31–46.

Foucault, M. (1979). *Discipline and punish*. London: Penguin.

Foucault, M. (1990). *The history of sexuality (Volume 1: An introduction)*. New York: Vintage.

Giddens, A. (1991). *Modernity and self-identity*. Cambridge, UK: Polity.

Giddens, A. (1992). *Transformation of intimacy*. Cambridge, UK: Polity.

Giddens, A., & Pierson, C. (1998). *Conversations with Anthony Giddens: Making sense of modernity*. Cambridge, UK: Polity.

Green, T., Harrison, B., & Innes, J. (1996). *Not for turning: An enquiry into the ex-gay movement*. London: Authors.

Greenberg, D. F. (1988). *The construction of homosexuality*. Chicago: University of Chicago Press.

Halperin, D. (1990). *One hundred years of homosexuality and other essays on Greek love*. New York: Routledge.

Hamilton, A. (1998, January). New law, new rights? *Gay Times*, pp. 31–37.

Harrocks, R. (1997). *An introduction to the study of sexuality*. Basingstoke, UK: Macmillan.

Harry, J. (1976). On the validity of typologies of gay males. *Journal of Homosexuality, 2*, 143–152.

Hartman, K. (1996). *Congregations in conflict: The battle over homosexuality*. New Brunswick, NJ: Rutgers University Press.

Hawkes, G. (1996). *A sociology of sex and sexuality*. Buckingham, UK: Open University Press.

Heelas, P. (1996). Introduction: Detraditionalization and its rivals. In P. Heelas, S. Lash, & P. Morris (Eds.), *Detraditionalization: Critical reflections on authority and identity*. Oxford, UK: Blackwell.

Hekma, G. (2000). Queering anthropology. In T. Sandfort, J. Schuyf, J. W. Duyvendak, & J. Weeks (Eds.), *Lesbian and gay studies: An introductory, interdisciplinary approach* (pp. 81–97). London: Sage.

Herdt, G. (1981). *Guardians of the flute*. New York: McGraw-Hill.

Herdt, G. (1984). *Ritualized homosexuality in Melanesia*. Berkeley: University of California Press.

Huston, M., & Schwartz, P. (1995). The relationships of lesbians and gay men. In: J. T. Wood & S. Duck (Eds.), *Understudied relationships* (pp. 89–121). London: Sage.

Isay, R. A. (1989). *Being homosexual: Gay men and their development*. Harmondsworth, UK: Penguin.

Jackson, S. (1999). *Heterosexuality in question*. London: Sage.

Jeffreys, S. (1990). *Anticlimax: A feminist perspective on the sexual revolution*. London: Women's Press.

John, J. (1993). *Permanent, faithful, stable: Christian same-sex partnerships*. London: Affirming Catholicism.

Johnson, A. N., Wadsworth, J., Wellings, K., Field, J., & Bradshaw, S. (1994). *Sexual attitudes and lifestyles*. Oxford, UK: Blackwell.

Jordan, M. D. (2000). *The silence of Sodom: Homosexuality in modern Catholicism*. Chicago: University of Chicago Press.

Jung, P. B., & Smith, R. F. (1993). *Heterosexism: An ethical challenge*. New York: New York University Press.

Katz, J. N. (1995). *The invention of heterosexuality*. New York: Dutton.

Kitzinger, C., & Wilkinson, S. (1994). Virgins and queers: Rehabilitating heterosexuality? *Gender and Society, 8*, 444–463.

Leupp, G. P. (1995). *Male colors: The construction of homosexuality in Tokugawa Japan*. Berkerley: University of California Press.

Mabry, M., & Theil, S. (1996, July 15). Getting used to it: Reality overtakes an old debate between gays in Europe. *Newsweek*, pp. 14–15.

Mackey, R. A., O'Brien, B. A., & Mackey, E. F. (1997). *Gay and lesbian couples: Voices from lasting relationships*. Westport, CT: Praeger.

Murray, S. O. (1995). *Latin American male homosexualities*. Albuquerque: University of New Mexico Press.

Murray, S., & Roscoe, W. (1997). *Islamic homosexualities: Culture, history, and literature*. New York: New York University Press.

Nelson, J. B. (1992). *Body theology*. Louisville, KY: Westminster John Knox Press.

Neumaier, J. (2000, October 15). Great to be gay? *The Observer (Focus Section)*, p. 18.

Oliver, J. (1996). Why gay marriage? *Journal of Men's Studies, 4*, 209–224.

Ponticelli, C. M. (1996). The spiritual warfare of Exodus: A postpositivist research adventure. *Qualitative Inquiry, 2*, 198–219.

Power, C. (1998). The outing of Europe. *Newsweek, 23*, 32–37.

Rich, A. (1980). Compulsory heterosexuality and lesbian existence. *Signs, 5*, 631–660.

Richardson, D. (1996). *Theorising heterosexuality*. Buckingham, UK: Open University Press.

Richardson, D. (1998). Sexuality and citizenship. *Sociology, 32*, 83–100.

Richardson, D. (2000). *Rethinking sexuality*. London: Sage.

Runzo, J., & Martin, N. M. (2000). *Love, sex and gender in world religions*. Oxford, UK: Oneworld.

Sample, T., & DeLong, A. E. (2000). *The loyal opposition: Struggling with the Church on homosexuality*. Nashville, TN: Abingdon.

Schmitt, A., & Sofer, J. (1992). *Sexuality and eroticism among males in Moslem societies*. New York: Harrington Park.

Seabrook, J. (1999). *Love in a different climate: Men who have sex with men in India*. London: Verso.

Segal, L. (1997). Sexualities. In K. Woodward (Ed.), *Identity and difference*. London: Sage.

Seow, C. L. (1996). *Homosexuality and Christian community*. Louisville, KY: Westminster John Knox Press.

Shallenberger, D. (1998). *Reclaiming the spirit: Gay men and lesbians come to terms with religion*. New Brunswick, NJ: Rutgers University Press.

Smart, C. (1996). Collusion, collaboration and confession: On moving beyond the heterosexuality debate. In D. Richardson (Ed.), *Theorising heterosexuality* (pp. 161–177). Buckingham, UK: Open University Press.

Stuart, E. (1995). *Just good friends: Towards a lesbian and gay theology of relationships*. London: Mowbray.

Stuart, E. (1996). Lesbian and gay relationships: A lesbian feminist perspective. In E. Stuart & A. Thatcher (Eds.), *Christian perspectives on sexuality and gender* (pp. 301–317). Leominster, UK: Gracewing.

Sullivan, A. (1997). *Same-sex marriage: Pro and con—a reader*. New York: Vintage.

Thadani, G. (1999). The politics of identities and languages: Lesbian desire in ancient and modern India. In E. Blackwood & S. E. Wieringa (Eds.), *Female desires: Same-sex relations and transgender practices across cultures*. New York: Columbia University Press.

Vanita, R., & Kidwai, S. (2000). *Same-sex love in India: Readings from literature and history*. New York: St. Martin's Press.

Waun, M. C. (1999). *More than welcome: Learning to embrace gay, lesbian, bisexual, and transgendered persons in the Church*. St. Louis, MO: Chalice Press.

Weeks, J. (1993). An unfinished revolution: Sexuality in the 20th century. In V. Harwood, D. Oswell, K. Parkinson, & A. Ward (Eds.), *Pleasure principles: Politics, sexuality and ethics*. London: Lawrence & Wishart.

Weeks, J. (1995). *Invented moralities*. Cambridge, UK: Polity.

Weeks, J., Donovan, C., & Heaphy, B. (1999). Everyday experiments: Narratives of non-heterosexual relationships. In E. B. Silva & C. Smart (Eds.), *The new family?* (pp. 83–99). London: Sage.

Weeks, J., Heaphy, B., & Donovan, C. (2001). *Same sex intimacies: Families of choice and other life experiments*. London: Routledge.

Whitehead, H. (1993). The bow and the burden strap: A new look at institutionalized homosexuality in native North America. In H. Abelove, M. A. Barale, & D. M. Halperin (Eds.), *The lesbian and gay studies leader* (pp. 498–527). New York: Routledge.

Williams, W. L. (1992). *The spirit and the flesh: Sexual diversity in American Indian culture*. Boston: Beacon Press.

Yip, A. K. T. (1997a). Dare to differ: Gay and lesbian Catholics' assessment of the official Catholic positions on sexuality. *Sociology of Religion, 58*, 165–180.

Yip, A. K. T. (1997b). *Gay male Christian couples: Life stories*. Westport, CT: Praeger.

Yip, A. K. T. (1997c). Attacking the attacker: Gay Christians talk back. *British Journal of Sociology, 48*, 115–129.

Yip, A. K. T. (1999). The politics of counter-rejection: Gay Christians and the church. *Journal of Homosexuality, 37*, 47–63.

Yip, A. K. T. (2000). Leaving the church to keep my faith: The lived experiences of non-heterosexual Christians. In L. J. Francis & Y. J. Katz (Eds.), *Joining and leaving religion: Research perspectives* (pp. 129–145). Leominster, UK: Gracewing.

IV
POWER-DISCREPANT RELATIONSHIPS

8

Inappropriate Therapist–Patient "Relationships"

Tanya Garrett
Reaside Clinic
and
University of Birmingham

Definitions

This chapter discusses the sexual abuse of patients by mental health professionals, principally psychotherapists. The term sexual *abuse* rather than sexual *relationships* is used because it is now commonly accepted that sexual contact between therapists and their patients, even, it may be argued, those who are discharged, is an abuse of the therapeutic relationship. There are a number of reasons for this, including the patient's emotional vulnerability and the negative effects of such sexual contact on the patient.

In this chapter, the terms *therapist* and *patient* are used, respectively, to describe a variety of professionals and the recipients of their services. To avoid repetition, the term *therapist* is intended to represent professionals, regardless of their professional background, who conduct what is referred to in the text as therapy (i.e., psychotherapy, psychological therapies, or counseling). The term *client* has frequently been advocated as an alternative to *patient*, but the latter is used here because of its traditional use in the psychotherapy literature, to which this research is most relevant, and because the professional–patient sexual contact considered here largely occurs in health service or medical settings.

In this chapter, reference is made to various levels of sexual interchange between therapist and patient. These include sexual attraction, sexual harassment, sexual contact, sexual violence, and sexual abuse. Sexual attraction toward patients occurs widely among therapists (Jehu, 1994) and is viewed as a natural process in therapy, provided it is not acted on. Sexual harassment is a broader issue, which may be defined as "unwelcome sexual advances, requests for sexual favours, and other verbal or physical conduct of a sexual nature" (Federal Register, 1980). Such behavior may be instigated by the therapist or by the patient, but such behavior on the therapist's part may be understood as an inappropriate use of the therapist's position. Thus, sexual harassment may be considered as an example of sexual abuse by therapists. Sexual contact with patients (e.g., kissing, genital exposure, touching the breasts, fondling the genital area, oral sex, and intercourse) is widely regarded as misconduct and is prohibited by most professional ethical codes (Jehu, 1994). Touching and hugging are less controversial and may not always include a sexual component (Jehu, 1994). Sexual violence may be defined as sexual contact by the therapist using physical force, threats, and/or intimidation (Pope & Bouhoutsos, 1986).

It has also been argued that there are parallels between therapist–patient sex, and rape and incest (Pope, 1990a). These include the power imbalance, secrecy and isolation (both emotional and physical), and the reaction of patients to sexual contact with their therapist, which includes guilt, shame, and self-blame (Bouhoutsos, 1985; Luepeker, 1989).

THE EXTENT OF THE PROBLEM

It is clear from North American research that sexual contact between psychotherapists and their patients is a significant problem, but that, like other forms of inappropriate sexual behavior such as rape and child sexual abuse, it is probably underreported. In the United States, half the money for professional malpractice cases is spent on complaints regarding sexual intimacy (Pope, 1991).

Approximately 13% of allegations of professional misconduct handled by the American Psychological Association insurance trust in 1981, and 18% of the complaints to the American Psychological Association ethics committee in 1982, involved sexual "offenses" against patients. Yet suits and complaints are rarely filed—in only about 4% of actual cases—and only half of these are completed (Bouhoutsos, 1985).

It would be reasonable to suggest that the studies discussed in this chapter provide important information, in terms of broad upper (e.g., Pope, Levenson, & Schover, 1979) or lower (e.g., Thoreson, Shaugnessy, Heppner,

& Cook, 1993) percentage levels, about the extent of the sexual abuse of patients by psychotherapists. However, there are a number of methodological limitations in the research that must be considered when interpreting it (Pope, 1990b).

Research studies in this area may include a number of biases, including cultural bias and volunteer bias. The most obvious bias is sampling bias—for example, the motivation of those who mail in surveys, in particular their motives to participate or not to participate. It is at present unclear how such factors may have influenced research findings. It might be argued, for example, that only those therapists who perceive their sexual contact with patients as having exerted a harmful effect on the patients would be motivated to participate, or indeed that only those therapists who viewed such contact in positive terms would be prepared to respond, perhaps because of their consequent lack of concern in disclosing.

In addition, the demographic characteristics of therapists who have sexual contact with their patients, particularly those who either do or do not return questionnaires, are unknown. Thus, it is problematic to draw inferences about the larger population of such therapists on the basis of such studies (Williams, 1992). In surveys, respondents may be prevented from responding at all, or from responding honestly by fear of lack of anonymity or confidentiality, even when these are assured by the researcher. Thus, the characteristics of those who do not respond to surveys are unknown, particularly in terms of the numbers who had sexual contact with patients. Furthermore, it is not clear how many of those who respond but claim to have had no sexual contact with patients may present a false picture in this respect. Those surveys offering a definition of sexual contact may inadvertently exclude some forms of therapist–patient sexual contact, thus restricting the "cases" reported.

Generally speaking, the U.S. epidemiological research has yielded no differences between the main statutory psychotherapy professions of psychology, psychiatry, and social work (Borys & Pope, 1989). There is a suggestion (Sonne & Pope, 1991) that the rate of sexual contact among marriage and family counselors and their patients may be significantly higher than that reported for psychologists, psychiatrists, and social workers. No information is as yet available to indicate the extent of sexual contact between other professionals or lay psychotherapists and counselors and their patients.

In North America at least, legal cases show that there have been approximately three times more malpractice cases involving psychiatrists than those involving psychologists (Perr, 1989), but this finding may be accounted for by the larger number of psychiatrists in practice. It would therefore be reasonable to consider the surveys of different professions as a whole.

Most surveys have found that, overall, under 10% of professional psychotherapists have had sexual contact with their patients. However, it is difficult to reach conclusions on the basis of these surveys. There are a number of reasons for this. Authors do not always distinguish between sexual contact with patients who were current and those who were discharged at the time of the sexual contact. Definitions of sexual contact differ from study to study, with some using sexual intercourse only as a definition (e.g., Holroyd & Brodsky, 1980), some offering less narrow definitions (e.g., Pope, Tabachnik, & Keith-Spiegel, 1987), and some allowing respondents to make their own definition (e.g., Pope et al., 1979).

Studies of psychiatrists, using various definitions of sexual contact, have generally found that some 6% to 7% disclosed that they had engaged in sexual contact with patients (e.g., Derosis, Hamilton, Morrison, & Strauss, 1987; Gartrell, Herman, Olarte, Feldstein, & Localio, 1986; Pope et al., 1979). The term *sexual contact* was not defined in Derosis et al. (1987) and Pope et al. (1979).

In surveys of psychologists, a rather broader range of figures have emerged, from 1.9% (Pope et al., 1987) through 4% (Rodolfa et al., 1994) to 6.5% (Pope, Keith-Spiegel, & Tabachnick, 1986). Although Holroyd and Brodsky (1980) found that 3.2% of respondents to their survey had had sexual intercourse with a patient, another 4.6% had engaged in other types of sexual behavior.

In a study of social workers, Gechtman (1989) found that 3.8% of respondents reported having "erotic" contact with clients. Although Thoreson et al. (1993) found that only 1.7% of their sample reported sexual intercourse or direct genital stimulation with current patients, a further 7% reported such contact with discharged patients. Presumably the figures would have been higher had a broader definition of sexual contact been adopted.

There is some suggestion that the rate of therapist–patient sexual involvement is declining in the United States (Pope, 1990b). However, this may depend on the way in which sexual contact is defined, and whether posttermination contacts are included in the figures. Most studies have not provided their respondents with specific instructions as to whether to include or exclude sexual contacts with patients in which the patient was already discharged when the sexual liaison began.

It is also problematic to draw inferences about actual changes in therapists' sexual behavior, because surveys do not specify when the sexual behavior occurred (Williams, 1992). In addition, reporting practices, particularly by male psychotherapists, may have changed over recent years (Stake & Oliver, 1991). This may be due to the increased publicity that has been accorded to the sanctions applied to sexually abusive professionals. Thus, Schoener (1991) concluded there is no evidence to suggest that a decline is taking place in the incidence/prevalence of therapist–patient sexual contact.

Williams (1992) suggested that a number of sources of information should be used when attempting to establish the prevalence of sexual contact. These include surveys of professionals, surveys of patients, and data from courts and professional ethics boards/state licensing boards (in the United States). There have been few published reports of the activities of state licensing boards. One notable exception is research by Gottlieb, Sell, and Schoenfeld (1988), who found that over a period of 3 years (1982–1985) the total number of complaints against psychologists of sexual impropriety *within* therapeutic relationships rose dramatically, by over 480%. In a fairly recent survey of the records of a large U.S. state's psychology licensing and disciplinary board over 28 months, Pope (1993) found 22 cases in which sexual contact with a patient led to the therapist being disciplined. In a survey of therapy clients who were clinical psychologists, it was found that almost 7% had been sexually involved with their therapists.

Few data are available regarding the problem of therapist–patient sexual contact in the United Kingdom. The only available data derive from the author's research with clinical psychologists (Garrett & Davis, 1998). The results of this survey, conducted in 1992, suggest a likely discrepancy between the rate of such contact as reported by therapists themselves and that reported by professionals in relation to their experience of other professionals and patients. Some 3.5% of respondents reported having had sexual contact with patients either in the course of therapy or following discharge. Almost a quarter reported that they had treated patients who had been sexually involved with previous therapists, and almost two fifths said that they knew (through sources other than patients) of other clinical psychologists who had had sexual contact with patients. A number of variables were associated with breach of sexual boundaries, of which three (homosexual orientation, sexual involvement with educators during postgraduate training, and longer postqualification professional experience) were significant predictors of sexual contact with patients.

SEXUAL ATTRACTION

It is well established in the literature that sexual attraction toward patients is very common. The research studies addressing this question have reported remarkably similar rates of such attraction, suggesting that only 12% to 15% of respondents never experience sexual attraction toward their patients.

Stake and Oliver (1991) found in their survey of licensed psychologists that 85% of respondents reported that they had felt sexually attracted to a patient. Pope, Keith-Spiegel, and Tabachnik (1987) noted that 86% of their psychologist respondents had experienced such attraction. In a survey of members of the American Psychological Association, Rodolfa et al. (1994) reported that only 12% of respondents reported never being attracted to any patient. Yet about half of those respondents who were attracted to patients reported that these feelings caused them discomfort, anxiety, or guilt. Similar frequencies of reported sexual attraction have been found among Dutch male gynecologists (85%) and ear, nose, and throat specialists (81%; Wilbers et al., 1992). In one study, a substantial proportion (68%) of respondents reported that if the particular patient was aware of their sexual attraction, they were more likely to view the therapy as harmed or impeded (Pope et al., 1986).

Rodolfa et al. (1994) reported that almost half of their psychologist respondents who had been sexually attracted toward patients felt that the attraction had, at least in some cases, been beneficial to the therapy. These assumed benefits included increased empathy for patients, enhanced awareness of transference and countertransference reactions, and improved awareness of patients' nonverbal behaviors. Slightly fewer believed that there had been some negative effects as a result of the sexual attraction. Examples of such negative effects were distraction from patient issues, problems in confronting patients, premature termination, or feelings of overinvolvement with the patient.

HISTORICAL PERSPECTIVE

The proscription of therapist–patient sexual contact can be traced back over many centuries to the Hippocratic oath, which states, "In every house where I come, I will enter only for the good of my patients, keeping myself far from all intentional ill-doing and all seduction, and especially from the pleasures of love with women and men" (cited in Pope & Bouhoutsos, 1986, p. 22).

In more recent times, the British mental health professions have maintained this prohibition indirectly by referring in their codes of ethics to the need for professional conduct that does not damage the interests of patients or public confidence in the profession (e.g., British Psychological Society, 1991). In Britain it is only very recently that sexual liaisons between therapists and their patients have been explicitly prohibited by some professional bodies (e.g., British Psychological Society Division of Clinical Psychology, 1996). In contrast, North American professions have for some time explicitly prohibited sexual contact with patients in their codes of conduct, and a number of American states have passed civil and/or criminal statutes making therapists' sexual involvement with patients an offense (Jorgenson & Schoener, 1994).

Historically, however, there were a number of sexual relationships between psychoanalysts and their patients in the early days of the development of psychoanalysis. Ferenczi, Horney, and Jung, for example, had sexual relationships with their patients (Field, 1999; Tansey, 1994). These behaviors were viewed at the time with mild disapproval among the psychoanalytic community. However, no sanctions were invoked against the offending therapists, although a sound theoretical basis for the taboo on therapist–patient sexual contact was well established in Freudian theory (Pope & Bouhoutsos, 1986). Freud concluded that analysis must be "carried though in a state of abstinence" (Field, 1999). Jeffrey Masson's important book *Against Therapy* (1988) documents some terrible sexual violations of patients by therapists. For example, Masson described legal action against John Rosen, a North American psychiatrist who apparently justified with therapeutic rationales coercive sex and other abuses with his patients. These included fellatio, forcing patients to eat his feces, and three-way sex with both adults and children.

In recent times in the United Kingdom, among the profession of clinical psychology at least and certainly within the recent extensive media coverage of the topic, it appears that the attitude toward sexual impropriety between therapists and their patients has begun to be regarded by some in quite pathological terms. Professionals who "offend" have become demonized and regarded as aberrant (e.g., Pilgrim, 1999). I have attempted to argue elsewhere (Garrett, 1999) that professional organizations should not "throw out the baby with the bathwater." Rather, attempts should be made to understand the process of the sexualization of the therapeutic relationship, particularly in the context of the lack of professional recognition of the problem, for example in training professionals. Evaluation systems should be in place to assess the "risk" of further inappropriate behavior by professionals and the prospect of occupational rehabilitation.

WHY SEX BETWEEN THERAPISTS AND PATIENTS IS INAPPROPRIATE

In recent years, there has accumulated an increasing body of empirical evidence to suggest that sexual contact between therapists and patients is usually harmful, and a burgeoning literature to argue its inappropriateness on a number of grounds.

Dual-Role Relationships

Sexual contact between therapist and patient is an example of a dual-role relationship (Kitchener, 1988). A dual-role relationship occurs when one or both members occupy two or more conflicting roles. Social psychology, and in particular role theory, has long recognized the strain caused by role conflict (Kitchener, 1988). Role conflict may arise from the stress experienced by the individual, from both incompatible obligations and different prestige and power associated with the roles. Failure to meet expectations regarding behavior, rights, and obligations that roles entail often leads to negative reactions in others. Kitchener (1988) asserted that those dual-role relationships that involve a high risk of harm to the client are unethical. In particular, Kitchener (1988) noted the finding from role theory that expectations are not consistently perceived; thus, a client may not share a professional's perception that his or her actions are consistent.

In the case of sexual contact between therapist and patient, the therapist fulfills the dual roles of therapist and lover. These roles are highly incompatible, and thus the therapist's objectivity and professional judgment are impaired. Role conflict may bring into question the ability of the professional to place the interests of the client above his or her own interests.

Parallels With Incest

Kardener (1974) argued that sexual contact between therapist and patient is similar to incest. Thus, it is suggested, as a consequence of the therapist's caretaker role with the patient, the patient is in a vulnerable position because of his or her disclosures to the therapist, his or her presenting problems, and the transference process (Pope & Bouhoutsos, 1986). Although the notion of a parallel between patients and children may be unpalatable in many respects, perhaps there are some useful parallels to be drawn that could strengthen the taboo on therapist–patient sexual contact.

Power Imbalance

Peterson (1992) maintained that boundary violations are the result of "the professional's attempts to equalise the power differential or discount the relationship. Such attempts alter the boundaries that protect the primacy of the client's needs" (Peterson, 1992, p. 4).

It may be argued that the power imbalance between therapist and patient renders any sexual contact exploitative. This power differential arises from the training, expertise, and social status of the therapist, versus the vulnerability of patients that results from needs they are unable to meet themselves (because of which they seek therapy). Even when the patient requests or initiates sexual contact, it is the duty of the treating professional to resist such advances in order to protect the patient (Sreenivasan, 1989). Sexual contact with a patient is usually connected with meeting the therapist's, rather than the patient's, needs (Hare-Mustin, 1974; Taylor & Wagner, 1976), which should never be the aim or purpose of therapy.

However, many professionals attempt to deny their authority or own their power, and this struggle with power is the primary psychological gateway through which boundary violations are created, argued Peterson (1992). Without the direction or leadership of the professional, the unreality of the client's expectations is not moderated. Consequently, the client may fill this void with his or her own agenda, thus paving the way for inappropriate behavior, as a direct result of the professional's refusal to accept the authority that is inherent in the role. If we eschew our authority as professionals, we falsely position ourselves and our clients as equal; thus, no one is in charge or responsible.

Unhelpful to Therapy

Saul (1962) maintained that sexual feelings toward the therapist should not be acted on because to do so would encourage the patient into a "blind alley" with regard to sexual and dependent needs for love. Rather, the patient needs to be helped by the therapist to find satisfaction in real life. Saul also suggested that sexual contact would be inappropriate because the essence of transference is the repetition of emotional patterns that cause patients difficulties. The therapist should, it may be argued, instead attempt to present a corrective image rather than repeat past maladaptive patterns.

Legal Issues

Sexual contact with patients is specifically legally prohibited, at least in some states in the United States (Pope & Bouhoutsos, 1986).

Impact on patients

There is considerable research evidence showing the damaging effects of sexual contact with a therapist on the patient (Pope & Bouhoutsos, 1986). Systematically gathered empirical data regarding the effects of therapist–patient sexual contact have only relatively recently become available. Traditionally, these relationships have been assumed to be harmful to patients (Marmor, 1972), but some writers have argued that such contact may be beneficial (e.g., McCartney, 1966). There is no evidence to suggest that sexual intercourse between a therapist and a patient is any more harmful than other forms of sexualized behavior, such as provocative statements or fondling (Keith-Spiegel & Koocher, 1985). Thus, all forms of behavior with sexual intent must be considered.

A review by Taylor and Wagner (1976) of every available case (34 in all at that time) in the literature of therapist–patient sexual contact, some reported by therapists, showed that the majority had negative or mixed effects on the patient, but 21% reportedly had positive effects.[1] However, this conclusion must be interpreted in the light of the empirical finding (Holroyd & Bouhoutsos, 1985) that psychologists who reported that no harm occurred to patients as a result of sexual encounters with their thera-

---

[1]The effects of sexual contact on the patient were established by Taylor and Wagner (1976) by rating "material presented in the case history, or by the patient's rating of the involvement" (p. 594).

pists are twice as likely themselves to have had sexual contact with a patient as are psychologists generally. Furthermore, psychologists who have been sexually intimate with patients are less likely to report adverse effects of sexual intimacy, either for patients or for therapy (Holroyd & Bouhoutsos, 1985).

In a survey of psychologists who treated patients who had been sexually intimate with a previous therapist, Pope and Vetter (1991) found that harm, both to the patient (e.g., adverse impact on personality functioning, psychiatric hospitalization) and to the therapist (e.g., marital breakdown, suicide attempts) had occurred in 90% of cases overall. Butler and Zelen (1977) concluded, on the basis of interviews with therapists who had had sexual contact with their patients, that "it was not a therapeutic experience for either patient or therapist" (p. 145). A similar conclusion was reached by Chesler (1972), who interviewed 11 women who had experienced sexual contact with their psychotherapist: "None of them was helped by their seductive therapists" (p. 144).

Feldman-Summers and Jones (1984) compared women who had had sexual contact with therapists, women who had had sexual contact with other health care practitioners, and women who had not had sexual contact with a professional. The first group had a greater mistrust of and anger toward men and therapists, and a greater number of psychological and psychosomatic symptoms than did the third group. The first two groups did not differ in terms of the psychological impact of the sexual contacts. The greater the reported prior sexual victimization (e.g., childhood sexual abuse or adulthood sexual coercion), the greater the impact of sexual contact with the professional. Mistrust of and anger toward men in general were greater when the abusive professional was married than when he was single. Patients who reported the greatest number of psychological and psychosomatic symptoms before treatment reported more symptoms after treatment with a professional with whom they had sexual contact than did those patients with fewer symptoms before treatment. Thus, the greater the historical emotional damage, the more devastating the impact of sexual contact with a therapist on the patient.

As a result of their work with patients who had sexual contact with their therapists, and of growing anecdotal reports in the literature (e.g., Schoener, Milgrom, & Gonsiorek, 1984) of the damaging effects of therapist–patient sexual contact, Pope and Bouhoutsos (1986) developed the concept of the "Therapist–Patient Sex Syndrome." This syndrome includes ambivalence (Schoener et al., 1984); guilt (Schoener et al., 1984); feelings of isolation and emptiness (Vinson, 1984, cited in Pope & Bouhoutsos, 1986); cognitive dysfunction (Vinson, 1984, cited in Pope & Bouhoutsos, 1986); identity/ boundary disturbance and inability to trust (Schoener et al., 1984; Voth, 1972); sexual confusion, lability of mood, and suppressed rage (Schoener et al., 1984) and increased suicidal risk (D'Addario, 1977, cited in Pope &

Bouhoutsos, 1986; Pope & Vetter, 1991). In addition, for patients with this syndrome, symptoms are increased (D'Addario, 1977, cited in Pope & Bouthoutsos, 1986; Voth, 1972) and hospitalization is frequently necessary (Pope & Vetter, 1991; Voth, 1972). Disturbances in patients' interpersonal relationships may also develop (Bouhoutsos, Holroyd, Lerman, Fover, & Greenberg, 1983; Voth, 1972).

THE ARGUMENT THAT THERAPIST–PATIENT SEXUAL CONTACT IS NOT INAPPROPRIATE

There have been a number of attempts to argue on theoretical grounds in favor of sexual contact with patients as a positive psychotherapeutic approach. McCartney (1966) argued for an extension of usual psychotherapy practice to include "overt transference" or allowing the patient to act on transference feelings by touching the therapist's body and, in some cases, engaging in sexual intercourse with the therapist. This, McCartney asserted, is appropriate in 10% to 30% of cases, where the patient needs to develop in maturity: here, the therapist is said to act as a parent-surrogate. McCartney suggested that such "treatment" should be restricted to heterosexual intercourse only.

A number of criticisms may be directed toward McCartney, calling into question his approach and theory. He rejected homosexuality as immature, neurotic, and adolescent, a view that holds little current credence in scientific circles, and he offered no other coherent argument for restricting therapist–patient sexual contact to heterosexual encounters. The validity of any therapy claiming that the therapist who engages in sexual contact with patients is acting as a parent-surrogate is undoubtedly questionable. There are many grounds for objecting to the view that sexual contact is necessary to enable patients to develop in maturity, not least is the damaging effect of such interactions (Taylor & Wagner, 1976). McCartney certainly took a limited perspective on the purposes and process of therapy, it would appear, to justify his aims. He provided grossly inaccurate information regarding the extent of his psychoanalytic practice, which, if true, would mean for example that he had spent more hours treating patients than are actually available in a working week. Tellingly, he was expelled from the American Psychological Association (Pope & Bouhoutsos, 1986).

Shepard (1971) concluded on the basis of interviews with patients who had been sexually intimate with their psychotherapists that "sexual involvement can be a useful part of the psychotherapeutic process" (p. 199). Indeed, it was so, he argued, in 8 out of 10 of the cases he considered. This conclusion was based on the patients' reports of the effect of the sexual contact, and on Shepard's own impression of whether or not the contact was helpful. He suggested guidelines for the therapist who is sexually involved with his or her patient to follow, and concluded that sexual involvement with patients should be "selective, meaningful and honest" (p. 208).

However, there is considerable evidence to demonstrate that therapist–patient sex is overwhelmingly harmful to the patient (e.g., Pope & Vetter, 1991). It is not clear whether Shepard himself engaged in sexual contact with his patients. If this was the case, his advocacy of therapist–patient sexual contact on the basis of his view that the outcome for the patient was positive may be questioned.

Another possible justification for sexual activity between patients and therapists is that such contact will prevent suicide in those vulnerable patients who are particularly likely to fall prey to sexual contact with their therapists (Gutheil, 1989). This argument was opposed by Eyman and Gabbard (1991), in a paper that aimed to show both that therapist–patient sexual contact actually led to a patient's suicide in one case, and that it cannot be justified as preventing suicide on legal, ethical, and clinical grounds.

It may be argued that to prohibit all sexual contact between therapists and patients, particularly former patients, is inconsistent with the promotion of equality between therapist and patient, and thus infantilizes the patient. Brown (1988) advanced several counterarguments to this viewpoint. First, and perhaps most important, it is largely therapists and not patients who advocate posttermination sexual contact as a mark of equality (Brown, 1988). Second, to draw a parallel between the therapist–patient relationship and the parent–child relationship, our society does not sanction sexual contact between parents and their adult children. This is because it is recognized that although the adult child may function in many respects as his or her parent's equal, there remains in their relationship some of the earlier significant power imbalance: "to make the former client's sexual availability to me serve as the hallmark of equality and complete recovery is a mockery of egalitarian principles" (Brown, 1988, p. 252).

Furthermore, when sexual contact occurs, the therapist's role changes and it is questionable whether he or she can retain appropriate therapeutic objectivity. It is also noteworthy that therapists are not qualified as competent lovers (if the rationale for the sexual contact is therapeutic) by virtue of their training (Hare-Mustin, 1974).

Therapists' Justifications

It appears that therapists may offer a distorted picture of the nature of their sexual contact with patients, in order to make it appear more acceptable, for example by inaccurately suggesting that the contact was initiated by the patient and began after termination of therapy. A number of rationalizations may be used by therapists to justify their actions, for example the notion that patients may actually benefit from sexual contact, as a "corrective emotional experience" (Herman, Gartrell, Olarte, Feldman, & Localio, 1987).

Sexual intimacy could be viewed by the therapist as acceptable, understandable, a mutual progression, or therapeutic. The therapist may fantasize that he or she is an exception to accepted ethical guidelines.

The responses given in surveys by those who state that sexual contact between therapists and their patients can be beneficial may assist the development of an understanding of the phenomenon. Herman et al. (1987) reported that 2% of their psychiatrist respondents believed that sexual contact with a patient can enhance the patient's self-esteem, provide a corrective emotional experience, treat a grief reaction, or change a patient's sexual orientation. Slightly more, 4.5%, believed that it could be useful in treating a sexual difficulty, and 4% believed that it could be appropriate if the patient and therapist were in love. Gechtman (1989) noted that 10% of social worker respondents believed that sex with a therapist may be beneficial to the patient. Some surveys report respondents' rationales for and evaluations of their own sexual involvement with patients. For example, Gartrell et al. (1986) found that most psychiatrists in their survey who reported sexual contact with their patients thought that the patients' experience of therapist–patient sex was positive. Pope and Bajt (1988) found that in 9% of such cases, psychologists argued that they had engaged in sexual relations with a patient for the treatment and welfare of that patient.

Of Butler and Zelen's (1977) 20 therapists who had had sexual contact with their patients, 90% reported that when the sexual contact occurred they were feeling vulnerable, needy, and/or lonely as a result of their own relationship difficulties. Some saw themselves as domineering and controlling (15%), but most (60%) viewed themselves as in a paternal relationship with the passive and submissive patient. Forty-five percent admitted to rationalizing in order to permit otherwise unacceptable behavior during therapy. Most experienced conflicts, fears, and guilt.

DISCHARGED PATIENTS

Sexual intimacy with discharged patients has, until recently, been little debated in the literature, and many surveys do not differentiate between sexual contact with current patients and with discharged patients.

In a study that did draw a distinction between current and former patients (Gartrell et al., 1986), 30% of respondents stated that they believed that posttermination sexual contact with patients would sometimes be acceptable. Interestingly, 74% of the psychiatrists in this study who had had sexual contact with patients believed that such contact would be acceptable, and indeed used this as a means of rationalizing their behavior. Indeed, it is possible that therapists may terminate treatment *in order* to engage in sexual contact with patients (Coleman, 1988).

In a survey of complaints regarding inappropriate sexual behavior filed to U.S. state licensing boards and psychological ethics committees between 1982 and 1983, psychologists were held to be in violation even when sexual contact with patients began after therapy was terminated (Gottlieb et al., 1988). Gottlieb et al. (1988) also noted that, at least for North American psychologists, their professional liability insurance extends to former patients with no time limit in respect of monetary settlements for sexual impropriety. In Britain, the situation is less clear.

In legal terms, at least in some U.S. states, the psychotherapist–patient relationship is held to continue in perpetuity for the purposes of the issue of sexual misconduct (Folman, 1991). This supports the view that sexual contact between a psychotherapist and a discharged patient is inappropriate, because the initial therapeutic encounter permanently and irrevocably establishes the prohibition against therapist–patient sexual contact on an "ethical contract" basis (Herman et al., 1987).

Many of the reasons for rejecting the legitimization of sexual contact with current patients are equally applicable to those who have been discharged, particularly in the light of the empirical finding (Pope & Vetter, 1991) that harm to patients occurred in 80% of the cases in which therapists engaged in sex with a patient after termination of therapy. The decision-making ability of discharged patients may continue to be compromised, either because of their presenting problems or because of residual transference (Applebaum & Jorgenson, 1991). This finding is supported by that of Grunebaum (1986), who interviewed patients whose sexual contact with their psychotherapist began after termination, and had been experienced as harmful. Brown (1988) suggested that the women she interviewed whose therapists had waited until after termination to become sexually involved with them experienced similar levels and types of harm to those patients whose therapists had sexual contact with them during therapy.

It may be argued that posttermination relationships between therapists and their patients can never be equal, because the therapist must always remain available for the patient to reenter therapy if necessary. Equally, the transference issues persist and would influence any relationship between the parties. In relation to this latter issue, it has been argued that the initial power imbalance between the therapist and the patient can never be erased (Herman et al., 1987).

Strean (1993) suggested that posttermination sexual contact involves unresolved transference and countertransference issues that are being acted out rather than discussed. This, he maintained, is particularly relevant in view of the fact that the goal of most therapies is separation between therapist and patient, not union. Vasquez (1991) asserted in a similar vein that an absolute ban on therapist–patient sexual contact after termination of therapy would allow the client and the therapist to use therapy as effectively as possible. The client would be freed to feel safe, open, and trusting when the option of sexual contact is not viable, and the therapist would be less likely to make errors in terminating therapy.

It has been proposed that in cases where the transference has been resolved (Coleman, 1988), or after a defined "cooling-off period" (Applebaum & Jorgenson, 1991), posttermination sexual contact may be appropriate. A number of professional bodies, in both the United Kingdom and the United States, have made recent amendments to their ethical codes, to allow for sexual contact between therapist and patient after a specified period following discharge. The time period varies from 12 weeks (British Association for Counselling, cited in Jehu, 1994) to 2 years under certain conditions (American Psychological Association, 1992; British Psychological Society, 1996).

Coleman (1988) also proposed in cases of discharged patients that if no harm occurs to the patient as a result of sexual contact with a therapist, there should be no prohibition on this behavior. However, of course the questions of who should determine whether the transference has been resolved and whether harm has occurred are crucial, because clear problems would arise if this was left solely to the treating psychotherapist. There is some research to suggest that patients' thoughts of the therapist continue for some years after the termination of therapy, and that many patients consider returning to therapy in the 5- to 10-year period following therapy (Buckley, Karasu, & Charles, 1981, cited in Shopland & VandeCreek, 1991). This would suggest that the notion of a cooling-off period may be inappropriate, unless it were of more than 10 years' duration.

A novel perspective on this issue is provided by the research of Geller, Cooley, and Hartley (1981–1982, cited in Vasquez, 1991), which suggests that improvement in psychotherapy patients is associated with their internal image of their therapist. Presumably, therefore, anything that interfered with this image of the therapist would have a negative impact on the client's progress after therapy, including, potentially, sexual contact (Vasquez, 1991).

Brown (1988) argued that female sexuality is such that the development of a sexual relationship is not, for women; "a demarcated phenomenon defined solely by genital contact, overt arousal, and orgasm. Rather, sexuality is perceived as developing along a continuum which begins with feelings of attachment and intimacy and expands over time to include physical and genital components" (Brown, 1988, p. 251).

Thus, in these terms, what is frequently referred to as a "posttermination" sexual or romantic relationship between therapist and patient, where one of the parties is female, is impossible because the onset of feelings of attraction occurred within the context of the therapeutic relationship: "The possibility that the client *might* become a lover has entered the process of therapy, and contaminated it, however subtly" (Brown, 1988, p. 251, original emphasis).

EXPLANATORY APPROACHES

Theoretical Perspectives

Strean (1993) asserted that the therapist's "psychotherapy family"—that is, the personnel of training programs—is central to the understanding of therapist–patient sexual contact. Strean suggested that the culture present in many psychotherapy training programs, in which traditional therapeutic barriers are crossed and candidates are infantilized, predisposes many therapists to "cross barriers with their own psychological sons and daughters" (p. 31) by giving their patients what they themselves desired, a love affair with their own therapist. Alternatively, the therapist may, like a child in a family, rebel against the family's values, displaying contempt by transgressing codes of conduct and having sexual contact with patients. Thus: "When boundaries are constantly crossed, when sadism and masochism are constantly being expressed, when strong wishes for narcissistic satisfaction are frequently being stimulated, the possibilities for sexual acting out by therapists are increased ... (and) therapists are not trained in any formal way not to act out sexually. It is something that is just assumed" (Strean, 1993, p. 32).

Training Issues

Pope et al. (1986) argued that educator–student sexual contact models later therapist–patient sexual involvement. For female respondents in their study, engaging in sexual contact with their educators while the respondents were still students was related to later sexual contact as professionals with patients: 23% as compared with 6% who had not had sexual contact with educators. For male respondents, the sample was too small to test the relationship. Thus, there is a suggestion from North American research that many therapists who have sexual relationships with their patients were themselves sexually involved with their own teachers, supervisors, or therapists (Folman, 1991; Pope, 1989). This proposition received support from the author's own research (Garrett & Davis, 1998).

Pope also noted (Pope & Bouhoutsos, 1986) that psychotherapists' training affords too little attention to the matter of sexual attraction to patients in general, and sexual countertransference in particular. Celenza (1995) suggested that the notion of countertransference love can be used inappropriately by therapists at an unconscious level, leading the therapist to assume that his or her feelings of love for the patient are in some way therapeutic. Tansey (1994) argued that the psychoanalytic profession (and presumably other psychotherapy professions) is "paralysed by phobic dread of countertransference that is sexual or desirous in nature" (p. 140).

He also noted that this dread paradoxically contributes to the occurrence of sexual contact between therapists and patients.

Gender Issues

Although research findings do not support the position that therapist–patient sexual contact is exclusively a problem of male therapists and female patients, there are nevertheless gender issues that may be relevant. Such issues have usually been considered in the literature in relation to male therapists and female patients, but other gender combinations do occur and thus require explanation. Some writers have begun to address same-sex therapist–patient sexual contact, and female therapist–male patient pairings, but further research and theoretical attention are necessary to these phenomena.

Brooks (1990) maintained that those male therapists who have sexual contact with their female patients may be overattached to traditional male gender roles. Thus, rather than viewing such therapists as aberrant, this perspective would regard them as an "unacceptable endpoint(s) on a psychological continuum, upon which all male psychologists have a place" (p. 345). In view of male socialization to inhibit emotional expression, Brooks argued, men might be more vulnerable to having difficulty in managing feelings arising as a result of the transference, and thus may potentially be more likely to mishandle the power and control imbalance in therapy.

Rutter (1989) extended this assertion, suggesting that psychological "wounds" from early childhood might contribute to inappropriate sexual contact with patients. Such wounds, Rutter proposed, derive from the loss of intimacy between father and son, as a result of which the male child fills the void with cultural myths about maleness and male sexuality. These myths include the view that men should act on their sexual tensions and that women will always be available as sources of physical, emotional, and sexual intimacy.

Additionally, the adult male may harbor anger at the lost intimacy between him and his mother, or because she made him feel powerless. What Rutter termed "merged" mothers may predispose their sons to believe that there is no boundary between their feelings, those of their sons, and those of other people. Conversely, "depriving" mothers who require their sons to take care of them yet simultaneously remain distant can raise men who need to retaliate against women who are vulnerable.

Few attempts have been made in the literature to understand the female therapist who becomes sexually involved with a male patient, or even sexual contact between the same-sex therapist and patient. Recent research suggests that more female therapists appear to be engaging in sexual contact with their patients. Stienstra (1988) argued that many of the issues that pertain to male offenders are also relevant in a consideration of female perpetrators. For example, women are no less subject to sexism than men, and are also in a position of power vis-à-vis patients (of both genders) in the therapeutic setting. Women therapists may be equally vulnerable on an emotional level to distress or personality difficulties that may predispose them to transgress the sexual boundary in therapy.

Marmor (1976) maintained that there are strong social and psychological disincentives to women to take the initiative sexually. However, Marmor argued, the incest taboo in respect of mothers and sons is more powerful than that between fathers and daughters. Thus, in the symbolism of the therapeutic relationship, the barriers against sexual acting out between the female therapist and the male patient are significant. Such an argument fails to consider female therapist–female patient sexual contact, and no discussion is available in the literature of male therapist–male patient pairings.

Stienstra (1988) noted that the age difference found between male therapist and the female patients with whom they become sexually involved tends to be absent in female therapist–female patient pairings. Female therapists are more likely, suggested Stienstra, to terminate therapy before commencing a sexual relationship with a patient, often anticipating that the relationship will be long term.

Benowitz (1994) hypothesized that those patients who explore their sexual orientation (particularly the possibility of bisexuality or lesbianism), and who discuss this openly in therapy may be at risk in relation to those therapists who are prone to becoming sexually involved with their patients. Although this argument was developed in relation to female therapist–female patient pairings, it may also apply to sexual contact between male therapists and male patients. Benowitz further suggested that although a female therapist may have a primary heterosexual orientation, she may still engage in sexual contact with female patients—indeed, that some such female therapists have their first same-sex encounter with a patient.

Benowitz (1994) also asserted that those female therapists who experience discomfort with their homosexual feelings may be at high risk of sexual inappropriateness with their female patients, or even that heterosexism may result in some therapists mislabeling nurturing feelings and behavior in sexual terms. Perhaps this is also true for male therapists who become sexually involved with their male patients. It would appear that the onset of female therapist–female patient sexual contact may occur at an earlier stage in therapy than may heterosexual contact, and that there is more socialization in such pairings (Benowitz, 1994). However, Stienstra (1988) argued the opposite. Clearly, further research is required in relation to the topic of homosexual sexual contact between patients and their therapists, and should consider the particular issue of onset of sexual contact.

It has been suggested (Gabbard, 1994) that the female professional who acts out sexually with her patients frequently believes that love is curative, and (unconsciously) that she can provide to the patient the nurturance which he or she failed to receive from his or her mother. Thus, an overidentification with the patient occurs. However, the extent to which this is also true of male therapists who have sexual contact with their patients, and whether there is any significant difference in this respect, is not clear. Data reported by Benowitz (1994) suggest that male and female therapists who report sexual contact with patients are very similar in their belief that sexual contact is less harmful and more beneficial to the patient, by comparison with therapists who do not become sexually involved with their patients.

A gender perspective is therefore an important one in developing an understanding of the processes of therapist–patient sexual contact. Such a gender perspective should not focus exclusively on the explanation of male therapist–female patient sexual contact. It also needs to contribute to an understanding of the reasons for sexual contact between same-sex therapists and patients, and between female therapists and their male patients. Little research has, however, been undertaken in this area, and the current understanding of gender issues is, at best, imperfect.

Supervision Issues

The notion that sexual contact with patients may occur as a failure of clinical supervision or as a consequence of lack of such supervision has some face validity. Such an argument would be based on the function of supervision as an opportunity to explore emotional issues in the therapeutic relationship, in particular countertransference reactions that, if neglected may lead to the sexualization of the therapeutic relationship. However, no research study has considered this question.

CONCLUSIONS

Sexual contact between therapists and patients remains a controversial area, with no definitive assessment available of its frequency or its appropriateness in the case of discharged patients. What is more certain is the psychological harm it usually does to the patients involved, including those who are discharged even at the time of onset of the sexual contact. There may be attempts by "offending" professionals to justify their behavior in terms of its supposed benefit to the patient. Harm to the patient is likely to occur because of role conflict, the power imbalance in the relationship between therapist and patient, and the unhelpfulness of sexual contact to the therapeutic endeavor. The few attempts to argue in favor of sexual contact between therapist and patient have been discredited. In many respects this is a little-understood phenomenon, although it appears relatively certain that therapists' training experiences, power, and gender issues are relevant. The lack of attention given in training programs to the essentially normal phenomenon of sexual attraction toward patients may indirectly have contributed to the problem.

Sexual abuse of patients has been extensively researched in the United States but such research has only relatively recently been instigated in the United Kingdom. In the United Kingdom a righteous and punitive approach has tended to be taken to those therapists who transgress the sexual boundary, rather than attempting to understand and resolve a problem that is little discussed in professional training (and is certainly not a requirement for inclusion in such training). Furthermore, such sexual contact has only relatively recently been explicitly prohibited by professional organizations, which have often failed to promulgate their ethical codes, including the relatively new, explicit prohibition on sexual contact between their members and patients. The professional approach to this problem must be a coordinated and coherent one. Training programs should compulsorily include issues of sexual attraction toward, and contact with patients and trainees, ethical codes should be promulgated, and individual cases should be accurately assessed in order to establish the most appropriate method of addressing the situation in each case.

SUMMARY

This chapter addresses the sexual abuse of patients by psychotherapists. It is argued that one cannot term such sexual contact a true "relationship" due to the power imbalance therein, and the consequent abusive nature of the contact. Sexual contact between therapists and their patients has been extensively researched in North America. Here, bearing in mind the likelihood of underreporting and the methodological and definitional problems in the research, it is likely that between 2% and 10% of professional therapists have had some kind of sexual contact with their patients.

Sexual attraction between therapist and patient, it is argued, is a normal part of the therapy process, but one that is too often ignored in professional training. Sexual contact between therapists and their patients has been proscribed indirectly until recently, and of late has been specifically mentioned in various professional ethical codes. However, the prohibition can be traced back to the Hippocratic oath. There were a number of famous violations in the early days of psychoanalysis, but despite a sound theoretical basis for the taboo, no strong disapproval was brought to bear on the transgressors. More recently, therapists who have sexually abused their patients have sometimes been pursued by the legal system. There is good evidence to consider sexual contact between therapist and patients as inappropriate, even after termination of therapy, for reasons including its harmful effect on the patient, its status as a dual-role relationship, its similarity to incest, and the power imbalance in the relationship. The attempts to argue in favor of sexual contact between therapist and patient have been few, and may be robustly criticized. Therapist–patient sexual contact may be understood in the context of the modeling effect of student–educator sexual contact, the training climate of the therapist, power and gender issues, and issues of supervision.

REFERENCES

American Psychological Association. (1992). Ethical principles of psychologists and code of conduct. *American Psychologist, 47,* 1597–1611.

Applebaum, P. S., & Jorgenson, L. (1991). Psychotherapist–patient sexual contact after termination of treatment: An analysis and proposal. *American Journal of Psychiatry, 148,* 1466–1473.

Benowitz, M. (1994). Comparing the experiences of women clients sexually exploited by female versus male psychotherapists. *Women and Therapy, 15*(1), 69–83.

Borys, D. S., & Pope, K. S. (1989). Dual relationships between therapist and client: A national study of psychologists, psychiatrists and social workers. *Professional Psychology: Research and Practice, 20,* 283–293.

Bouhoutsos, J. (1985). Sexual intimacy between psychotherapists and clients: Policy implications for the future. In L. Walker (Ed.), *Women and mental health policy* (pp. 207–227). Beverly Hills, CA: Sage.

Bouhoutsos, J., Holroyd, J., Lerman, H., Fover, B. R., & Greenberg, M. (1983). Sexual intimacy between psychotherapists and patients. *Professional Psychology: Research and Practice, 14*(2), 185–196.

British Psychological Society. (1991). *Code of conduct, ethical principles and guidelines.* Leicester: British Psychological Society.

British Psychological Society Division of Clinical Psychology. (1996). *Professional practice guidelines.* Leicester: British Psychological Society.

Brooks, G. R. (1990). The inexpressive male and vulnerability to therapist–patient sexual exploitation. *Psychotherapy, 27*(3), 344–349.

Brown, L. S. (1988). Harmful effects of posttermination sexual and romantic relationships with former clients. *Psychotherapy, 25,* 249–255.

Butler, S., & Zelen, S. L. (1977). Sexual intimacies between therapists and patients. *Psychotherapy: Theory, Research and Practice, 14,* 139–145.

Celenza, A. (1995). Love and hate in the countertransference: Supervisory concerns. *Psychotherapy, 32*(2), 301–307.

Chesler, P. (1972). *Women and madness.* New York: Avon.

Coleman, P. (1988) Sex between psychiatrist and former patient: A proposal for a "no harm, no foul" rule. *Oklahoma Law Review, 41*(1), 1–52.

Derosis, H., Hamilton, J. A., Morrison, E., & Strauss, M. (1987). More on psychiatrist–patient sexual contact. *American Journal of Psychiatry, 144*(5), 688–689.

Eyman, J. R., & Gabbard, G. O. (1991). Will therapist–patient sex prevent suicide? *Psychiatric Annals, 21*(11), 669–674.

Federal Register. (1980). *Equal opportunity guidelines on sexual harassment, 45*(72), 25025.

Feldman-Summers, S., & Jones, G. (1984). Psychological impacts of sexual contact between therapists or other healthcare practitioners and their clients. *Journal of Consulting and Clinical Psychology, 52*, 1054–1061.

Field, N. (1999). O tell me the truth about love. In D. Mann (Ed.), *Erotic transference and countertransference: Clinical practice in psychotherapy* (pp. 99–110). London: Routledge.

Folman, R. Z. (1991). Therapist–patient sex: Attraction and boundary problems. *Psychotherapy, 28*(1), 168–173.

Gabbard, G. O. (1994). Psychotherapists who transgress sexual boundaries with patients. *Bulletin of the Menninger Clinic, 58*(1), 124–135.

Garrett, T. (1999). Sexual contact between clinical psychologists and service users: A response to Pilgrim. *Clinical Psychology Forum, 132*, 13–14.

Garrett, T., & Davis, J. (1998). The prevalence of sexual contact between British clinical psychologists and their patients. *Clinical Psychology and Psychotherapy, 5*, 253–263.

Gartrell, N., Herman, J., Olarte, S., Feldstein, M., & Localio, R. (1986). Psychiatrist–patient sexual contact: Results of a national survey, I: Prevalence. *American Journal of Psychiatry, 143*(9), 1126–1131.

Gechtman, L. (1989). Sexual contact between social workers and their clients. In G. O. Gabbard (Ed.), *Sexual exploitation in professional relationships* (pp. 27–38). Washington, DC: American Psychiatric Press.

Gottlieb, M. C., Sell, J. M., & Schoenfeld, L. S. (1988). Social/romantic relationships with present and former clients: State licensing board actions. *Professional Psychology: Research and Practice, 19*(4), 459–462.

Grunebaum, H. (1986). Harmful psychotherapy experience. *American Journal of Psychotherapy, 40*(2), 165–177.

Gutheil, T. G. (1989). Borderline personality disorder, boundary violations and therapist–patient sex: Medicolegal pitfalls. *American Journal of Psychiatry, 146*(5), 597–602.

Hare-Mustin, R. T. (1974). Ethical considerations in the use of sexual contact in psychotherapy. *Psychotherapy: Theory, Research and Practice, 11*, 308–310.

Herman, J. L., Gartrell, N., Olarte, S., Feldman, M., & Localio, R. (1987). Psychiatrist–patient sexual contact: Results of a national survey, II: Psychiatrists' attitudes. *American Journal of Psychiatry, 144*(2), 164–169.

Holroyd, J. C., & Bouhoutsos, J. (1985). Biased reporting of therapist–patient sexual intimacy. *Professional Psychology: Research and Practice, 16*(5), 701–709.

Holroyd, J. C., & Brodsky, A. M. (1980). Does touching patients lead to sexual intercourse? *Professional Psychology, 11*, 807–811.

Jehu, D. (1994). *Patients as victims: Sexual abuse in psychotherapy and* counselling. Chichester, UK: Wiley.

Jorgenson, L. M., & Schoener, G. R. (1994). Regulation in the U.S.A. In D. Jehu (Ed.), *Patients as victims: Sexual abuse in psychotherapy and counselling* (pp. 27–35). Chichester, UK: Wiley.

Kardener, S. H. (1974). Sex and the physician–patient relationship. *American Journal of Psychiatry, 131*, 1134–1136.

Keith-Spiegel, P., & Koocher, G. P. (1985). *Ethics in psychology: Professional standards and cases.* New York: Random House.

Kitchener, K. S. (1988). Dual role relationships: What makes them so problematic? *Journal of Counseling and Development, 67*, 217–221.

Luepeker, E. T. (1989). Sexual exploitation of clients by therapists: Parallels with parent–child incest. In G. R. Schoener, J. H. Milgrom, J. C. Gonsoriek, E. T. Luepeker, & R. M. Conroe (Eds.), *Psychotherapists' sexual involvement with clients: Intervention and prevention* (pp. 73–79). Minneapolis: Walk-In Counselling Center.

Marmor, J. (1972). Sexual acting out in psychotherapy. *American Journal of Psychoanalysis, 32,* 3–8.

Marmor, J. (1976). Some psychodynamic aspects of the seduction of patients in psychotherapy. *The American Journal of Psychoanalysis, 36,* 319–323.

Masson, J. (1988). *Against therapy.* London: Collins.

McCartney, J. (1966). Overt transference. *Journal of Sex Research, 2,* 227–237.

Perr, I. N. (1989). Medicolegal aspects of professional sexual exploitation. In G. O. Gabbard (Ed.), *Sexual exploitation in professional relationships* (pp. 211–228). Washington, DC: American Psychiatric Press.

Peterson, M. (1992). *At personal risk: Boundary violations in professional–client relationships.* New York: Norton.

Pilgrim, D. (1999). On keeping a disorderly house. *Clinical Psychology Forum, 124,* 4–7

Pope, K. S. (1989). Malpractice suits, licensing disciplinary actions, and ethics cases: Frequencies, causes and costs. *Independent practitioner, 9*(1), 22–26.

Pope, K. S. (1990a). Therapist–patient sexual involvement: A review of the research. *Clinical Psychology Review, 10,* 477–490.

Pope, K. S. (1990b) Therapist–patient sex as sex abuse: Six scientific, professional and practical dilemmas in addressing victimisation and rehabilitation. *Professional Psychology: Research and Practice, 21*(4), 227–239.

Pope, K. S. (1991). Rehabilitation plans and expert testimony for therapists who have been sexually involved with a patient. *Independent Practitioner, 22*(3), 31–39.

Pope, K. S. (1993). Licensing disciplinary actions for psychologists who have been sexually involved with a client: Some information about offenders. *Professional Psychology: Research and Practice, 24*(3), 374–377.

Pope, K. S., & Bajt, T. C. (1988). When laws and values conflict: A dilemma for psychologists. *American Psychologist, 43,* 828.

Pope, K. S., & Bouhoutsos, J. C. (1986). *Sexual intimacy between therapists and patients.* New York: Praeger.

Pope, K. S., Keith-Spiegel, P., & Tabachnick, B. G. (1986). Sexual attraction to clients: The human therapist and the (sometimes) inhuman training system. *American Psychologist, 41,* 147–158.

Pope, K. S., Levenson, H., & Schover, L. R. (1979). Sexual intimacy in psychology training: Results and implications of a national survey. *American Psychologist, 34*(8), 682–689.

Pope, K. S., Tabachnik, B. G., & Keith-Spiegel, P. (1987). Ethics of practice: The beliefs and behaviors of psychologists as therapists. *American Psychologist, 42*(11), 993–1006.

Pope, K. S., & Vetter, V. A. (1991). Prior therapist–patient sexual involvement among patients seen by psychologists. *Psychotherapy, 28*(3), 429–438.

Rodolfa, E., Hall, T., Holms, V., Davena, A., Komatz, D., Antunez, D., & Hall, A. (1994). The management of sexual feelings in therapy. *Professional Psychology: Research and Practice, 25*(2), 168–172.

Rutter, P. (1989). *Sex in the forbidden zone.* London: Unwin Hyman.

Saul, L. J. (1962). The erotic transference. *Psychoanalytic Quarterly, 31,* 54–61.

Schoener, G. R. (1991, January). Therapist–client sexual involvement—incidence and prevalence. *Minnesota Psychologist,* pp. 14–15.

Schoener, G., Milgrom, J. H., & Gonsiorek, J. (1984). Sexual exploitation of clients by therapists. *Women and Therapy, 3,* 63–69.

Shepard, M. (1971). *The love treatment: Sexual intimacy between patients and psychotherapists.* New York: Wyden.

Shopland, S., & VandeCreek, L. (1991). Sex with ex-clients: Theoretical rationales for prohibition. *Ethics and Behavior, 1*(1), 35–44.

Sonne, J. L., & Pope, K. S. (1991). Treating victims of therapist–patient sexual involvement. *Psychotherapy, 28*(1), 174–187.

Sreenivasan, U. (1989). Sexual exploitation of patients: The position of the Canadian Psychiatric Association. *Canadian Journal of Psychiatry, 34*, 234–235.

Stake, J. E., & Oliver, J. (1991). Sexual contact and touching between therapist and client: A survey of psychologists' attitudes and behavior. *Professional Psychology: Research and Practice, 22*(4), 297–307.

Stienstra, R. (1988). *Sexual abuse in the female therapist–female client relationship.* Holland: Central Inspectorate for Public Health/Central Inspectorate for Mental Public Health. (Unofficial translation by Jeannet Renfree.)

Strean, H. S. (1993). *Therapists who have sex with their patients: Treatment and recovery.* New York: Brunner Mazel.

Tansey, M. J. (1994). Sexual attraction and phobic dread in the countertransference. *Psychoanalytic Dialogues, 4*(2), 139–152.

Taylor, B. J., & Wagner, N. N. (1976). Sex between therapists and clients: A review and analysis. *Professional Psychology, 7*, 593–601.

Thoreson, R. W., Shaugnessy, P., Heppner, P. P., & Cook, S. W. (1993). Sexual contact during and after the therapeutic relationship: Attitudes and practices of male counsellors. *Journal of Counseling and Development, 71*, 429–434.

Vasquez, M. J. T. (1991). Sexual intimacies with clients after termination: Should a prohibition be explicit? *Ethics and Behavior, 1*(1), 45–61.

Voth, H. (1972). Love affair between doctor and patient. *American Journal of Psychotherapy, 26*, 394–400.

Wilbers, D., Veerstra, G., Van de Wiel, H. B. N., & Schulz, W. C. M. W. (1992). Sexual contact in the doctor–patient relationship in the Netherlands. *British Medical Journal, 304*, 1531–1534.

Williams, M. H. (1992). Exploitation and interference: Mapping the damage from therapist–patient sexual involvement. *American Psychologist, 47*(3), 412–442.

9

Over My Dead Body: On the Histories and Cultures of Necrophilia

Dany Nobus[1]
Brunel University

I can imagine many a reader wondering about the appropriateness of including a chapter on the histories and cultures of necrophilia in a scholarly volume on inappropriate relationships. Isn't necrophilia more indicative of the limitlessness of human fantasy than of the problematic extent of sexual misconduct within contemporary society? Aren't there more pressing relational imbalances to be addressed than that of a human being indulging in sexual intercourse with a cadaver? Although few will presumably doubt that necrophilia ranks among the most inappropriate behaviors conceivable—if not from a moral perspective, at least from a psychological point of view—the accepted rarity of its occurrence, in combination with the global prevalence of sexual harassment at work,

---

[1]Dany Nobus is a Senior Lecturer in Psychology and Psychoanalytic Studies at Brunel University. He is the editor of *Key Concepts of Lacanian Psychoanalysis* (The Other Press, 1999) and author of *Jacques Lacan and the Freudian Practice of Psychoanalysis* (Routledge, 2000), as well as numerous papers on the theory and practice of psychoanalysis, and the history of psychiatry.

child sexual abuse, and domestic violence may indeed invest my contribution with an aura of suspicion, impropriety, and bad taste. It is even questionable to classify necrophilia as a type of relationship when taking account of the fact that the necrophiliac's partner is not able to show and reciprocate any feelings whatsoever—the anticipated mutuality of human interactions purportedly forcing dead-lovers to avoid all conventional forms of bonding with living people. Instead of epitomizing an inappropriate relationship, necrophilia indeed seems more tantamount to a severely disordered state of mind, regardless of whether the individual has "live" encounters with the dead or merely cherishes the fantasy as a sexual prop.

In this chapter, I first situate the notion of necrophilia within its original historical context, demonstrating how its diagnostic confusion with necrosadism and lust murder continues to inform contemporary views on the subject. In an attempt to assess the prevalence of necrophilia, I subsequently argue that the historical association of the disorder with the desecration and mutilation of corpses may be partly responsible for the widespread portrayal of necrophilia as an extremely rare phenomenon. Broad definitions of necrophilia as a practiced and/or fantasized love for dead bodies are likely to inflate the estimates of its occurrence, whereas very narrow designations will inevitably deflate the figures. Yet, as becomes obvious in statements obtained from the Association for Necrophiliac Research and Enlightenment, those who entertain and promote necrophilia in its broadest sense do not always agree with its sexual overtones. Paradoxically, self-defined necrophiliacs may emphasize the inappropriateness of necrophilia as a sexual relationship.

In the second part of this chapter, I first concentrate on the issue of sexual consent and its significance for the evaluation of necrophilia in relation to ethical standards. Drawing on the recent case of Diane Blood, who insisted on being inseminated with the sperm of her dead husband, I simultaneously argue that the opposition between the cultural sacralization of the corpse and the sensuousness of human sexuality is at least as important for a judicious consideration of necrophilia as the factor of sexual consent, and that this opposition generates questions that are applicable to a wide range of social dilemmas.

LONG LIVE THE DEAD!

The history of necrophilia as a diagnostic label, a bizarre sexual behavior and a deviant social phenomenon remains largely unexplored, and many source materials on the subject are littered with inaccuracies as to the origin and applications of the term. This observation alone could warrant a detailed investigation of the historical backdrop of necrophilia, yet a historical approach is also a prerequisite for any understanding of how the term has been used as an umbrella for a variety of different patterns and profiles, and how in its broad conception necrophilia is presumably much more prevalent than commonly assumed.

Merely retracing the origin of the term *necrophilia* has often posed insuperable problems to researchers, with some of the most judicious accounts simply providing the reader with details about its etymology. As such, one can find in Spoerri (1959), von Hentig (1964), and Fromm (1973) that necrophilia is derived from the Greek words *nekros* (corpse, dead body) and *philia* (love, friendship), without any supplementary information about when and where the notion was first introduced.

Although the most widely respected English dictionaries remain dead silent about the origin of necrophilia, the renowned *Trésor de la Langue Française* (Centre National de la Recherche Scientifique, 1986) attributes the first occurrence of the concept to an 1861 textbook of general pathology (Monneret, 1861). However, it suffices to verify the passage in Monneret's book in order to discover that he himself associated the term *necrophilia* with the name of a certain Guislain: "One has to align these sad disorders of the reproductive instinct [onanism, nymphomania, satyriasis] with the depraved tastes that prompt certain individuals to profane female and even male cadavers, and to exercise their ghastly passion on them (necrophilia, Guislain)" (Monneret, 1861, p. 54). Guislain also featured as the intellectual father of necrophilia in a number of recent French studies (Dansel, 1991; De Gaudenzi, 1998), yet without any specific mention of the actual source. Dansel (1991) and De Gaudenzi (1998) appear to have drawn their information from Epaulard (1901), who indeed conceded that the term *necrophilia* "was created by Guislain, a Belgian alienist from the middle of the nineteenth century" (p. 9). Unfortunately, Epaulard also refrained from offering any further data. As far as I know, the only English-language source in which Guislain has been acknowledged as the inventor of the term *necrophilia* is Rosario (1997), yet this author also satisfied himself by (deceptively) referring the reader to Epaulard for additional details.

Owing to this impenetrable jungle of unspecified references, it seemed necessary to me to pinpoint and elucidate the birth of necrophilia in the writings of Joseph Guislain, who was indeed—as Epaulard stated—a mid-19th century Belgian alienist, but also a highly respected clinical reformer whose lifelong advocacy of a more humane treatment for institutionalized mental patients at one point earned him the title of "Belgian Pinel." The coveted passage in which Guislain coined *necrophilia* figures in his *Leçons Orales sur les Phrénopathies*, in the transcription of a lecture that was probably delivered some time during the winter of 1850:

> It is within the category of the destructive madmen [*aliénés destructeurs*] that one needs to situate certain patients to whom I would like to give the name of NECROPHILIACS [*NÉCROPHILES*]. The alienists have adopted, as a new form, the case of [S]ergeant Bertrand, the disinterrer of cadavers on whom all

the newspapers have recently reported. However, don't think that we are dealing here with a form of phrenopathy which appears for the first time. The an-
cients, in speaking about lycanthropy, have cited examples to which one can
more or less relate the case which has just attracted the public attention so
strongly. (Guislain, 1852, p. 257)

This fragment was not published until 1852, and it would take at least
another decade for the term *necrophilia* to enter the professional vocabulary of French and German psychiatrists. Instrumental for the wider acceptance of necrophilia as an alternative to vampirism and lycanthropy was
Bénédict-Augustin Morel, an influential French alienist who was well acquainted with Guislain's work and who also acknowledged him as the
source of necrophilia within an extensive reevaluation of the infamous case
of the sergeant quoted by Guislain (Morel, 1857).

If Guislain has rarely been referenced as the intellectual father of
necrophilia, this case of Sergeant François Bertrand has definitely entered
world history as the morbid template for grave robbers, profanators, body
snatchers, and ghouls across the globe. So paradigmatic is Bertrand's case
that it is even questionable whether the term *necrophilia* would have existed altogether had his story not come to the attention of the medical establishment and excited the imagination of the general public. The
extraordinary events in the case of François Bertrand took a dramatic turn
around 11:30 p.m. on Thursday, March 15, 1849, when a 25-year-old man
dragged himself to the Val-de-Grâce hospital in Paris suffering from serious gunwounds on his right side (Dansel, 1991). News about Bertrand's
predicament spread rapidly among the military, and when a gravedigger of
the Montparnasse cemetery accidentally overheard a conversation between soldiers stationed nearby, he suddenly realized that this man could
only be the notorious "vampire" of Montparnasse, whom some of his colleagues had just managed to hit with their ingenious booby trap. Arrested
while still recovering from his injuries in the hospital, one of François
Bertrand's surgeons, the honorable Dr. Marchal de Calvi, ultimately obtained a full written confession of his patient, which he carefully reproduced at the young man's trial in July 1849.

In this document, Bertrand admitted with amazing candor to a long list
of desecrations in various graveyards across the country, during which he
had surrendered himself to horrendous acts of eviscerating and dismem-
bering both male and female corpses. In his testimony, Marchal de Calvi intimated that the young soldier's destructive "monomania" also involved an
even more repulsive component, yet he refrained from specifying the pre-
cise nature of this complication. However, for contemporary alienists, it
was clear that the surgeon had alluded to Bertrand's sexual involvement
with the exhumed corpses, which was sufficient to trigger a heated debate
about what could possibly drive a young man to commit such hideous acts
(Brierre de Boismont 1849; Lunier, 1849; Michéa 1849).

Although the case of Sergeant Bertrand has been adduced as the most important historical record of necrophilia, it does not require great acumen to observe that his interest did not merely lie in the sexual violation of cadavers. As he himself explained in a detailed response to Michéa (1849), he was principally concerned with the physical mutilation of corpses, masturbation occurring only as a secondary phenomenon in relation to his contemplation of the dismembered bodies. It is quite debatable, therefore, to promote his story as a paragon of necrophilia, the more so because Bertrand's mutilation of the corpses reflects more a profound hate than an ardent love for the dead bodies, unless one is happy to entertain Oscar Wilde's idea that each man kills the thing he loves.

Nonetheless, the idea that necrophilia may be something of a misnomer when applied to stories such as Bertrand's has not deterred professionals as well as self-identified necrophiliacs from expanding the list of founding fathers with similar vignettes. For instance, on one of the main pages of the Necroerotic Web site (NecroErotic, 2000), the survey of "founding influences" encompasses, alongside the vicissitudes of Sergeant Bertrand, brief descriptions of the murderous careers of Victor Ardisson (Belletrud & Mercier, 1903), Ed Gein (Schechter, 1989), and Jeffrey Dahmer (Masters, 1993; Norris, 1992). Although honesty obliges me to concede that less murderous and more sexually oriented cases—such as those of Count Karl von Cosel (Foraker, 1976) and Karen Greenlee (Morton, 1987)—also tend to feature prominently in contemporary charts of famous necrophiliacs, the spurious identification of necrophilia with necrosadism and lust murder often continues to pervade popular and scientific accounts alike.

Using necrophilia as a synonym for necrosadism and lust murder not only poses a nosological and diagnostic problem, but also affects the estimates of its prevalence throughout history and across cultures. Many authors who have written on the subject since the emergence of the spectacular case of François Bertrand have argued that necrophilia is an extremely rare disorder that hardly ever appears in the consultation room of mental health professionals, and that is more strongly rooted in sexual fantasies and the literary imagination than in real-life events. No doubt necrophilia, in its broad definition of the love for dead bodies, has stimulated the creative impulsive of many an artist, especially during the 19th century (Dijkstra, 1986; Kramer, 1997; Praz, 1970), yet also in more recent times. Literary examples of how the corpse of a dead woman can ignite the sexual desire of a man can be found in the works of Edgar Allan Poe, Théophile Gautier, and Emily Dickinson (Paglia, 1990), yet some contemporary creations continue this historical tradition with great verve and pizzazz (Bortnick, 1997; Davis, 1997; De Wargny, 1965; Wittkop, 1998).

In a scholarly review of the literature, Burg (1982) challenged the common belief that necrophilia is an extremely rare phenomenon: "The rarity of necrophilia is a conclusion drawn from the limited number of cases that have come to the attention of medical or legal authorities. That conclusion is based on no reliable data; there is no information on the frequency of undetected necrophilia or on the frequency of necrophilial fantasies, whether broadly or narrowly defined, among any population group" (p. 242). Burg is of course right in pointing out that clinical and forensic data offer no reliable indication for assessing the prevalence of necrophiliac behaviors and fantasies, for there is of course no reason to believe that all necrophiliacs will eventually seek help, whereas we do have good reason to assume that many are likely to choose professions that will give them ready access to dead bodies, without the risk of being detected by law enforcers. If the educational system offers an exquisite professional playground for pedophiles, necrophiliacs will probably endeavor to work as gravediggers, morticians, hospital orderlies, funeral parlor employees, undertakers, morgue attendants, emergency medical technicians, and so on. Apart from the obvious dark number (the hidden cohort) associated with one's reliance on clinical data, the reported rarity of necrophilia also stems from the relative inaccessibility of the available literature and the narrowness with which necrophilia has generally been approached. Burg himself emphasized that despite "this frequent complaint about the unavailability of material, the quantity of published research on necrophilia, in fact, is now fairly substantial, particularly when considered in conjunction with the large body of psychological theory on the topic that has developed over the years" (Burg, 1982, p. 242). In an attempt to produce an exhaustive overview and analysis of all vignettes of necrophilia mentioned in the literature, Rosman and Resnick (1989) subsequently identified no fewer than 88 cases, yet even this comprehensive survey circumvents the historical instances reported by Guislain (1852), a substantial number of cases discussed by Stekel (1929), and some German materials adduced by Hirschfeld (Koestler, 1938). But even more important than the relative obscurity of the available books and articles, is the authors' own restrictive definition of necrophilia as a behavior for which the vignettes of Sergeant Bertrand, Victor Ardisson, Ed Gein, and Jeffrey Dahmer serve as paradigms. When necrophilia is extended to include all instances of love for the dead—sexual as well as platonic—the practice may be much more frequent than commonly assumed.

As Burg suggested, it is difficult to find reliable evidence for this claim beyond the boundaries of clinical and legal documents. In a recently published interview, Leilah Wendell—the founder of The American Association for Necrophiliac Research and Enlightenment, coordinator of the Westgate/Azrael Project, and proprietor of The House of Death in New Orleans, Louisiana (Westgatenecromantic, 2000)—reported that her biannual newsletter reaches 25,000 people across the globe, although only 1% of this audience self-identify as necrophiliacs (Hensley, 2000). However, it should be noted that the Westgate/Azrael Project does not cater for those who are predominantly in search of sexual gratification from an encounter with the dead. As Wendell herself put it:

> I don't believe in sex with the dead. I believe that the body can be a catalyst for a spirit to come through to you because it is an empty shell.... I do not believe you should just go out, dig up a stiff, and have your way with it. I'm very, very much against that.... Just digging up a body is not what it's all about. That's a violation. Today's modern concept of necrophilia is not at all what I think about the subject. Taken from a ritualistic point of view, the dead body is a secret altar. A contact point for the Death energy. Something tangible, something to touch. (Hensley, 2000, pp. 286–287)

Wendell's outlook on necrophilia, which defines sex with the dead as an inappropriate behavior from a pseudoreligious and mystical perspective, seems strangely paradoxical. Who would expect the founder and leader of an organization for necrophiliac enlightenment to condemn sexual involvement with cadavers as an inappropriate violation of a sacrosanct object? Wendell's view on necrophilia, which strips all sexual aspects from the love for the dead, is simultaneously reminiscent of some peculiar Tantric rituals mentioned by Bullough (1976), whereby cult members have a habit of meditating on the forces of death, decay, and putrefaction. Bullough did not fail to indicate that some of these rituals do have sexual connotations, with practitioners sitting in cemeteries and pressing a human skull between their legs, yet he stated that only in the so-called black ritual does the penis become erect (of the corpse, of the cult member?) and ejaculation ensue.

Judging by the extent of Wendell's readership, a much higher proportion of the public is ostensibly interested in deriving mental strength from mixing with the dead than in actual sexual intercourse with cadavers. Because her conception of necrophilia explicitly repudiates sexual love, Wendell has also been branded a necrophony, a necrofraud, and a necrophobic of the worst kind (Pirog, 2000a). More interesting, the author of these accusations, who is the editor of *The NecroErotic*, a newsletter devoted entirely to the promotion of sex with the dead, admitted without blushing that he himself has never had any sexual contact with a corpse, which does not preclude his harboring a strong desire for doing so (Pirog 2000b). In addition, he did not provide any information as to how frequent the practice is, and the only interview with a self-identified necrophiliac he produced is anything but specific, because it concerned Nicolas Claux, a French mortuary assistant nicknamed the "Vampire of Paris" who in 1997 was convicted to 12 years imprisonment for murdering a 35-year-old man, committing a dozen grave desecrations, and eating the flesh of the exhumed bodies (Claux 2000; Pirog 2000c).

When asked about the likings of his fellow morticians, Claux proclaimed that nobody else in the morgue was interested in necrophilia

(Pirog, 2000c), yet Karen Greenlee disclosed that necrophilia within funeral homes is much more common than people imagine (Morton 1987). Based on her own experience as a mortician before she was convicted for abducting the dead body of a 33-year-old man in December 1979, Greenlee stated that many necrophiliac activities in funeral homes pass unnoticed and that in those cases where evidence of sexual activity does come to the attention of funeral directors, they are often reluctant to report it out of fear for bad publicity (Morton, 1987). The prevalence of necrophilia among morticians is confirmed by one of Eurydice's interviewees, a male mortician from a nonspecified Los Angeles suburb: "A hell of a lot of people would be into this if they had easy, private access to fresh bodies. I suspect half the people who come in contact with corpses play with them. They're hard not to take advantage of, lying there passive—you can act out any fantasy with them, you have access to the most taboo places and notions" (Eurydice, 1999, p.185).

For those necrophiliacs whose professions do not facilitate easy access to cadavers, it was suggested by Hirschfeld (Koestler, 1938) that brothels in which prostitutes play the part of a corpse often provide some form of solace: "The luxury brothels of the European capitals have not only torture chambers, but also 'mortuaries,' in which prostitutes lying in an open coffin submit to coitus and ill-treatment by necro-sadists" (p. 529). Yet the most extraordinary piece of information comes from an investigative study conducted by Hennig (1979), in which a young German man testified to having participated in a necrophiliac scenario in a clandestine New York brothel that sold sexual intercourse with a fresh corpse for the price of $200.00. Urban myth or painful reality? The only confirmation of this story I have been able to find comes from Bosworth's biography of Montgomery Clift, in which the famous actor revealed that he was acquainted with an American plastic surgeon and abortionist who earned some money on the side by supplying dead bodies to a secret place in New York where people could pay to have sex with them (Bosworth, 1978).

A GRAVE TABOO

The popular image of necrophilia as a highly unusual, exceedingly bizarre, and thoroughly perverse sexual disturbance has generally been confirmed by the scientific literature since the birth of sexology at the end of the 19th century. In one of his famous *Studies in the Psychology of Sex*, the British sexologist Havelock Ellis commented on the sensational case of Victor Ardisson as described by Belletrud and Mercier (1903) in the following terms:

> But when so highly abnormal an act [sexual intercourse with a corpse] is felt as natural we are dealing with a person who is congenitally defective so far as the

finer developments of intelligence are concerned. It was so in this case of necrophily; he was the son of a weak-minded woman of unrestrainable sexual inclinations, and was himself somewhat feeble-minded; he was also, it is instructive to observe, anosmic. (Ellis, 1937a, p. 82)

Echoing the opinion of fellow researchers, Ellis added in a later study: "Necrophily, or a sexual attraction for corpses, is sometimes regarded as related to pygmalionism [people falling in love with statues]. It is, however, a more profoundly morbid manifestation, and may perhaps he [sic] regarded as a kind of perverted sadism" (Ellis, 1937b, p. 188).

Written almost a century ago, against the background of a sociomoral climate still heavily infected with repressive Victorian sexual attitudes, these glosses on necrophilia do not differ significantly from those employed within contemporary accounts of the subject. In his acclaimed study of bizarre behaviours, Prins argued that people "who commit necrophilic acts will have grossly disordered personalities. Some may be suffering from psychotic states, such as schizophrenia, and others may be of impaired intelligence" (Prins, 1990, p. 86). In their contribution to a comprehensive textbook of forensic psychiatry, Grubin et al. pointed out that, for many authors, "sexual deviation is always symptomatic of some other disturbance," agreeing that this "must surely be the case with necrophilia" because "individuals usually show a range of personality difficulties that include obsessional traits, narcissism, sadism and a preoccupation with destruction. Most have poor reality testing and a few are frankly psychotic. The disorder is rare, of no known specific aetiology and can be treated in the context of a broad approach to the patient's personality" (Grubin, Gudjonssen, Gunn, & West, 1993, pp. 553–554). Yet descriptions of necrophilia as an utterly revolting form of sexual expression that is generally associated with a severe personality disorder are not restricted to the medicoforensic literature. A recent feminist companion to sexuality defines the practice as "the ultimate social taboo, surpassing even cannibalism. So repulsive is the concept that it rarely appears as a crime on the statute books" (Gilbert, 1993, p. 182).

The latter point deserves some elaboration in its own right, because the author of the entry (Elizabeth Young) suggested that the violation of dead bodies is often not inscribed in criminal law precisely because of its repugnant nature. Indeed, similar to criminal proceedings in many other countries, the English penal code allows for necrophiliacs to be charged with outraging public decency, committing acts of malicious damage, or engaging in tomb violation, but it does not prohibit as such the sexual involvement with corpses. When implying that it is the intrinsic abhorrence of these activities that has enabled their escape from criminal laws, Young not only contended that certain behaviors may be so outrageous that they cannot even be named within a symbolic system of justice—thus challenging the idea that legal prohibitions weigh on all acts that are considered socially offensive, morally wrong, or contravening human rights—she also surmised that disgust may be the prime motivating factor behind the legislators' resolution *not* to take legal action. Young's speculation stands in radical opposition to a recent argument made by Nussbaum (1999), who underscored, again with reference to necrophilia, that the emotions of disgust and indignation inform many a law enforcer's decision to make an act illegal.

In keeping with the aforementioned designation of necrophilia as a bizarre inclination that signals an underlying personality disorder, one could of course argue that criminal law does not apply to individuals who are not accountable for their acts, owing to the fact that they suffer from a debilitating mental disorder. Instead of a criminal offense, necrophilia thus becomes a potential "excuse" within the criminal justice system, as well as a central issue when assessing a defendant's good cause for pleading not guilty by reason of insanity. This is exactly what was at stake during the sensational trial of Jeffrey Dahmer, the Wisconsin serial killer accused of murdering and mutilating 15 men between 1978 and 1991 (Masters, 1993; Norris, 1992; Schwartz, 1992; Tithecott, 1997). During Dahmer's trial, Dr. Becker tried to convince the jury that Dahmer "suffered from necrophilia such that he was unable to control his impulses to have sex with dead bodies" (quoted in Reznek, 1997, p. 289). Testifying for the prosecution, Dr. Dietz challenged his colleague's opinion by relying on the presupposed controllability of the paraphilic impulse, whether the latter concerns necrophilia or some other type of abnormal sexual preference: "Paraphilia is a description of what is sexually exciting. Whether one acts to seek out that image in varying ways is not determined by the paraphilia but by other aspects of one's life.... [I]t is important to point out that acquiring a paraphilia is generally not a matter of choice.... What humans do choose is whether they will act on their sexual interests or not" (Reznek, 1997, p. 289). Eventually, Dahmer was found guilty and sentenced to 957 years in prison, his punishment ending prematurely when he was killed by a fellow inmate shortly after being admitted to jail.

However compelling Dietz's plea in the Dahmer case may have been, it opens a much more complex debate about the exact status of necrophilia as an inappropriate sexual practice. Although the expert managed to convince the jury that the defendant's "choice" to act on his fantasies was proof of his accountability, the expert still regarded the sexual interest in corpses as a clinically abnormal condition, confirming its tabulation as a paraphilia within contemporary psychiatric manuals.

In this respect, the current *Diagnostic and Statistical Manual of Mental Disorders* (DSM-IV) classifies necrophilia as a "paraphilia not otherwise specified" (category 302.9), whereby paraphilia is defined on the basis of two criteria: "recurrent, intense sexually arousing fantasies, sexual urges, or behaviors generally involving 1) nonhuman objects, 2) the suffering or humiliation of oneself or one's partner, or 3) children or other nonconsenting persons, that occur over a period of at least 6 months (Criterion A)," and causing "clinically significant distress or impairment in social, occupational, or other important areas of functioning (Criterion B)" (American Psychiatric Association, 1994, pp. 522–523). However, necrophilia is presumably the most exquisite test case for the validity of these criteria. To what extent does it make sense to claim that the objects to which the necrophiliac feels attracted are essentially nonhuman? Is it really possible to inflict pain and/or suffering on a dead body? And in light of the fact that the necrophiliac's "partner" is dead, is it appropriate to evaluate the act in terms of its violation of the fundamental principle of sexual consent? Regarding Criterion B, doesn't the small number of case studies of necrophiliacs in the clinical literature suffice to dispute the high level of psychosocial distress caused by the disorder? Isn't the remarkable scarcity of medicopsychological reports on necrophiliacs who have not espoused the Dahmer option of self-manufactured corpses, or who have not been involved in snatching bodies from the local cemetery, an indication of the relative social competence of the necrophile individual?

These questions evidently raise important ethical issues, which some moral philosophers have actually tried to address within the context of more general reflections on consensuality and sexual health. In *Sexual Consent*, Archard (1998) pondered the interesting possibility of necrophilia being morally wrong because a person's interests could be extended beyond the boundaries of his or her biological existence, regardless of the act's indirect traumatizing effect on the dead person's relatives and its transgression of whatever taboos a community may impose on the bodies of its deceased members. Of course, this consideration is not only significant within the context of necrophilia, because it also pervades the contentious practice of the medical removal of organs from a dead person's body. Whereas in some European countries this practice is inscribed by law—although relatives should always be informed about it and always maintain the right to object—the scandal at Liverpool's Alder Hey hospital in January 2001, whereby it was discovered that the organs of more than 800 children had been stocked for medical purposes without their parents' consent, demonstrates how a country without strict regulations on medical organ removal does not seem to bother about potentially harming the interests of dead people, or those of their families.

To solve the ethical problem of organ removal, donor cards have been introduced on which people give their full consent to being medically "dismantled" after their death. But do we really want to consider the creation of "necrocards" such as those advocated by the Neoist Alliance and reproduced in the pages of *Apocalypse Culture II* (Parfrey, 2000)? If it is not inconceivable, as Archard (1998) maintained, for Sue to consent before her demise to Harry's sexual involvement with her body after her death (an antemortem agreement that could safeguard her postmortem interests), Sue will nonetheless be unable to revoke her decision during the sexual act. Archard could only conclude that it "would be all the more important, therefore, to ensure that any expression of consent to post-mortem use of their body was considered, made in full knowledge of its implications, and was indeed, and in every sense of the word, their final word on the subject" (Archard, 1998, p. 72).

The famous case of Diane Blood, whose legal battle with the Human Fertilisation and Embryology Authority regularly filled the headlines of British newspapers for almost 3 years during the second half of the 1990s, illustrates how problematic the matter of consent can be when the subject happens to be a dead body. Her husband having entered a state of coma after contracting meningitis, Mrs. Blood managed to convince the doctors to extract a sperm sample from his body, yet when she asked to be inseminated with the cells following his death, she was faced with the fact that there was no signed note of informed consent in which he had agreed to his sperm being used posthumously. Despite huge public backing, Mrs. Blood's request was turned down by the High Court, yet in February 1997 the Court of Appeal eventually granted her the opportunity to undergo artificial insemination with the exported semen of her dead husband in the Centre for Reproductive Medicine at the Free University of Brussels. Liam Stephen Blood was born in December 1998, nearly 4 years after his father's death.

Because Mrs. Blood did not have sexual intercourse with her dead husband, she can hardly be accused of performing a contrived act of necrophilia, at least not in the traditional sense of the word, and if only because such an act would probably have excluded the possibility of conception in the first place. I wish to emphasize the word *probably* here, because in July, 1998 newspapers also revealed that an American woman had become pregnant with sperm cells taken from her husband 24 hours *after* his death. Nonetheless, when Liam Stephen was conceived, his father had already been buried for more than 3 years, so that one could reasonably argue that the conception epitomized a sexual act during which the paternal agency was unquestionably dead.

Moreover, on top of there not being a written consent note justifying the sexual act after his death, Mr. Blood had not even given consent to his sperm being tapped from his body when lying in a coma. Interestingly, the judges concentrated on the issue of consent in relation to Mrs. Blood's artificial insemination, apparently endorsing the *medical* removal of sperm cells from a psychically dead body. Again, it is awkward to pigeonhole the latter event as a technologically sophisticated type of necrophilia in the traditional sense of the word, unless one would also include comatose individuals among the necrophiliac's preferred objects of attraction, and unless one would permit the doctors to derive some form of enjoyment from the act. Nonetheless, when the semen was collected, Mr. Blood had no discretion whatsoever to either agree with or protest against the invasion of his body, such that one could reasonably argue that the removal of his sperm epitomized an intrusive act involving an essential component of human sexuality on an unconscious, helpless, and totally unresponsive body. Apart from exemplifying the difficulty of applying notions of consent with regard to dead or unconscious bodies, the case of Diane Blood thus equally elicits cardinal questions about the boundaries of necrophilic activity, not to mention its presumed association with severe personality disorders.

Archer's provisional solution to the vexed issue of consensuality in the case of necrophilia drew extensively on the work of Belliotti (1979, 1993), whose philosophical explorations of what it means to participate (in)voluntarily in sexual activities have informed many an exchange on sexual ethics. Assessing the relevance of Belliotti's outlook, Soble criticized his view for making "an assumption ... that a person can—logically and morally— consent to a sexual act in advance of the time it occurs, even if one has no firm idea when it might occur. Belliotti's view ... resembles a principle of Pauline marriage: one consents on the day of marriage to sex acts that will occur some indefinite time in the future" (Soble, 1996, p. 31). Soble intimated here that the solution of the antemortem consent is problematic not only because the interference of death makes it impossible for the person to change his or her mind during the act, but also owing to the time lapse between the consent and its operationality. Put differently, consent does not only engage the continuous possibility of revocation, for which the participant evidently needs to be alive, but also the temporal occurrence of the acts to which one has consented.

Of course, the entire discussion about the consensuality of the "partner" within a necrophiliac "relationship" becomes futile, if not to say ridiculous, as soon as one agrees that corpses should not be judged with the same criteria as living (human and nonhuman) creatures. Soble remarked deservedly that "if to masturbate on a rug is not to sexually use the rug involuntarily, against its will, we cannot say that masturbating on or in a corpse involves its 'involuntary participation' " (Soble, 1996, pp. 30–31). Yet, unlike the rug, the corpse is likely to have had the capacity of exercising a will, whether or not the person had reached the legal age of consent before his or her death, which makes the issue slightly more complicated ·than Soble accepted. In addition, to the best of my knowledge there is no such thing as a culture in which rugs are the objects of multifarious social and religious taboos, or in which they feature as the centerpiece of elaborate funeral rites.

Here we touch on a configuration that is at least as fundamental as that of consent when it comes to dissecting necrophilia as an inappropriate relationship. Since times immemorable, human beings have distinguished themselves from their nonhuman counterparts by developing all kinds of death rituals. This typically human attitude toward death, dying, and the dead (Ariès, 1974) has crystallized in the design of cemeteries and burial places; the organization of funerary ceremonies; the erection of tombs, vaults, cenotaphs, shrines, and mausoleums; the construction of morgues and funeral homes, and the staging of public executions.

Underneath the welter of forms these death rituals have assumed across cultures and throughout history, two central motives stand out: a constitutive concern to dispose of the dead body in the most effective way, and an equally fundamental desire to preserve what has animated it (Ragon, 1983). Quite often these two motives are linked, inasmuch as the techniques of disposal (burial, cremation, mummification, etc.) and the funerary customs (weeping, chanting, waking, etc.) stem from a particular set of beliefs about how the body's spiritual force can be sustained. The dead body itself is usually treated with a peculiar mixture of animosity and veneration (Helmers, 1989), because it is simultaneously regarded as impure and unclean, as entitled to care and respect in order to ensure the best possible conditions for the afterlife or the reincarnation of the soul, and as a serious disturbance for the living in its potential return as an undead ghost—hence the elaborate anthropopytheics in premodern as well as industrialized communities (Barber, 1988). Although based on Frazer's extensive collection of ethnographic myths and tales, much of Freud's (1912–1913) ideas concerning the social "taboo upon the dead" therefore also remain applicable to many Western cultures and to large historical periods. Across the widest array of religious beliefs and funerary practices, the dead body appears as both sacred and untouchable, divine and malignant, inviolate and awesome, solemn and troubling (Giovannini, 1998; Ulybin, 1995).

When the necrophiliac indulges in sexual intercourse with a corpse, he or she therefore not only ventures on a body whose consensual power is highly problematic, but also on a corporeal structure whose sociocultural and religious status is exceedingly complex, as reflected in the sophisticated arrangements of funeral rites and death cults. Some funerary customs also seem to have been specifically motivated by the awareness of a likely desecration of the body by necrophiliacs, or a possible violation of its tomb by grave robbers. In what is generally referenced as the first historical mention of necrophilia, a passage that Bullough (1976) perhaps too quickly discarded as an "unverified bit of gossip about necrophilia in ancient Egypt" (p. 67), Herodotus (1990) divulged that "Wives of notable men, and women of great beauty and reputation, are not at once given over to the embalmers, but only after they have been dead for three or four days; this is done, that the embalmers may not have carnal intercourse with them. For it is said that one was found having intercourse with a woman newly dead, and was denounced by his fellow-workman" (p. 373). Similarly, Ragon (1983) argued that a dead body's mandatory consumption by fire in many religious traditions not only facilitates the release of its animating spiritual force and prevents the corpse from rotting, but also serves as an excellent protection against its profanation.

Over and above its psychiatric diagnosis as a mental disorder, it thus seems to me that any characterization of necrophilia as an inappropriate relationship should necessarily take account of the two criteria of informed consent and the social taboo on the dead. The latter criterion is usually overshadowed by the former—in the Diane Blood case only one reader of *The Independent* expressed her unease at the lack of dignity with which Mr. Blood's body had been treated (Arbuthnot, 1996)—and many psychoanalytically oriented researchers (Brill, 1941a; Calef & Weinshel, 1972; Jones, 1951) quoted the "possession of an unresisting and unrejecting partner" (Rosman & Resnick, 1989, p. 160) as the prime motivating factor behind necrophilia. They have thereby often taken for granted patients' own reflections on the origin of their sexual condition, a self-assessment that was expertly summarized by Franzini and Grossberg:

> They [necrophiliacs] frequently mention the desirability of a partner who is helpless, unresistant, and completely at their mercy. The dead lover never rejects caresses and is always available when required; makes no demands, is never unfaithful, and never rejects you. This lover does not compare your love-making skills with others', will go along with any sort of kinky sex, and, if things go too far, cannot be harmed and will never file a complaint against you. (Franzini & Grossberg, 1995, p. 232)

Taking my bearings from Freud (1912–1913), I believe that the social taboo on the dead should also be taken into account here. This factor may even constitute a more important motive for the occurrence of necrophilia than the actual helplessness of the corpse. Also, the desire and enjoyment that necrophiliacs experience before or during their sexual involvement with cadavers is easier to explain in relation to the sociocultural prohibitions that weigh on the dead than in terms of the unresponsiveness of the corpse. Isn't the greatest satisfaction obtained from the transgression of the most vehemently defended cultural taboos? Isn't the most ardent desire experienced in the face of the most powerful cultural prohibitions?

CONCLUSION

What can be learned from this deliberately concise and inevitably incomplete study of necrophilia as an inappropriate relationship? First of all, it is extraordinarily onerous to pinpoint what exactly should be included under the heading of necrophilia. The etymology of Guislain's invention refers to a love for the dead, yet this framework provides room for extensive nosological maneuvering. Traditionally, necrophilia has been associated with the cases of Sergeant Bertrand, Victor Ardisson, and other grave violators, despite the fact that these people seemed more interested in mutilation than sexual intercourse and/or masturbation.

When the definition of necrophilia is expanded to include all acts of love vis-à-vis the dead, one is almost forced to admit that the term should also be applied to those people who have difficulty separating from their loved ones after they have died, and some authors have indeed gone so far as to say that necrophilia is at stake in people's desire to preserve close contact with the deceased body of their beloved partner or sovereign. In this respect, Roach (1996) did not hesitate to qualify the honorable Samuel Pepys as a necrophiliac, owing to his self-reported kiss on the mouth of Katherine of France's remains at Westminster Abbey, during the afternoon of February 23, 1669. Whether they were aware of Pepys' case or not, it is highly unlikely that Masters and Lea (1963) would have accepted such events as instances of necrophilia for their gallery of necrophiles, necrosadists, and necrophagists. Roach's designation demonstrates how far researchers are willing to go when employing the term *necrophilia*, and the case of Diane Blood may push the nosological issue even further, apart from its unquestionable significance for the ethical debate surrounding the coincidence of death and sexuality.

Depending on the scope with which necrophilia is used, estimates of its prevalence will vary immensely, yet the dark number is likely to remain firmly in place. Which mortician will be happy to divulge that his or her profession functions merely as a cover for sexual intercourse with the dead? How many people will be ready to admit that they secretly cherish fantasies of sexual activity with corpses? And how many mortals will concede that they have considered snooping around graveyards for the sole purpose of sexual enjoyment? Recently, some high-profile advocates of necrophilia have provided valuable information concerning the general interest in love relationships with the dead, and the extent of sexual activities with corpses within the private confines of funeral homes. The reliability of these data is almost impossible to ascertain, and until a researcher is found who is willing to engage in extensive participant observation, speculation about the frequency of necrophilia will continue to loom large over professional accounts of the subject.

Finally, rather than endorsing one or another of the multitude of explanations for necrophilia—a welter of different views expertly summarized by Burg (1982)—I have decided to reconsider necrophilia as an "inappropriate relationship" from the dual perspective of informed consent and the social taboo on the dead. The latter criterion has hardly been taken into account when assessing the psychic mechanisms underlying necrophilia, yet to me it seems at least as important as the more common criterion of consent. Furthermore, when viewed from the angle of the taboo on the dead, the designation of necrophilia as an "inappropriate relationship" may acquire a new meaning, because it can be argued that the necrophiliac is more driven by a certain relationship with the reigning symbolic prohibitions concerning the status of dead bodies within a particular culture, than with the lifeless partner on which his or her sexual interest has attached itself.

REFERENCES

American Psychiatric Association. (Ed.). (1994). *Diagnostic and statistical manual of mental disorders* (4th ed.). Washington, DC: APA.

Arbuthnot, F. (1996, October 23). Letter: Unease over widow's fight. *The Independent*, p. 135.

Archard, D. (1998). *Sexual consent*. Boulder. CO: Westview.

Ariès, P. (1974). *Western attitudes toward death: From the middle ages to the present*. Baltimore, MD: Johns Hopkins University Press.

Barber, P. (1988). *Vampires, burial, and death: Folklore and reality*. New Haven, CT: Yale University Press.

Belletrud & Mercier. (1903). Perversion de l'instinct génésique. Anosmie—Affaire Ardisson. *Annales d'hygiène publique et de médecine légale, 49*(6), 481–490.

Belliotti, R. (1979). A philosophical analysis of sexual ethics. *Journal of Social Philosophy, 10*(3), 8–11.

Belliotti, R. (1993). *Good sex: Perspectives on sexual ethics*. Lawrence: University Press of Kansas.

Bortnick, B. (1997). *Deadly urges*. New York: Kensington.

Bosworth, P. (1978). *Montgomery Clift: A biography*. New York: Harcourt Brace Jovanovich.

Brierre de Boismont, A. J. F. (1849, July 21). Remarques médico-légales sur la perversion de l'instinct génésique. *La Gazette médicale de Paris*, pp. 555–564.

Brill, A. A. (1941a). Necrophilia. *Journal of Criminal Psychopathology, 2*, 433–443.

Brill, A. A. (1941b). Necrophilia. *Journal of Criminal Psychopathology, 3*, 51–73.

Bullough, V. L. (1976). *Sexual variance in society and history*. Chicago: University of Chicago Press.

Burg, B. R. (1982). The sick and the dead: The development of psychological theory on necrophilia from Krafft-Ebing to the present. *Journal of the History of the Behavioral Sciences, 18*(3), 242–254.

Calef, V., & Weinshel, E. M. (1972). On certain neurotic equivalents of necrophilia. *International Journal of Psychoanalysis, 53*, 67–75.

Centre National de la Recherche Scientifique. (Ed.). (1986). *Trésor de la langue française. Dictionnaire de la langue du XIXe et du XXe siècle (1789–1960)*, (vol. 12). Paris: Gallimard.

Claux, N. (2000). The vampire manifesto. In A. Parfrey (Ed.), *Apocalypse culture II* (pp. 443–445). Venice, CA: Feral House.

Dansel, M. (1991). *Le Sergent Bertrand: Portrait d'un nécrophile heureux*. Paris: Albin Michel.

Davis, C. A. (1997). *Shrouded*. London: Do-Not Press.

De Gaudenzi, F. (1998). Nécropolis. In G. Wittkop, *Le nécrophile*, (pp. 99–158). Paris: La Musardine.

De Wargny, G. (1965). *La bête noire*. Paris: Le Dinosaure.

Dijkstra, B. (1986). *Idols of perversity: Fantasies of feminine evil in fin-de-siècle culture*. New York: Oxford University Press.

Ellis, H. (1937a). Erotic symbolism—the mechanism of detumescence—the psychic state in pregnancy. In *Studies in the psychology of sex* (vol. 2, pp. 1–279). New York: Random House.

Ellis, H. (1937b). Sexual selection in man. In *Studies in the psychology of sex* (vol. 1.). New York: Random House.

Epaulard, A. (1901). *Vampirisme. Nécrophilie, nécrosadisme, nécrophagie.* Lyon, France: A. Storck.

Eurydice. (1999). *Satyricon USA: A journey across the new sexual frontier.* New York: Scribner.

Foraker, A. G. (1976). The Romantic Necrophiliac of Key West. *Journal of the Florida Medical Association, 63*(8), 642–645.

Franzini, L. R., & Grossberg, J. M. (1995). *Eccentric and bizarre behaviors.* New York: Wiley.

Freud, S. (1912–1913). Totem and taboo. In *The standard edition of the complete psychological works of Sigmund Freud* (vol. 13). London: Hogarth Press and the Institute of Psycho-Analysis.

Fromm, E. (1973). *The anatomy of human destructiveness.* New York: Holt, Rinehart & Winston.

Gilbert, H. (Ed.). (1993). *The sexual imagination: From Acker to Zola.* London: Jonathan Cape.

Giovannini, F. (1998). *Necrocultura: Estetica e culture della morte nell'immaginario di massa.* Rome: Castelvecchi.

Grubin, D., Gudjonsson, G., Gunn, J., & West, D. J. (1993). Disordered and offensive sexual behaviour. In J. Gunn & P. J. Taylor (Eds.), *Forensic psychiatry: Clinical, legal and ethical issues* (pp. 522–566). Oxford, UK: Butterworth-Heinemann.

Guislain, J. (1852). *Leçons orales sur les phrénopathies, ou Traité théorique et pratique des maladies mentales. Cours donné à la clinique des établissements d'aliénés à Gand.* Gand, Belgium: L. Hebbelynck.

Helmers, S. (1989). *Tabu und Faszination: Uber die Ambivalenz der Einstellung zu Toten.* Berlin: D. Reimer.

Hennig, J.-L. (1979). *Morgue. Enquête sur le cadavre et ses usages.* Paris: Editions Libres-Hallier.

Hensley, C. (2000). My lips pressed against the decay. In A. Parfrey (Ed.), *Apocalypse culture II,* (pp. 277–287). Venice, CA: Feral House.

Herodotus. (1990). *Histories* (A. D. Godley, trans.). Cambridge, MA: Harvard University Press.

Jones, E. (1951). *On the nightmare.* New York: Liveright.

Koestler, A. (Ed.). (1938). *Sexual anomalies and perversions: Physical and psychological development and treatment. A summary of the works of the late professor Dr. Magnus Hirschfeld.* London: Torch.

Kramer, L. (1997). *After the lovedeath: Sexual violence and the making of culture.* Berkeley: University of California Press.

Lunier, L. J. J. (1849). Examen médico-légal d'un cas de monomanie instinctive. Affaire du sergent Bertrand. *Annales Médico-Psychologiques, 2*(1), 351–379.

Masters, B. (1993). *The shrine of Jeffrey Dahmer.* London: Coronet.

Masters, R. E. L., & Lea, E. (1963). *Perverse crimes in history: Evolving concepts of sadism, lust-murder, and necrophilia—from ancient to modern times.* New York: Julian.

Michéa, C.-F. (1849). Des déviations maladives de l'appétit vénérien. *Bulletin de l'Union Médicale, 3,* 338–339.

Monneret, E. (1861). *Traité de pathologie générale, Tôme troisième: Séméiologie—pronostic—étiologie.* Paris: Béchet Jeune.

Morel, B.-A. (1857, March 13). Considérations médico-légales sur un imbécile érotique convaincu de profanation des cadavres. *Gazette hebdomadaire de médecine et de chirurgie,* pp. 345–378.

Morton, J. (1987). The unrepentant necrophile: An interview with Karen Greenlee. In A. Parfrey (Ed.). *Apocalypse culture* (pp. 27–34). New York: Amok.

NecroErotic. (2000). http://home.earthlink.net/~john30/public.html/ (accessed on December 14, 2000).

Norris, J. (1992). *Jeffrey Dahmer*. New York: Pinnacle.

Nussbaum, M. C. (1999). "Secret Sewers of Vice": Disgust, Bodies and the Law. In S. A. Bandes (Ed.), *The passions of law: Critical America* (pp. 19–62). New York: New York University Press.

Paglia, C. (1990). *Sexual personae: Art and decadence from Nefertiti to Emily Dickinson*. New Haven, CT: Yale University Press.

Parfrey, A. (Ed.). (2000). *Apocalypse culture II*. Venice, CA: Feral House.

Pirog, J. (2000a). Westgate/The Azrael Project: Necrophonies, necrofrauds, and necrophobics of the worst kind. http://home.earthlink.net/~john30/public.html/westgate.htm (accessed on December 3, 2000).

Pirog, J. (2000b). Ghoulish introspection. http://home.earthlink.net/~john30/public.html/ introspection.htm (accessed on December 3, 2000).

Pirog, J. (2000c). Interview with a ghoul! http://home.earthlink.net/~john30/public.html/nicointerview.htm (accessed on December 3, 2000).

Praz, M. (1970). *The romantic agony* (A. Davidson, trans.). New York: Oxford University Press.

Prins, H. (1990). *Bizarre behaviours: Boundaries of psychiatric disorder*. London: Tavistock/Routledge.

Ragon, M. (1983). *The space of death: A study of funerary architecture, decoration, and urbanism* (A. Sheridan, trans.). Charlottesville: University Press of Virginia.

Reznek, L. (1997). *Evil or ill? Justifying the insanity defence*. London: Routledge.

Roach, J. (1996). History, memory, necrophilia. In P. Phelan & J. Lane (Eds.). *The ends of performance* (pp. 23–30). New York: New York University Press.

Rosario, V. A. (1997). *The erotic imagination: French histories of perversity*. New York: Oxford University Press.

Rosman, J. P., & Resnick, P. J. (1989). Sexual attraction to corpses: A psychiatric review of necrophilia. *Bulletin of the American Academy of Psychiatry and the Law, 17*(2), 153–163.

Schechter, H. (1989). *Deviant: The shocking true story of Ed Gein, the original "psycho."* New York: Pocket Books.

Schwartz, A. E. (1992). *The man who could not kill enough: The secret murders of Milwaukee's Jeffrey Dahmer*. New York: Birch Lane Press.

Soble, A. (1996). *Sexual investigations*. New York: New York University Press.

Spoerri, T. (1959). *Nekrophilie. Strukturanalyse eines Falles*. Basel, Switzerland: Karger.

Stekel, W. (1929). *Sadism and masochism: The psychology of hatred and cruelty* (authorized English version by L. Brink). New York: Liveright.

Tithecott, R. (1997). *Of men and monsters: Jeffrey Dahmer and the construction of the serial killer*. Madison: The University of Wisconsin Press.

Ulybin, V. (1995). *Smert' pogrebal'nykh obriadakh na Rusi ot proslavian do postsovetskogo perioda: Istoriko-literaturnoe issledovanie*. Sankt-Petersburg, Russia: TOO Firma Kredit-Servis.

von Hentig, H. (1964). *Der Nekrotrope Mensch: Vom Totenglauben zur morbiden Totennähe*. Stuttgart: F. Enke Verlag.

Westgatenecromantic. (2000). http://www.westgatenecromantic.com (accessed on November 10, 2000).

Wittkop, G. (1998). *Le nécrophile*. Paris: La Musardine.

10

The Inappropriateness of Relational Intrusion

Brian H. Spitzberg
San Diego State University

William R. Cupach
Illinois State University

Most conceptions of "relationships" envision such qualities as intimacy, openness, trust, and fulfillment (Floyd, 1998). Explicit or implicit in most of these perspectives is an assumption that there is some degree of conjunction between the participants' definitions and objectives in the relationship. That is, the very notion of "relationship" tends to elicit ideas of mutuality and exchange. There are classes of relationships, however, that are more disjunctive in the ways the participants define their connection. Sexually harassing, coercive, abusive, codependent, and enslaving relationships all reflect examples of fundamentally disjunctive relationship preferences. In such relationships, there is a behavioral conjunction, but a psychological disjunction: The partners have divergent, even mutually exclusive, preferences for the trajectory of the relationship. Generally, one of the "participants" prefers to end the relationship altogether, whereas the other participant prefers to pursue an escalation of the relationship, and may not even recognize the divergence. The party evading the relationship is likely to perceive the pursuer's actions as highly inappropriate, whereas the pursuer is unlikely to comprehend the inappropriateness of his or her activities. Such disjunctive relationships are likely to be sites of contention over the appropriateness of interpersonal behavior, and therefore provide a useful domain of discovery in the understanding of inappropriate relationships. One of the purest exemplars of such disjunctive relational states is the obsessively intrusive relationship, in which a person persistently pursues greater intimacy with another person who explicitly does not desire such intimacy. This chapter offers an examination of the process of obsessive relational intrusion and its conceptual cousin, stalking, as forms of inappropriate relationship.

THE NATURE OF OBSESSIVE RELATIONAL INTRUSION

History

In 1990, in response to some sensationalized murder cases in which celebrities had been pursued by mentally disturbed strangers, California passed the first antistalking legislation. The connection of stalking with celebrities seemed to catalyze this stereotype in the public and media consciousness, despite the fact that all available evidence indicates that cases of ordinary people being stalked are far more prevalent than celebrity stalking. By the mid-1990s, there still was virtually no social scientific research on the stalking phenomenon. Indeed, the fact that stalking only became recognized in the 1990s as a significant type of inappropriate relationship suggests that models and research are in their infancy. It is also noteworthy that by the end of the 1990s, all 50 states in the United States and several other countries (e.g., Canada, Australia, Great Britain) had begun to pass or strengthen criminal harassment and stalking legislation, despite a dearth of solid scientific research on the phenomenon being criminalized (Department of Justice, 1998). Many questioned the constitutionality of such legislation, because behaviors such as writing letters, using telephone lines, following, and occupying public spaces are all forms of protected speech in many countries (Bradburn, 1992; Welch, 1995). Regardless, the legislation has generally withstood constitutional tests, and has now generally been normalized within the routines of most law enforcement jurisdictions, however unevenly (Department of Justice, 1998).

Stalking and Obsessive Relational Intrusion

Stalking is generally defined as a legal concept referring to "the willful, malicious, and repeated following and harassing of another person that threatens his or her safety" (Meloy & Gothard, 1995, p. 258). Implicit in this definition are conditions of intent (i.e., willful, malicious), persistence (i.e., repeated), troublesome intrusion (i.e., following and harassing), and threat (i.e., safety). Each of these legal standards poses a significant burden of proof for law enforcement, and illustrate some of the difficulty of establishing the action as criminal. These standards also provide ample opportunity for stalkers to craft their activities so as to make such standards difficult to prove.

Obsessive relational intrusion (ORI) is the repeated and unwanted pursuit and invasion of one's sense of physical or symbolic privacy by another person, either stranger or acquaintance, who desires and/or presumes an intimate relationship (Cupach & Spitzberg, 1998; Cupach, Spitzberg, & Carson, 2000; Spitzberg, Nicastro, & Cousins, 1998). It is closely related to what has been referred to as "relational stalking" (Emerson, Ferris, & Gardner, 1998), "domestic stalking" (Dunn, 1999), or "intimate partner stalking" (Tjaden & Thoennes, 2000). ORI involves a person pursuing intimacy with another that the other explicitly disprefers. ORI ranges from relatively mild activities such as calling and mailing notes of affection or desire, to more severe activities such as property invasion, spying, coercion, kidnapping, and endangerment (Cupach & Spitzberg, 2000). As a process, much of ORI is likely to emulate relatively normal courtship practices in the form of persistent displays of attraction, provision of tokens and gifts of affection, and frequent attempts to communicate a desire for a more intimate relationship. What makes such activity inappropriate is the disjunctive preference possessed and expressed by one of the persons involved in this "relationship."

ORI and stalking are overlapping but not isomorphic sets of activities. In 1993, the National Institute of Justice published a model antistalking code that entailed four necessary major elements:

- A course of conduct involving repeated physical proximity (following) or threatening behavior or both; …
- The occurrence of incidents at least twice;
- Threatening behavior, including both explicit and implicit threats;
- Conduct occurring against an individual or family members of the individual. (Department of Justice, 1998, pp. 26–27)

As of 1998, 32 states required that the pursuit behavior entail an intent to instill fear, and 14 more states required demonstration that the pursuit is purposeful. Six states involve a legal test that a "reasonable person" would be afraid of the pattern of behavior (Department of Justice, 1998). Thus, stalking requires that fear and/or threat be credible or intended, both potentially difficult legal standards. Furthermore, although it is a minority of all cases, stalking can be entirely nonrelational, as when an assassin pursues a target for a hit. Finally, stalking sometimes involves a former relationship in which there is no intent to pursue a further relationship. A jilted former lover or spouse may simply seek pure revenge and destruction of the former partner.

In contrast, ORI activity may be bothersome, annoying, or harassing, but not threatening. Furthermore, ORI specifically entails, at least at some point in the process, a pursuit of some form of intimacy with the object of pursuit. Despite these differences, stalking and ORI are largely overlapping sets of behavior. Studies of such obsessive relational intrusion behavior reveal that when it is unwanted, even normatively benign behaviors tend to be perceived as at least moderately threatening (Cupach & Spitzberg, 2000). Most stalking occurs in the context of previous relationships (Tjaden & Thoennes, 1998, 2000). Thus, ORI and stalking represent largely overlapping but not isomorphic domains. Much of obsessive intrusion constitutes a form of stalking, even if it may (or may not) meet the legal standards of the crime. Given their degree of overlap, this chapter examines the research on both activities as forms of inappropriate relational intrusion, understanding that stalking on occasion is not "relational" in nature.

Significance of Unwanted Intrusion

As a recognized process, stalking is still a relatively recent phenomenon. ORI, as one of the "dark sides" of close relationships, has been relatively neglected due to the more dominant ideology of intimacy in the social sciences (Cupach & Spitzberg, 1998). Consequently, the research agenda has only recently begun to lift the veil on the processes of unwanted relational intrusion. Based on data available from over 50 studies of stalking and obsessive relational intrusion, some basic conclusions about the nature and scope of such inappropriate relationships are becoming clear (Spitzberg & Cupach, 2001).

According to the only representative survey, performed in the United States, about 8% of females and 2% of males have been stalked in their lifetime, and .5% of women and .2% of men have been stalked in the past year (Tjaden & Thoennes, 2000). These rates are even higher when a self-defined criterion is employed (Tjaden, Thoennes, & Allison, 2000). This study employed a relatively strict screening criterion. When the questions are relaxed a bit to include persistent following and ORI, or when people have simply been asked if they have been stalked, the rates have tended to be much higher, although to date almost all such estimates have been obtained from convenience samples. For example, in college samples, rates of obsessive harassment and/or stalking have ranged from 5% to 15% (Fisher, Cullen, & Turner, 1999; McCreedy & Dennis, 1996), to even 20% to 30% (Coleman, 1997; Cupach & Spitzberg, 1998; Sinclair & Frieze, 2000; Spitzberg et al., 1998). Almost 100% of people who have been broken up with in unrequited love relationships admit to engaging in unwanted pursuit behaviors (Langhinrichsen-Rohling, Palarea, Cohen, & Rohling, 2000).

Before ORI and stalking were recognized as important phenomena, some studies found that substantial percentages of college students had experienced behaviors that may have been facets of these phenomena. For example, Leonard et al. (1993) found 91% of graduate students, 69% of undergraduate students, 84% of faculty, and 67% of staff had experienced "unwanted letters, calls, visits, pressure for meetings, dates, etc., where personal interest in you was implied, but no sexual expectations were stated" (p. 176). Similarly, in a study of harassment by jilted dating partners among adolescents, Roscoe, Strouse, and Goodwin (1994) found that 16% to 23% of males and females had received unwanted and harassing calls, letters, pressure for dates, and sexual advances from the former partner.

Other studies examine more specialized or focused populations. For example, Burgess and colleagues found that 30% of domestic violence cases they examined involved stalking (Burgess et al., 1997). Only 4% of a small sample of human resources staff reported being stalked (Eisele, Watkins, & Matthews, 1998), whereas almost 6% of counselors claimed to have been stalked by clients (Romans, Hays, & White, 1996). In contrast, almost 68% of medical workplace violence episodes in one study involved some amount of stalking (Feldman, Holt, & Hellard, 1997). Given the variance among these studies and their distinct populations and operationalizations, it is difficult to generalize with much precision regarding the prevalence of stalking and ORI. However, given the lowest estimate of 2% for males, it is still clear that this phenomenon affects millions of people. However, this is obviously a conservative estimate, and the lifetime population parameter is almost certainly much higher.

ARE STALKING AND ORI "CLOSE RELATIONSHIPS"?

A legitimate question arises when examining stalking and obsessive relational intrusion in the context of close relationships theory: Do these phenomena constitute close relationships? The answer to this question needs to be established in steps.

To begin with, not all stalkers are seeking relational closeness. Excluding these cases, we believe that the vast majority of the remaining instances of stalking and obsessive relational intrusions can be legitimately conceptualized as close relationships, for the following reasons.

Relational History

First, the vast majority of stalking and obsessive intrusion cases arise out of some prior established relationship. Averaging across slightly disparate relationship labels in 15 studies of stalking/ORI, approximately 15% were married; 13% cohabiting; 21% dating seriously; 15% dating casually; 23%

friends; 5% relatives; 24% coworkers, classmates, or in a professional relationship; and 25% acquaintances. Indeed, an average of 15% reported currently being in the relationship with the person pursuing them. In contrast,
13% reported the pursuer as a stranger, and 7% reported the target as a
public figure.[1] McCreedy and Dennis (1996) reported that 40% and Fisher
et al. (1999) reported that 53% of their respondents claimed to know the
suspect "well." In their nationally representative study of 16,000 persons,
Tjaden and Thoennes (1998) reported that 59% of female and 30% of male
stalking victims were pursued by a former or present intimate partner. In
short, a substantial majority of stalking and obsessive pursuit phenomena
emerge from existing or previous ongoing relationships.

Second, from a structural perspective, close relationships can be defined
in terms of several specific dimensions. In a classic exposition on what constitutes a "close relationship," four basic criteria were isolated: duration of
interconnections, frequency of interconnections, strength of interconnections (i.e., amount of change P—pursuer—causes in O—object), and diversity of interconnections (Kelley et al., 1983). A case can be made for each of
these criteria in the paradoxical world of obsessional pursuit.

Duration

Only a few studies have inquired as to the duration of stalking or ORI. The
ranges reported show that stalking tends to mimic relatively durable relationships. The average median across three diverse studies is 12.7 months
(Brewster, 1998; Fisher et al., 1999; Pathé & Mullen, 1997), and the average mean across three diverse studies is 4.6 months (Fisher et al., 1999;
Spitzberg & Cupach, 1996; Spitzberg & Rhea, 1999). However, the largest
and most representative sample reports a mean of 1.8 years per stalking relationship, with 9% of the population reporting being stalked for over 5
years (Tjaden & Thoennes, 1998). Whereas many of these processes of
pursuit may be relatively ephemeral, clearly many of them are very long-
standing processes of interaction.

Frequency

What is oddly hidden in the statistics of duration is the frequency with
which the stalking and ORI intrude into the person's life over these spans

---

[1]The 15 studies were Brewster (1998), Burgess et al. (1997), Fisher et al. (1999), Fremouw,
Westrup, and Pennypacker (1997), Gill and Brockman (1996), Hall (1997), Harmon et al.
(1995), Hills and Taplin (1998), Kienlen et al. (1997), Kong (1996), Mullen et al. (1999), New
Jersey State Police (1997), Nicastro et al. (2000), Pathé and Mullen (1997), and Spitzberg and
Rhea (1999). The percentages add to more than 100% because different studies employed different categories. In cases in which a generic label was employed (e.g., "former intimate partner"),
the statistic reported in the original study was divided evenly among the categories of "married,"
"cohabiting," "seriously dating," and "casually dating."

of time. For example, Fisher et al. (1999) found that 13% of victims claimed to have experienced daily events, and 41% experienced 2 to 6 events per week. Kienlen, Birmingham, Solberg, O'Regan, and Meloy (1997) reported that 32% had been contacted between 10 and 19 times, 32% had been contacted between 20 and 49 times, and one fifth were contacted over 80 times. In a sample of abused women, when asked if their partner had "stalked you" in the past month, 15% claimed to have been stalked one to two times, 5% claimed once to twice a week, 5% claimed several times a week, and 3% claimed daily victimizations (Mechanic, Weaver, & Resick, 2000).

Placed in the context of these duration findings, the frequency data indicate that these are persistent, ongoing, and reasonably durable relationships. Indeed, although there is little systematic basis for the inference, it may well be that stalking and ORI relationships display higher average duration and frequencies of contact than do many reciprocal relationships! As to whether or not stalking and ORI meet the remaining strength and diversity criteria of close relationships, it is important to examine two additional domains of the intrusion phenomenon: the impact of victimization (i.e., strength) and the tactical diversity of pursuit.

Strength

One of the interpretations of the strength of a relationship is the extent of change each person can effect in the other (Kelley et al., 1983). The very notion of "obsession" suggests the strength of the object's effect on the pursuer. The data reviewed previously also demonstrate the amount of investment of time that pursuers are willing or compelled to commit to the pursuit of the relationship. Conversely, there is increasing evidence to indicate that the objects of pursuit are affected significantly by the process of pursuit.

Brewster (1998) reported that 99% of objects experienced "quality of life" costs due to the pursuit, including such tendencies as constantly looking over one's shoulder, fear or terror, distrust or suspicion, paranoia, nervousness or jumpiness, anger, depression, insomnia, and frustration. In addition, evidence of strength is indicated by the finding that 64% of these respondents reported changing their activity patterns, and 80% reported financial costs associated with stalking victimization. Nicastro, Cousins, and Spitzberg (2000) found that 80% of their cases reported feeling fearful, 43% threatened, 33% nervous, 29% angry, 11% physically ill, and 9% depressed. Tjaden and Thoennes (1998) found that 20% to 30% of stalking victims sought counseling, lost time from work, were more concerned with safety, and more likely to carry something to defend themselves.

Finally, physical or sexual violence or injury occurs at least a small percentage of the time (i.e., < 10%; e.g., Kong, 1996; Zona, Sharma, & Lane,

1993), but may occur in as much as 15% to 30% of cases (Brewster, 1998; Burgess et al., 1997; Fisher et al., 1999; Gill & Brockman, 1996; Hall, 1997; Kienlen et al., 1997; Mullen, Pathé, Purcell, & Stuart, 1999; Nicastro et al., 2000; Tjaden & Thoennes, 1998). Not surprisingly, given this array of injuries and insults to a person's life, over 95% of objects of persistent pursuit or stalking claim they are injured emotionally or psychologically (Fisher et al., 1999; Romans et al., 1996). In summary, if the effect on someone's life is taken as a measure of the strength of relationship, stalking and ORI clearly portray a consistent picture of a strong relationship.

Diversity

Diversity refers in part to the various facets and contexts of interaction experienced in a relationship. To the extent that pursuit exploits a wide variety of places, tactics, and motives, it provides evidence of diversity. The research itself is seldom consistent in its operationalization of these characteristics, but the data are consistent in displaying diversity of interaction. Stalkers and pursuers reveal impressive ingenuity in their tactical repertoires. Pursuit commonly occurs in the form of persistent telephone calls at home, work, and on cellular telephone; e-mails; watching from afar; following in a car and on foot; visiting work; appearing at social events; interrupting conversations; driving or walking by the object's home; trespassing; breaking into a home or car; theft of identity; sending of gifts; surveillance of home; property damage; sexual propositions; and approaches in public places (Brewster, 1998; Burgess et al., 1997; Fisher et al., 1999; Gill & Brockman, 1996; Hall, 1997; Kienlen et al., 1997; Meloy & Gothard, 1995; Mullen et al., 1999; Nicastro et al., 2000; Pathé & Mullen, 1997; Tjaden & Thoennes, 1998). In addition, across most studies, more than half of stalking cases involve threats made directly against the object or against the object's valued pets, friends, family, and/or possessions (Brewster, 1998; Fisher et al., 1999; Gill & Brockman, 1996; Kienlen et al., 1997; Meloy & Gothard, 1995; Mullen et al., 1999; Nicastro et al., 2000; Pathé & Mullen, 1997; Tjaden & Thoennes, 1998).

The motives underlying these actions display both the socioemotional ambivalence of stalking and the variegation of the process itself. The motives or causes of stalking have been attributed by respondents to relationship breakup, reconciliation, incompetence, jealousy, new boy/girlfriend, intimidation, anger/revenge, resentment, possessiveness, dependency, obsession, infatuation, drug abuse, and of course, mental illness (Brewster, 1998; Hall, 1997; Harmon, Rosner, & Owens, 1995; Kienlen et al., 1997; Mullen et al., 1999; Nicastro et al., 2000). Stalking and obsessive relational pursuit run a wide gamut of motives, tactics, and contexts. Consequently, stalking and obsessive relational pursuit constitute highly diverse forms of interaction.

In conclusion, stalking and obsessive relational intrusion tend to emerge from prior or extant relationships, and the process of pursuit tends to be durable, frequent, diverse, and strong. Consequently, ORI and stalking appear to meet the criteria of "close relationships." Yet, there is clearly something different about these relationships from what is normally understood as close relationships. We believe that one of the key differences is that obsessive pursuit and intrusion are part of a class of disjunctive relationships. Close relationships are typically considered close in part because both partners share some mutual interest in the pursuit of the relationship and the rewards it brings, either actually or potentially, directly or indirectly. In stalking and ORI, however, one of the parties explicitly does not want to pursue the relationship, and yet finds him- or herself a captive of the relationship, playing a game, the rules of which are only vaguely perceived, and in which the ability to quit is elusive. Generally speaking, "the phenomenon of stalking is marked exactly by radical disjuncture between the perspectives and understandings of victims and pursuers" (Emerson et al., 1998, p. 294).

ORI FROM AN INTERACTIONAL-RELATIONAL PERSPECTIVE

Nascent Relational Concepts in Dominant Models

Most current models of stalking and obsessive pursuit have been clinical and forensic in approach. There are at least three dominant sets of clinical/forensic models that attempt to explain and/or describe stalking behavior. The first set consists of approaches that rely on attachment and object relations theories. The second set of models provides typologies of stalker types, generally based on some underlying dimension presumed to have explanatory, predictive, or descriptive value. The third set of models attempts to place stalking into a sequential or stage-based process. These sets of models are generally neither fully developed nor mutually exclusive. Their value to establishing an interactional-relational perspective is that each of these sets of models contains within it implicit relational themes.

Developmental Models. To date, developmental models have relied primarily on attachment theory, with occasional nods to the complementary theory of object relations (Cupach et al., 2000; Meloy, 1992). Attachment is an affectional bond resulting from attachment behavior patterns that develop between persons. Attachment behavior consists of proximity maintenance activities, ranging from physical contact to eye contact and auditory responsiveness (Bowlby, 1980). Attachment and attachment behaviors are thought to form a homeostatic behavior system.

Attachments are formed in infancy with adults, most significantly the primary caregiver. Over time, attachment patterns form collective systems of cognition considered working relationship models or schemata, which in turn organize perceptions and expectations regarding attachment behavior. Thus, if a primary caregiver is consistently available, responsive, affectionate, and nurturing, the infant tends to develop into adulthood with relatively *secure* attachment models. Those with secure working models tend to develop self-esteem, popularity, generalized trust, sociability, and an ability to balance autonomy and intimacy (Feeney & Noller, 1996). As adults, those with secure working models tend to describe love as happy, friendly, trusting, and accepting (Shaver, Hazan, & Bradshaw, 1988). In contrast, when primary caregivers are inconsistent, intrusive, or interfering in their affections, infants become more *anxious-ambivalent* about affection. Those with anxious-ambivalent working models tend to be suspicious of others' motives, distrusting, apprehensive, and interpersonally distant (Feeney & Noller, 1996). Anxious-ambivalent adults tend to describe love in terms of a need for union, obsessive preoccupation, jealousy, and emotional extremes (Shaver et al., 1988). Alternatively, if the primary caregiver rejects or ignores the infant, the infant will tend to develop an *avoidant* working model. Those with an avoidant working model tend to become fatalistic, dependent, afraid of rejection, lacking in self-confidence, and yet desirous of extreme intimacy (Feeney & Noller, 1996). Adult avoidants tend to describe love in terms of a fear of intimacy, emotional extremes, and jealousy (Shaver et al., 1988).

More recent work has identified two underlying dimensions of adult attachment, resulting in four working models rather than three. The first dimension, *discomfort with closeness*, corresponds to the extent to which a person is basically negative or positive regarding others (Roberts & Noller, 1998). The second dimension, conceptualized as *anxiety over abandonment*, corresponds to a dimension of negative or positive feelings about self (Roberts & Noller, 1998). These dimensions create a taxonomy of four attachment styles (Bartholomew & Horowitz, 1991; Becker, Billings, Eveleth, & Gilbert, 1997). *Secures* possess a positive model of self and a positive model of others. *Preoccupieds* possess a negative model of self and a positive model of others. *Dismissives* possess a positive model of self and a negative model of others. Finally, *fearful-avoidants* possess a negative model of self and a negative model of others.

There are several potential overlaps between attachment-based working models and the phenomena of stalking and obsessive pursuit (Cupach et al., 2000; Langhinrichsen-Rohling et al., 2000). The first area of overlap concerns attachment styles as they influence love styles and orientations to romantic relationships. Secures are unlikely to feel sufficiently inadequate to develop an obsession or a fixation on another as a potential source of self-fulfillment. Conversely, dismissives are unlikely to need or desire intimacy, and are therefore unlikely to pursue anyone for the sake of a relationship. Fearful-avoidants tend to endorse passionate and game-playing styles of love that are low on intimacy, passion, and commitment. Thus, they may enjoy the manipulative aspect that characterizes some stalking, and are likely to lack the empathy with the object of pursuit that might deter more threatening kinds of action. But their negative view of others is unlikely to sustain a personally costly campaign of pursuit of another who represents a source of anxiety. Anxious-ambivalents, in contrast, tend to endorse manic, desperate, and possessive love (Levy & Davis, 1988; Sperling & Berman, 1991), and can be expected to fixate and pursue an object of affection with passion. Thus, it is expected that stalkers and obsessive pursuers will be most likely to reveal an anxious-ambivalent attachment style, with a smaller percentage of stalkers and pursuers revealing an avoidant attachment style.

Another source of overlap between attachment styles and obsessive pursuit is through psychopathology and borderline personality disorder. Bowlby (1980) described psychopathology as the progression through a deviant pathway of attachment experiences (see also Fonagy et al., 1995). Loss of a significant caregiver, as well as consistently punishing, abusive, or unreliable caregiving, are thought to inculcate a withdrawal into self, and thereby an inability to engage in reflective meta-cognition or perspective taking. This leads to formation of borderline personality. People with borderline disorder tend to have disturbed interpersonal relations characterized as "fundamentally disordered, short-lived, chaotic yet extremely intense" (Fonagy et al., 1995, p. 259).

Furthermore, turning inward can produce narcissism as a defensive approach to the world. Narcissism entails a grandiose sense of self that is ironically generally seated in a deeper sense of unworthiness. This pathological narcissism, combined with the inability to experience others as fully articulated individuals, leads to a tendency to view others as mere "objects" for gratifying self (Meloy, 1998). A pattern of interpersonal hypersensitivity, suspicion, and distrust results, in which "the mildest criticism or the slightest rebuff" can turn submissiveness into "disparagement and rage" (Fonagy et al., 1995, p. 260). Such persons become "extraordinarily sensitive to rejection and the feelings of shame or humiliation that accompany it" (Meloy, 1998, p. 19). By turning inward, such persons are left without a "meaningful inner experience of human contact. This may account for the 'neediness' of borderline personality individuals" (Fonagy et al., 1995, p. 259). It is in the nexus of such disturbed attachments and personality development that people can become coercive and violent (Fonagy et al., 1995; Roberts & Noller, 1998), especially in the face of an object of affection turning away from the pursuer.

Finally, attachment theory and obsessive pursuit overlap because people with insecure attachment styles (i.e., anxious-ambivalents, avoidants) are also likely to be hypersensitive to significant stressors and relational losses. Thus, research indicates that stalkers are likely to have recently experienced some significant stress, including relational losses (Kienlen et al., 1997; Meloy, 1996). Such losses may prime the insecurities experienced since childhood, and lead to defensive reactions that include either pursuit of intimacy, pursuit of revenge, or both.

Descriptive Typologies.   Given the spectacular ways in which the crime of stalking first began to enter the public psyche, it is small wonder that attempts to understand the phenomenon have relied heavily on clinical and "type of relationship" classifications (e.g., Harmon et al., 1995; Kienlen et al., 1997; Roberts & Dziegielewski, 1996). Many of these typologies identified types based on the underlying psychological characteristics of the stalker. It is informative to note the extent to which many of the typologies "pathologize" stalking, thereby defining such activities as abnormal and deviant, and therefore implicitly inappropriate. For example, one of the more prominent typologies was formulated and refined by Zona and others (e.g., Zona et al., 1993), who identified three basic types. The *simple obsessional* consists of persistent pursuit by someone who has some previous relationship or knowledge of the object of pursuit. The *love obsessional* consists of a person pursuing an object with whom no previous relationship existed. The most common subtype is the celebrity or public figure stalker. *Erotomanics* are delusionally convinced that their object loves them. Although a small minority of all stalkers, erotomanics have captured the imagination of much of the scholarly clinical and stalking literatures (e.g., Harmon et al., 1995; Zona et al., 1993).

Spitzberg and Cupach (2001) formulated a formal typology based on the intersection of two dimensions: motive and mode (see Fig. 10.1). The mode can be controlling or expressive in nature. Controlling modes of pursuit involve planned activities to influence certain outcomes. Expressive modes of pursuit are more affective and spontaneous. Motives can be based on love (i.e., affection, intimacy, caring, etc.) or hate (i.e., fear inducement, revenge, pain, etc.). When crossed, these dimensions identify two types of pursuer and two types of stalker: annoying pursuer (expressive mode, love motive), intrusive pursuer (controlling mode, love motive), organized stalker (controlling mode, hate motive), and disorganized stalker (expressive mode, hate motive).

Emerson et al. (1998) identified five types of stalking, one of which is particularly relevant to inappropriate relational pursuit. Three types involve relative strangers: unacquainted stalking, pseudoacquainted stalking, and semi-acquainted stalking. Revenge stalking consists of pursuit designed to intimidate, express hostility, and/or aggression. Relational stalking entails "unilateral pursuit linked to some admiring or romantic interest in, or implied or specific assertions of rights to, a continuing, close or inti-

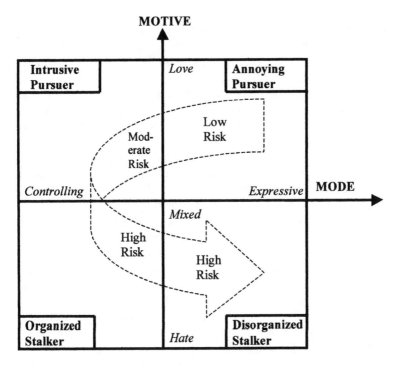

FIG. 10. 1.   A formal typology of obsessive pursuer types.

mate relationship with another" (p. 295). There are two unique character-izations of this type of stalker: first, the one-sidedness of the pursuit; and second, the existence of meta-relational troubles, in which interaction fo-cuses on "words and actions that define and comment upon whatever pre-vious relationship the parties have had, and what the parties should be to and for one another in the future" (p. 296).

Stagic and Phasic Models.   To date, there have been only two at-tempts to outline specific stages through which stalking is likely to pro-ceed. In their analysis of stalking case files, Burgess et al. (1997) found that certain activities tended to occur before others. They discovered an aver-age ranked order as follows: anonymous phone calls, hang-up calls, of-fender tries to discredit victim, contact at residence, contact at work, love turns to hate, contact at public place, contact others regarding victim, fol-low victim to car, send flowers/gifts, and entering residence. In speculating about this and other results from their analysis, Burgess et al. formulated a formal flow model for partner abuse and stalking. In this model, an abuser who seeks to dominate a partner engages first in forms of psychological and/or physical aggression (e.g., isolation, sexual coercion, physical abuse, etc.), then escalates this aggression to higher levels of threat and abuse. At some point, separation of the partners creates a situation in which the abuser's need to control the partner extends into stalking, which takes one of three forms: open attempts at contact, conversion of positive emotion to negative emotion, and escalation into violence in the partner's residence or workplace.

In contrast, Emerson et al. (1998) interviewed people who had been followed or sought temporary restraining orders. Based on these qualitative data, a general set of phases of activities was discerned. The authors noted that many of these stages occur in a larger stage that might be considered "prestalking," in the sense that they are recognized as stalking only in retrospect. The phases consisted of (a) pursuer follows victim, (b) pursuer restricts, extracts, or controls information from or about victim, (c) pursuer makes initial proposals to victim who provides initial rejections, (d) pursuer persists to the point that victim recognizes the pursuit as excessive or intrusive, and (e) pursuer's orientation shifts to revenge, hostility, jealousy, rage, and violence. These phases have a strong intuitive coherence, and accord somewhat with traditional models of relationship development (e.g., Battaglia, Richard, Datteri, & Lord, 1998), to a point. That is, there is a sense of a traditional courtship script up to the point of the recognition that the pursuit is excessive. At the point the object's rejection creates a significant face or identity issue for the pursuer, this rebuff is likely to serve as a trigger that shifts affection to aggression.

The data thus far regarding stages of stalking are very interpretive in nature. Stages are difficult to test empirically. One conjecture, however, would be that if stalking progresses in stages as normal relationships do, stalking behavior might differ in quantity or quality according to the type of relationship a person has with the pursuer. At least one study found no significant differences in a wide array of stalking behaviors in a sample of acutely battered women on the basis of whether or not their relationship with the partner was described as dating, married, cohabiting, or separated/divorced (Mechanic et al., 2000). Such a finding needs to be replicated in diverse populations to see if the stage of relationship reflects shifts in the nature of stalking activity, or if stalking activities operate by an entirely different type of relational clock.

ORI From an Interactional-Relational Perspective

ORI as Communicative and Interactional.   An interactional-relational perspective on ORI begins with the assumption that obsessive relational intrusion is borne out of symbolic behavior. Pursuit behaviors are largely intentional and strategic in nature. The pursuer is striving for a concrete relational goal and communicative plans to achieve the goal are designed, modified, and implemented. All pursuer contact with the object evokes meanings for both the pursuer and object. Early on, even before the object realizes that pursuit will become obsessive, the object interprets the actions of the pursuer in various ways, and the pursuer interprets the reactions of the object. Even at the point where an object attempts to avoid responding to a pursuer, the pursuer derives meaning from the object's "noncommunication" (cf., Watzlawick, Beavin, & Jackson, 1967). It follows that the object's appraisals of the inappropriateness of the pursuer's behavior will be an important meaning in determining how direct and proactive relational extraction will be. Likewise, pursuer's appraisals of the inappropriateness of the object's avoidance will likely influence the pursuer's aggressiveness of pursuit. Some of the dynamics of such appraisals and processes are elaborated in the context of an interactional-relational perspective toward obsessive pursuit and stalking.

The actions of both pursuer and object are interconnected and manifested in a temporal pattern. A single action or reaction does not define ORI, nor does a single "episode" of pursuit constitute ORI. Rather, ORI has a serial quality, such that pursuer and object behaviors are thematically and sequentially connected. The actions of the pursuer influence the subsequent actions of the object, which in turn affect the subsequent actions of the pursuer, and so on. Thus, pursuer and object possess, at some point in the progression of events, a mutual awareness of each other, and pursuer–object behaviors are mutually contingent over time. This combination of mutual awareness, mutual influence (contingency), and temporal symbolic continuity constitute the defining features of a relationship (e.g., Hinde, 1997).

ORI as a Disjunctive Relational Form.   As we argued earlier, ORI satisfies the criteria to qualify as a type of close relationship. However, the nature of the relationship between pursuer and object is distinctive in its disjunctive nature. The pursuer and the object possess conflicting relationship goals, and the definition of the relationship is nonmutual (cf., Morton, Alexander, & Altman, 1976). Pursuer and object are relationally bound up in a dialectical unity of opposites. Misperception and miscommunication perpetuate this disjunctive connection.

ORI as Dysfunctional and Inappropriate.   The disjunction that results from ORI renders the relationship between pursuer and object dysfunctional and inappropriate. Both parties are unhappy with the nature of the relationship, as the pursuer strives for more connection and intimacy whereas the object seeks disconnection and distance. Because of the pursuer's egocentric focus on personal goals for a relationship with the object, the pursuer rationalizes pursuit as appropriate, even when object resistance is repeated and unequivocal (Langhinrichsen-Rohling et al., 2000; Sinclair & Frieze, 2000). The relationship is inappropriate, however, to the extent that the pursuer's actions entrap the object in an unwanted relationship—a type of relationship that is culturally defined as voluntary. In other words, the pursuer seeks a relationship that requires mutuality and conjuctivity to be viable and appropriate. Yet the object's participation in the relationship is involuntary; the pursuer inappropriately imposes the relationship on the object.

The exact point at which relational pursuit becomes obsessive and inappropriate often is not precisely definable (Sinclair & Frieze, 2000). This is due, in part, to the fact that ORI emerges out of ordinary, normative behaviors designed to negotiate relationships (Cupach et al., 2000; Emerson et al., 1998; Spitzberg & Cupach, 2001). Affinity-seeking, information-seeking, self-disclosure, ingratiation, expressions of regard, and so on constitute normal and pervasive everyday relational activities. Some degree of persistence in relational pursuit is expected and accepted, and terminated relationships are frequently repaired or reconciled after repeated and concerted efforts. Normal relationship pursuit becomes obsessive and inappropriate when the pursuer persists despite overt and repeated rejection by the object (Cupach & Spitzberg, 1998). Exaggerated and excessive forms of developing intimacy therefore symptomize ORI.

Using prototypical dimensions of relationship intimacy, Table 10.1 provides a comparison of "normal" intimate relationships versus relationships characterized by ORI. For example, using the prototypical intimacy dimensions of self-disclosure and closeness, we expect that normal relationships develop by way of cautious and progressive disclosure. Disclosure is more positive than negative, and occurs in reciprocal increments. Familiarity develops progressively and mutually. In a relationship marked by ORI, on the other hand, disclosure is premature, excessive, and incommensurate with the level that is reciprocated. Familiarity is engineered through violations of privacy, and closeness is imposed through hyperactive possessiveness. Considering all of the prototypical dimensions of intimacy indicated in Table 10.1, ORI relationships are characterized by forms of intimacy that are distorted, exaggerated, accelerated, more intense, and more desperate compared to the normal prototype for developing intimacy. Although the same dimensions of intimacy that characterize normal relations apply to ORI relations, their manifestations are more forced, fabricated, prematurely escalated, and disinhibited in ORI relations. In the section that follows, we present a model to account for how normal relational pursuit becomes exaggerated, excessive, obsessive, and inappropriate.

TABLE 10.1

Comparison of "Normal" and Obsessive Relational Intrusion (ORI) Intimate Relationships Along Prototypical Dimensions of Intimacy. (Dimensions adapted from Floyd, 1998; Roscoe, Kennedy, & Pope, 1987; Waring, Tillman, Frelick, Russell, & Weisz, 1980).

Intimacy Dimension	"Normal" Relations Prototype	ORI Relations Prototype
Self-disclosure	Disclose cautiously/progressively; significantly higher ratio of positive to negative disclosures	A spillway of relatively unregulated disclosure
Emotional expression	Steady progression of personal feelings and direct expression of affection	Attempts to elicit disclosures from O re: feelings toward P through P's own incessant disclosures of feelings for O
Closeness	Seek progressive but punctuated increase in time together and "familiarity" with other	Hyperactive possessiveness and immediate sense of total familiarity illustrated through privacy invasions
Liking/loving	Displays of affection, caring, empathy, but consistent with stage of progression for the relationship	Showering of O with gifts, tokens, notes, calls, etc., generally all oriented to expressing affection for O
Commitment	Measured negotiation of acceptable or desired level of relational exclusivity	Instantaneous and frequent insistence on relational exclusivity and fidelity
Trust and loyalty	Low but steady progression of faith that each other will "be there" for the other, through "thick and thin"	Intense ambivalence of P due to O's avoidance/rejection, leading to P's frequent conflicts with O regarding O's faithfulness
Interests and activities	Individual interests are shared and nurtured to develop common spheres of mutual interest	P "takes up" O's interests as a way "into" O's life, and to fabricate coincidental meetings
Compatibility	Gradual interpenetration of activities and negotiation of mutually consistent values and/or agreements to disagree	Frequent assertions of how "fate" made P and O "perfect" for each other

(continued on next page)

207

TABLE 10.1   *(continued)*

Intimacy Dimension	*"Normal" Relations Prototype*	*ORI Relations Prototype*
Physical interaction	Escalation of frequency, comfort, intimacy, sexuality, and publicness of bodily contact	P expresses desire for physical contact that O denies to P; P provides graphic descriptions of past or imagined physical trysts
Interaction comfort	Development of conversational rapport, interaction rituals, and behavioral synchrony	Ongoing "strain" attempting to develop rapport by P, made difficult by O's avoidance and/or rejection
Autonomy	Each person brings out the "best" in the other, and helps other fulfill individual objectives unrelated to the relationship	P feels complete only if O joins P; P behaves unilaterally or coercively to fulfill own autonomy and self
Lack of conflict	Conflict is generally limited in intensity and frequency, and when it does occur it serves to advance the relationship	Conflict is unpleasant, but P views it as necessary evil to make O realize P's correctness

P = Pursuer, O = Object of pursuit.

A Model of Obsessive Relational Intrusion

Figure 10.2 offers a tentative model of ORI. The model does not capture all of the dynamic and serial qualities that attend ORI. However, it does focus on proximal cognitive and behavioral elements that account for the persistence and obsessiveness of some pursuit.

Pathways to Pursuit: The Pursuer–Object "Event."   ORI begins with the pursuer acquiring a goal to establish an intimate relationship of some sort with the object. This goal emerges from one of three possible "events" that trigger the pursuer's interest in the object. Perhaps the most common path occurs when pursuer and object previously shared a mutual, conjunctive relationship. The pursuer holds the goal of keeping (or restoring) the relationship, even though the former partner now relinquishes that connection. Domestic stalking during marital separation or divorce represents a common example of this path (e.g., Coleman, 1997). Although the former relationship is typically romantic in nature (i.e., dating

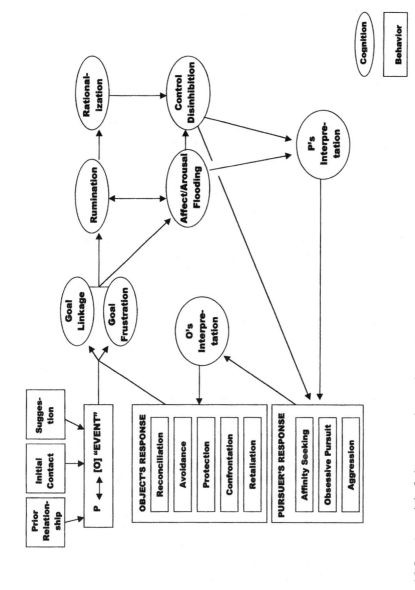

FIG. 10.2.   A model of obsessive relational intrusion.

or married), it is not necessarily so. Pursuers sometimes desire to maintain a friendship or collegial relationship that is terminated by the object.

An alternative path for the pursuer developing a relational goal occurs when the pursuer and the object share some nominal interaction, such as in a chance meeting at work or in a public place. During such an encounter, the pursuer's immediate attraction to the object leads to the development of the pursuer's goal to establish a more intimate connection with the object. The object may be unaware for some time that subsequent, seemingly coincidental contacts with the pursuer are actually motivated by the pursuer's unstated relational goal. The pursuer may take any cordial and polite interaction with the object as reciprocation and reinforcement for the relational goal.

A third, less common, pathway to the formation of a relational goal by a pursuer can occur even though the pursuer and object have never directly communicated with one another. Under this scenario, the pursuer observes the object from a distance, or learns about the object from members of the pursuer's social network, or through depictions of the object in the media. Pursuers may suffer from erotomania, in which they develop delusional beliefs that their affection for the object is reciprocal, even though the pursuer is a complete stranger to the object. Many cases of celebrity stalking follow this path where observation of the object from a distance suggests to the pursuer the desire and possibility for a relationship with the object.

The Pursuer's Goal Frustration and Goal Linkage.   An individual's goals are hierarchically organized. Goals that are lower in the hierarchy are less important, so they are more easily abandoned compared to higher-order goals when barriers thwart their achievement. In normal cases of relational pursuit, the pursuer will abandon the goal of a relationship with the object after a modicum of rejection. Depending on the level of attraction the pursuer experiences, some degree of persistence is expected and promoted by social scripts and cultural norms regarding the pursuit of relationships (e.g., Bratslavsky, Baumeister, & Sommer, 1998). But eventually, most pursuers "get the message" that their relational goal is not shared by the object, and pursuit terminates before it reaches obsessive levels.

Some pursuers, however, are *linkers* (McIntosh & Martin, 1992). They link the goal of a relationship with the object to a higher-order goal such as life happiness (McIntosh & Martin, 1992) or self-worth (Pyszczynski & Greenberg, 1987). In other words, pursuers who are linkers perceive that fulfilling the goal of a relationship with the object is necessary in order to achieve a higher-order goal, such as life happiness. Such higher-order goals are very difficult to forsake. Hence, pursuit of the connected lower-order goal persists despite repeated failure to make desired progress in achieving the goal. Obsessive pursuers persist in striving for a relationship with the object, even in the face of substantial rejection, because failure to obtain the relationship translates into inherent failure in life happiness (or some other higher-order goal).

The Pursuer's Rumination and Negative Affect. When an important goal remains frustrated, it causes the goal pursuer to ruminate (Martin & Tesser, 1996; Millar, Tesser, & Millar, 1988). Thus, linking a lower-order goal (e.g., a relationship with the object) to a higher-order goal (e.g., life happiness) stimulates rumination (McIntosh & Martin, 1992). In this case, rumination consists of repeated, distressing, intrusive, and aversive thoughts. The obsessive pursuer becomes mentally preoccupied with the fact that the relational goal remains blocked. The pursuer's thoughts regarding the object and the desired relationship become hyperaccessible. As goal frustration continues, rumination intensifies over time and the negativity of thoughts polarizes. Rumination is aversive, but it is relieved only by goal achievement or goal abandonment. Because the obsessive pursuer holds the relational goal to be so important (by virtue of linking it to a higher-order goal), goal abandonment is unlikely. Consequently, rumination reinforces the pursuer's commitment to the relational goal and spurs the pursuer on to persist and intensify efforts to develop or restore intimacy with the object (Cupach et al., 2000; Spitzberg & Cupach, 2001).

Rumination is emotionally distressing. Ongoing thoughts about the thwarting of an important goal are associated with feelings of negative arousal. As rumination intensifies, the pursuer feels emotionally flooded (i.e., overwhelmed with and absorbed by negative feelings). Moreover, the negative feelings constantly inform the pursuer that the relational goal is unmet, thereby intensifying rumination (Martin & Tesser, 1996). Distressing rumination and emotional flooding are self-perpetuating insofar as they exacerbate each other over time (Cupach et al., 2000).

One method a pursuer might employ to relieve the distress of rumination and negative affect is to suppress unwanted thoughts. Paradoxically, this strategy backfires because attempts to suppress unwanted thoughts contribute to their persistence (e.g., Wegner, 1994). Although thought suppression works for a brief time if the pursuer manages to engage in a distracting task, a rebound effect ultimately amplifies rumination. As long as a relationship with the object remains an important goal for the pursuer, ruminative thoughts about relational pursuit remain hyperaccessible in the pursuer's memory.

The Pursuer's Rationalization and Disinhibition. As pursuit progresses, the pursuer finds that insufficient goal progress requires intensified effort. In fact, most obsessive pursuit probably follows an escalatory trajectory whereby pursuit behaviors become increasingly intrusive and aggressive over time. Fueled by ever-increasing rumination and negative affect, the pursuer must find ways to rationalize such investment in an unobtained goal (Cupach et al., 2000). The pursuer may engage in any number of rationalizations, including: (a) exaggerating positive character-istics attributed to the object, thereby bolstering attraction to the object; (b) interpreting signs of affection and reciprocation from the object when none are intended by the object; (c) misconstruing rejection by the object as being "misguided" ("She'll change her mind when she knows me better"); (d) mistaking rejection as a sign of affection; (e) misconstruing avoidance as encouragement; (f) ignoring or downplaying the negative con-sequences of persistent pursuit for the object; and (g) justifying persis-tence on the basis of noble motives (e.g., love for the object).

The effect of rationalization on the pursuer is to disinhibit the pursuer's sense of propriety. Under normal circumstances, a pursuer would realize when persistence is excessive, inappropriate, and deviant. Social norms and legal sanctions normally would deter a pursuer from carrying pursuit too far. In other words, counterbalancing risks and moral imperatives even-tually would supersede and extinguish the relational goal. Fueled by goal linkage and rumination, however, the obsessive pursuer short-circuits ele-ments that would guide more rational (instead of rationalized) decision making. Rationalizations permit the pursuer to escalate persistence be-cause they disincline the pursuer to be regulated by the social and legal constraints that keep normal pursuers in check. In a sense, the pursuer loses control over his or her behavior because normal constraints on exces-siveness are undermined by rationalization.

The Object's Interpretation and Response to Pursuer. As we indi-cated previously, pursuers have a diverse repertoire of pursuit tactics that are available to them. A pursuit relationship that is on the trajectory to becom-ing obsessive usually begins with affinity-seeking behaviors that are consid-ered normal and appropriate, such as calling, sending e-mails, leaving notes, self-disclosures, and reasonable attempts to escalate relational intimacy. Ob-jects may at first enjoy such attention if they are ambivalent about repro-cating a relationship with the pursuer (Dunn, 1999). Even when the object decides that such relational bids are unwanted, however, the object does not usually perceive these normal courtship behaviors to be very threatening (Cupach & Spitzberg, 2000), and indeed may even view such attention as flattering (Dunn, 1999). These milder forms of pursuit may be annoying, but they are accepted as reasonable attempts at relationship development. Later on, after the escalation of pursuit occurs, the object may reinterpret these behaviors as obsessive and/or threatening, in retrospect (Emerson et al., 1998). But as long as pursuit seems within the bounds of normality, the object either tolerates it, avoids it, or politely rejects the pursuer.

Objects begin to see pursuit as being excessive when (a) normal pursuit behaviors persist despite repeated and unequivocal rejections by the object, or (b) pursuit behaviors escalate in intensity, are more intrusive on the object's privacy, and become more threatening in nature (Emerson et al., 1998; Sinclair & Frieze, 2000). Invasions of privacy and overt threats are more upsetting to objects than are the overt but normal attempts to establish intimacy (Cupach & Spitzberg, 2000). Several responses by the object are possible, including avoidance of the pursuer, direct confrontation of the pursuer, retaliation against the pursuer, obtaining protection against the pursuer, or any combination or sequential pattern involving these responses (Cupach & Spitzberg, 2000; Spitzberg & Cupach, 2001).

Avoidance is a common relational termination strategy (e.g., Baxter, 1985), so it should not be surprising that it is employed to reject unwanted relationship pursuit. Avoidance involves minimal effort, and it allows the pursuer to infer rejection before it is communicated directly, and thereby allows the pursuer to save face. Forms of avoidance include ignoring pursuer messages, hinting disinterest, restricting or blocking the pursuer's access, ignoring the pursuer's behavior, and refraining from showing any signs of reciprocity or interest (Spitzberg & Cupach, 2001). Because pursuers tend to rationalize, avoidance is often not interpreted as rejection. Yet, the relational goal fails to be realized, so rumination, rationalization, and persistence escalate.

An object's direct confrontation of the pursuer involves admonishing the pursuer, asking the pursuer to refrain from further contacts, attempting to reason with the pursuer, and seeking the pursuer's understanding and empathy. This strategy is more likely to work if it is employed relatively early in the progression of pursuit—particularly before pursuit escalates to threatening behavior (de Becker, 1997). Nevertheless, direct confrontation may be construed by the pursuer as promising. If direct confrontation occurs multiple times, it shows the pursuer that persistence buys further contact with the object, which is a necessary condition to achieve relational intimacy. Obsessive pursuers do not easily take "no" for an answer and tend to respond to direct rejections with escalated pursuit and more clandestine behaviors that are not easily monitored by the object.

Retaliation attempts to punish the pursuer, and consequently disincentivize pursuit. Threatening the pursuer with physical or reputational harm, and belittling or shaming the pursuer, represent forms of retaliation. Retaliation may threaten the face of the pursuer to such an extent that it is difficult for the pursuer to continue to imagine that reciprocity from the object is possible. However, such face threat can produce sufficient shame and anger that the pursuer counterretaliates, becoming abusive and violent.

Objects can seek protection from obsessive pursuit in a number of ways. Friends or law enforcement officials may be asked to intervene, restraining orders made be obtained, locks may be changed, and so on. This strategy may afford a degree of security for the object. However, orders of protection are routinely violated (e.g., Brewster, 1998; Hall, 1997; Nicastro et al.,

2000; Tjaden & Thoennes, 1998). There are even fears that the formality and seriousness of obtaining a restraining order might trigger the pursuer's anger and aggressiveness, although there is little evidence to support such fears (cf. Nicastro et al., 2000). Especially if pursuit has escalated to intrusiveness and threat, and if the relationship was previously intimate, then the object's attempts to control the pursuer's access may result in anger and concerted attempts to overcome the obstacles erected by the object.

Summary.   The model proposed here identifies specific processes proximal to the negotiation of relationships that turn otherwise normal affinity-seeking or relationship restoration into excessive and obsessive relationship pursuit. We propose that obsessive pursuers view the goal of a relationship with the object as being essential to the attainment of a higher-order goal, such as life happiness or self-worth. This goal linkage effectively makes the relationship goal extraordinary in its importance to the pursuer. To the extent that this relational goal is frustrated, the pursuer experiences aversive rumination and negative affect. Rumination and negative emotional arousal intensify over time as the relational goal continues to be thwarted. Moreover, the pursuer develops a variety of rationalizations that disinhibit pursuit behaviors that otherwise would be perceived as inappropriate. Over time, rumination, negative arousal, and rationalizations lead to increasingly aggressive pursuit. Object responses are interpreted by the pursuer in ways that fuel rumination and rationalization, thereby intensifying efforts by the pursuer to establish intimacy with the object. At some point, the pursuer may realize the futility of the relational goal. Because of the pursuit investment, and because of the shame experienced in having to abandon such an important goal, the pursuer may stalk the object with the motive of revenge.

CONCLUSION

"The fundamental paradox, forced upon us in daily tragedies, is the bitter reality that we maintain a world of atrocity by refusing to acknowledge the role of dark desires in our own communities and individual lives" (Moore, 1990, p. 185). The increasing interest in the paradoxical processes of obsessive relational pursuit and stalking is a welcome step for cultural and individual self-reflection (e.g., Spitzberg & Cupach, 2001). Cultures that overlay images of success on the process of relational persistence need critical examination. Research in the areas of sexual coercion and violence have already demonstrated that the "acceptability" or appropriateness of such activities is contingent on a variety of contextualizing frames (e.g., sex of aggressor, sex of victim, what the aggression is in response to, etc.). For example, aggressors in general perceive their own actions as more appropriate than do the targets of such actions (Mummendey, Linneweber, & Löschper, 1984). Aggression is normatively perceived as more appropriate when it is viewed as punishment for deviance, reciprocal, defensive, or part of a "fair fight" (Felson, 1981). Male aggression against females tends to be viewed as less appropriate than female aggression against males (Arias & Johnson, 1989).

If aggression is often perceived as culturally appropriate, then various aspects of obsessive pursuit and stalking also may be perceived as appropriate, even if often in disjunctive ways. For example, Dunn (1999) found that stalking and persistent forcible interaction were ingrained in the cultural milieu of college women in the form of icons of courtship. In other words, college women tended not to see such behavior as inappropriate when couched in the trappings of courtship. Ultimately, society will increasingly have to grapple with the implications of disjunctive relationships and the cultural processes that enable them. Perhaps understanding the process by which people construct disjunctively unwanted relationships will provide better insights into the dark side in all of us. As Simon (1996, p. 3) suggested, "The basic difference between what are socially considered to be bad and good people is not one of kind, but one of degree, and of the ability of the bad to translate dark impulses into dark actions."

REFERENCES

Arias, I., & Johnson, P. (1989). Evaluations of physical aggression among intimate dyads. *Journal of Interpersonal Violence, 4,* 298–307.
Bartholomew, K., & Horowitz, L. M. (1991). Attachment styles among young adults: A test of a four-category model. *Journal of Personality and Social Psychology, 61,* 226–244.
Battaglia, D. M., Richard, F. D., Datteri, D. L., & Lord, C. G. (1998). Breaking up is (relatively) easy to do: A script for the dissolution of close relationships. *Journal of Social and Personal Relationships, 15,* 829–845.
Baxter, L. A. (1985). Accomplishing relationship disengagement. In S. Duck & D. Perlman (Eds.), *Understanding personal relationships* (pp. 243–265). London: Sage.
Becker, T. E., Billings, R. S., Eveleth, D. M., & Gilbert, N. W. (1997). Validity of scores on three attachment style scales: Exploratory and confirmatory evidence. *Educational and Psychological Measurement, 57,* 477–493.
Bowlby, J. (1980). *Attachment and loss: Vol. 3. Loss, sadness and depression.* New York: Basic Books.
Bradburn, W. E., Jr. (1992). Stalking statutes. *Ohio Northern University Law Review, 19,* 271–288.
Bratslavsky, E., Baumeister, R. F., & Sommer, K. L. (1998). To love or be loved in vain: The trials and tribulations of unrequited love. In B. H. Spitzberg & W. R. Cupach (Eds.), *The dark side of close relationships* (pp. 307–326). Mahwah, NJ: Lawrence Erlbaum Associates.
Brewster, M. P. (1998). *An exploration of the experiences and needs of former intimate stalking victims.* Final report submitted to the National Institute of Justice (NCJ 175475). Washington, DC: U.S. Department of Justice.
Burgess, A. W., Baker, T., Greening, D., Hartman, C. R., Burgess, A. G., Douglas, J. E., & Halloran, R. (1997). Stalking behaviors within domestic violence. *Journal of Family Violence, 12,* 389–403.

Coleman, F. L. (1997). Stalking behavior and the cycle of domestic violence. *Journal of Interpersonal Violence, 12*, 420–433.

Cupach, W. R., & Spitzberg, B. H. (1998). Obsessive relational intrusion and stalking. In B. H. Spitzberg & W. R. Cupach (Eds.), *The dark side of close relationships* (pp. 233–263). Mahwah, NJ: Lawrence Erlbaum Associates.

Cupach, W. R., & Spitzberg, B. H. (2000). Obsessive relational intrusion: Incidence, perceived severity, and coping. *Violence and Victims, 15*, 357–372.

Cupach, W. R., Spitzberg, B. H., & Carson, C. L. (2000). Toward a theory of obsessive relational intrusion and stalking. In K. Dindia & S. Duck (Eds.), *Communication and personal relationships* (pp. 131–146). New York: Wiley.

de Becker, G. (1997). *The gift of fear: Survival signals that protect us from violence.* Boston: Little, Brown.

Department of Justice. (1998). *Stalking and domestic violence* (Third Annual Report to Congress under the Violence Against Women Act, NCJ 172204). Washington, DC: U.S. Department of Justice.

Dunn, J. L. (1999). What love has to do with it: The cultural construction of emotion and sorority women's responses to forcible interaction. *Social Problems, 46*, 440–459.

Eisele, G. R., Watkins, J. P., & Matthews, K. O. (1998). Workplace violence at government sites. *American Journal of Industrial Medicine, 33*, 485–492.

Emerson, R. M., Ferris, K. O., & Gardner, C. B. (1998). On being stalked. *Social Problems, 45*, 289–314.

Feeney, J., & Noller, P. (1996). *Adult attachment.* Thousand Oaks, CA: Sage.

Feldman, T. B., Holt, J., & Hellard, S. (1997). Violence in medical facilities: A review of 40 incidents. *Journal of Kentucky Medical Association, 95*, 183–189.

Felson, R. B. (1981). An interactionist approach to aggression. In J. T. Tedeschi (Ed.), *Impression management theory and social psychological research* (pp. 181–199). New York: Academic.

Fisher, B. S., Cullen, F. T., & Turner, M. G. (1999). *The extent and nature of the sexual victimization of college women: A national-level analysis.* Final Report submitted to the National Institute of Justice (NCJ 179977). Washington, DC: U.S. Department of Justice.

Floyd, K. (1998). Intimacy as a research construct: A content-analytic review. *Representative Research in Social Psychology, 22*, 28–32.

Fonagy, P., Steele, M., Steele, H., Leigh, T., Kennedy, R., Mattoon, G., & Target, M. (1995). Attachment, the reflective self, and borderline states: The predictive specificity of the Adult Attachment Interview and pathological emotional development. In S. Goldberg, R. Muir, & J. Kerr (Eds.), *Attachment theory: Social, developmental, and clinical perspectives* (pp. 233–278). Hillsdale, NJ: Analytic Press.

Fremouw, W. J., Westrup, D., & Pennypacker, J. (1997). Stalking on campus: The prevalence and strategies for coping with stalking. *Journal of Forensic Sciences, 42*, 664–667.

Gill, R., & Brockman, J. (1996). *A review of section 264 (criminal harassment) of the Criminal Code of Canada.* Working document WD 1996 7e. Ottawa, Ontario, Canada: Research, Statistics and Evaluation Directorate, Department of Justice, Canada.

Hall, D. M. (1997). *Outside looking in: Stalkers and their victims.* Unpublished doctoral dissertation, Claremont Graduate School, Claremont, CA.

Harmon, R. B., Rosner, R., & Owens, H. (1995). Obsessional harassment and erotomania in a criminal court population. *Journal of Forensic Sciences, 40*, 188–196.

Hills, A. M., & Taplin, J. L. (1998). Anticipated responses to stalking: Effect of threat and target–stalker relationship. *Psychiatry, Psychology and Law, 5*, 139–146.

Hinde, R. A. (1997). *Relationships: A dialectical perspective.* East Sussex, UK: Psychology Press.

Kelley, H. H., Berscheid, E., Christensen, A., Harvey, J. H., Huston, T. L., Levinger, G., McClintock, E., Peplau, L. A., & Peterson, D. R. (Eds.). (1983). *Close relationships*. New York: Freeman.

Kienlen, K. K., Birmingham, D. L., Solberg, K. B., O'Regan, J. T., & Meloy, J. R. (1997). A comparative study of psychotic and nonpsychotic stalking. *Journal of the American Academy of Psychiatry and Law, 25,* 317–334.

Kong, R. (1996). Criminal harassment. *Juristat, 16* (12, Statistics Canada: Canadian Centre for Justice Statistics), 1–13.

Langhinrichsen-Rohling, J., Palarea, R. E., Cohen, J., & Rohling, M. L. (2000). Breaking up is hard to do: Unwanted pursuit behaviors following the dissolution of a romantic relationship. *Violence and Victims, 15,* 73–90.

Leonard, R., Ling, L. C., Hankins, G. A., Maidon, C. H., Potorti, P. F., & Rogers, J. M. (1993). Sexual harassment at North Carolina State University. In G. L. Kreps (Ed.), *Sexual harassment: Communication implications* (pp. 170–194). Cresskill, NJ: Hampton.

Levy, M. B., & Davis, K. E. (1988). Lovestyles and attachment styles compared: Their relations to each other and to various relationship characteristics. *Journal of Social and Personal Relationships, 5,* 439–471.

Martin, L. L., & Tesser, A. (1996). Some ruminative thoughts. In R. S. Wyer (Ed.), *Ruminative thoughts* (pp. 1–47). Mahwah, NJ: Lawrence Erlbaum Associates.

McCreedy, K. R., & Dennis, B. G. (1996). Sex-related offenses and fear of crime on campus. *Journal of Contemporary Criminal Justice, 12,* 69–80.

McIntosh, W. D., & Martin, L. L. (1992). The cybernetics of happiness: The relation of goal attainment, rumination, and affect. In M. S. Clark (Ed.), *Emotion and social behavior* (pp. 222–246). Newbury Park, CA: Sage.

Mechanic, M. B., Weaver, T. L., & Resisk, P. A. (2000). Intimate partner violence and stalking behavior: Exploration of patterns and correlates in a sample of acutely battered women. *Violence and Victims, 15,* 55–72.

Meloy, J. R. (1992). *Violent attachments*. Northvale, NJ: Jason Aronson.

Meloy, J. R. (1996). A clinical investigation of the obsessional follower: "She loves me, she loves me not...." In L. Schlesinger (Ed.), *Explorations in criminal psychopathology* (pp. 9–32) Springfield, IL: Charles C. Thomas.

Meloy, J. R. (1998). The psychology of stalking. In J. R. Meloy (Ed.), *The psychology of stalking* (pp. 2–24). San Diego, CA: Academic.

Meloy, J. R., & Gothard, S. (1995). Demographic and clinical comparison of obsessional followers and offenders with mental disorders. *American Journal of Psychiatry, 152,* 258–263.

Millar, K. U., Tesser, A., & Millar, M. (1988). The effects of a threatening life event on behavior sequences and intrusive thought: A self-disruption explanation. *Cognitive Therapy and Research, 12,* 441–457.

Moore, T. (1990). *Dark eros: The imagination of sadism*. Woodstock, CT: Spring.

Morton, T. L., Alexander, J. F., & Altman, I. (1976). Communication and relationship definition. In G. R. Miller (Ed.), *Explorations in interpersonal communication* (pp. 105–125). Beverly Hills, CA: Sage.

Mullen, P. E., Pathé, M., Purcell, R., & Stuart, G. W. (1999). Study of stalkers. *American Journal of Psychiatry, 156,* 1244–1249.

Mummendey, A., Linneweber, V., & Löscher, G. (1984). Aggression: From act to interaction. In A. Mummendey (Ed.), *Social psychology of aggression: From individual behavior to social interaction* (pp. 69–106). New York: Springer-Verlag.

New Jersey State Police. (1997). *Domestic violence: Offense report*. Trenton: New Jersey Department of Law & Public Safety.

Nicastro, A. M., Cousins, A. V., & Spitzberg, B. H. (2000). The tactical face of stalking. *Journal of Criminal Justice, 28,* 69–82.

Pathé, M., & Mullen, P. E. (1997). The impact of stalkers on their victims. *British Journal of Psychiatry, 170*, 12–17.

Pyszczynski, T., & Greenberg, J. (1987). Self-regulatory perseveration and the depressive self-focusing style: A self-awareness theory of reactive depression. *Psychological Bulletin, 102*, 122–138.

Roberts, A. R., & Dziegielewski, S. F. (1996). Assessment typology and intervention with the survivors of stalking. *Aggression and Violent Behavior, 1*, 359–368.

Roberts, N., & Noller, P. (1998). The associations between adult attachment and couple violence: The role of communication patterns and relationship satisfaction. In J. A. Simpson & W. S. Rholes (Eds.), *Attachment theory and close relationships* (pp. 317–350). New York: Guilford.

Romans, J. S. C., Hays, J. R., & White, T. K. (1996). Stalking and related behaviors experienced by counseling center staff members from current or former clients. *Professional Psychology: Research and Practice, 27*, 595–599.

Roscoe, B., Kennedy, D., & Pope, T. (1987). Adolescents' views of intimacy: Distinguishing intimate from nonintimate relationships. *Adolescence, 22*, 511–516.

Roscoe, B., Strouse, J. S., & Goodwin, M. P. (1994). Sexual harassment: Early adolescent self-reports of experiences and acceptance. *Adolescence, 29*, 515–523.

Shaver, P., Hazan, C., & Bradshaw, D. (1988). Love as attachment: The integration of three behavioral systems. In R. J. Sternberg & M. L. Barnes (Eds.), *The psychology of love* (pp. 68–99). New Haven, CT: Yale University Press.

Simon, R. I. (1996). *Bad men do what good men dream.* Washington, DC: American Psychiatric Press.

Sinclair, H. C., & Frieze, I. H. (2000). Initial courtship behavior and stalking: How should we draw the line? *Violence and Victims, 15*, 23–40.

Sperling, M. B., & Berman, W. H. (1991). An attachment classification of desperate love. *Journal of Personality Assessment, 56*, 45–55.

Spitzberg, B. H., & Cupach, W. R. (1996, August). *Obsessive relational intrusion: Victimization and coping.* Paper presented at the International Society for the Study of Personal Relationships Conference, Banff, Canada.

Spitzberg, B. H., & Cupach, W. R. (2001). Paradoxes of pursuit: Toward a relational model of stalking-related phenomena. In J. Davis (Ed.), *Stalking crimes and victim protection: Prevention, intervention, threat assessment, and case management* (pp. 97–136). Boca Raton, FL: CRC Press.

Spitzberg, B. H., Nicastro, A. M., & Cousins, A. V. (1998). Exploring the interactional phenomenon of stalking and obsessive relational intrusion. *Communication Reports, 11*, 33–48.

Spitzberg, B. H., & Rhea, J. (1999). Obsessive relational intrusion and sexual coercion victimization. *Journal of Interpersonal Violence, 14*, 3–20.

Tjaden, P., & Thoennes, N. (1998). *Stalking in America: Findings from the National Violence Against Women Survey.* Washington, DC: National Institute of Justice and Centers for Disease Control and Prevention (NCJ 169592).

Tjaden, P., & Thoennes, N. (2000). Prevalence and consequences of male-to-female and female-to-male intimate partner violence as measured by the national violence against women survey. *Violence Against Women, 6*, 142–161.

Tjaden, P., Thoennes, N., & Allison, C. J. (2000). Comparing stalking victimization from legal and victim perspectives. *Violence and Victims, 15*, 7–22.

Waring, E. M., Tillman, M. P., Frelick, L., Russell, L., & Weisz, G. (1980). Concepts of intimacy in the general population. *Journal of Nervous and Mental Disease, 168*, 471–474.

Watzlawick, P., Beavin, J. H., & Jackson, D. D. (1967). *Pragmatics of human communication: A study of interactional patterns, pathologies, and paradoxes.* New York: Norton.

Wegner, D. M. (1994). *White bears and other unwanted thoughts.* New York: Guilford.

Welch, J. M. (1995). Stalking and anti-stalking legislation: A guide to the literature of a new legal concept. *Reference Services Review, 23,* 53–58, 68.

Zona, M. A., Sharma, K. K., & Lane, J. (1993). A comparative study of erotomanic and obsessional subjects in a forensic sample. *Journal of Forensic Sciences, 38,* 894–903.

11

Social Exclusion— Pedophile Style

Dennis Howitt
Loughborough University

Relationships exist and are seen, interpreted, and experienced within a complex of ideologies. No single, universal ideological position governs how relationships are regarded, and there may be conflicts among the competing ideologies. Although relationships are rarely discussed in terms of ideology, their fundamentally ideological character is readily seen. Television talk shows graphically demonstrate such ideological components. Aspects of these ideologies may be shared between the general public and counselors/therapists, but inevitably they remain fundamentally ideological as 'social facts' must:

> Close relationships promote psychological well being.
> It is good to talk.
> People in good sexual relations are closer than the closest of close friends.
> Openness and honesty are fundamental and essential to satisfactory relationships.
> Even if rules, of say, faithfulness, are violated, partners in close relationships share emotional empathy.

Violence in close relationships is prohibited, and failure in this respect should lead to "walking out."

These are not facts, but instead components of a modern ideology of relationships—different cultures and times would emphasize quite different features of relationships. For example, compare the romantic concept of marriage with the broadly South Asian system that may involve parental arrangement. People do not plan their beliefs on the basis of research findings; so, in a sense, questions of formal psychological support simply do not apply. However, in social constructionist terms, counselors and therapists form an influential elite that both mediates and creates social knowledge about relationships. This also applies in terms of pedophilic relationships—the general animosity toward pedophiles is not, for example, based on evidence, although it is fed and influenced by the views and ideas of professionals working with pedophiles and the children involved with them.

Researchers into close relationships might object that some of these ideologically derived notions have been supported by research. Whether or not this is the case, this is not the reason why people generally accept them. The knowledge created by researchers is only applicable within the very ideological context in which research is carried out. It is impossible to plan research to test the veracity of the components separate from their ideological acceptance. If I believe that openness of communication is the *sine qua non* of a good relationship, then its lack may be distressing; but if I believe that my marriage is important for the community's respect for my family, then the lack of closeness may be an irrelevance. Thus, it is not possible to separate what we get out of relationships from what we believe constitutes a good relationship (Owusu-Bempah & Howitt, 2000).

Because relationships exist within frameworks of ideology, to understand relationships fully requires an understanding of these frameworks. Speculatively, it might be proposed that inappropriate relationships are those in which two or more distinct ideological perspectives are brought into proximity and, consequently, conflict. Adultery, for example, is problematic insofar as it joins the ideology of romantic love—with its emphasis on openness and closeness—with an exploitative, almost Machiavellian view of relationships. Lies, manipulation, and deceit are essential for an adulterous relationship to be maintained even briefly. Prostitution could be seen as an inappropriate relationship because, for example, the ideology of commerce and capital is involved directly and intimately in an act that, from another ideological perspective, is a sharing, giving, and mutual experience. Of course, yet other ideological perspectives may be involved apart from these.

If this is so, the careful analysis of inappropriate relationships helps us to understand the ideological foundations of relationships in general. Answers to the question "What is unacceptable about a particular relationship or type of relation?" help us to formulate the characteristics of acceptable relationships—and those of unacceptable ones. Naturally, there are other ways of gaining knowledge about what is considered a good or satisfactory relationship. Nevertheless, a working assumption of this chapter is that the study of inappropriate relationships constitutes a *methodologically* sound basis for exploring the ideological foundations of *all* relationships. This information is often not readily available from the study of appropriate relationships: They fail to provide the dilemmas that highlight critical aspects of relationships, and so-called normal relationships such as marriage for the most part lack extreme dilemmas. The study of inappropriate relationships is not merely a somewhat worthy and novel research area, but also an important key to a deeper understanding of the ideology of relationships in general.

An acid test of this proposal lies in the study of adult–child sexual contacts—generally called *pedophilia* in this chapter. We should learn something about normatively appropriate relationships from the study of pedophilia's inherent ideological conflicts (Billig et al., 1988). An objection might be raised. Surely, pedophilia represents the grossest perversion of interpersonal and sexual relationships? Are not pedophiles perverts who prey on the innocent and vulnerable—people who sully childhood by forcing premature sexual relationships on innocent children with disastrous consequences for the normal development of any child involved with them? Furthermore, do they not lie, cheat, and manipulate to achieve their ends? It is not merely that pedophiles exhibit behaviors that are the reverse of what we expect in "normatively" approved relationships—that is too simple to be the full picture and, to a degree, is misleading. Things cannot be defined effectively simply in terms of what they are not. Ideas about pedophiles and their activities are not simply the negation of what we expect decent people to do.

From a social psychological perspective, no single viewpoint exists from which to study and understand pedophilia. Consequently, it is necessary to regard the dominant position of professionals working in the field of child sexual abuse as merely that. They promote the following ideas *inter alia*:

1. Children are victims of and damaged by sexual contacts with adults.
2. No good comes to the child from sexual contact with adults.
3. Sex offenders against children are evil and manipulative, and any attempt to understand them is to collude with abuse.

This common analysis relies greatly on a consensual account of the nature of pedophile relationships. It presents us with little opportunity for further analysis. Although this perspective is practically universal within the writings of professionals, there is little recognition that these are not incontrovertible factual matters but instead value-laden judgments. This makes the comments of David Finkelhor particularly insightful, especially given his intellectual dominance in the field of child sexual abuse: "Ultimately, I do continue to believe that the prohibition on adult–child sexual contact is primarily a moral issue. While empirical findings have some relevance they are not the final arbiter" (Finklhor, 1991, p. 314).

So what are the values that underlie what Finkelhor suggested be described as a moral matter?

PEDOPHILE IDEOLOGY

Most of us have little opportunity to read propedophilia arguments, despite the organizations committed to the dissemination of pedophile viewpoints. Pedophiles are currently excluded from many channels of communication—consequently, we find it harder to understand their sexual contact with children (Howitt, 1995). By failing to understand adult sexual interest in children, prevention is made much more difficult. The difficulty is, of course, that some points of view, especially those of pedophiles, are offensive to the majority. For example, most of us are not regularly exposed to the promotional activities of propedophilia activists. For one thing, this material is relatively scarce and sanctions against it may be strong. PIE (the Paedophile Information Exchange, formed in the UK in the 1970s) was effectively shut down a few years later (Howitt, 1995). Elsewhere, however, it is still possible to find Internet sites belonging to propedophile groups such as the Danish Paedophile Association and the North American Man–Boy Love Association:

> Amidst the near-holocaust proportion of anti-pedophile hysteria, a number of facts about man/boy love have been ignored. Consensual sexually expressed friendships between boys and men exist. Age of consent laws and prosecutorial attitudes treat all man/boy contacts as abuse although there is no justification to do so. True pedophile desire is built around the boy's pleasure. Prohibition of all pedophile acts is unjust and implies the persecution of a minority. Even worse than the hatred expressed toward boylovers is the complete ignorance of the positive aspects of sexually expressed friendships between boys and men. Religious "sexual morality" commonly opposed to boylove, as highly questionable as it is on a scholarly basis, cannot be legislated by the state. Current laws violate boys' rights to sexual self-determination. Lawmakers should remove age of consent laws and vigilantly prevent intervention into voluntary relationships. Many boys possess very natural "expressed needs" for sexual attention from a person of their own choosing: an adult male friend who instills trust, courage, love and affection through the intimate sexual friendship, a friend who treats the boy as an equal and in doing so boosts the boy's feeling of self-esteem and self-worth. (Benjamin, 1997)

More generally, there are a number of themes common to propedophile writings. Major themes include:

The special and pure relationship involved in man–boy love.

The libertarian aspect in which the repression of children, sexually and otherwise, by the family and the community is contrasted with the freedom of choice and feelings involved in the man–boy relationship. The personal growth and emotional gain to be obtained by partners in man–boy relationships.

Exposed to such propedophile ideas for the first time, most of us will probably recoil in disbelief. There is no reason to accept them as "true," and moral rejection is an appropriate response to such material. That is not central in terms of the present argument. Crucial is the radically different perspective presented in propedophile writings compared with what most of us have assimilated from modern child sexual abuse writers and others. Prior to the 1980s—the point at which child sexual abuse emerged as a significant social and professional issue—writings on pedophilia adopted this generally positive tone (Howitt, 1995). This is no longer the case. Anyone wishing to explore this type of writing might be advised to consult the special edition of the *Journal of Homosexuality* (1991, parts 1 & 2). This, controversially, provided a forum for one edition in which propedophile writers could put forth their point of view.

The viewpoint expressed there and elsewhere is singularly a romantic one. Indeed, if not for the fact that we are discussing pedophilic acts, the sentiments seem worthy and attractive. It could almost be the scenario of *Romeo and Juliet*. In terms of nonpedophilic relationships, however, the viewpoint would generally be seen as unrealistic and idealized. Of course, in the pedophile discourse, issues of exploitation are not raised. The pedophile view tends to be supported by a number of arguments. The special and pure nature of the man–boy relationship is presented as an essential something that has to be experienced. Statements attributed to the boys involved are used to reinforce the viewpoint:

> Examination of ninety-two letters 8 of one boy (sic), Nate, to his older friend indicates a strong need for the relationship. The letters do not explicitly mention sexual contact, but Nate's ultimate desired expression of affection was being masturbated by his older friend. Such contacts took place in the beginning of the friendship, but soon ended; his older friend was not a pedophile and turned away his expressed need for love. (Benjamin, 1997)

Public statements of pedophile ideology are often accompanied by quotations that purport to represent the views of eminent persons. Thus, social scientists might be surprised to find pedophile organizations quoting the work of Michel Foucault, the eminent French philosopher psychologist, apparently expressing this libertarian sentiment about pedophilia: "It is quite difficult to lay down barriers [particularly since] it could be that the child, with his own sexuality, may have desired the adult" (cited in Radow, 2000). The passage hints at a contrast between a 'liberal' ideology and repressive ideologies surrounding childhood and childhood sexuality. In other words, it puts an ideological slant on the fact that most professionals working in the field of child protection who would describe such relationships as exploitative and damaging.

HATRED OF PEDOPHILES

Remember: "The only good paedophile is a dead paedophile!" (King-Ky Ron, 2000, italics added)

Most would agree that adult–child sexual relationships are among the most fiercely condemned of the relationships that might be considered inappropriate. The evidence for this is all around us in the news media. More systematically, Brown (1999) studied community attitudes to the treatment of pedophiles in the community and elsewhere. A large percentage of people expressed the view that pedophiles need to be locked up in prison, and that treatment is inappropriate. Among those willing to accept the treatment of sex offenders in special units in the community, support was fairly muted and few would actively join demonstrations to support of such special units. In conjunction with the evidence of vigilante attacks on pedophiles reported in newspapers from time to time, there would seem little doubt that emotions against pedophiles are much stronger and more common than are sympathetic responses.

Should the phrase "inappropriate relationship" include the sort of adult–child sexual relationship being discussed here? Are such liaisons regarded as being merely inappropriate (after all, they can result in life sentences in prison for offenders), and are they indeed relationships? (The professional literature, e.g., tends to regard them as one-sided attacks rather than as acts involving mutuality or reciprocity.) Reading the man–boy love literature on the World Wide Web or elsewhere, we find presented a version of the romantic ideal. Molesters and victims are portrayed as being in reciprocal, caring, beneficial, and deep relationships. If anything, it is the boy who is presented as the prime beneficiary. For the pedophile, but probably for few or no others, this is a completely positive, appropriate relationship. To pedophiles, it is merely society's response to such episodes that creates the problem. According to the pedophile organizations, everyone is to blame except the pedophile.

What are the features of relationships that justify us describing them as inappropriate? The word *inappropriate* implies that there is something not proper about the relationships. Not-proper relationships might mean two different things. The first is whether or not it is a true relationship—that is, does it have the characteristics of a (good) relationship? As indicated, from the point of view of the professional literature on pedophilia, there is no relationship if reciprocity is the criterion. The other possibility is that there is a recognizable relationship but some other feature of the relationship makes it not proper or inappropriate—the actors involved being the most obvious example. This means that the study of inappropriate relationships involves understanding both what constitutes a relationship and who constitute appropriate actors in this relationship. Thus, adulterers are clearly inappropriate actors in a relationship. but their relationship itself may demonstrate features of good relationships—for example, passion, loving, caring, giving, and so forth. Indeed, what is wrong with an adulterous relationship may lie in it being satisfactory compared to the marital relationship. However, the case of pedophilia actually illustrates the difficulty in accepting the independence of the two components. The professional child abuse worker would see the actors in the pedophile episode as inappropriate (an adult and a child), and also either deny that there is a relationship or claim that it is exploitative and damaging. The advocate, say, of man–boy love would see both the actors and the relationship as satisfactory. The lack of total consensus does not, however, prevent us from exploring the factors that make a relationship appropriate in some perspectives and inappropriate in the eyes of others.

If we hold that adult–child sexual episodes constitute inappropriate relationships, then the task is to explain why this is so. Trepidation is appropriate when dealing with issues of this sort. Major shifts occurred in the way in which society regarded sex and sexuality—and children—in the latter decades of the last century. Because the *study* of sexual abuse is largely a phenomenon of the last quarter of the 20th century, it is difficult to capture the change other than anecdotally. As a young psychology student in the 1960s, I became interested in the issue of incest. The topic was hardly central to the psychology of the time and, generally, provoked a slightly embarrassed but jocular response. I do not remember the sort of response of disgust that became common more recently when, say, I explained my research on pedophiles to colleagues and others. One thing stands out in my memory of these times: an occasion when I was giving a talk as a graduate student on my initial choice of topics for my doctoral dissertation—incest. At this meeting, my professor asked the question—it sounded serious, whether or not it was meant to be provocative—why she shouldn't have sex with her beautiful brother. In a sense, it is not the question that was crucial but that it could be asked. As an indicator of how much thinking has changed, there was then a seemingly incontrovertible rebuttal to the question. The danger of incest lay in its profound risk to the health of the genetic stock through inbreeding (Lindzey, 1967). This argument has little currency nowadays, despite most of us being aware of the dangers of inbreeding. Anyway, cross-cultural and historical research had suggested the virtual universality of the incest taboo. Exceptions are few—the primary one being associated with Egyptian pharaoh classes (De Mause, 1976).

The near-universality of the incest taboo might be taken to stress the biological necessity of incest avoidance. Nevertheless, there are serious flaws in this view. In particular, it confuses incest avoidance with ineligibility for marriage. This is clearly fundamental and has some equivalence to the gay marriage debate, in which sexual activity may be perfectly legal but marriage not possible. The virtual universality of prohibitions against incest does not prove that its basis was the fear of weakening the genetic stock. Same-sex adult–child sexual relations, for example, would not cause genetic risk for obvious reasons, but are no more acceptable. Furthermore, genetics can carry no explanatory force when nonfamily adult–child relationships are under consideration, irrespective of the genders of the child and adult.

The relationship between incest taboo and eligibility for marriage is far from simple. For example, under United Kingdom law there are a number of relationships that are prohibited from marriage. Some of these are determined by the age of consent, and others by there being a close genetic relationship (e.g., an aunt–nephew marriage). Nevertheless, many of the prohibitions are inexplicable in genetic terms. For example, a man may not marry his stepdaughter, former stepdaughter, daughter-in-law, former daughter-in-law, adoptive daughter, or former adoptive daughter. Similar laws apply to mother and the equivalent son relationships. There is clearly no simple genetic rule that explains these prohibitions—many of them involve no genetic connection at all. This is made confusing by other exceptions. A man may marry his daughter-in-law *if* both his son's mother and his son are dead. Cousin marriage is perfectly legal despite the greater genetic closeness.

By the 1980s, such explanations of sexual taboos had changed. By extension of the feminist politic of the dangerousness of male power that is expressed, in part, through violence and sex (especially in rape), the belief in the adverse consequences of powerlessness for the victim of a predator gained ascendance. The language also changed: There were *victims* and *perpetrators* who constituted a rigid dyad of powerlessness versus power. In this formulation, inappropriate relationships are a function of the inappropriate use of power. The definition of power from this viewpoint is complex, although little explored. Power can be seen simply as the use of physical force to achieve a certain end; however, power also resides in certain sorts of social relationships. One hidden assumption of this is that the parent–child relationship involves power in the sense of authority, although this is not easily separated from the potential for the use of violence in the relationship.

HISTORICAL RELATIVISM

There is a further difficulty in drawing pedophilia into a discussion of normal relationships. Seen from a historical perspective, the sanctions against pedophilia remain strong—probably stronger than they have ever been in recent history. Indeed, there is a case for the argument that the pedophilic relationship is one that has reversed the trend for other relationships, leading those other relationships to become increasingly sanctioned. This cannot be said about many of the other inappropriate relationships discussed in this book. Adultery, for example, is less severely punished than once it was and, certainly in the West, is no longer regarded as a crime. Instead, it is treated as a matter for the partners involved rather than a matter for the community or family. Parents, friends, and others are expected to keep an appropriate distance and, apart for the provision of social support, not become emotionally involved in the relationship's crisis. Similar patterns have been followed for homosexuality and illegitimacy. It would be a brave soul who would suggest that our treatment of pedophiles is repressive but temporary—that more enlightened future generations will regard pedophilia more positively.

Is it even possible to apply historical relativism to adult–child sexual relationships? The historical record on pedophilia is not extensive, and instances of its acceptance are relatively difficult to find cross-culturally. According to De Mause (1976), the sexual use of boys by older men was common in Ancient Greece and Rome. In most cities, boy brothels existed. The license to abuse younger boys seems to have been greater when the boy involved was a slave. Bleibreu-Ehrenberg (1991) claimed that people in parts of Papua New Guinea and Melanesia regarded a boy who had not been initiated sexually by a male guardian as not being capable of the status of adult man. The lack of a more general record, historically, suggests that these are exceptions rather than the rule.

The relative liberality applied currently to adulterous relationships, marriage involving divorcees, and gay and lesbian relationships contrasts markedly with dominant responses to adult–child relationships. It is impossible to quantify this, but it would seem that we have become increasingly condemnatory of adults involved in adult–child relationships. Changes in legislation, perhaps, capture some of this change. The sparse historical record suggests that even as recently as the late 19th century, antichild views were held in relation to this issue. Children in such relationships were condemned as seducers or liars (Baartman, 1992). Reversals can also be seen in the physical punishment of children. Modern ideology is pushing toward the criminalization of adults physically punishing children, which can be contrasted with the "spare the rod, spoil the child" view of earlier generations.

These shifts in the ideological basis of views of childhood involve broader changes. Hence, for example, the condemnation of physical discipline for children is partly associated with an ideological shift from conceptualizing childhood as different and children as the property of their parents for the parents to do with virtually what they could. The emancipation of children to the status of persons with rights, especially to self-determination, and the right to a voice in what happens to him or her has not been complete. Alongside the view that children have the right to be treated as people, consulted and conversed with, is the view that children need protection from dangers, whether or not of their own making. This alternative ideology involving protection for the child's own good irrespective of the child's wants is inevitably repressive. Given that childhood has a component of sexuality, it is equally inevitable that childhood can be regarded as being subject to sexual repression. Howitt (1995) pointed to the potential contradiction in the writings of Kitzinger when she advocated greater rights in childhood that would include the right for a child to decide for him or herself when to engage in sexual relations: "The mainstream campaigns conspicuously fail to take any overall stand against the structural oppression of children. They are, therefore, not only severely limited in what they can achieve, but they also often reinforce the very ideologies which expose children to exploitation in the first place" (Kitzinger, 1988, p. 85).

It is, then, hardly surprising to find that spokespersons for groups subject to sexual repression should raise painful issues intended to highlight issues of the repression of children. This includes pedophilia advocates. Nevertheless, these arguments, largely irrespective of their source, are eagerly seized on by propedophilia organizations. Some of these are assembled together by propedophile groups on their Web sites, such as the following from Radow (2000):

> When does a youngster have the right and the power to make his own sexual decisions? How are laws against intergenerational sex used specifically to target gay men? (Preston, 1991, cited in Radow, 2000)

> The statutory structure of the sex laws has been identified as oppressive and insulting to young people. A range of sexual activities are legally defined as molestation, regardless of the quality of the relationship or the amount of consent involved. (Gayle Rubin, lesbian feminist, 1978, cited in Radow, 2000)

Irrespective of the bandwagon jumping of the pedophiles, such statements as those by Preston and Rubin raise important and difficult questions for our views of childhood and the transition from childhood into a more mature state in which the individual is deemed capable of making sexual choices. The mere fact that a minority of writers is disposed to raise such issues is evidence of fundamental ideological conflicts that rarely surface. Responses to these quotations may be intense, but their intensity indicates the strength of our commitment to ideologies of childhood, which are seldom challenged. Their ideological nature means that these are not matters of fact—their relative value cannot be determined by even a myriad of research studies. We may be much more comfortable with the familiar but rigid professional rhetoric that brands adult–child sexual relationships as acts of abuse and molestation.

Suggestions that the child might be a willing partner are deemed distorted thinking—the perverse views of pedophiles. This is a common charge in the professional literature on pedophiles (Jenkins-Hall, 1989). It also entrains the idea that there is a right way of thinking.

The competing ideological perspectives on childhood (or old age for that matter) do not establish with any certainty that historical relativism would place our present dominant ideology of childhood merely as a temporary and geographically limited viewpoint. Historical relativism does apply to adult–child relationships if we define childhood in strict age terms, but this may be to confuse differing concepts of childhood with different ideas about the appropriateness of adult–child sex. The issue is easily illustrated by asking simple questions such as the following: Are there or have there been societies that have approved of sex between adults and children under 5? To my knowledge, the answer is no. Are there societies that have approved of sexual intercourse and children of 10? This question is harder to answer, because there have been societies that permitted marriage at this age. It may be mistaken to assume that this gave approval to marriages between 10-year-olds and much older persons. Approval may have been restricted to marriages between similar aged youngsters, other unions being regarded with horror. Furthermore, care should be taken not to assume that the time of marriage is synonymous with the beginning of sexual relations in such marriages.

There are many historical and cultural issues, but it cannot be assumed that complete historical relativism necessarily applies to adult–child sexual relationships. Because the historic record on pedophilia is not immense, it is difficult to assess the extent to which matters of detail alter the broad issues much. For example, there have been variations in the ages of consent in different communities in different historical periods. To what extent does this variation undermine the broad principle that adult–child sexual unions have rarely, if ever, been approved? Who is defined as a child, incapable of marriage, may have varied in terms of time and geography, but that merely reinforces that the concept of being too youthful for sexual relationships is somewhat universal.

Furthermore, it tells us nothing of how sexual activities at this age outside of marriage would have been regarded. Some authors point out that the historical record mentions examples of adult–child sexual activities that were not taken seriously. For example, there are examples of French royalty engaging in sex play with very young children (Howitt, 1992). It should further be considered that the minimum ages of marriage and consent are not in themselves normative in the sense that they prescribe when marriage can rather than will take place—it cannot be assumed that they were ever seen as ideal ages for marriage. Thus, in this context, it is worthwhile noting that legislation has, at times, defined two different ages for marriage—one unfettered and the other if parental consent has been given.

Similarly, in the Western world in modern times, the marriage of teenagers, despite its legality, is regarded as being risky and, possibly, ill advised. The point is that even where the partners are equally matched in terms of age, doubts are cast on the advisability of youthful sexual encounters—or, more to the point, youthful sexual encounters involving long-term expectations.

A number of troubling issues emerges out of investigations of the pedophile given other relationships that have been historically, if not presently, condemned. Once again, homosexual relationships are probably the best example of this. One hardly needs to catalogue society's intolerance of homosexuality—which extended in the West into the responses of psychology and the other social sciences. Do we even dare question now that adult homosexual relationships are appropriate? Yet this change has occurred over a period of less than half a century. Homosexuality is now regarded as a sexual orientation rather than a sexual perversion. The suggestion is not that homosexuality is universally accepted as a healthy, fulfilling, and appropriate lifestyle, but that the consensus that appeared united against it no longer is so effectively and coherently voiced. Homosexuality, rather than something to be cured or punished, is now seen as being as integral to the core of the individual as heterosexuality is. So why not pedophilia?

There are several reasons for regarding pedophilia as a sexual orientation rather than as a perverse act of an evil manipulator of children (Howitt, 1995). One of these is that the pedophile orientation is formed by the age of young adulthood or late adolescence—much as homosexual orientation is. To be sure, some homosexuals may be confused by a number of factors into failing to recognize this identity. Some pedophiles may attempt, and even be successful up to a point, at heterosexual relationships, but the same may well be true of a homosexual person.

THE AGE STRUCTURING OF RELATIONSHIPS

> Your local paedophile,
> Patiently leans and watches.
> And your children play,
> Under his guilty gaze,
> While he plots to rob them,
> Of their innocence.
> (Clan of Hate, 2000)

> A convicted paedophile banned from walking puppies and from displaying teddy bears in his windows has left South Wales (BBC News Online, 1998)

Accounts of the activities of pedophiles tell an interesting story. In particular, they describe the process of "grooming." This includes the methods and strategies used by the pedophiles to involve themselves with youngsters. The public's conception of pedophiles as violent predators, taking children by force, is not the typical pattern of pedophile acts (Cupoli & Sewell, 1988; Nash & West, 1985). The research literature is less than clear about the extent of the use of violence by pedophiles, partly because of problems defining what is meant by "violence." Clearly gross acts of violence such as those of pedophiles who murder their sexual victims do exist but they are atypical of the mass of pedophile acts, just as rape-murders are atypical of sexual assaults on adult women.

Much more important than force and violence are the interpersonal techniques used by pedophiles and other offenders against children to contact children for sexual purposes. Grooming techniques vary widely—say, from encouraging neighboring children to visit by offering drinks and snacks, to moving into the homes of adult women who already have children of the age attractive to the pedophile. Threats may be involved—such as "Don't tell your mummy or...." Of course, grooming has some parallels with the courting rituals that adult heterosexuals employ as part of the dating process. But despite the similarity, the points of difference are also clear. For example, for adult dating there is a range of acceptable places and points of contact between the adults—clubs and discos, pubs, gay bars, dating agencies, and so forth. These are recognized and accepted points of heterosexual and homosexual sexual contact. Of course, there are other less salubrious places (e.g., public parks and toilets). In contrast, adult–child sexual episodes lack any such recognized or accepted locations; they are not generally initiated in most of the locations just mentioned.

The absence of accepted adult–child contact locations may be of more significance than at first appears. It may seem ludicrous to suggest that adult–child sexual contacts are difficult, solely on the basis of the notion that pedophile contacts with children involve considerable effort. One reason for scepticism might be the numbers of instances of child sexual abuse taking place annually. If abuse is so common, then contact cannot be difficult. Furthermore, surely it is one of the characteristics of childhood that there is continuous dependence of young people on adults? The home and school are both environments in which children and adults interact.

Thus, in a sense, the argument fails at first base. Adults and youngsters are in continued interaction. This, on the other hand, does not mean that we are dealing with open social systems that lack rigid constraints. Schools, for example, are not the environs of just any adult. Their access is confined to a limited number of classes of adults—parents, teachers, and ancillary staff such as janitors, and the occasional visiting tradesperson. Anyone else would have no place being at the school and their presence would be regarded with some suspicion. The family, similarly, is not an open social system, but instead one in which access is fairly rigidly controlled. Put it another way, just how easy would it be for a pedophile to gain unfettered contact with the children of any family with which one is familiar? Babysitting might sometimes be an exception. Certainly, within a family there are a number of adults who have such relatively unfettered access to children—grandparents being the clearest example. However, in the sexual abuse literature, it is the more distant relations and 'social' uncles, for example, who seem particularly common among perpetrators (Russell, 1983).

There are other exceptions, obviously, such as youth club leaders who have access to young people, although these are formal roles and free mingling of adults and children in these settings is not possible. Priests, especially in previous less secular eras, would also have access to children and their families. It is notable, however, that these are the very sorts of roles that have attracted pedophiles, because they offer greater opportunities of access to children. All of this is another way of saying that the mixing of adults and children, apart from parents and their children, is not great. This is especially the case when we exclude collective adult–child contacts such as the case of playgroups in which pools of adults and children intermingle on a collective basis.

The ways in which age structures relationships are not commonly discussed in research on interpersonal relationships. It may be that such age structuring is such a self-evident feature of relationships that it scarcely warrants attention. Much as this may be so, it is surprising nevertheless that if researchers are aware of structuring they have not chosen to explore its features. For example, does the age structuring differ for different types of relationships? What is it about age that makes it such a key variable? What factors militate against age structuring? If most of the relationships experienced by individuals are striated by age with a degree of rigidity, is this surprising in terms of the institutional structures of Western society?

Nevertheless, most of the close relationships if not all types of relationship experienced by individuals seem to be fairly rigidly age striated. Social institutions at every stage force similarly aged persons into contact. In these circumstances, not surprisingly, friendships and other relationships are roughly age compatible. The toddler is rejected as a regular playmate by older children and largely has other toddlers, who are also children of their parents' friends, with whom to play—adults are in a relatively informal teaching role. Age rules determine admission to playgroups, school, and college, as well as departure from them. Even within this age structuring there is further structuring. Schools are structured by chronological age, with passage through the institution virtually exclusively determined by chronological age. A child or young adult leaves these institutions at times largely determined by age. Entry into the adult world of bars, clubs, and discos is effectively determined, within a few years, by laws concerning these institutions. Entry into the world of work shows very similar characteristics. Most of us enter work immediately after school or after college, at roughly similar ages. Furthermore, the promotion structure of employment ensures that the older workers will tend to have supervisory responsibility allied to a degree of social distance over younger workers. Although not quite so close, matters such as beginning parenthood for the vast majority occurs within a band of several years. No matter the exceptions, it is a matter of simple observation that the majority of relationships demonstrate these age-banded characteristics. Retirement has another pattern.

Of course, the significance of age banding has not totally escaped relationship researchers. For example, Cramer (1998) discussed four studies that explored age similarity in spouses. The correlation between the ages of husbands and wives over a range of studies was impressively large—ranging between about 0.9 and 0.7, depending on study and type of sample. These correlations exceed those for all other measures of similarity between couples quite substantially. Although not so important in this context, Cramer pointed out that research has suggested there is a greater degree of similarity between the ages of still-married partners than there is between no-longer-married partners. In other words, age similarity is functional as well as normative within an age-banded community. Presumably, there may be a variety of factors associated with age similarity that encourage successful relationships.

In an age-striated society, certain individuals are permitted to cross age boundaries. Some, such as teachers and youth workers, as we have seen, are allowed to do so under a form of license. Others—such as elderly people and young children—can do so in less clear-cut and defined circumstances. Almost as if there is an affinity between elderly people and children, elderly people are excused their interest in children—perhaps the age differential is of such a span that sexually they are no threat. Alternatively, it may be the consequence of the recognition of the social isolation and loneliness that old age may bring. Other possible explanations are readily found. Childhood and old age are both regarded as periods of powerlessness in Western society. Dependence on others is another shared feature. In this sense, old people are seen to have a legitimate interest in young children, because they share a similarity of social status in the West. Significantly, one common explanation of pedophilia involves the idea of emotional empathy or congruence between the perpetrator and the child (Araji & Finkelhor, 1986). Although research essentially fails to support this idea (Howitt, 1995), the fact that such explanations are used suggests that "normal" adults have no such empathy with children. In other words, adults (apart from parents), generally are expected to find relationships with children unsatisfactory.

THE UNILLUMINATING ISSUE OF AGE OF CONSENT

The age at which a youngster is held capable of consenting to heterosexual activity and, by implication, the youngest age at which that youngster may marry varies widely. In the United States, according to the most recent available figures, the range appears to vary from a low of 12 years of age (Delaware) to 13 years (New Mexico), 14 years (e.g., Iowa, Georgia), 16 years (Kansas), 17 years (New York, Texas), and 18 years (e.g., Arizona, Florida). Parental consent is often required at the lower age ranges. On a worldwide scale, including nations at various stages of economic development, the variability is also great and no obvious patterns are to be found that might determine whether a nation has a younger or older age of consent.

These figures are interesting as much for their variability as for any trends they reveal. They reflect a 6-year spread that seems to have little relationship to key variables such as the age of puberty, the start of menstruation in girls, and similar indicators of physical maturity. Also, it is clear that what might be a licit adult–youngster relationship in one geographical location would be illicit in another geographical location. Why should there be a differential of 6 years in terms of the age at which youngsters in different countries are allowed to choose whether to engage in sexual intercourse or marriage? Because of the paucity of the historical record, historical trends are difficult to elicit.

There is an argument, popular among those who advocate man–boy love, that is worth recounting here. It makes the case that ages of consent (and perhaps the need for an age of consent) are related to the needs of industrial society. Industrial society requires an increasingly educated workforce in order to function. Consequently, young people are defined as schoolchildren for a much longer period—well into age groups that previous generations would see as adults. Characteristically, schoolchildren are financially dependent on their parents—a state that extends well into adulthood for numbers of young people. Such dependency would be made intolerable, for example, by a need for that same family to support a further family. The evidence to support this view is overall rather weak. For one thing, it would imply great pressures to raise the age of consent in the most industrialized societies. Generally, it is not possible to discern any such pattern. However, a study of Swiss Cantons during the late 19th century provides, perhaps, an exception (Killias, 1991). These different administrative sections of Switzerland had different levels of development of the educational system (perhaps an indicator of industrial development). The different areas had different levels of control on young people's sexual activities and adults' sexual activity with young people. A relationship was found between the level of development of the educational system and age of consent. This might be seen as some support for the view that age of consent was a product of industrialization—to do with the needs of capitalism rather than those of the individual child.

However, there is a general lack of evidence pertinent to this issue, and it is impossible to discern trends for ages of consent to vary in line with this argument by comparing countries with different levels of industrialization in terms of age of sexual consent. Attempting to do so seems to produce no clear pattern. Hence, in the United Kingdom the age of consent is 16, in the United Arab Emirates it is 18, in Pakistan it is 21, in Mexico it is 18, and so forth. That is, there is no discernible trend. Furthermore, any argument that the age of consent is set to prevent dependent children producing dependants of their own cannot explain trends in homosexual age of consent. In many nations these are identical but sometimes homosexual age of consent is higher than heterosexual age of consent.

Despite encouragement otherwise from the man–boy love movement, we should not assume uncritically that there is a rationality underlying legislation concerning sexual matters of this sort. Indeed, it might be safer to assume that issues of homosexual ages of consent may be better regarded as peculiarly modern phenomena rather than as a matter that has affected legislators historically. Nevertheless, because the idea that the age of consent might vary with the needs of capitalism has been seized on by propedophilia campaigners as evidence of unacceptable economic forces coming between true love (albeit love across age boundaries), the fragility of the idea has to be stressed. Indeed, the lack of other supporting evidence makes the argument specious.

PEDOPHOBIC AMBIENCE

"Suffer little children to come unto me." Jesus Christ, if he said that now he'd be on the paedophile register. (Stockton, 1997)

Another theme, the pedophobic ambience, interweaves with issues to do with pedophilia such that general family life becomes the focus of attention. This is basically the idea that adult–child relationships have been effectively blocked and, in a sense, destroyed because of the fear of the risk of accusations of sexual abuse. There is a range of issues that have been associated with this; in particular, the issue of parent–child contact and, even more publicly, the legitimacy of bathtime and beach photographs taken by parents of their offspring. Once in a while these issues have gained great public notoriety. Fundamental to all of this is the view that there was once an idyllic time when adult–child relationships, especially within the family, could proceed without concerns about physical matters being mistaken for sexual abuse. This fear is probably out of all proportion to any cases where such matters ever materialize. However, it is probably more to do with public beliefs about the power of social workers to launch draconian actions against families on the basis of the most trivial of evidence (Howitt, 1992).

Perhaps the most graphic way to illustrate the issue lies in the example of the British newsreader, Julia Somerville, who was arrested along with her partner when a photo-lab worker reported bathtime photos of the couple's 7-year-old daughter naked. The equation of child nudity with child pornography "has contributed to a culture in which adults are scared of intimacy even with their own children" (*The Guardian*, January 13, 1996, p. 12). The point is not that there was an overwhelming condemnation of the couple for their activities, but instead there was sympathy with the predicament of parents in the modern climate. The debate was essentially around the innocence portrayed by such family snapshots against the fear of state intervention into normal physical closeness between parent and child.

In terms of this analysis, the difficulty lies in knowing the extent to which such pictorial records of family life reflect modern ideas and the extent to which they have deep cultural and historic associations in our culture. Without knowing this, it is impossible to assess whether we are considering factors that might have destroyed an important aspect of family life and parent–child interaction. The issue is whether adult–child relationships have become fettered in modern times, or whether there was truly a period when such relationships were common and if they necessarily included this aspect of physical closeness. Unfortunately, the answer to the question requires ethnographic knowledge of family and community life for periods of our history for which the record is, once again, lacking. The importance of physical closeness of parent with child may merely reflect the ideology surrounding the modern family and what is a good family. For example, the 'modern' family discusses what is wrong about a child's behavior—it does not slap. Adults and children maintain discourse at a level that might have been impossible when families were typically much larger.

THE HARMFULNESS OF SEX

Pedophile organizations argue that relations with children involve reciprocity and are beneficial to boys. This contrasts directly against major ideological threads in professional thinking since the 19th century. There is a tradition, certainly dating from that period, for sex to be regarded as dangerous by those professions dealing with social problems.

Professionalization during this period gave medicine a collective voice on a wide variety of issues. *The Society for the Study and Cure of the Inebriated*, for example, was a typical example of how the profession brought a distinctive medical perspective to the study of social problems (Berridge, 1989). Perhaps even more remarkable were the numerous 19th-century medical writings around the topic of sex. Reflecting wider societal concerns about the dangers of sex, medics wrote treatises describing its harmfulness. The dangers ranged enormously. Masturbation was held to be debilitating and greatly in need of control. Apparatuses were designed to prevent the possibility of a child masturbating—strapping, mittens, and the like were all made available. Girls were discouraged from bicycle riding because of the risk of arousing contact with the bicycle saddle. Clitorectomy was performed by Western medics well into the 20th century (Haller & Haller, 1974).

It should be stressed that all forms of sexual activity were regarded as potentially harmful. Thus, for example, marital sex was regarded as debilitating for the general health. It was also socially bad—the consequences for the young unmarried woman who became pregnant were often extreme. Nevertheless, this sexually repressive atmosphere was evident well into the middle of the 20th century and most clearly so in relation to children. For some, the sexual repression of childhood may be still with us in altered, modern forms. Perhaps that is the taboo that the pedophile breaks. One way of regarding this is that childhood innocence is a euphemism for the sexual repression of childhood, part of the general repression of children that some have discerned in childrearing practices. For example, physical punishment of children is regarded as an outmoded but still legitimated form of violence.

The debate on adult–child sexual relations substantially involves the idea that adult–child sexual activity is harmful. The clinical literature is full of this. In other words, the ideologically founded idea of the harmfulness of sex is incorporated into the modern literature on child sexual abuse. And there can be little doubt that the clinical literature is dominated by evidence in support of this view (Howitt, 1995). However, once again the potentially ideological nature of this is apparent if we consider alternatives. As might be expected, pedophile proponents have such a view. This opposing conception recently returned into focus with the publication of a meta-analysis of studies of effects of adult–child sex (Rind, Tromovitch, & Bauserman, 1998). This study of studies concluded essentially that overwhelmingly the studies of adult–child sex tend to reinforce the view that no negative psychological effects occurred in the children. The public response in the United States was so intense that a spokesperson for the American Psychological Association, publishers of the offending article, had to deny its scientific worth. This is another fraught area that needs to be encroached with trepidation. Nevertheless, the issue is fairly simple, really—that of consent or consensuality.

The professional literature on child sexual abuse frequently stresses the adverse consequences of adult–child sex on the personality and social development of what is always construed as the victim in this literature. Clinical evidence of the damage done by adult–child sexual relationships is abundant (Howitt, 1995), but clinical samples are by their nature highly selected samples—selected because of the psychiatric and psychological problems shown. Typically, the explanation of the negative effects of adult–child sexual activity is held to be the result from matters related to power and the victim's lack or loss of control. Propedophile reviews of such studies are highly critical of the methodological artefacts involved in obtaining research evidence in this field. They prefer to stress studies that use a slightly more systematic methodology—putatively. A number of studies can be cited that conclude that adult–child sexual activity may be less harmful than the professional literature suggests. These studies, unusual for social research, can be found described on the Internet despite their age (Bauserman, 1991; Brongersma, 1991; Mrazek, 1985; Sandfort, 1982, 1987; Sonenschein, 1987). However, many of these employ suspect methodologies of their own, such as interviewing boys in current relationships with men. Not surprisingly, a high degree of satisfaction is found with the experience. Indeed, the pro-man–boy love groups may claim that the research evidence shows that man–boy relationships are not harmful (Fredericksen, 2000)—although man–girl relationships may well be!

Howitt (1995) pointed out that studies using a broad definition of sexual abuse find little evidence that children are damaged by abuse, but because this includes the milder forms of abuse (e.g., exposing a child to sexual talk), then perhaps this is to be expected. More convincing evidence of the dangers of adult–child sexual activity comes from studies of cycles of sexual abuse or cycles of pedophilia. The evidence is much stronger here—penetrative sexual acts by certain sorts of adults are virtually universal in pedophiles' childhood. There are also surveys that present a slightly subtler view than either extreme. Sandfort (1988, 1989), for example, showed that consent was an important variable in determining whether or not sexual activity between adults and (adolescent) children was harmful. The findings were essentially that nonconsensual adult–child sexual relationships were associated with poorer psychosexual development, whereas consensual adult–child sexual relationships were associated with better psychosexual adjustment in adulthood.

To avoid the argument being misconstrued, my interpretation of the literature is that it is not surprising that no measurable harm comes to some teenagers who knowingly consent to an involvement with adults just a few years older than themselves. In some communities with different laws, they might be old enough to be free to engage in sexual relations. We do not necessarily have to read into these cases any element of force or pressure. However, this does not mean that all adult–young person sexual relations are invariably nondamaging—or that it is possible to predict 'harmless' ones with any confidence. Feeling exploited, not being a willing partner, being lied to, being manipulated, and many similar adverse features may well turn healthy youngsters into damaged adults. This, in no sense, is an argument for underage sex, merely a recognition that adolescents will differ in respect of their readiness for adult relationships. (These are issues at the margins between adolescence and adulthood—we are not considering adults having full sexual relations with, say, a 5-year-old.)

This presents a different picture of pedophile relationships compared to virtually every other type of relationship, which are generally seen as beneficial in a number of ways—marriage, in particular. Of course, we generally accept that and regard it as evidence in support of the beneficial consequences of relationships as being well established. There are characteristics of good relationships and different ones for bad relationships. Violent, sexually or emotionally abusive relationships may be seen from the outside as harmful, and eventually by the victim in the same way, but generally speaking relationships are held to be positive despite their faults and inadequacies. Not so the pedophile and his victim, according to the general, public perception, which suggests that any adult–child contact is harmful.

CONCLUSION

It is beyond doubt that the study of adult–child sexual contacts demands that we understand something of the role of ideology in the way we view relationships. Relationships are not simply personal matters, but instead relate to broader sets of beliefs organized as fairly identifiable ideologies. The study of inappropriate relationships such as pedophilia helps us identify aspects of the ideologies that underlie relationships more generally. The public voice of pedophiles justifies pedophile activity in terms that translate readily into dominant romantic ideologies. Nevertheless, we are a long way from knowing whether this is what is felt or whether it is merely rhetoric calculated to appeal to the wider audience in its own terms.

Pedophilia is held in horror in ways that other relationships once were. Nevertheless, this does not encourage us to regard it any less unfavorably. We have become much more tolerant of a wide variety of sexual relationships—even those that involve the sexual behavior of the relatively young. Perhaps we are even more accepting of underage sex between youngsters than marriage between teenagers. As the chronological graph of outrage over time goes down for such a wide variety of relationships, it seems to be rising for pedophilia. Yet there does not appear to be a simple reason why. It cannot be a growing intolerance of the sex activity involving the young, because such activities—apart from the pedophilic ones—show the less punitive trend. This can be regarded as reason to emphasize the importance of understanding relationships in the light of their ideological bases.

REFERENCES

Araji, S., & Finkelhor, D. (1986). Abusers: A review of the research. In D. Finkelhor (Ed.), *A Sourcebook on child Sexual Abuse* (pp. 89–119). Beverly Hills, CA: Sage.

Baartman, H. E. M. (1992). The credibility of children as witnesses and the social denial of the incestuous abuse of children. In F. Losel, D. Bender, & T. Bliesener (Eds.), *Psychology and law: International perspectives* (pp. 345–351). Berlin: de Gruyter.

Bauserman, R. (1991). Objectivity and ideology: Criticism of Theo Sandfort's research on man–boy sexual relations. *Journal of Homosexuality, 20*(1/2), 297–312.

BBC News Online UK. (1998, March 17). "'Paedophile' protesters arrested." http://news1.thls.bbc.co.uk/low/english/uk/newsid_66000/66271.stm.

Benjamin, J. (1997, November 25). On boys and boylovers. http://www.demon.nl/freespirit/fpc/pages/boy-muse/report.html.

Berridge, V. (1989). Historical issues. In S. McGregor (Ed.), *Drugs and British society* (pp. 20–35). London: Routledge.

Billig, M., Condor, S., Edwards, D., Gane, M., Middleton, D., & Radley, A. R. (1988). *Ideological dilemmas*. London: Sage.

Bleibreau-Ehrenberg, G. (1991). Pederasy among primitives: Insitutionalzied initiation and cultic prostitution. *Journal of Homosexuality, 20*(1/2), 13–30.

Brongersma, E. (1991). Boy-lovers and their influence on boys: Distorted research and anecdotal observations. *Journal of Homosexuality, 20*(1/2), 145–175.

Brown, S. (1999). Public attitudes toward the treatment of sex offenders. *Legal and Criminological Psychology, 4*(2), 239–252.

Clan of Hate. (2000). http://www.julius.ndirect.co.uk/Clan%20of%20Hate.html

Cramer, D. (1998). *Close relationships: The study of love and friendship*. London: Arnold.

Cupoli, J. M., & Sewell, P. M. (1988). One thousand fifty-nine children with a chief complaint of sexual abuse. *Child Abuse and Neglect, 12*, 151–162.

De Mause, L. (1976). *The history of childhood: The evolution of parent–child relationships as a factor in history*. London: Souvenir.

Finkelhor, D. (1991). Response to Bauserman. *Journal of Homosexuality, 20*(1/2), 313–315.

Frederiksen, A. (2000). A criticism of sex abuse research. http://www.digiweb.com/igeldard/LA/pamphlets/rad-fem.htm

The Guardian. (1996, January 13), p. 12.

Haller, J. S., & Haller, R. M. (1974). *The physician and sexuality in Victorian America*. Urbana: University of Illinois Press.

Howitt, D. (1992). *Child abuse errors*. Hemel Hempstead, UK: Harvester Wheatsheaf.

Howitt, D. (1995). *Paedophiles and sexual offences against children*. Chichester, UK: Wiley.

Jenkins-Hall, K. D. (1989).Cognitive restructuring. In D. R. Laws (Ed.), *Relapse prevention with sex offenders* (pp. 207–215). New York: Guilford.

Journal and Research Reports on Pedophilia (1994). http://qrd.rdrop.com:80/qrd/orgs/NAMBLA/journal.and.research.reports

Journal of Homosexuality, 20(1/2). [Special issue]. (1990).

Killias, M. (1991). The historic origins of penal statutes concerning sexual activities involving children and adolescents. *Journal of Homosexuality, 20*(1/2), 41–46.

King-Ky Ron. (2000). The anti-paedophile site. http://kingron.8m.com/ (August 3, 2000).

Kitzinger, J. (1988, Spring). Defending innocence: Ideologies of childhood. *Feminist Review, 28*, 77–87.

Lindzey, G. (1967). Some remarks concerning incest, the incest taboo, and psychoanalytic theory. *American Psychologist, 22*, 1051–1059.

Mrazek, D. (1985). Science, politics, and ethic: Issues in the study of the sexual use of children. *Contemporary Psychology, 30*(1), 37–38.

Nash, C. L., & West, D. (1985). Sexual molestation of young girls: A retrospective survey. In D. J. West (Ed.), *Sexual victimisation: Two recent researches into sex problems and their social effects* (pp. 1–94). London: Gower.

Owusu-Bempah, K., & Howitt, D. (2000). *Psychology beyond Western perspectives*. Leicester, UK: British Psychological Society Books.

Radow, R. (2000). What people are saying about NAMBLA and man/boy love. http://qrd.rdrop.com:80/qrd/orgs/NAMBLA/quotes

Rind, B., Tromovitch, P., & Bauserman, R. (1998). A meta-analytic examination of assumed properties of child sexual abuse using college samples. *Psychological Bulletin, 124*(1), 22–53.

Russell, D. E. H. (1983). The incidence and prevalence of intrafamilial and extra-familial sexual abuse of female children. *Child Abuse and Neglect, 7*, 133–146.

Sandfort, T. (1982). *The sexual aspect of paedophile relations: The experience of twenty-five boys.* Amsterdam: Pan/Spartacus.

Sandfort, T. (1987). *Boys on their contacts with men: A study of sexually expressed friendships.* Elmhurst, NY: Global Academic.

Sandfort, T. G. M. (1988). *The meanings of experience: On sexual contacts in early youth, and sexual behaviour and experience in later life.* Utrecht: Homostudies.

Sandfort, T. G. M. (1989, July). *Studies into child sexual abuse: An overview and critical appraisal.* Paper presented at the 1st European Congress of Psychology, Amsterdam.

Sonenschein, D. (1987). On having one's research seized. *Journal of Sex Research, 23,* 408–414.

Stockton, E. (1997). Lady Godiva home page. http://www.users.zetnet.co.uk/stockton/136-contents.htm

V
EPILOGUE

12

Inappropriate Relationships in a Time of Social Change … Some Reflections on Culture, History, and Relational Dimensions

Robin Goodwin
Brunel University

Duncan Cramer
Loughborough University

CATEGORIZING RELATIONAL INAPPROPRIATENESS

In the introductory chapter of this book, Steve Duck and Lise VanderVoort proposed three levels of inappropriateness that they called the unconventional, the disapproved, and the forbidden, and which are listed in order of increasing social disapproval. Of the detailed examples of inappropriateness covered in this text, they put within the first category cross-gender friendships (Baumgarte, chap. 6) and culturally disparate marriages (Adams & Rosen-Grandon, chap. 5). Within the second category, they place therapist–patient sexual relationships (Garrett, chap. 8) and marital affairs (Allen &

Harrison, chap. 3), whereas in the third category, they include pedophilia (Howitt, chap. 11) and obsessional relational intrusion (Spitzberg & Cupach, chap. 10). Instances of inappropriateness, which they think may be placed anywhere along this continuum or even off it according to the view of the individual, are same-sex relationships (Yip, chap. 7) and interracial relationships (Gaines & Leaver, chap. 4).

To explore the degree to which these types of relationships were recognized in a student population, 100 undergraduates at a British university were asked to write "Who would it be inappropriate to have a relationship with?" Students were permitted to write as many characteristics as they wished, with most listing three or four relationships. Most frequently cited were those relationships involving a "forbidden" feature. Other relationships less frequently mentioned could largely be classified as "disapproved" or "unconventional." Some 91% of these students mentioned a relationship with a relative or family member (including foster parents). Age was a major criterion, with 39% citing someone considerably younger or a child (hinting at forbidden pedophilia) and 34% a much older partner (a relationship that Duck & VanderVoort termed as "unconventional"). About 38% reflected norms of fidelity by claiming it was inappropriate to have a relationship with someone already married or seriously involved with another, which may be characterized as a "disapproved" relationship. This fidelity rule was also reflected in the 21% who cited a partner of a friend, which could probably also be classed as "unconventional."

Taboos surrounding power inequalities were noted by the 32% who mentioned a teacher, with 20% citing a boss, and 4% of respondents noting an employee. Nine percent of our students cited priests and nuns, two mentioned prohibitions concerning the doctor–patient relationship, and two addressed professional colleagues. All these latter relationships involve power inequalities that Duck and VanderVoort claimed are likely to be disapproved and may damage social reputation due to the violation of prescribed roles. Homosexuality (placed in varying categories in the Duck/VanderVoort taxonomy) was cited by 7% of the students, whereas taboos concerning those that are very close to the individual (such as good friends and housemates) were cited by a further 11% of the students. Finally, relationships with animals (surely forbidden in most cultures) and relationships with criminals (most likely categorized as suspicious and unconventional) were each cited by 9% of the students.

Inappropriate relationships may also be classified in terms of the extent to which they occur that may not directly correspond with the degree to which they are disapproved. Estimates of prevalence may vary due to differences in the way the behavior is defined, and there may be a tendency to underreport behaviors that are disapproved more strongly.

Several of the contributors to this book have provided figures of the prevalence of the inappropriate relationships that were their concern.

Garrett (chap. 8) reported the extent to which sexual contact may occur between psychotherapists and their patients during treatment as well as after it has ended. American studies suggest that under 7% of psychotherapists have stated that they have had such contact (e.g., Holroyd & Brodsky, 1980; Pope, Keith-Spiegel, & Tabachnick, 1986; Thoreson, Shaugnessy, Heppner, & Cook, 1993). This figure corresponds with the percentage of patients disclosing such contact (Pope & Feldman-Summers, 1992), although as these patients were clinical psychologists it is not known how representative this figure is of the typical psychotherapy patient. Garrett's own study noted that less than 4% of British clinical psychologists reported having sexual contact with their patients (Garrett & Davis, 1998). Spitzberg and Cupach (chap. 10) noted that a representative survey in the United States found that 8% of females and 2% of males have been stalked in their lifetime, using a legal definition of stalking (Tjaden, Thoennes, & Allison, 2000). These rates were higher when a self-defined criterion was applied, with about 12% of the women and 6% of the men saying they had been stalked. The prevalence of people who have stalked others does not appear to have been asked. If someone who has stalked another person is likely to have stalked more than one other individual, then the prevalence of stalkers will be lower than that of those who have been stalked.

Gaines and Leaver (chap. 4) record that only 2% of European Americans are in "interracial" marriages (Alba, 1995). We can provide more detailed figures of marriages between White and Black people using the 1990 census data (Goldstein, 1999). Needless to say, this percentage will be smaller when it is expressed as a function of the majority than of the minority group. Thus, the percentage of Black wives with White husbands is about 1.54 of Black wives and about 0.10 of White husbands. The percentage of Black husbands with White wives is about 3.66 of Black husbands and about 0.25 of White wives. Kalmijn (1993) found that the number of Black–White marriages increased in the United States in the years from 1968 to 1986. In Britain, the number of Black people is smaller than in the United States. Consequently, the percentage of Black–White unions will be higher when expressed as a function of the relevant Black group. Using the 1991 census data (Coleman & Salt, 1996, p. 198), the percentage of Black women married or cohabiting with White men is about 18.09 of the Black group and about 0.16 of the White group. The percentage of Black men married or cohabiting with White women is about 26.99 of the Black group and about 0.27 of the White group.

In the International Social Survey Program for 1986 was a question on the gender of your best or closest friend, excluding your partner or family members (Finch, 1989, p. 94). This question was asked in seven different countries (Australia, Austria, Britain, Hungary, Italy, the United States, and West Germany). The percentage of women with a cross-gender best friend ranged from 7% in Britain to 13% in Austria, Hungary, and Italy. The percentage of men with a cross-gender best friend varied from 0% in Hungary to 21% in Austria. Although restricting the question to best friend has the advantage of selecting an important and distinctive personal relationship, it is likely to provide an underestimate of the prevalence of cross-gender friendships in general.

From 1991 onward a question on whether the respondent has ever had sex with someone other than their spouse has been asked in certain years as part of the General Social Survey in the United States (*www.icpsr.umich.edu/GSS*). The number of people answering "Yes" to this question is likely to provide an overestimate of the proportion of people who have had affairs, because this figure will include those who have had sex with a prostitute or who have had a one-night stand. Many people might not see these types of sex as constituting an affair as such. About 17% of Americans have admitted to having sex with someone other than their spouse. In the National Survey of Sexual Attitudes and Lifestyles carried out in 1990/1991 in Britain, about 2% of wives and 6% of husbands reported having more than one heterosexual partner in the past year (Johnson, Wadsworth, Wellings, & Field, 1994). These figures are likely to be higher if a period longer than the past year had been used.

Perhaps the most appropriate way of determining whether one is homosexual is in terms of self-definition, which was included in the National Health and Social Life Survey carried out in 1992 on a national representative sample of 18- to 59-year-old Americans (Laumann, Gagnon, Michael, & Micheaels, 1994). About 1.4% of the women and 2.8% of the men identified themselves as homosexual or bisexual. These percentages, together with those of people having same-gender sex partners in the last year, were the lowest for the various questions on same-gender sexuality. However, because homosexuality is generally disapproved of, some individuals may not wish to see themselves as homosexual, may not engage in same-gender sexual behavior, or may deny their homoerotic desires.

In addition, representative surveys may give an underestimate of homosexuality if those with homosexual tendencies are not uniformly distributed throughout the population but are more likely to be concentrated in certain areas, such as particular cities or particular areas of cities. There was evidence from the National Health and Social Life Survey that the percentage of men identifying themselves as either homosexual or bisexual was over three times greater in the central cities of the 12 largest metropolitan areas of the United States than the sample average. For women it was less than twice as big. In the National Survey of Sexual Attitudes and Lifestyles conducted on 16- to 59-year-olds in the United Kingdom in 1990/1991, about 0.4% of the women and 1.1% of the men reported that they had had at least one homosexual partner in the last year (Johnson et al., 1994, p. 191). These figures are slightly lower than the comparable ones for the United States. More than twice as many men in London reported having had homosexual experience as did men elsewhere. In support of Yip's comment that penetrative anal sex is relatively uncommon in male same-sex sexual behavior, the highest percentage of those reporting ever engaging in such acts in this survey was 25%. This was for the 16- to 34-year-olds having insertive anal sex with a same-gender partner in the last year, which compares with about 7% for cross-gender anal sex for the same age group.

There have been nationally representative surveys of pedophilia or adult–child sexual behavior in several Western countries (e.g., Edgardh & Ormstad, 2000; Finkelhor, 1994). The results of only the first two studies, conducted in Great Britain (Baker & Duncan, 1985) and the United States (Finkelhor, Hotaling, Lewis, & Smith, 1990), are briefly reported here. In the British survey, respondents who were over 15 years old were presented with a definition of child sexual abuse. This was specified as any activity carried out with a person under 16 years old by a sexually mature individual that led to the latter's sexual arousal. About 12% of females and 8% of males reported having such an experience. This involved no physical contact in 55% of the females and 48% of the males. A stranger perpetrated the abuse in 56% of the females and 43% of the males. The abuse had been a single experience for 66% of the females and 59% of the males. In other words, the typical experience of child sexual abuse seemed to be a single incident with a stranger involving no physical contact.

In the American survey, respondents were over 17 years old and child sexual abuse was determined on the basis of four questions asking whether they had various experiences under 19 years of age that they would now consider sexual abuse such as someone trying to touch, grab, kiss, or rub up against them. About 27% of the women and 16% of the men said they had had such experiences. If the percentage of individuals reporting this as occurring between 16 and 18 years of age is excluded to make the data more comparable with those of the British survey, 21% of the women and 10% of the men considered themselves to have been sexually abused. A stranger committed the offense in 21% of all females and 40% of all males abused. The experience was a single incident for 64% of the women and 73% of the men. For 98% of the women and 83% of the men, the perpetrator was male.

Although the prevalence and nature of childhood sexual abuse will vary according to the way it is defined and measured (Gorey & Leslie, 1997), some indication of these aspects is given by these two studies. As was the case with stalking, there do not appear to have been any studies that have attempted to estimate the number of people who sexually abuse children, which may be expected to be less than the number so abused if people who abuse one person tend to abuse others.

HISTORICAL AND CULTURAL PERSPECTIVES

In this book, we have striven to show that the very definition of "inappropriate relationship" is likely to be highly dependent on the cultural and subcultural setting in which it occurs. We believe that any comprehensive account of inappropriate relationships needs to provide an explanation of historical and cultural differences. Unfortunately, such analyses are still relatively uncommon, particularly by social psychologists, although the introduction of surveys on representative samples at intermittent intervals over the last 30 or so years has enabled some monitoring of attitudes toward some of these forms of inappropriate relationships.

Interracial Relationships

Interracial relationships were punishable by internment and death during the Nazi regime in Germany. Gaines and Leaver (chap. 6) noted that all remaining antimiscegenation laws were rendered null and void in the United States only as recently as 1967. A question on attitudes toward interracial marriage has been asked in the United States since 1963 (Schuman, Steeh, & Bobo, 1985) and in Britain since 1983 (Brook et al., 1992), although the question asked was very different in the two countries. In the United States, the question was "Do you think there should be laws against marriages between (Negroes/Blacks/African-Americans) and Whites?" In Britain, it was "Would you mind if one of your close relatives were to marry a person of Black/West Indian or Asian origin?" The term "Asian" in Britain refers to people who originated from the Indian subcontinent. Participants were either asked about their views on Asian or on Black or West Indian people, but there was little difference in their attitude to these two groups. There has been a decrease in agreement to these questions in both countries.

In the United States, the percentage of people who agreed there should be antimiscegenation laws declined from about 37% in 1972 to about 10% in 1996 (www.icpsr.umich.edu/GSS). In Britain, the percentage of people who said they would "mind a lot" if one of their close relatives were to marry a person of Black or Asian origin decreased from about 32% in 1983 (Brook et al., 1992) to about 15% in 1996 (Jowell et al., 1997). When a question similar to the British one was asked in the United States in 1977, about 42% of White Americans said they would be "very uneasy" if a close relative of theirs was planning to marry a Negro or Black (www.icpsr.umich.edu/GSS).

Extramarital Relationships

A question on the wrongness of extramarital sexual relations and homosexuality has been periodically surveyed in the United States since 1970 (Smith, 1990; see www.icpsr.umich.edu/GSS) and in Britain since 1983

(Scott, 1998), with the two questions being asked together in the same surveys. With respect to extramarital sexual relationships, there is little U.S. evidence suggesting a marked double standard in the attitude to such behavior in the sense that men were only slightly more likely to approve of such affairs than women (Scott, 1998). There was also little apparent or consistent change in the disapproval of such behavior over the years surveyed, the last of which was 1994. Although the percentage of people saying that such relationships were "always" or "almost always" wrong varied from one point of assessment to another; in general, this level of disapproval was about 86% in the United States (Smith, 1990). A direct comparison with Britain needs to be made cautiously, because of slight differences in the question asked, particularly in the number and wording of the response options. However, the percentage of people thinking that such behavior was "always" or "mostly" wrong appeared to be similar at about 84%. It should be noted that sexual fidelity is thought to be important not only in marriage, but also in a regular sexual relationship (Johnson et al., 1994) with some 80% of women and 69% of men holding this view.

Disapproval was somewhat lower for same-sex than extramarital sexual relationships throughout this same period, over which there appeared to be little change up until 1994. The percentage disapproving was about 76% in the United States (Smith, 1990) and about 68% in Britain (Brooks et al., 1992). Women were generally less disapproving than men (Scott, 1998). Since 1994, there appears to have been a decrease in disapproval. In 1998, about 60% disapproved of same-gender sexual relationships in the United States (*www.icpsr.umich.edu/GSS*), and about 50% did so in Britain (Jowell et al., 1999).

Cross-Cultural Perspectives

The categorization of behaviors may also vary in different cultures. For example, some sexual acts are illegal in certain states and countries (e.g., *www.ageofconsent.com; www.ilga.org/Information/Legal_survey/ilga_ world_legal_survey*), and adultery may be punished by death in some fundamentalist Muslim countries. Age of sexual consent is, as Dennis Howitt discussed in his chapter on pedophilia (chap. 11), likely to vary not only across cultures but even within societies such as the United States. The tripartite distinction proposed by Duck and VanderVoort accords well with the traditional demarcation of custom, morality, and law (e.g., Benn & Peters, 1959; Cramer, 2000; MacIver, 1949), and the categorization of the examples covered in this book seems most applicable in contemporary Western societies. Just as the Deadhead subculture discussed by Rebecca Adams and Jane Rosen-Grandon in chapter 5 helps demarcate the nature of interactions within this group, wider cultural boundaries serve to guide, frustrate, regulate, and sanction relational behaviors (Goodwin, 1999). Indeed, if culture can be at least partially defined as "the rules of the game" (Rohner, 1984), then at least some of these regulations are likely to include relationship formation and behavior.

The acceptance of same-sex friendships, considered by Roger Baumgarte in chapter 6, is also culturally variable, with the rejection of these relationships (and the classification of these relationships as "forbidden" rather than "unconventional") most likely in those societies where such friendships pose an apparent threat to established relationship arrangement agreements. Patient–therapist relationships are predicated on a broad set of cultural understandings rooted in shared notions of confidentiality and vulnerability, as well as broader societal conceptualizations of relationship equity. It is not difficult to imagine, however, societies where the "power" of the therapist to unfairly exploit his or her charge would be less widely acknowledged (and certainly less legally sanctioned). Furthermore, in a society where male assertion is valued, "relational persistence" (which might also mean stalking) may attract lesser sanctions and may even receive approval from some sections of society (provided it is the man—and probably a powerful one—who is the persistent party). Thus, in sexually violent societies, sexual assaults may be either permitted or ignored (Sanday, 1981). In societies where there is apparent free choice in relationship partner, women are frequently caught in a double-bind situation, being both attracted to their partner but having to deal with the possibility of unwanted advances (Burgoyne & Spitzberg, 1992). This situation often leads to equivocation, misunderstandings, and potential aggression. At the same time, as a relationship develops, cultural variations might be reduced (Baumgarte, Kulich, & Lee, 1998; Gudykunst, 1994). Thus, inappropriate behaviors, such as the discussion of confidences with another (Argyle, Henderson, Bond, Iizuka, & Contarello, 1986), may be more universally disapproved than variations in behavior with more distant relationship interactants.

Minturn, Grosse, and Haider (1969) found homosexuality to be condemned or ridiculed in nearly half (48%) of the 52 nonindustrial societies they analyzed. In contrast, in Melanesian societies, sexual contacts between males may occur as part of male initiation, suggesting a quite different attitude toward both homosexuality and child sexual activity than in Britain (Greenberg, 1995; Schlegel & Barry, 1991). Questions on extramarital sex and homosexuality were asked in 1994 in a number of countries as part of the International Social Survey Programme (see *www.issp.org*), enabling comparisons to be made across more countries than just the United States and Britain. Scott (1998) compared disapproval rates for six Western countries differing in sociopolitical and religious traditions. These countries were Britain, the United States, Ireland, (West and East) Germany, Sweden, and Poland. Disapproval for extramarital sex was generally high, ranging from about 82% in West and East Germany to about 93% in the United States, Ireland, and Sweden. Disapproval of same-gender sexual relationships was more varied, ranging from about 52% in West Germany to about 82% in Poland.

In chapter 1, Duck and VanderVoort argued that there has been a gradual separation over time between stable and personal attributions (viewing an individual as plain "evil" for his or her behavior) and identifying the *behavior* of that person as inappropriate (or just wrong). However, this separation may not always be universal, especially during times of high anxiety—research into social representations of sexual disease, for example, demonstrates the very close proximity between the rejection of high-risk sexual behaviors and a wider condemnation of the individuals or groups seen as responsible for those behaviors (Joffe, 1996; Markova, 1992; Markova & Wilkie, 1987; Sontag, 1989). Such a tendency for outgrouping blame allows others to feel protected (Joffe, 1996), with AIDS having led to the development of intense feelings and marked divisions in social relationships (Herzlich & Pierret, 1989) and a condemnation of fringe, "pariah" groups whose indulgent, immoral behavior was responsible for their infection (Buckley, 1993; Sontag, 1989). Such condemnations are likely to be related to other persisting representations of morality in a society, which in turn are likely to reflect religious beliefs and broader societal values (Paez et al., 1991).

Furthermore, the general egalitarian trend identified by Duck and VanderVoort, in which a wider range of relationships practiced by all social classes might be condemned as "inappropriate" might be of lesser significance in societies where the rules for behavior are very much created by the elite. In such high power-distance cultures (Hofstede, 1980), otherwise "inappropriate" behaviors (e.g., the maintenance of multiple sexual partners) are likely to be tolerated simply because they appeal to the whims of a powerful ruling class. Such an elite may be able, of course, to define the rules of appropriateness and, through their control over public sources of communication, stop "inappropriate" behaviors from ever becoming public knowledge.

NAUGHTY BUT NICE? WHY DO WE FIND INAPPROPRIATE RELATIONSHIPS SO HARD TO END?

In his majestic novel *Love in the Time of Cholera*, Gabriel García Márquez told a passionate tale of the unrequited love of the principal protagonist, Florentino Ariza, for a married woman (Fermina Daza). Although once, in Fermina's premarried days, the pair were sweethearts, for more than 50 years Florentino has been forced to worship Fermina from afar, with very little encouragement from the object of his affection. Why does he persist, despite the pain it causes him and the apparent hopelessness of his situation? Indeed, why do individuals persist in or pursue inappropriate relationships when the costs to them are so high, and when these relationships may lead to social retribution, loss of employment, prosecution, or worse?

Inevitably, the reasons for this persistence are likely to be complex. One possibility, of course, is that the situation may not be defined as "inappropriate," or the laws or regulations (moral or legal) that so define this relationship may be seen by the individual(s) involved as irrelevant or just plain wrong. Thus, the homosexual may reject the legal or moral framework imposed or implied by others. Other individuals may have less knowledge of regulations, particularly legal restrictions, or may be motivated to conveniently "forget" or "reinterpret" legislation, or they may turn to others for support in their own interpretation of this legislation (such as the pedophile who turns to other pedophiles for support for their activities). Although this may allow for a feeling of "us" and "them" to develop among the transgressing group, as Duck and VanderVoort noted in chapter 1, inappropriate relationship participants rarely enjoy a large social network.

A second possibility rests on the personality of the individual concerned. Particular individuals seek and openly embrace the excitement and challenge of inappropriate relationships. Sensation seekers, for example, might enjoy the thrill of the forbidden. Certainly, the literature on multiple partnerships and personality suggests that hedonists and sensation seekers report more partners (Cooper, Agocha, & Sheldon, 2000; Goodwin et al., in press). Furthermore, the paradox between searching for excitement and the desire for safety is well known in the relationship literature, and images of love as passionate, uncontrollable, and irrational (and therefore dangerous and often leading to inappropriate behaviors) are common across cultures (Doherty, Hatfield, Thompson, & Choo, 1994; Jankowiak & Fischer, 1992; Sternberg, 1998). In addition, leaving a relationship can often require considerable cognitive resources and coping styles that allow the individual to resolve his or her situation, resources that are not equally available to all.

A third interpretation comes from the sociobiological approach discussed by Pam Regan in chapter 2. From this viewpoint, each species is seen as having a genetically organized set of strategies and tactics for survival, growth, and reproduction (Kenrick & Keefe, 1992). At the core of this is gene replication through sexual interaction. Although sociobiologists focus on those traits that maximize gene replication (Thiessen & Gregg, 1980), they are generally less concerned with the social mores that might develop or restrict the choice of partners—insofar as these choices do not interfere with this gene transference process. From this perspective, therefore, "inappropriate" relationships such as opposite-sex friendships are potentially highly appropriate *because* of their sexual overtones. Similarly, opposite-sex prisoner–guard relations, relationships between socially marginalized groups, and the like are seen as functional inasmuch as they allow for successful gene transfer.

A fourth possibility can be interpreted in terms of social exchange processes. Exchange theory is an adaptation from economic concepts popular in the late 1950s (Homans, 1961; Thibaut & Kelley, 1959), and there are now numerous exchange theories examining exchanges within an established relationship, although all share the assumption that social behavior is determined by rewards and costs or the expectation of such rewards and costs (Hinde, 1997). Gordon and Donat (1992) suggested that a strong ethos of social exchange may lead certain men to feel that once they have kept "their side of the bargain" (having paid for a meal, taken the woman out in their car, etc.), then their partner should also keep hers (namely, engage in sexual intercourse). Failure may lead to the man feeling "justified" in sexually assaulting or stalking the woman, and one can envisage situations in which an inappropriate (and often dangerous) obsession with another might follow a sense of injustice on the part of one party, however mistaken ("I have done so much for her, I *deserve* her love"). Inevitably, such relational problems are likely to reflect significant power inequalities in societies where economic dependency by women make them less able to challenge and leave inappropriate relationships (Goodwin, 1999).

As such theories have developed, they have also recognized the significance of individual perceptions in the exchange process and the central role of perceived equitability of exchange between the partners (equity theory; e.g., Adams, 1965). From a social interdependence approach (Thibaut & Kelley, 1959), individuals compare their existing relationships with other possible and real relationships. Inappropriate relationships may of course represent the only relationship open to an individual with poor relationship alternatives elsewhere. Such alternatives are negatively correlated with relationship commitment (Rusbult, Morrow, & Johnson, 1986), and insofar as no more attractive alternative is available we would then predict that this relationship would persist despite the apparent low levels of satisfaction gained.

Finally, and perhaps most interesting of all, is a cognitive consistency approach. From the perspective of equity theory (Walster & Walster, 1978), those in inequitable relationships (which can include ones from which they overbenefit) will attempt to restore equity by leaving the relationship, or by manipulating the actual or perceived rewards and costs to themselves or their partner. From a balance theory perspective (Heider, 1958), we can envisage a problematic triangle where an actor (P) positively appraises not only the inappropriate relationship (O) but also the group that imposes sanctions (X) or the wider societal mores or regulations that forbid the relationship. In such a situation of imbalance, cognitive consistency approaches would lead us to expect a) a rejection of the inappropriate relationship (O); b) a rejection of the sanctioning body or group or, where this is self-imposed, a change in personal mores (X); c) a redefinition of the relationship O (perhaps as not inappropriate) or a redefinition of the relationship between O and X. Thus, an individual might end an inappropriate relationship for fear of sanction, may distance him or herself from a religious group condemning the relationship, or, as is the case for many stalkers, redefine the relationship as a "normal" nonintrusive one. Of course, as Duck and VanderVoort noted in their chapter, inappropriate relationships frequently demand considerable work and commitment. From a cognitive dissonance perspective (Festinger, 1957), such cognitive commitment might make future abandonment of the relationship difficult and costly in itself.

Such balance models presume considerable "cognitive gymnastics" (Berscheid, 1983), and it is questionable whether we consider such factors in such a rational manner or whether, to rephrase Heider's famous observation, emotions "engulf the field" (Heider, 1958). There is also cross-cultural evidence to suggest that such cognitive inconsistency is not necessarily problematic (Triandis, 1995). Nevertheless, such a balance approach may be informative not only for comprehending the manner in which individuals define their relationships, but also in the way in which outside audiences attribute the behavior of others. For example, in the Bill Clinton infidelity scenario that inspired this book, a generally well-respected and popular President was caught performing in an unacceptable and immoral manner. Few would suggest that he was unaware of the risks and potential consequences of his manner and the morality issues that accompanied it (even if he himself was less willing to make this immoral attribution). It was therefore perhaps not surprising to find some prominent commentators talking of Clinton's activity as "obsessive sexual behavior," providing a clinical (and to some extent external) attribution to the apparent paradox between an intelligent, important man and apparently unintelligent, immoral behavior.

How, then, are we to attribute the behavior of Florentino Ariza, the hero of García Márquez's profound novel, based partly on the story of his parents' own involvement? Certainly Florentino recognizes the inappropriate nature of his love for Fermina, and from his description he does not seem to be an active sensation seeker. There is no indication in the novel of a problematic childhood, difficulties for our protagonist in comprehending social rules and rituals, or broader social pathology.

Furthermore, although his desire for sexual relations with his heroine may be appropriate from a sociobiological perspective, he also has many other sexual admirers and partners and important social and economic power (he becomes the director of a shipping company), but the considerable time and energy he spends pursuing one, apparently "hopeless" case does not seem a suitable investment. Although his investment in her cause is considerable (in the dozens of unanswered love proclamations, etc.) he does not, as stated earlier, lack attractive alternatives. Instead, his very agony seems to stem from the imbalanced triangle of his emotions, caught between love for another and not only his inability to violate the rules of marriage but also the ambivalence of the object of his affection. Unable even to escape into fantasy, he creates his own "story" of an impossible but overwhelming love (Sternberg, 1998) that engulfs his daily life. And although of course García Márquez is telling a partly fictional tale, it is our ability to embrace this story and empathize with this hero that, from a "cold" social cognitive perspective, provides us with many challenges about the emotional, apparently irrational nature of our relationships. As such, the study of inappropriate relationships provokes us to challenge further our assumptions in this relationships field and to better appreciate the emotional and conflictual nature of relationship thoughts and actions.

SOME IMPLICATIONS

When we began this book, we saw the issue of what was and was not an inappropriate relationship primarily as an intellectual puzzle, and, as we developed our ideas and contacted potential contributors, it became clear we could have included a very wide range of inappropriate relationships not discussed here (indeed, the topic of "inappropriate relationships" could have formed the basis for a whole series of books).

One theoretically challenging issue that began to emerge was the problematic chestnut of what constitutes a relationship, discussed by Steve Duck and Lise VanderVoort in their introductory chapter. It soon became clear to us that when considering many of the relationships in this book, what one individual considers to be his or her "relationship" with another is often quite differently defined by the other, thereby challenging the implicit boundaries imposed by many of us when inquiring about and researching relational processes. The important role of both explicit and implicit subcultural and cultural regulation also led us to challenge many of the assumptions we make about relationships as a *public* act, declared in often ritualized performances before a largely uncritical audience. For many of the more "subterranean" relationships explored in this book these performances must remain hidden, but we as researchers are largely unaware of the consequences of this concealment on their dynamics and potential outcomes. We suspect that by studying just the openly acknowledged and performed—and the mutually defined and proclaimed—relationship researchers are neglecting a whole underbelly of relationship dynamics that, as we hope our example from *Love in the Time of Cholera* illustrates, is likely to have a whole set of cognitive and emotional challenges and rules of its own.

Such considerations should act as more than just a critique of theoretical trends in relationship research. We believe an understanding of what many of these relationships have in common can also help us deal with many of the very real problems some of these relationships can produce for both their interactants and their wider social groups and societies. First, consider the historical and cultural variations we discussed earlier in this chapter and that are alluded to throughout this text. Cultural relativism is far from an uncontroversial topic (and several of the relationships considered here are, as we have noted, universally condemned), but at the same time it is clear that an awareness of cultural and ethnic group sensibilities for many relational dilemmas is likely to be important for lawmakers, enforcement agencies, and other policymakers and support services dealing with multiple ethnic groups, and even different generations. Coupled with this, an understanding of the malleability of some of the relational dimensions discussed by Steve Duck and Lise VanderVoort can give us valuable insights into the different ways in which different societies and ethnic groups may view what others may consider as "self-evidently" appropriate or inappropriate. In addition, an understanding of prevalence statistics can be used to challenge existing dogmas, or may highlight real but neglected areas of policy concern (e.g., some of the alarming statistics for relational intrusion discussed by Spitzberg and Cupach).

A second practical issue that emerged from our discussions concerned the role played by power discrepancies, both institutional and economic. Many of the discussions in this book underlined the power inequalities present in many inappropriate relationships, and the difficulties these raise for both the sustenance of a relationship (e.g., in the case of the patient–therapist relationship) or the withdrawal from it (e.g., in the case of the pedophiliac relationships). Although relationship researchers are unlikely to have any profound influence on power distributions in society, they can (and should) be more explicit in their educational role in considering the influence of power imbalances on relational processes and outcomes. By discussing these power issues in an informed manner, some of the continuing anxieties raised by a range of relationships (including some not discussed in this volume, such as those between professor and student or secretary and boss) can hopefully be better resolved.

Of course, as we draw to the end of this book, many questions remain. What happens, for example, when an individual is involved in more than one "inappropriate relationship" (does transgression of one regulation lead to further transgressions?)? What are the social group demarcations in societies that allow "inappropriate" relationships to be tolerated? (For some relationships, marginalized groups might almost be expected to engage in "inappropriate behaviors"; for other relationships, social power can protect boundary transgressions.) What role do wider societal bodies such as the media play in framing relational boundaries and "appropriate" behaviors? We hope this book has stimulated the reader to consider these and many more questions—and, of course, to reflect on his or her own relationship experiences with respect to this fascinating and challenging topic.

REFERENCES

Adams, J. (1965). Inequity in social exchange. In L. Berkowitz (Ed.), *Advances in experimental social psychology* (vol 2., pp. 267–299). New York: Academic.

Alba, R. D. (1995). America's quiet tide. *Public Interest, 119*, 3–18.

Argyle, M., Henderson, M., Bond, M., Iizuka, Y., & Contarello, A. (1986). Cross-cultural variations in relationship rules. *International Journal of Psychology, 21*, 287–315.

Baker, A. W., & Duncan, S. P. (1985). Child sexual abuse: A study of prevalence in Great Britain. *Child Abuse and Neglect, 9*, 457–467.

Baumgarte, R., Kulich, S. J., & Lee, N. (1998, June). *Friendship patterns among college students in four cultures.* Paper presented at the 9th International Society for the Study of Personal Relationships, Saratoga Springs, NY.

Benn, S. I., & Peters, R. S. (1959). *Social principles and the democratic state.* London: Allen and Unwin.

Berscheid, E. (1983). Emotion. In H. H. Kelley et al. (Eds.). *Close Relationships* (pp. 110–168). San Francisco: Freeman.

Brook, L., Hedges, S., Jowell, R., Lewis, J., Prior, G., Sebastian, G., Taylor, B., & Witherspoon, S. (1992). *British social attitudes cumulative sourcebook.* Aldershot, UK: Gower.

Buckley, M. (1993). *Redefining Russian society and polity.* Boulder, CO: Westview.

Burgoyne, S., & Spitzberg, B. (1992, July). *An examination of communication strategies and tactics used in potential date rape episodes.* Paper presented at the Sixth International Conference on Personal Relationships, Maine.

Coleman, D., & Salt, J. (Eds.). (1996). *Ethnicity in the 1991 census: Volume one: Demographic characteristics of the ethnic minority populations.* London: HMSO.

Cooper, M. L., Agocha, V. B., & Sheldon, M. S. (2000). A motivational perspective on risky behaviors: The role of personality and affect regulatory processes. *Journal of Personality, 68*, 1059–1088.

Cramer, D. (2000, June). *Towards a conceptual framework for studying 'inappropriate' relationships and relationship behaviours?* Paper presented in the Symposium on Inappropriate Relationships at the Second Joint Conference of the International Society for the Study of Personal Relationships and the International Network on Personal Relationships, Brisbane, Australia.

Doherty, R. W., Hatfield, E., Thompson, K., & Choo, P. (1994). Cultural and ethnic influences on love and attachment. *Personal Relationships, 1*, 391–398.

Edgardh, K., & Ormstad, K. (2000). Prevalence and characteristics of sexual abuse in a national sample of Swedish seventeen-year-old boys and girls. *Acta Paediatrica, 89*, 310–319.

Festinger, L. (1957). *A theory of cognitive dissonance.* Evanston, IL: Row, Peterson.

Finch, J. (1989). Kinship and friendship. In R. Jowell, S. Witherspoon, & L. Brook (Eds.), *British social attitudes: Special international report: The 6th report* (pp. 87–103). Aldershot, UK: Gower.

Finkelhor, D. (1994). The international epidemiology of child sexual abuse. *Child Abuse and Neglect, 18*, 409–417.

Finkelhor, D., Hotaling, G., Lewis, I. A., & Smith, C. (1990). Sexual abuse in a national survey of adult men and women: Prevalence, characteristics, and risk factors. *Child Abuse and Neglect, 14*, 19–28.

Garrett, T., & Davis, J. (1998). The prevalence of sexual contact between British clinical psychologists and their patients. *Clinical Psychology and Psychotherapy, 5*, 253–263.

General Social Survey. (n.d.). Retrieval September 24, 2001, from www.icpsr.umich.edu/GSS.

Goldstein, J. R. (1999). Kinship networks that cross racial lines: The exception to the rule? *Demography, 36,* 399–407.

Goodwin, R. (1999). *Personal relationships across cultures.* London: Routledge.

Goodwin, R., Realo, A., Kwiatkowska, A., Kozlova, A., Nguyen Luu, L. A., & Nizharadze, G. (in press). Values and sexual behavior in central and eastern Europe. To appear in *Journal of Health Psychology.*

Gordon, S., & Donat, P. (1992, July). *Social exchange and influence strategies in dyadic communication: Applications to research on acquaintance rape.* Paper presented at the 6th ICPR, Orono, ME.

Gorey, K. M., & Leslie, D. R. (1997). The prevalence of child sexual abuse: Integrative review adjustment for potential response and measurement biases. *Child Abuse and Neglect, 21,* 391–398.

Greenberg, D. F. (1995). The pleasures of homosexuality. In P. R. Abramson & S. D. Pinkerton (Eds.), *Sexual nature, sexual culture* (pp. 223–256). Chicago: University of Chicago Press.

Gudykunst, W. B. (1994). *Bridging differences: Effective intergroup communication.* (2nd ed.). Thousand Oaks, CA: Sage.

Heider, F. (1958). *The psychology of interpersonal relations.* New York: Wiley.

Herzlich, C., & Pierret, J. (1989). The construction of a social phenomenon: Aids in the French press. *Social Science and Medicine, 29,* 1235–1242.

Hinde, R. A. (1997). *Relationships: A dialectical perspective.* London: Psychology Press.

Hofstede, G. (1980). *Culture's consequences: International differences in work-related values.* Beverly Hills, CA: Sage.

Holroyd, J. C., & Brodsky, A. M. (1980). Does touching patients lead to sexual intercourse? *Professional Psychology, 11,* 807–811.

Homans, G. (1961). *Social behavior: Its elementary form.* New York: Harcourt.

International lesbian and gay association. (n.d.). Retrieval September 24, 2001, from www.ilga/information/legal_survey/ilga_world_legal_survey

Jankowiak, W. R., & Fischer, E. F. (1992). A cross-cultural perspective on romantic love. *Ethology, 31,* 149–155.

Joffe, H. (1996). AIDS research and prevention: A social representation approach. *British Journal of Medical Psychology, 69,* 169–190.

Johnson, A. M., Wadsworth, J., Wellings, K., & Field, J. (1994). *Sexual attitudes and lifestyles.* London: Blackwell.

Jowell, R., Curtice, J., Park, A., Brook, L., Thomson, K., & Bryson, C. (1997). *British social attitudes: The 14th Report.* Aldershot, UK: Gower.

Jowell, R., Curtice, J., Park, A., Thomson, K., Jarvis, L., Bromley, C., & Stratford, N. (1999). *British social attitudes: The 16th Report.* Aldershot, UK: Ashgate.

Kalmijn, M. (1993). Trends in black/white intermarriage. *Social Forces, 72,* 119–146.

Kenrick, D. T., & Keefe, R. C. (1992). Age preferences in mates reflect sex differences in human reproductive strategies. *Behavioral and Brain Sciences, 15,* 75–133.

Laumann, E. O., Gagnon, J. H., Michael, R. T., & Michaels, S. (1994). *The social organization of sexuality: Sexual practices in the United States.* Chicago: University of Chicago Press.

Legal age of consent. (n.d.). Retrieval September 24, 2001, from www.ageofconsent.com

MacIver, R. M. (1949). *Society: An introductory analysis.* London: Macmillan.

Markova, I. (1992). Scientific and public knowledge of AIDS: The problem of their integration. In M. Von Cranach, W. Doise, & G. Mugny (Eds.), *Social representations and the social bases of knowledge* (pp.179–183). Lewiston, UK: Hogrefe & Huber.

Markova, I., & Wilkie, P. (1987). Representations, concepts and social change: The phenomenon of AIDS. *Journal for the Theory of Social Behaviour, 17*, 389–409.

Marquez, G. G. (1989). *Love in the time of cholera.* Harmondsworth, UK: Penguin.

Minturn, L., Grosse, M., & Haider, S. (1969). Cultural patterning of sexual beliefs and behavior. *Ethnology, 8*, 301–313.

Páez, D., Echebarria, A., Valencia, J., Romo, I., San Juan, C., & Vergara, A. (1991). AIDS social representations: Contents and processes. *Journal of Community and Applied Social Psychology, 1*, 89–104.

Pope, K. S., & Feldman-Summers, S. (1992). National survey of psychologists' sexual and physical abuse history and their evaluation of training and competence in these areas. *Professional Psychology: Research and Practice, 23*, 353–361.

Pope, K. S., Keith-Spiegel, P., & Tabachnick, B. G. (1986). Sexual attraction to clients: The human therapist and the (sometimes) inhuman training system. *American Psychologist, 41*, 147–158.

Rohner, R. (1984). Toward a conception of culture for cross-cultural psychology. *Journal of Cross cultural Psychology, 15*, 111–138.

Rusbult, C., Morrow, G., & Johnson, D. (1986). Predicting satisfaction and commitment in adult romantic involvements: An assessment of the generalizability of the investment model. *Social Psychology Quarterly, 49*, 81–89.

Sanday, P. R. (1981). The socio-cultural context of rape: A cross-cultural study. *Journal of Social Issues, 37*, 5–27.

Schlegel, A., & Barry, H., III. (1991). *Adolescence: An anthropological inquiry.* New York: Free Press.

Schuman, H., Steeh, C., & Bobo, L. (1985). *Racial attitudes in America: Trends and interpretation.* Cambridge, MA: Harvard University Press.

Scott, J. (1998). Changing attitudes to sexual morality: A cross-national comparison. *Sociology, 32*, 815–845.

Smith, T. W. (1990). The polls—a report: The sexual revolution? *Public Opinion Quarterly, 54*, 415–435.

Sontag, S. (1989). *AIDS and its metaphors.* New York: Doubleday.

Sternberg, R. J. (1998). *Love is a story: A new theory of relationships.* Oxford, UK: Oxford University Press.

Thibaut, J., & Kelley, H. (1959). *The social psychology of groups.* New York: Wiley.

Thiessen, D., & Gregg, B. (1980). Human assortative mating and genetic equilibrium: An evolutionary perspective. *Ethology and Sociobiology, 1*, 111–140.

Thoreson, R. W., Shaugnessy, P., Heppner, P. P., & Cook, S. W. (1993). Sexual contact during and after the therapeutic relationship: Attitudes and practices of male counselors. *Journal of Counseling and Development, 71*, 429–434.

Tjaden, P., Thoennes, N., & Allison, C. J. (2000). Comparing stalking victimization from legal and victim perspectives. *Violence and Victims, 15*, 7–22.

Triandis, H. C. (1995). *Individualism and collectivism.* Boulder, CO: Westview.

Walster, E., & Walster, G. (1978). *A new look at love.* Reading, MA: Addison-Wesley.

Author Index

X

Xu, X., 34

Y

Yi, J., 74, 75
Yip, A. K. T., 126, 130, 136, 138

Z

Subject Index

A

Adaptive problems, 26
Adultery, 222, 227, 229
  cultural views of, 45–7
  terminology 49
Age structuring, 232–235
AIDS, 255
Ambiguity, 58–60
American Psychological Association, 239
Anal sex, 251
Assortative mating, see homogamy
Attachment theory, 27–28, 199–201
  styles, 74–75. 200–201
Attributional biases, 70, 71, 72, 75

B

Behavior/relationship distinction, 8, 9,
  10, 12, 15
Betrayal, 55–6
Borderline personality, 201

C

Christian, 126–129, 134–138, 140
Church, 125, 136–138, 141
  Roman Catholic, 126, 128, 134
  Vatican, 138
Cicero, 13
Client, see patients
Clinical issues, 95–97, 98
  identification of, 96–97
  language, 97
  and trust, 95–96
Clinton, Bill 7, 8, 12, 46
Clitorectomy, 238
Close relationships, 231
  nature of, 195–196

stalking and, 199
Commitment, 73
Companionate marriage, 47
Confluent love, 48
Context for behavior, 15
Cook, Robin, 46
Cross-cultural perspectives, 253–255
  on friendship, 75, 106–107, 118
Cross-gender friendship, 247, 249–250
Cultural values, 75

D

Demographic change, 47
Disapproval, 14
Disapproved relationships, 18–19
Disinhibition, 211–212
Disjunctive relationships, 191–192, 199,
  205
Double standard, sexual, 253
Dual-role relationships, 153–154, 165
Duty, 4

E

Emotional instability, see neuroticism
Endogamy, 34
Enemies, 17
Equity, 4
Evolutionary models of human mating,
  26–27
Evolutionary psychology, 26
Exclusivity, 34–36
  adaptive significance of, 34, 36
  as a cultural universal, 35
Extramarital sexual relationships,
  252–255
Exogamy, 34